ANTIQUE GUNS
THE COLLECTOR'S GUIDE

ANTIQUE GUNS
THE COLLECTOR'S GUIDE

JOHN E. TRAISTER

STOEGER PUBLISHING COMPANY

COVER DESIGN and PHOTO: Ray Wells

BOOK DESIGN and PRODUCTION: Charlene Cruson Step

Published by Stoeger Publishing Company
55 Ruta Court
South Hackensack, New Jersey 07606

ISBN: 088317-144-9
Library of Congress Catalog Card No.: 88-60403
Manufactured in the United States of America

Distributed to the book trade and to the sporting goods
trade by Stoeger Industries, 55 Ruta Court, South
Hackensack, New Jersey 07606.

In Canada, distributed to the book trade and to the sporting
goods trade by Stoeger Canada, Ltd., Unit 16, 1801
Wentworth Street, Whitby, Ontario L1N 5S4.

PREFACE

My research on **Antique Guns—The Collector's Guide** started some 30 years ago, although I was not aware of it. It was about the time I was allowed to carry a gun into the field, and about the time I bagged my first white-tailed deer. My appreciation for and respect of firearms stemmed from my associations with my Dad and uncles, who were all accomplished hunters. Shooting that deer, however, was my coming of age. It was exhilarating for many reasons. But most important, it kindled a curiosity about the types of weapons hunters use. I'd got a taste of what a modern shotgun could do in the Virginia woods, but what was it like in Colonial days shooting with a flintlock?

So the reading began. For years, I devoured everything printed about firearms that I could put my hands on. This naturally grew into trading guns, repairing and smithing guns (I started my own business about 10 years ago), and finally I started to write about them.

Five years ago, I wrote **How to Buy and Sell Used Guns** (another Stoeger book), which is the predecessor to this one. It discusses in detail how to inspect antique (and modern) arms and determine their authenticity, firearms price trends and how to collect for investment, firearms to avoid, restoring arms and whether to do it, and how to protect your collection, among other related topics.

This title, **Antique Guns—The Collector's Guide,** covers the specific pre-1900 firearms that most antique arms collectors are interested in. It was conceived in response to the enormous demand I've encountered among collectors and shooters for a detailed guide to identifying and pricing antique firearms—a guide that is not so long and wordy that it takes hours to pour through it, nor a guide so skimpy that you can't determine exactly which item among similar models is listed.

In a concise, easy-to-follow format, I have tried to include the basics—the essential specifications necessary to make an accurate identification, some historical notes about specimens of particular interest, hundreds of photos and/or drawings for I.D. purposes, and a suggested monetary value, based on the average trading price. For rare items, collectors, dealers and museums were consulted.

The antique arms are arranged into three broad categories: handguns, rifles and shotguns. Within those groupings, the guns are listed alphabetically by name of gunmaker or manufacturer, which ultimately makes any item relatively easy to find. At the end of the groupings are several smaller, obvious categories, such as American Kentucky Flintlock Rifles (at the end of the Rifle Section) and Confederate Handguns (at the end of Handguns). In any of my books, I've never wanted the reader to be bogged down with too much verbiage, and my objective in this title was to achieve a healthy balance between words and information.

Several other things, I believe, make this book different from a few books you may currently find in the marketplace on antique arms. One is the inclusion of guns of foreign origin. American arms are fascinating to be sure. But our heritage, after all, is derived from many countries around the world. I have tried to give this book international scope by highlighting the craftsmanship of British gunmakers, for example, Belgian, French, Italian, Canadian, German, Chinese, and others.

Another difference from other volumes is the Blackpowder Replica Section. This is an extensive listing that encompasses contemporary reproductions of antique arms. Why is it included?

Three reasons: 1) descriptions of these guns may prevent the novice collector from getting scalped by the purchase of replicas posed as originals; 2) the prices of replicas, the Colt Dragoons, for example, are more affordable than the originals—and while the "real thing" is most desirable, a replica may be a beginning for some collectors; 3) no other book, to my knowledge, has such a complete, up-to-date identification/pricing guide for these models.

Another feature of this book is a detailed listing of Obsolete Cartridges, an area for some collectors that is a direct outgrowth of their collecting of antique arms. This section includes centerfire rifle cartridges, obsolete metric cartridges, rimfire cartridges, and obsolete shotshells—all well illustrated.

Finally, a complete cross-referenced index is provided to assist you in finding whatever or whomever it is you need to locate in regards to your collecting.

In a volume of this scope, it is difficult to include everything pertinent to every collector. I have endeavored to include the major U.S. gunmakers and manufacturers and a number of foreign gunmakers, as mentioned earlier, that are most often encountered in gun trading circles. This book in no way reflects an attempt to include every model and every variation of firearm ever made prior to 1900.

In addition, the prices listed within are intended to be the average selling price as found through my "poll" throughout the country. They are not engraved in stone and can be arbitrary at times because of various contributing factors, which are discussed at length in the section "Collecting Antique Guns." As the on-press date approached, it became difficult to find certain items. Rather than list a misleading value, I chose, instead, simply to indicate lack of information by using three asterisks. In the next edition, we plan to supply the missing values, as well as adding to the overall listings as they are encountered in our research.

Hopefully, all collectors—aspiring or established—will discover this book as a vital reference. In addition, I hope it will prove to be a valuable resource for gunsmiths—especially those involved in repairing and restoring antique weapons—as well as museum curators, auctioneers, appraisers and insurance adjusters.

ACKNOWLEDGMENTS

The resources for a volume of this kind are endless. I couldn't possibly list or remember all the books and articles I've read that have helped me compile this. However, the printed sources I've used most recently are listed in the Bibliography. As far as experts I've spoken to, they have been numerous, and I would specifically like to thank Turner Kirkland of Dixie Gun Works, Dave Condon, Fred Goodwin, Dick Reyes, and the many gun dealers all over the country that I've consulted with at length. Also to the associations and curators of all the museums listed below who provided me with information from their collections and allowed me to try to photograph rare specimens for this book (which was not always successful).

I'd like to extend my thanks to all the firearms manufacturing companies who assisted in providing and clarifying information and/or supplying photographs, especially Colt Industries and Savage Arms; Beeman, CVA, Hopkins & Allen, Navy Arms, Shiloh, Thompson/Center and all the other blackpowder reproduction manufacturers.

Obtaining photographs of antique arms is a full-time pursuit in itself, and I would like to thank John Denner of North Lancaster, Ontario, Canada, for the use of hundreds of his photos, Andrew Larson of the General Robert E. Lee Museum in Gettysburg, Penn., for taking photos especially for this volume, Ken Longe, the research specialist of the Union Pacific Historical Museum, the other museums who contributed negatives and photos, R. Bruce McDowell for loaning us antique arms from his collection to photograph for the cover, and Ray Wells for doing such a superb photography job with the cover.

Finally, I'd like to thank the editors of Stoeger Publishing for their enormous enthusiasm and editorial dedication, and to everyone else who was in any way involved with the project.

— John E. Traister

U.S. MUSEUMS AND ASSOCIATIONS
Antietam National Battlefield, Sharpsburg, MD
Arkansas State University, Jonesboro, AR
Arizona Historical Society, Tucson, AZ
Bangor Historical Society, Bangor, ME
Colonial National Historical Park, Yorktown, VA
DAR Museum, Washington, DC

Douglas County Historical Society, Omaha, NE

Ft. Davis Nat'l. Historic Site, Ft. Davis, TX

Gettysburg Nat'l. Military Park, Gettysburg, PA

Harpers Ferry Nat'l. Historical Park, Harpers Ferry, WV

Higgins Armory Museum, Worcester, MA

Historical Society of the Militia and National Guard, Washington, DC

Hubbell Trading Post National Historic Site, Ganado, AZ

Independence Nat'l. Historical Park, Philadelphia, PA

J. M. Davis Gun Museum, Claremore, OK

Kampeska Heritage Museum, Watertown, SD

Kentucky Military History Museum, Frankfort, KY

Maine Historical Society, Portland, ME

Manassas National Battlefield Park, Manassas, VA

Maritime Philadelphia Museum, Philadelphia, PA

National Museum of American History, Washington, DC

National Museum of History and Technology, Washington, DC

National Rifle Association (NRA) Firearms Museum, Washington, DC

Naval War College, Newport, RI

New Market Battlefield Park, New Market, VA

Old Washington Historic State Park, Washington, AR

Patriots Point Development Authority, Mt. Pleasant, SC

Pendleton District Historical & Recreational Commission, Pendleton, SC

Petersburg National Battlefield, Petersburg, VA

Richmond National Battlefield Park, Richmond, VA

Rutherford B. Hayes Presidential Center, Fremont, OH

Shasta State Historic Park, Shasta, AR

Springfield Armory National Historic Site, Springfield, MA

State of Rhode Island and Providence Plantations, Providence, RI

The Museum of the Confederacy, Richmond, VA

U.S. Marine Corps Museum, Washington, DC

Union Pacific Historical Museum, Omaha, NE

Virginia Historical Society, Richmond, VA

Warren Rifles Confederate Museum, Front Royal, VA

Washington County Historical Museum, Ft. Calhoun, NE

West Point Museum, West Point, NY

Woolaroc Museum, Bartlesville, OK

CANADIAN MUSEUMS AND ASSOCIATIONS

F. T. Hill Museum, Rivershurst, Saskatchewan

Fort Howe Blockhouse, Saint John, New Brunswick

Fort Macleod Historical Assn., Fort Macleod, Alberta

Ft. Rodd Hill Nat'l. Historic Park, Victoria, British Columbia

Halton Region Museum, Milton, Ontario

London Historical Museums, London, Ontario

Montreal Military & Maritime Museum, Montreal, Quebec

Museum of Northern British Columbia, Prince Rupert, British Columbia

New Brunswick Museum, New Brunswick

Pacific National Exhibition, Vancouver, British Columbia

Princess Patricia's Canadian Light Infantry Regimental Museum, Calgary, Alberta

Regimental Museum, New Westminster, British Columbia

ABOUT THE AUTHOR

John Traister has collected and traded antique and modern firearms ever since he was about 13 years old living in Front Royal, Virginia. His father and uncles were accomplished hunters and outdoorsmen, and naturally John followed in their footsteps.

After attending college in Boston, Traister served a hitch in the U.S. Marine Corps that he completed in the mid-1960s. He then became involved in the construction business as a principle with Engineering Associates Ltd. until 1975. It was during this period that he wrote his first book of a technical nature.

Not content with writing about engineering problems, he began writing about his collecting hobby—firearms. In 1978, he turned the gun hobby into a full-fledged vocation by launching a gun-trading/gunsmithing business of his own in his present home town of Bentonville, Va.,—and continued to write about the arms as well.

To date Traister has authored more than 100 different books, at the rate of about seven or eight titles per year. Most notably those books include **How to Buy and Sell Used Guns, Basic Gunsmithing, Professional Care and Finishing of Guns,** and **Learn Gunsmithing: The Trouble-Shooting Method.** He has written hundreds of articles for such magazines as American Rifleman, Handloader's Digest, Fishing World and Fur-Fish-Game. Most recently he has plunged into the publishing end of the business. With the help of computer technology, he sends out monthly tabloids called Winchester Gun Trader and American Gunsmith. And of course he is working on several

new firearms books. In addition, he is a firearms consultant for Stoeger Industries, Inc.

CONTENTS

COLLECTING ANTIQUE GUNS

Anyone engaged in buying, selling or trading antique firearms should be and can become competent in three major areas. First, the firearm in question must be identified. Second, a knowledge of the gun's characteristics must be known to recognize any modifications or fakes and, of course, a value must be placed on the gun.

Since the beginning of the firearms industry in the 15th century, thousands of different models of rifles, muskets, shotguns and handguns have been crafted. In the earliest years, seldom did two guns ever turn out alike—even those made by the same gunmaker. This greatly complicates identification. Furthermore, markings on many older firearms were nonexistent or else are not recognizable due to aging and wear. Still, there are several characteristics to look for in any firearm, and the knowledgeable person can at least determine the approximate era of manufacture and also the approximate value from the quality of workmanship and from dealing in similar firearms.

Experts have spent the majority of their lifetimes studying old gun catalogs, museum collections and hundreds of reference books; they know not only the maker and model of a particular firearm, but can also readily identify the variations, and oftentimes pinpoint the manufacture date to within a year or two. Furthermore, they can usually tell if a particular gun has been altered, refinished or faked. Such knowledge cannot be acquired from any one book or within a short period of time. It takes years of study and experience to develop the required skills.

The term "antique" as used in this book encompasses all firearms manufactured prior to 1900. Let's take a closer look at several factors that are involved in the evaluation of any antique firearm: collector interest, scarcity and condition.

COLLECTOR INTEREST

A primary factor that influences the value of a firearm is collector interest. Was the gun made by somebody famous, owned by somebody famous, or was it fired in an important historical conflict, such as the Revolutionary War? Answers to these questions have a direct effect on the demand for any firearm. Conversely, where there is meager collector interest, demand will be low.

Although most antique firearms have collector interest to some extent, certain models are naturally more in demand than others. Few collectors will argue that Winchester and Colt firearms have been the blue chips of gun collections for the better part of this century. However, today almost any antique firearm is interesting to some collector. This situation has been brought about by the hearty increase in the number of active collectors and the correspondingly growing number of dealers who cater to them. With this growth a wide diversity in collecting interest has developed. Firearms that held little appeal a few years ago are now becoming extremely popular. Typical examples are the small-bore Stevens and Winchester rifles, single-shot pistols, the cheap cartridge revolvers; even the old single-shot, break-open shotguns are fascinating to many collectors.

Specialization, however, parallels the overall popularity of gun collecting. Individual collectors will concentrate on, say, pre-1900 lever-action rifles, while others on one brand of shotgun. These specialized fields embrace the entire range of firearms development, including such accessories as loading tools, bullet molds and gunsmith's tools. And the often-ignored rusted battlefield relics have their devotees, too. Armed with only a metal detector, many collectors enjoy hours of pleasure combing the old Civil War battlefields in search of lead bullets, buttons and other artifacts.

SCARCITY

As certain firearms become more difficult to find, their value almost always increases; an original Confederate Schneider & Glassick Revolver, for example, is almost impossible to come across casually; it will take work to obtain it for your own collection. Consequently, paying thousands of dollars for it, when found, may not be surprising.

Having established the fact that a firearm interests a particular collector, that it may or may not be a scarce commodity, the final factor to consider—and the one open to infinite debate between seller and buyer—is condition.

CONDITION

Condition is the major criterion in determining the value of an antique firearm. For example, your neighbor's grandmother discovered a Remington 1858 Army Revolver in the attic that her grandfather used during the Civil War. It did not see heavy service, so nearly 90 percent of the original finish is intact. This would command a premium price. On the other hand, if the gun had been dug up in an old garbage pit and it had a rusted barrel, heavily scratched wood grip and a missing trigger, what would you be willing to pay for it?

NRA Standards of Condition for Antique Firearms. Recognizing that the parties concerned seldom agree on the condition of a used firearm, the National Rifle Association has made available "Standards of Condition for Antique Firearms," which are probably the most popular and most often used in determining condition. They are largely based on the percentage of original finish, as follows.

Factory New: all original parts; 100% original finish; in perfect condition in every respect, inside and out.

Excellent: all original parts; over 80% original finish; sharp lettering, numerals, and design on metal and wood; unmarred wood; fine bore.

Fine: all original parts; over 30% original finish; sharp lettering, numerals, and design on metal and wood; minor marks in wood; good bore.

Very Good: all original parts; none to 30% original finish; original metal surfaces smooth with all edges sharp; clear lettering, numerals,

and design on metal; wood slightly scratched or bruised; bore disregarded for collector firearms.

Good: some minor replacement parts; metal smoothly rusted or lightly pitted in places, cleaned, or reblued; principal lettering, numerals, and design on metal legible; wood refinished, scratched, bruised, or minor cracks repaired; in good working order.

Fair: some major parts replaced; minor replacement parts may be required; metal rusted, may be lightly pitted all over, vigorously cleaned, or reblued; rounded edges of metal and wood; principal lettering, numerals, and design on metal partly obliterated; wood scratched, bruised, cracked, or repaired where broken; in fair working order or can be easily repaired and placed in working order.

Poor: major and minor parts replaced; major replacement parts required and extensive restoration needed; metal deeply pitted; principal lettering, numerals, and design obliterated, wood badly scratched, bruised, cracked, or broken; mechanically inoperative; generally undesirable as a collector firearm.

These standards, however, were compiled a number of years ago, and current dealers have found that they need to articulate the condition of a firearm even more finitely than the NRA did. Nowadays, for example, an antique arm considered in "Excellent" condition may have 95 percent original finish (not just the "over 80%" as prescribed by the NRA), and that 15 percent between the 80 and 95 would make the difference between a selling price of $500 versus $5,000. So you will find that most gun dealers today try to break down that percentage of original finish even more finely.

DETERMINING GUN VALUES

While the worth of any antique firearm involves condition, relative scarcity, historical significance, and collector demand, the "true value" of any firearm is not what a collector thinks his or her gun is worth. Nor is it the price the seller asks. It is not just what the buyer is willing to pay, either. The true value is determined when the amount the seller will accept coincides with the amount the buyer is willing to pay. This, and only this, is the true value of any gun.

However, for purposes of determining the value of firearms in this book, all arms are considered to be in "Excellent" condition, as defined by the NRA Standards. If they fall below this category, then the price you might expect to receive for a particular gun will be lowered. The prices on the following pages have been established by averaging the prices polled from around the country through printed sources, gun dealers, museums, and the like.

General demand for collector firearms is constantly increasing, and any guns's worth rises in proportion to the demand for it. Demand is also influenced by articles that appear in periodicals or by well-prepared gun books that describe and classify firearms of a particular maker or manufacturer.

Also remember that gun values may vary from region to region around the country and from dealer to dealer.

Even with the NRA Standards of Condition as a guide, it is difficult to appraise or evaluate the general condition and mechanical features of any firearm with precise accuracy unless you can examine it personally. It is unlikely that anyone unfamiliar with firearms would know if parts had been replaced or altered, or if a gun had been refinished, made up from two or three specimens, or was a rare variation or a transitional type. Thus, in correspondence, such points may be overlooked. Identifications or appraisals by mail may be both inaccurate and unfair to the owner or to the one being asked to identify or evaluate the gun unseen. All that can be done under the circumstances is to give a probable value of the model or type.

Keep in mind that collector values tend to rise steeply in the "Fine" and "Excellent" categories. This is particularly true of older firearms that are rarely encountered in top condition. Some of the great rarities are almost never encountered in any but worn condition, yet their values are not severely lessened by their condition.

Anyone interested in antique firearms and their values should own not only this book, **Antique Guns—The Collector's Guide,** but also read every other book you can obtain. A perusal of classified ads that appear in firearms publications such as Shotgun News, Gun List, Winchester Gun Trader, etc., will also keep you up-to-date as to value trends on specific or comparable firearms. Attending gun shows where guns are bought, sold or traded is another excellent way to acquaint you with current selling prices and trends.

It should be obvious that the serious collector must be a firearms student. Any gun worth having is worth learning about. A book for every gun is the policy of many successful collectors. With the wide availability of fine articles and books published today and the numerous gun shows that are held, no one need be uninformed of any old gun or its value.

CHAPTER ONE
HANDGUNS

The handgun has traditionally been a weapon of self-defense. The early smoothbore flintlock pistols, for example, were carried by travelers to protect themselves from highwaymen or other lawless persons. The pistol also played an important role in settling disputes of the day, either in the form of duels or shootouts. There is no doubt that some shooters used their handguns to take game on occasion; sometimes they were used to finish off a wounded deer or antelope, rather than use another precious rifle cartridge. But, still, the handgun was used primarily to defend one's self or possessions.

Most of the early pistols were of single-shot design, although double-barreled varieties were also seen. As firearms evolved into the 19th century, the number of barrels multiplied into three, four or more and became known as pepperboxes. One distinguishing feature of firearms of the 1800s is their remarkable diversity. It seemed to be a period of prolific invention, during which all types, shapes and novelties were produced: cane guns, hand cannons, saw handles, exotic wood, pearl or ivory grips, spur triggers. You name it, it was there. Many of these guns are not merely weapons, however; they are works of art and leaps of the imagination that have been preserved by and for collectors.

Samuel Colt is often credited with the first successful revolving pistol. Note the use of the term "pistol" here. You will find on the following pages many revolvers that are referred to as pistols. Remember that during this period, the revolver was a new entity, with "pistol" being a carryover from an earlier time. Nowadays, firearms aficionados easily distinguish between pistols and revolvers, but it took a while for people to make that distinction. During the last half of the century, revolvers were rapidly adopted by law enforcement personnel and, after much persuasion, by soldiers. Once accepted, they acquired great popularity with the Army and Navy as service weapons. In addition to Colt, manufacturers such as Remington, Harrington & Richardson, and Smith & Wesson soon followed with their own revolver models, some of which continue to be manufactured today.

For ease in locating a particular firearm, the Handgun Section is arranged in four basic groupings:

ADAMS REVOLVING ARMS CO.
New York, New York

Although the main office of this firm was in New York City, its percussion revolvers were actually manufactured by the Massachusetts Arms Company of Chicopee Falls, Mass. The Adams Patent Revolvers were based on English patents owned by Robert Adams (*see* separate listing) and were manufactured under license; these were undoubtedly used during the Civil War, probably by both sides, although ordnance records of the time do not substantiate their official use.

Adams Patent Percussion Revolver **$375**
Calibers: 36, some 31. Five-shot cylinder. Barrels: about 3, 4 or 6 inches. Solid frame. Sliding safety. Walnut grips. Blued finish. Based on the Beaumont-Adams revolver design, this was made during the late 1850s.

ROBERT ADAMS
London, England

Robert Adams (1809–1870) was a British gunmaker of reknown. During the 1850s, his self-cocking, five-shot revolver became a chief competitor to the Colt of similar design. Service tests, in fact, were conducted comparing the two guns and, although the Adams stood up well in the testing, it was rejected in favor of the Colt because it lacked a sturdy loading ramrod. Adams solved this problem and patented the improvement in 1854 along with an improved self-cocking lock mechanism of Beaumont design (1855). This improved gun did pass British ordnance tests and replaced the Colt as a service arm. The Massachusetts Arms Co. licensed the patent designs and manufactured an Adams Patent Revolver, of different calibers, for use in the U.S.

Adams Revolver **$395**
Calibers: 38, 54. Barrels: 4¹/₂, 6¹/₄, 7¹/₂ inches; octagonal. Five-shot cylinder. Solid frame. Loaded with a wadded bullet pressed in by the thumb. Manufactured by George & John Deane of London, and often called the Deane-Adams Model (1851).

Beaumont-Adams Revolver

Beaumont-Adams Revolver **$375**
Calibers: 38, 54. Five-shot cylinder. Sliding safety. Cylinder-pin release. Carried the improved lock mechanism patented by Lt. F.B.E. Beaumont (1855) and an improved lever rammer patented by James Kerr (1855). Manufactured by the London Armoury Company and supplied to the British military services until about 1867.

AETNA ARMS COMPANY
New York, New York

Aetna Pocket Revolver **$245**
Caliber: 22 RF. Seven-shot tip-up revolver. Barrel: 3¹/₈ inches, octagonal. Brass frame with spur trigger. Blade front sight, rear notch sight. Walnut or rosewood grips. Blued or plated finish. Made from 1880 to 1890.

ALLEN & THURBER
Worcester, Massachusetts

Ethan Allen secured his first U.S. patent in 1837 for what eventually became the well-known pepperbox-type of multiple firing pistol. He set up shop with his brother-in-law, Charles Thurber, in Grafton, Mass., from 1837 to 1842. They relocated to Norwich, Conn., from 1842 to 1847, then made a final move to Worcester, where Allen & Thurber, the company, remained until 1865. (*See* also Allen & Wheelock and Ethan Allen & Co.)

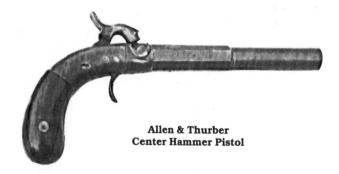

**Allen & Thurber
Center Hammer Pistol**

Allen & Thurber Center Hammer Pistol **$185**
Caliber: 34. Center hammer. Barrel: 6 inches; half-round, half-octagonal. Made circa 1840 to 1860.

Allen & Thurber Pepperbox **$550**
Caliber: 31. Six-shot cylinder. Barrel: 3³/₄ inches. Engraved frame and nipple shield. Hammer stamped "ALLEN'S PATENT 1845." Made circa 1845 to 1855.

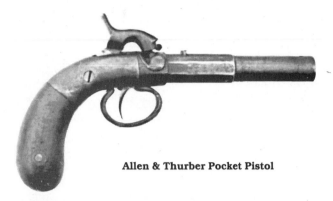

Allen & Thurber Pocket Pistol

Allen & Thurber Pocket Pistol **$185**
Caliber: 50. Center hammer. Barrel: half-round, half-octagonal. Trigger guard. Round walnut grip. Made circa 1840.

ALLEN & WHEELOCK
Worcester, Massachusetts

Upon Charles Thurber's retirement in 1856, Ethan Allen formed a partnership with his other brother-in-law, Thomas P. Wheelock. Under the name Allen & Wheelock, the company produced pepperbox pistols and a variety of revolvers from 1856 to 1865. In about 1865 after Wheelock's death, the company name was changed again to Ethan Allen & Co., when Allen's sons-in-law, Henry C. Wadsworth and Sullivan Forehand, became partners. (*See* also Allen & Thurber, Ethan Allen & Co., U.S. Military Revolvers.)

Allen & Wheelock Pocket Pepperbox **$395**
Calibers: 25, 28, 31, 43. Four-, five- and six-shot cylinders. Barrels: 2¹/₂ to 4 inches, fluted. Bar hammers or hammerless, which command a premium.

Allen & Wheelock Percussion Pistol

Allen & Wheelock Single Shot Percussion Pistol. **$395**
Calibers: 31, 36 and 38. Single shot. Barrel: 3 to 6 inches; octagonal and half-octagonal. Fixed sights. Walnut grips. Blued finish.

ETHAN ALLEN & CO.
Worcester, Massachusetts

After their Uncle Tom Wheelock died, Sullivan Forehand and Henry Wadsworth became the "& Co." principals of Ethan Allen & Co., formerly Allen & Wheelock. Both Forehand and Wadsworth married Allen's daughters and continued the family business with their father-in-law, producing pepperboxes, underhammer pistols, revolvers and rifles. After Allen died in 1871, his sons-in-law carried on the gunmaking legacy, which endured almost until the turn of the century. (*See* also Forehand & Wadsworth, Allen & Wheelock.)

Ethan Allen & Co.
Center Hammer Single Shot Pistol

E. Allen & Co. Single Shot Pistol **$300**
Caliber: 32 RF. Center hammer. Barrel: 4 inches, with auto ejector. Iron frame. Made from 1865 to 1871.

AMERICAN ARMS COMPANY
Boston, Massachusetts

American Arms Co. Hammerless Revolver. . . . **$195**
Caliber: 32. Five-shot. Top break. Barrel: 3¹/₄ inches; round, ribbed. Hard rubber grips with monogram at top. Nickel finish.

American Arms Co. Revolver (DA) **$150**
Caliber: 38 S&W. Double action. Top break.

American Arms Co. Revolver (SA) **$165**
Caliber: 38 S&W. Five-shot cylinder. Single action. Top break.

American Arms Co. Wheeler Pat. O/U Pistol (I) **$795**
Caliber: 22 Short RF, 32 Short RF. Double barrel. Brass frame. Spur trigger. Made from 1866 to 1878.

American Arms Co. Wheeler Pat. O/U Pistol (II) **$575**
Caliber: 32 Short RF. Barrel: 3 inches, double. Brass frame. Spur trigger. Made from 1866 to 1878.

American Arms Co. Wheeler Pat. O/U Pistol (III) **$775**
Caliber: 41 Short RF. Barrel: 2⁵/₈ inches, double. Brass frame. Finger spur trigger. Square butt grips. Made from 1866 to 1878.

AMERICAN STANDARD TOOL CO.
Newark, New Jersey

American Standard Tool Co. Hero. **$210**
Caliber: 34. Percussion. Screw barrel. Center hammer. Spur trigger. Made from 1865 to 1870.

American Standard Tool Co. Revolver **$410**
Caliber: 32 Short RF. Seven-shot cylinder. Spur trigger. Tip-up type. Made from 1865 to 1870.

ARABIAN FLINTLOCKS
Various Manufacturers

Arabian Flintlock Pistol **$490**
Caliber: ⁵/₈-inch bore. Barrel: 13 inches, round. Overall length: 20 inches. Markings on lock plate, some inlays in stock. Brass trim.

G.H. AVELEY & WHEAKS
Great Britain

Aveley & Wheaks
British Coat Pistol

Aveley & Wheaks Percussion Coat Pistol. **$495**
Calibers: various. Barrel: varied, but 5 inches common; octagonal. German silver furniture. Capbox in butt. Sterling silver escutcheon on grip, usually with initials and Scottish thistles. Made circa 1835.

BABCOCK REVOLVER
Address Unknown

Babcock Revolver. **$175**
Caliber: 32 Short RF. Five-shot cylinder. Single action. Spur trigger. Solid frame. Made circa 1880.

BACON ARMS COMPANY
Norwich, Connecticut

Bacon Arms Co. Pepperbox

Bacon Arms Co. Pepperbox Revolver **$880**
Caliber: 22 RF. Six-shot cylinder. Barrel: 2¹/₂ inches, fluted. Iron frame. Spur trigger. Rosewood grips. Blued finish. Made in the early 1860s.

Bacon Arms Co. Pocket Revolver. **$210**
Caliber: 32 Short RF. Five-shot cylinder. Barrel: 4 inches, round. Spur trigger. Rounded iron frame. Bird's-head butt with walnut grips. Blued finish. Made circa 1865.

Bacon Arms Co./GEM Pocket Revolver. **$525**
Caliber: 22 Short RF. Seven-shot cylinder. Barrel: 1¹/₄ inches, octagonal. Iron frame. Spur trigger. Plated finish. Bird's-head butt with walnut or ivory grips. Made from 1878 to 1881.

Bacon Arms Co./Governor Pocket Revolver. . . **$175**
Caliber: 22 Short RF. Seven-shot cylinder. Barrel: 3 inches, round. Spur trigger. Walnut grips. Blued finish. Made from 1869 to 1873.

BACON MANUFACTURING COMPANY
Norwich, Connecticut

This company was operational in the mid-1850s and '60s and turned out a number of prototypical 19th-century arms.

Bacon Mfg. Co. "Boot Gun" Pistol $355
Caliber: 34 percussion. Barrel: half-octagonal. Under-hammer.

Bacon Mfg. Co. Derringer $380
Caliber: 32 RF. Side-swing barrel. Spur trigger. Made in the early 1860s.

Bacon Mfg. Co. Navy Revolver. $550
Caliber: 38 Long RF. Six-shot cylinder. Barrel: 7$\frac{1}{2}$ inches, octagonal. Single action. Large-size iron frame. Spur trigger. Square butt. Blued finish with walnut grips. Made early 1860s.

Bacon Mfg. Co. Pocket Revolver. $215
Caliber: 22 Short RF. Seven-shot cylinder. Barrel: 2$\frac{1}{2}$ inches, octagonal. Spur trigger. Solid frame. Made in the early 1860s.

Bacon Mfg. Co. Revolver (I) $325
Caliber: 32 Short RF. Six-shot swing-out cylinder. Barrel: 4 inches, octagonal. Spur trigger. Walnut grips. Blued finish. Made 1860 to 1865.

Bacon Mfg. Co. Revolver (II) $300
Caliber: 32 Short RF. Single action. Six-shot cylinder. Barrel: 4 inches, octagonal. Solid frame. Trigger guard. Made in the early 1860s.

Belgian 7mm Pinfire
Revolver

Belgian Pinfire Revolver (I). $185
Caliber: 7mm pinfire. Octagonal barrel. Checkered grips.

C.H. BALLARD & CO.
Worcester, Massachusetts

C.H. Ballard Single Shot Derringer. $475
Caliber: 41 RF. Barrel: 2$\frac{13}{16}$ inches; part octagonal, part round; blued or silver-plated. Brass frame with silver-plated finish. Bird's-head butt with walnut grips. Made circa 1861 to 1870.

Belgian 7mm Pinfire Revolver
Engraved

Belgian Pinfire Revolver (II) $125
Caliber: 7mm pinfire. Engraved frame.

BELGIAN HANDGUNS
Various Manufacturers

Belgian Double Barrel Pistol $300
Caliber: 58. Barrels: 4$\frac{3}{4}$ inches. Rib engraved "CANON A DAMAS" (among others.) Clam shell-type cap box in butt. Iron furniture nicely engraved. Checkered grip. Silver escutcheons. Made circa 1850.

Belgian Over/Under Percussion Travelling Pistol. $375
Caliber: 63. Barrels: about 6 inches with Damascus pattern. Checkered grip and lightly engraved iron fittings. Made circa 1860.

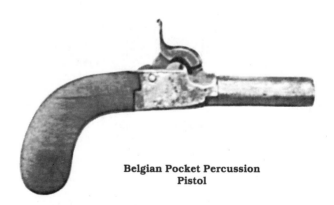

Belgian Pocket Percussion
Pistol

Belgian Pocket Percussion Pistol $150
Caliber: 44 percussion. Flip-down trigger.

Belgian Pocket Percussion
Pistol

Belgian Pocket Percussion Pistol **$200**
Caliber: 45. Barrel: 3³/₄ inches, octagonal. Engraved silver band around butt with silver escutcheons in butt and on checkered grip. Engraved box lock. Flip-down trigger. Made circa 1850.

Belgian Saloon Pistol

Belgian Saloon Pistol **$175**
Caliber: 22. Checkered grip with silver escutcheon. Blued barrel. Iron furniture. Finger spur trigger guard. Made circa 1860.

Belgian Target Pistol

Belgian Target Pistol **$495**
Caliber: 44. Barrel: about 6 inches; Damascus; 20-groove rifling. Iron furniture. Adjustable front sight. Single-set trigger. Engraving usually dense; wood usually shows some relief carving. Silver escutcheon behind barrel tang.

DAVID BENTLEY
Birmingham, England

David Bentley Bulldog
Revolver

David Bentley Revolver. **$165**
Caliber: 44. Barrel: 3 inches. Address engraved on top strap. Made circa 1880.

GUILLAUME BERLEUR
Liège, Belgium

Berleur was a Belgian gunmaker who lived from 1780 to 1830.

Berleur Cavalry Pistol

Berleur Cavalry Pistol. **$465**
Caliber: 70. Percussion lock. Brass furniture. Lock engraved "G. BERLEUR FST. D'ARMES A LIÈGE."

BILLINGS
Address Unknown

Billings Vest Pocket Single Shot Pistol **$750**
Caliber: 32 RF. Barrel: 2¹/₂ inches, round. Oversized handle with walnut grips. Blued finish. Rare. Made in the mid-1860s.

F. D. BLISS
New Haven, Connecticut

F. D. Bliss Pocket Revolver **$295**
Caliber: 25 RF. Six-shot cylinder. Barrel: 3¼ inches, octagonal. Spur trigger. Blued finish. Smooth walnut or rosewood or checkered hard rubber grips. Made early to mid-1860s.

HORACE A. BRIGGS
Norwich, Connecticut

H. A. Briggs Single Shot Pistol **$750**
Caliber: 22 RF. Barrel: 4 inches; part round, part octagonal. Square butt with walnut grips. Blued finish. Made in the early 1850s.

BRITISH PISTOLS
Various Manufacturers

The following listings contain a variety of British-made flintlock and percussion pistols. They are placed together here because they are representative of particular types of guns and also because the specific manufacturers are unknown. In cases where a gunmaker is identified, those entries are detailed separately, by name of manufacturer/gunmaker, elsewhere in the Handgun Section.

British Flintlock Belt Pistol **$550**
Calibers: various. Barrel: brass; engraved "LONDON." Belt hook on left side. Brass lockplate and furniture. Made circa 1800.

British Flintlock Blunderbuss Coach Pistol . . **$560**
Caliber: ⅞-inch at muzzle. Barrel: 6½ inches, brass. Overall length: 11½ inches. Flat wood butt. Center hammer. Engraved guard that pulls back to release bayonet.

British Flintlock Holster Pistol

British Flintlock Holster Pistol **$475**
Calibers: various. Checkered grip. Sliding safety. Plain iron furniture. Roller on frizzen spring. Silver wedge escutcheons. Platinum touch hole. Made circa 1780.

British Flintlock Pistol **$475**
Calibers: various, but ⅝-inch bore common. Barrel: 2 inches, round. Overall length: 6 inches. British proof marks on barrel.

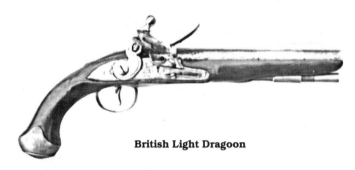
British Light Dragoon

British Light Dragoon Flintlock Pistol **$535**
Calibers: various. Made circa 1805.

British New Land Pattern
Pistol

British New Land Pattern Pistol **$550**
Calibers: various. Tower with crown and G.R. engraved on lockplate. Also called a "Horse Pistol," this was introduced circa 1790 and was the standard weapon for the cavalry.

British Overcoat Flintlock Pistol **$750**
Caliber: ¹¹/₁₆-inch bore. Barrel: 4½ inches, round. Overall length: 9½ inches. Swivel ramrod. Lockplate stamped "BARNETT."

British Flintlock Pocket Pistol

British Pocket Flintlock Pistol **$300**
Caliber: 45. Brass trigger guard. Made circa 1750.

British Percussion Pocket Pistol

British Pocket Percussion Pistol (I) **$200**
Caliber: 41. Round barrel. Engraved box lock. Checkered stock with silver escutcheon. Made circa 1850.

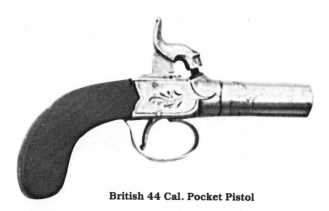

British 44 Cal. Pocket Pistol

British Pocket Percussion Pistol (II) **$150**
Caliber: 44. Percussion ignition. Large oval trigger guard. Engraved lock. Made circa 1840.

British Pocket Percussion Pistol (III) **$200**
Caliber: 45. Octagonal barrel. Flip-down trigger. Engraved silver band around butt with silver escutcheons in butt and on grip. Checkered grip. Engraved box lock. Made circa 1850.

British Flintlock Trade Pistol

British Trade Flintlock Pistol **$475**
Caliber: 61. Flintlock ignition. Barrel: octagonal, brass. Brass furniture. Top stamped "LONDON." Side stamped "EXTRA PROOF" with proof mark. Belgian-made lock.

British Percussion Trade Pistol

British Trade Percussion Pistol **$200**
Caliber: 70. Percussion ignition. Brass trigger guard and butt cap with iron barrel band. All furniture is of Continental pattern. Lockplate stamped "TOWER." May have been made for the African trade circa 1850.

British Volunteer Lancer's Pistol **$450**
Caliber: 79. Percussion ignition. Lock has crown and "TOWER" stamped on it. Brass furniture. Made circa 1840.

B. BROOKE
London, England

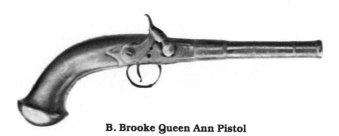

B. Brooke Queen Ann Pistol

B. Brooke Queen Ann Pistol (Percussion Conversion) **$100**
Originally flintlock, but many have been converted to percussion. The value of the flintlock should be about 50 percent higher. Made circa 1600 to 1720.

BROOKLYN ARMS CO.
Brooklyn, New York

Designed by Frank Slocum, the April 1863 patent for his front-loading revolver was one of the several attempts in the late 1850s and early 1860s to outmaneuver the Rollin White-S&W monopoly on rear-loading rimfire revolvers. The chambers in Slocum's gun can actually be opened at the sides for insertion of the cartridges.

Brooklyn Arms/Slocum Pocket Revolver (I)... $435
Caliber: 32 RF. Five-shot cylinder. Barrel: 3 inches, round. Sliding chambers. Spur trigger. Engraved brass frame with silver plate. Oval-shaped butt with walnut grips. Made from 1863 to 1867.

Brooklyn Arms/Slocum Pocket Revolver (II).. $535
Caliber: 32 RF. Six-shot, straight, unfluted cylinder. Barrel: 3 inches, round. Brass frame. Spur trigger. Flat butt flared at rear. Walnut grips. Made 1863 to 1867.

BROWN MANUFACTURING CO.
Newburyport, Massachusetts

Originally made by Merrimack Arms Mfg. Co. (*see* separate listing).

Brown Mfg. Co. Southerner Derringer $325
Caliber: 41 RF. Barrel: 2½ inches; octagonal, side swing. Brass frame, silver-plated. Spur trigger. Plated or blued iron barrel. Walnut or rosewood grips. Made 1869 to 1873.

CALDERWOOD
Dublin, Ireland

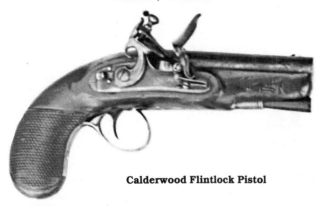

Calderwood Flintlock Pistol

Calderwood Flintlock Pistol $675
Calibers: various. Sliding safety on lock. Round, checkered grip. Made circa 1815.

CANADIAN PISTOLS
Various Manufacturers

Canadian P 1858 Cavalry Pistol

Canadian Percussion Model 1858 Pistol $795
Calibers: various. Barrels: 4 to 7 inches, round. Lock stamped 1855 over Tower with crown and VR. Proof and inspector's marks. Termed "Cavalry Pistol." Made circa 1858.

Canadian Webley MK III
Model 1897 Presentation

Canadian Presentation Webley MK III M. 1897.................................... $950
Caliber: 455. The pistols pictured were presented to Capt. H.S. Greenwood V.D. by the citizens of Peterborough, Ontario, upon his departure for South Africa with the second Canadian contingent. Other presentation Webley pistols should have approximate value; price shown is for the pair.

G. AND J. CHAPMAN
Philadelphia, Pennsylvania

G. & J. Chapman Pocket Revolver $600
Caliber: 32 RF. Seven-shot cylinder. Barrel: 4 inches, round. Brass frame. Blued barrel and cylinder. Bird's-head butt with walnut grips. Rare. Made circa 1860.

CHICAGO FIREARMS COMPANY
Chicago, Illinois

Chicago Firearms Co. Protector Palm Pistol . **$880**
Caliber: 32 extra short RF. Squeezer-type with rotary chambers. Nickel-plated finish standard; blued finish on some. Hard rubber grip plates, although some had pearl or ivory plates.

CHINESE HANDGUNS
Various Manufacturers

Ancient Chinese Hand Cannon

Ancient Chinese Hand Cannon. **$1200**
Barrel: 12 inches; diameter is 1 inch at smallest point. Overall length: 22 inches. Diameter at the breech: 1³/₄ inches. Barrel is supported by an additional piece of wood secured with bamboo wrappings. Swivel is intended for support against a wall or for firing from a boat.

Ancient Chinese Hand Cannon
Pistol

Ancient Chinese Hand Cannon Pistol. **$1795**
Hand-fired ancient pistol with bronze ornamentation. Overall length: 3¹/₂ inches. Very rare.

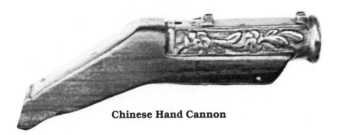

Chinese Hand Cannon

Chinese Hand Cannon. **$250**
Calibers: varied, but 75 common. Bronze barrel with scroll work. Made circa 1850.

COLT'S PATENT FIRE ARMS MFG. CO.
Hartford, Connecticut

Samuel Colt whittled out the first model of a new revolving firearm, with automatic revolution and locking cylinder, while signed aboard the Brig *Corlo* on a return voyage from India. Shortly after returning to America, Colt obtained a patent on his invention, and in 1831 he commissioned a gunsmith to work on his first models. During the years between 1832 and 1836, several Colt pistols, rifles and one shotgun were produced in Albany, Baltimore and Hartford.

Colt's first factory was opened in Paterson, N.J., on March 5, 1836, in an unused section of a silk mill—calling it the Patent Arms Manufacturing Co. But due to lack of business, the Paterson operation failed and closed permanently in 1842, although valuable experience was gained in the process.

The Colt revolving system is said to have been the first practical system of its kind, as it used a pawl on the hammer engaging a ratchet on the end of the cylinder to rotate the cylinder automatically during firing.

Samuel Colt died on January 10, 1862, but Colt Industries in Hartford is still producing fine firearms based on Colt's original 1830s' patents.

See also U.S. Military Handguns of Colt Manufacture and Blackpowder Replicas.

Colt Bisley Model 1894

Colt Bisley Model Single Action Revolver
Calibers: about 18 different ones, ranging from 32 Colt to 455 Eley. Same general specifications as the Single Action Army Model (*see* separate listing), except has longer grips with a sharper drop, lower and flatter hammer and larger trigger guard with curved trigger. Made 1894 to 1912.
Standard Bisley Model **$1050**
Flat Top Target Model. **2050**

Colt Deringer—First Model. **$850**
Caliber: 41 RF. Single shot. All metal. Barrel: 2¹/₂ inches. Overall length: 4¹/₄ inches. Weight: 9 ounces. Barrel turns to side to eject fired cases; thumb catch on right side of frame. Sharply curved metal butt. Lightly engraved. Originally designed by Daniel Moore and made by National Arms Co. (*see* separate listing). Made by Colt from 1870 to about 1890.

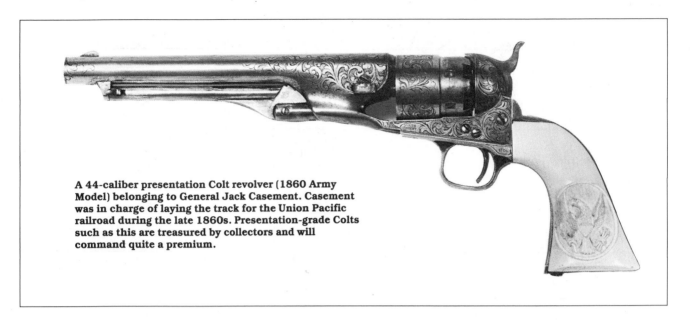

A 44-caliber presentation Colt revolver (1860 Army Model) belonging to General Jack Casement. Casement was in charge of laying the track for the Union Pacific railroad during the late 1860s. Presentation-grade Colts such as this are treasured by collectors and will command quite a premium.

Colt Deringer—Second Model. **$1000**
Caliber: 41 RF. Single shot. Barrel: 2¹/₂ inches; oval, flat top. Overall length: 5¹/₄ inches. Weight: 9 ounces. Barrel lock button on right. Lightly engraved. Bird's-head butt with wood or ivory grips. Originally made by National Arms Co., Colt manufactured it from 1870 to about 1890.

Colt Third Model (Thuer)
Deringer

Colt Deringer—Third Model (Thuer)
Designed by Colt engineer F. Alexander Thuer. Caliber: 41 RF. Single shot. Barrel: 2¹/₂ inches, avg., although other lengths made; round. Overall length: 4¹/₂ inches. Weight: 7¹/₂ ounces. Barrel turns to side to eject fired cases. Spur trigger. Bird's-head butt. Wood grips. Made from 1875 to about 1912.
First Issue (straight hammer spur) **$1050**
Second Issue (backward-inclining hammer
spur). **575**
Third Issue (largest butt). **475**
London Marked **900**

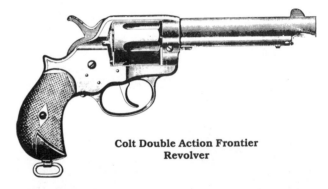

Colt Double Action Frontier
Revolver

Colt Double Action Frontier Revolver. **$950**
Model 1878 Frontier or Double Action Army. Similar to the Model 1877 Lightning, but built on a heavier frame of slightly different shape, round disc on left side of frame and lanyard loop in butt. Calibers: 32-20, 38-40, 44-40 ("Frontier Six-Shooter"), 45 Colt. Six-shot cylinder. Barrels: 3¹/₂ and 4 inches without ejector; 4³/₄, 5¹/₂ and 7¹/₂ inches w/ejector. Overall length: 12¹/₂ inches w/7¹/₂-inch bbl. Weight: 39 ounces w/7¹/₂-inch bbl. Fixed sights. Hard rubber bird's-head grips. Blued or nickel finish. Made 1878 to 1905.

Colt "House Pistol"— Cloverleaf House SA Revolver
The first Colt revolver designed specifically for metallic cartridges. Caliber: 41 RF. Single action. Four-shot cloverleaf-shaped cylinder with recessed chambers. Barrels: 1¹/₂ inches, round or octagonal; 3 inches, round. Overall length: 5¹/₄ inches w/1¹/₂-inch bbl. Weight: 14 ounces. Brass frame. Spur trigger. Straight-up hammer. Wooden bird's-head grips. Rod ejector. Made 1871 to 1876.
With 1¹/₂-inch round bbl. **$700**
With 1¹/₂-inch octagonal bbl.. . . . .**925**
With 3-inch round bbl.. . . . .**485**

Colt "House Pistol" SA Revolver **$1050**
Caliber: 41 RF. Single action. Five-shot round cylinder. No ejector. Barrel: 2⅝ inches, round. Weight: 15 ounces. Made 1871 to 1876.

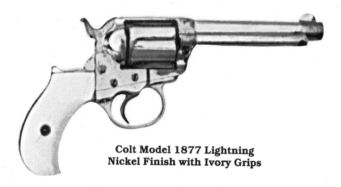

Colt Model 1877 Lightning
Nickel Finish with Ivory Grips

Colt Model 1877 Lightning
with Holster

Colt Lightning Central Fire DA Revolver **$510**
Model 1877 Lightning, the first in the line of popular double-action Colts. Interestingly, Sam Colt would not endorse the concept of double-action arms before his death, asserting that accuracy was not possible. This gun was designed by William Mason, a Colt engineer, who worked out the "bugs." Calibers: 38 and 41 centerfire (41 cal. called the "Thunderer"). Six-shot cylinder. Barrels: 1½, 2½, 3½, 4½ and 6 inches w/o ejector; 4½, 5 and 6 to 10 inches w/ejector. Overall length: 8½ inches w/3½-inch bbl. Weight: 23 ounces w/3½-inch bbl. Fixed sights. Hard rubber bird's-head grips. Blued or nickel finish. Made 1877 to 1909.

**Colt Model 1855 Root Percussion
Handgun (I)** **$780**
Named after Elisha King Root, Colt's old friend and superintendent/top engineer at the Colt Armory in Hartford; also called "Pocket Pistol" and "1855 Sidehammer Colt" because the hammer is on the right side of the frame. Caliber: 256 (designated 28). Five-shot, straight, round, engraved cylinder. Barrel: 3½ inches, octagonal; marked "Colt's Pat. 1855—Address Col. Colt, Hartford, Ct. U.S.A." Overall length: 8 inches. Weight: 17 ounces. Solid, blued steel frame with spur trigger. Loading lever. No trigger guard. Made 1856 to 1861.

Colt London Cased 31 Caliber
Model 1855 Root Percussion
Revolver

**Colt Model 1855 Root Percussion
Handgun (II)** **$780**
A continuation of the 1855 Root (Sidehammer) series, except in 31 caliber with round or octagonal barrels of 3½ or 4½ inches. Most have full fluted cylinders, some with roll engraved scenes. Made 1861 to 1870.

Colt Model 1872 Single Action Revolver
Also called the Open Top .44. Caliber: 44 Henry RF. Six-shot engraved cylinder. Barrel: 7½, 8 inches. Overall length: 13½ to 14 inches. No strap above cylinder. Iron or brass grip straps. Similar to Colt 1860 Army percussion, but not a conversion. Total of approx. 7,000 made about 1872.
Army-style Grip-frame **$2700**
Navy-style Grip-frame **3000**

Colt New House Single Action Revolver **$450**
Calibers: 38 Long Colt, 41 RF, (32 rare). Five-shot cylinder with long flutes. Barrels: most 2¼ inches without ejector rod; left side stamped "COLT HOUSE" or "NEW HOUSE." Squared butt with checkered hard rubber or plain wood grips, "COLT" on upper part. One model in the "New Line Pistol" series (*see* below). Made 1880 to 1886.

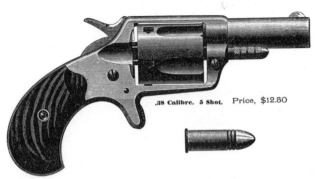

.38 Calibre. 5 Shot.   Price, $12.50

Colt New Line Pocket Revolver

Colt New Line Pocket Revolver **$480**
Calibers: 22, 30, 32, 38 and 41 RF; 32 Short Colt, 38 Short Colt, 38 Long Colt, 41 centerfire. Five-shot cylinder (7-shot in 22 cal.). Barrels: 2¼ inches to 10 inches (custom), round; 22 cal. with flat-sided barrel. Sheath trigger. Bird's-head grip. Made about 1873 to 1884.

Colt New Line Police Single Action Revolver . **$425**
Caliber: 38 Long Colt. Five-shot unmarked cylinder. Barrels: 4½, 5 and 6 inches, round; marked "New Police .38." Overall length: 9 inches. Side rod ejector and loading gate. Square butt with hard rubber grips. Made 1882 to 1886.

Colt New Navy Model 1889 DA Revolver **$500**
Calibers: 38 Short Colt, 38 Long Colt, 41 Short Colt, 41 Long Colt (civilian version only). Six-shot, full fluted, swing-out cylinder. Barrels: 3, 4½ and 6 inches. Overall length: 11¼ inches w/6-inch bbl. Fixed sights, knifeblade and V-notch. Walnut or hard rubber grips. Blued or nickel-plated finish. Made 1889 to 1894.

Colt New Navy Model 1892 DA Revolver **$350**
Also known as "New Army" Models 1892, 1894, 1895, 1896, 1901 and 1903, and were improved versions of the New Navy Model 1889. Calibers: 38 and 41 Colt. Same general specifications as above. Made 1892 to 1907. These were superseded in 1908 by the New Army Special revolvers, which continued the serial numbers.

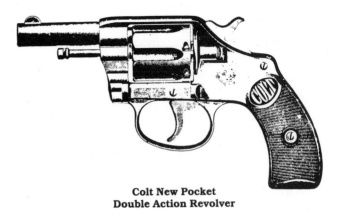

**Colt New Pocket
Double Action Revolver**

Colt New Pocket DA Revolver **$320**
Calibers: 32 Short and Long Colt "central fire," 32 S&W. Double action. Six-shot, swing-out cylinder. Small, jointless solid frame. Barrels: 2½ to 6 inches, round. Overall length: 10 inches w/6-inch bbl. Blued or nickel-plated finish. Marked "Colt's New Pocket." Made 1893 to 1905. This model replaced the S.A. New Line revolvers and, in turn, were superseded by the Pocket Positive model in 1905.

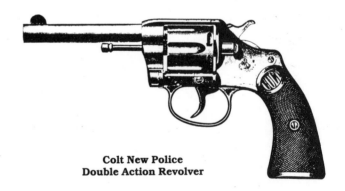

**Colt New Police
Double Action Revolver**

Colt New Police DA Revolver **$290**
Calibers: 32 Colt, 32 S&W. Six-shot swing-out cylinder. Barrels: 2½, 4, 6 inches; round. Overall length: 10½ inches w/6-inch bbl. Weight: about 19 ounces w/6-inch bbl. Blued or nickel-plated finish. Marked "Colt's New Police." In 1896, about 4500 were purchased by the New York City Police Dept., of which Theodore Roosevelt was commissioner; he was given Serial No. 1 for testing. Made 1896 to 1905.

**Colt New Service Double
Action Revolver, Military Issue**

Colt New Service DA Revolver. **$360**
The largest framed double-action with swing-out cylinder in the Colt repertoire. Calibers: 18 different, ranging from 38 Short Colt to 476 Eley. Barrel: 8 lengths, ranging from 2 to 7½ inches. Weight: 42 ounces, avg. Blued or nickel-plated finish. Lanyard loop in butt. Many variations exist. Made 1898 to 1944.

Colt Open Top Pocket Pistol

Colt Old Line Single Action Pocket Revolver
Also known as Open Top Pocket Pistol. Caliber: 22 RF. Seven-shot unmarked cylinder. Barrel: 2³/₈ or 2⁷/₈ inches. Overall length: 6½ inches. No strap on frame over cylinder. With or without rod ejector. Wood bird's-head grip. Made 1871 to 1877.
First Model w/ejector **$875**
Second Model w/o ejector **375**

**Colt Paterson—"Baby" or No. 1 Pocket Percussion
Handgun**
Caliber: 28. Five-shot engraved cylinder with rounded cylinder stops. Barrel: length varies; octagonal. Overall length: 7 to 7⁷/₈ inches. Smooth, straight walnut grips. This is the first handgun manufactured by Colt in Paterson, N.J., based on his original patent of Feb. 25, 1836. Made late 1836 to 1838, some altered in 1840 to include loading lever.
Without loading lever, 4-inch bbl. **$3925**
With loading lever, 3-inch bbl. **4300**

**Colt Paterson—"Baby" Percussion
Handgun.** **$3800**
Same general specifications as above models, but with 4¼-inch barrel. Low blade front sight; rear sight on hammer nose. Two rounded bands extend around the engraved cylinder. Made between 1836 and 1838.

Colt Paterson No. 2 Belt Pistol
Caliber: 31 percussion. Five-shot engraved cylinder with square nipple separations. Barrel: avg. 4¼ to 4³/₄ inches; octagonal. Overall length: 8 to 8½ inches, avg. Weight: about 20 ounces. No loading lever. Straight walnut grips. Made about 1838 to 1840, some altered in 1840 to include loading lever.
Without Loading Lever. **$3950**
With Loading Lever. **4350**

Colt Paterson No. 3 Belt Pistol. **$3950**
Same general specifications as the Paterson No. 2 Belt Pistol, except has flared walnut grips. With the factory loading lever attached (done on some models in 1840), this is a rare item and will command a premium.

Colt Paterson No. 2 or No. 3 Belt, Cased **$5500**
Same revolvers as above, except cased in original Paterson Colt mahogany case with extra cylinder, bullet mold, combination tool, cleaning rod and priming device, and combination bullet and powder flask.

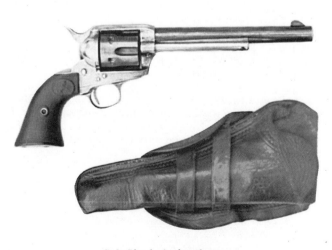

**Colt Single Action Army
with Holster**

Colt Single Action Army Revolver
Dubbed "Peacemaker," "Six-Shooter," "Frontier," "Equalizer," "Sheriff's Model," and "Storekeeper's Model" to name but a few, this is by far the most famous of the Colt revolvers. It was used by such legendary figures as Gen. George Custer, Bat Masterson, Teddy Roosevelt and George S. Patton. Calibers: 30 different ones, from 22 RF to 476 Eley, those most frequently encountered 32-20, 38-40, 41, 44-40 and 45. Six-shot fluted cylinder. Barrels: 4³/₄ to 16¹/₈ inches, with ejectors; 2 to 7¹/₂ inches, often without ejectors. Solid, casehardened frame. Blued finish. Oil-finished walnut grips standard. Many variations of the S.A.A. exist, some with exquisite engravings and custom grips, etc. The Flattop Target Model, a major variation, was introduced in 1888 and the Bisley, another, was produced between 1894 and 1912 (*see* separate listing). In 1900, the revolvers were constructed to handle smokeless powder. Total production spanned from 1873 to 1940.

Artillery Model, 5¹/₂-inch bbl.,
    screw-retained cylinder **$2100**
Flattop Target Model. **3200**
Indian Scout Model, screw-retained cylinder. . . **3550**
Long-barreled Models, 8- to 16-inch bbl. **2100**
Long-barreled Models w/folding rear sight **4300**
Rimfire Calibers. **2100**
Standard Calvary Model, Ser. Nos. under
    15000. . . . . **3100**
Standard S.A.A. Model **1200**
Storekeeper's Model, short bbl., no ejector **3250**

D. D. CONE
Washington, D. C.

D. D. Cone was allegedly a trade name used by William Uhlinger on his 1860s-produced revolvers, which were in violation of the Rollin White patent owned by S&W regarding bored-through cylinders.

D.D. Cone Revolver (I) **$200**
Caliber: 22 Long RF. Six-shot cylinder. Barrel: 2³/₄ or 3 inches; octagonal. Spur trigger. Solid iron frame. Square butt. Blued finish. Rosewood or walnut grips. Made circa 1861 to 1865.

D.D. Cone Revolver (II) **$235**
Caliber: 32 Long RF. Six-shot cylinder. Barrel: 5, 6 or 7 inches; octagonal. Single action. Spur trigger. Solid iron frame. Plated or blued finish. Walnut or rosewood grips. Made circa 1861 to 1865.

CONNECTICUT ARMS COMPANY
Norfolk, Connecticut

One of the several attempts to produce a successful front-loading revolver in the mid-1860s.

Connecticut Arms Co. Pocket Revolver **$340**
Caliber: 28 cup primed. Six-shot cylinder. Barrel: 3 inches, octagonal, tip-up. Spur trigger. Brass frame. Silver-plated finish. Steel parts blued. Square butt with walnut grips. Made circa mid-1860s.

CONNECTICUT ARMS & MFG. CO.
Naubuc, Connecticut

Connecticut Arms & Mfg. Co. Bulldog Pistol . **$330**
Pivoting breechblock. Caliber: 44 RF. Barrel: 4 inches, octagonal. Spur trigger. Iron frame with casehardened finish. Blued barrel. Made 1866 to 1868.

Connecticut Arms & Mfg. Co. Bulldog Pistol . **$490**
Same general specifications as above, except with much longer barrel.

CONTINENTAL ARMS COMPANY
Norwich, Connecticut

Continental Arms Co. Continental 1 . . . . **$510**
Caliber: 22 RF. Seven-shot pepperbox. Barrels: 2¹/₂ inches. Spur trigger. Sold iron frame. Square butt. Made 1866 to 1867.

Continental Arms Co. Continental 2 . . . . **$615**
Caliber: 32 RF. Five-shot pepperbox. Spur trigger. Solid iron frame. Made 1866 to 1867.

JOSEPH ROCK COOPER
Birmingham, England

In 1840 J. R. Cooper patented his self-cocking, six-barreled pepperbox, the popular arm of that day. By 1850 he had established a sales outlet not only in Birmingham, but also in New York City, which imported his English-made guns.

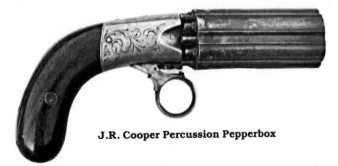

J.R. Cooper Percussion Pepperbox

J. R. Cooper Percussion Pepperbox **$485**
Caliber: 38. Six shots. Barrels: 3¹/₂ inches. Overall length: about 8 inches. Some engraved with fern design. Made from 1840 to 1853.

FRANK COPELAND
Worcester, Massachusetts

F. Copeland Pocket Revolver (I) **$220**
Caliber: 22 Short RF. Seven-shot cylinder. Barrel: 2¼ inches, octagonal. Brass frame. Spur trigger. Walnut or rosewood grips. Bird's-head butt. Made 1868 to 1874.

F. Copeland Pocket Revolver (II) **$245**
Caliber: 32 Short RF. Seven-shot cylinder. Barrel: 2¼ inches, octagonal. Brass frame. Spur trigger. Walnut or rosewood grips. Bird's-head butt. Made 1868 to 1874.

COWLES AND SON
Chicopee, Massachusetts

Cowles & Son Single Shot Pistol **$265**
Calibers: 22 and 30 RF. Barrel: 3¼ inches; round, side swing, blued. Brass frame with silver-plated finish. Spur trigger. Bird's-head butt. Walnut grips. Made 1871 to 1876.

SILAS CRISPIN
New York, New York

Based on Silas Crispin's patent of 1865, the Smith Arms Co. of New York City apparently produced this revolver. It is one of the several attempts to thwart the restrictions posed by the Rollin White/S&W patent regarding rear-loading revolvers. In this version, the cylinder is split about three-quarters of the way in to allow for inserting of the cartridges. The arm is considered scarce, and dangerous.

Silas Crispin Revolver **$3675**
Caliber: 32. Six-shot cylinder. Barrel: 5 inches, octagonal. Split cylinder. Iron frame with blued finish. Made circa late 1860s.

O. S. CUMMINGS
Lowell, Massachusetts

O. S. Cummings Pocket Revolver **$200**
Caliber: 22 RF. Seven-shot cylinder. Barrel: 3 inches, ribbed. Iron frame with nickel finish. Spur trigger. Rosewood or walnut grips. Bird's-head butt. Made circa 1870s.

GEORGE HENRY DAW
London, England

Although handguns were a part of G. H. Daw's firearms trade, shotguns were a major interest. In fact, he is credited with the first hammerless shotgun using modern-type cartridges, which he patented in 1862. His firm was active until the early 1890s.

Daw British Sea Service
Pistol

Daw British Sea Service Pistol **$385**
Caliber: 58. Percussion ignition. Contract piece by G. H. Daw, London. Name engraved on barrel and lockplate. Belt hook on left side. Brass furniture. Lanyard ring in butt.

HENRY DERINGER JR.
Philadelphia, Pennsylvania

Henry Deringer Jr. was born in Easton, Penn., on October 26, 1786. At age 20, he set up shop at 612 North Front Street in Philadelphia, producing flintlock pistols and muskets under Government contracts for the U. S. Army.

Deringer also catered to the civilian market with flintlock and percussion hunting rifles, along with cased dueling pistols. In 1831, he developed the percussion pistol or short-rifled barrel with heavy caliber that became the prototype of what is known as the "derringer." (Note the one "r" in the surname vs. the two in the pistol name.)

The Deringer Pocket Pistol experienced large sales in the South, and this market spread to the Pacific Coast during the gold rush years. Deringer's pistols were copied, and even his name and trademark were stamped on the lockplate and breech of the barrel. These circumstances led to the famous lawsuit of Henry Deringer vs. A. J. Plate. Unfortunately, before the suit was settled, Deringed died in Philadelphia on February 26, 1868, in his 81st year. The damages were awarded to his estate in the final settlement.

The firm continued for a while under the direction of Dr. Jonathan Clark, a son-in-law, and other relatives (*see* Deringer Rifle & Pistol Works).

Deringer Pocket Pistol

Deringer Pocket Pistol **$845**
Calibers: 36 to 54, with 41 caliber being the most popular. Barrels: less than 1 inch to over 4 inches. Overall lengths: 3³/₄ to 15 inches. Lockplate was inscribed "DERINGER PHILADELA." These pistols were not serial numbered, but the various parts were stamped with matching assembly numbers or letters. A Deringer derringer was used by John Wilkes Booth to assassinate President Abraham Lincoln.

Deringer Dueller Pistols **$1695**
Calibers: various, but 41 most common. Barrel: various lengths, from 6 to 10 inches or more. German silver mounts, cased pair. Made from 1806 to 1868.

Deringer Dueller Pistols (Gold Mounts) **$5700**
Same general specifications as the standard duellers, except with gold mounts rather than German silver. Made from 1806 to 1868.

Deringer Dueller Pistols (Silver Mounts) **$2100**
Same general specifications as standard duellers, except with sterling silver mounts rather than German silver. Made from 1806 to 1868.

DERINGER RIFLE & PISTOL WORKS
Philadelphia, Pennsylvania

After Henry Deringer's death in 1868, relatives continued the manufacture of metallic cartridge revolvers for about 10 years.

Deringer Centennial '76 Revolver **$400**
Caliber: 38 Long RF. Five-shot cylinder. Single action. Spur trigger. Tip-up barrel.

Deringer Pocket Model 1 Revolver **$375**
Caliber: 22 Short RF. Seven-shot straight, unfluted, cylinder. Barrel: 3 inches; octagonal, ribbed, tip-up. Spur trigger. Walnut grips. Bird's-head butt. Made 1873 to 1879.

Deringer Pocket Model 2 Revolver **$340**
Caliber: 22 Short RF. Seven-shot, spur trigger, semi-fluted cylinder. Barrel: 3 inches; round, ribbed. Fluted sides. Spur triggers. Walnut grips. Bird's-head butt. Made 1873 to 1879.

Deringer Pocket Revolver **$340**
Caliber: 32 Long RF. Five-shot cylinder. Barrel: 3¹/₂ inches; round, tip-up. Brass or iron frame. Silver or nickel plated. Spur trigger. Walnut grips. Bird's-head butt. Made late 1870s.

E. L. & J. DICKINSON
Springfield, Massachusetts

E. L. & J. Single Shot Pocket Pistol (I) **$425**
Caliber: 22 RF. Barrel: 3³/₄ inches; octagonal, pivoting, rack ejector. Brass frame, silver plated. Spur trigger. Walnut grips. Square butt. Made 1868 to 1872.

E. L. & J. Dickinson Single Shot Pocket Pistol (II) **$320**
All specifications the same as above model, except made in 32 rimfire caliber.

J. B. DRISCOLL
Springfield, Massachusetts

J. B. Driscoll Single Shot Pocket Pistol **$475**
Caliber: 22 RF. Barrel: 3¹/₂ inches; octagonal, blued, pivots downward for loading. Brass frame with silver-plated finish. Spur trigger; also has trigger-like latch release under barrel. Walnut grips. Square butt. Made circa 1870.

EAGLE ARMS COMPANY
New York, New York

Eagle Arms Co. Revolver (I) **$380**
Caliber: 28 cup primed. Six-shot cylinder. Single action. Spur trigger. Solid frame. Made in 1865.

Eagle Arms Co. Revolver (II) **$375**
Caliber: 28 cup primed. Six-shot cylinder. Single action. Spur trigger. Tip-up. Made in 1865.

Eagle Arms Co. Revolver (III) **$350**
Caliber: 30 cup primed. Six-shot cylinder. Barrel: 3¹/₂ inches; octagonal, ribbed. Spur trigger. Solid brass frame with silver-plated finish. Barrel and cylinder blued. Made in 1865.

Eagle Arms Co. Revolver (IV) **$400**
Same general specifications as revolver (III), above, except is tip-up model.

Eagle Arms Co. Revolver (V) **$325**
Caliber: 42 cup primed. Six-shot cylinder. Barrel: 6 inches; octagonal, ribbed. Single action. Spur trigger. Solid frame. Made in 1865.

Eagle Arms Co. Revolver (VI) **$465**
Caliber: 42 cup primed. Six-shot cylinder. Barrel: 6 inches; octagonal, ribbed. Spur trigger. Tip-up model. Made in 1865.

DURS EGG
London, England

Durs Egg (1748–1831) distinguished himself as a gunmaker by handcrafting fine flintlock arms. He supplied handguns and long arms to the military service and even provided many of the guns used by British volunteers during the Revolutionary War against the "Colonies."

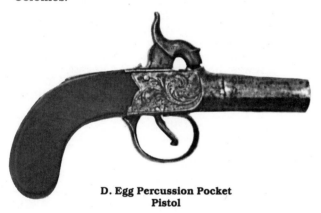

D. Egg Percussion Pocket
Pistol

Durs Egg Percussion Pocket Pistol **$175**
Caliber: 49. Engraved boxlock with silver escutcheon on grip. One of Egg's latest production pieces, this was made circa 1830.

EUROPEAN PISTOLS
Various Manufacturers

European Cavalry Flintlock Pistol

European Cavalry Flintlock **$575**
Caliber: 73. Barrel: about 6 inches, half-octagonal; stamped "EX." Inside of lock stamped "RUIZ." Brass furniture. Made circa 1800.

European Percussion Pistol **$250**
Caliber: 52. Barrel: 8 inches; octagonal, engraved. Abstract rampant lion on lockplate. Captive ramrod capbox in butt. Iron-mounted. Made circa 1840.

FABRIQUE NATIONALE D'ARMES DE GUERRE
Liège, Belgium

Located in the heart of the Belgian firearms-producing area, Fabrique National is a long established arms manufacturer. It is still engaged in arms production under the name Fabrique Nationale Herstal, a suburb of Liège from which it takes its name.

FN Browning Model 1900 Pocket Auto Pistol **$400**
Caliber: 32 automatic (7.65 mm). Seven-shot magazine. Barrel length: 4 inches. Overall length: 6½ inches. Weight: 22 oz. Fixed sights. Hard rubber stocks. Blued finish. Made 1899 to 1910.

FOREHAND ARMS COMPANY
Worcester, Massachusetts

See Forehand & Wadsworth.

FOREHAND & WADSWORTH
Worcester, Massachusetts

The Forehand & Wadsworth Company began operation in 1871, being successors and sons-in-law to Ethan Allen, who operated Ethan Allen & Co. from 1865 to 1871. In 1890, H. C. Wadsworth retired and the firm changed its name to The Forehand Arms Co. and operated under this designation from 1890 to 1902. Both firms were known primarily for their shotguns and revolvers, but the firms did produce a few rifles also.

Forehand & Wadsworth British Bulldog (I) . . . **$105**
Caliber: 38 S&W. Six- or seven-shot cylinder. Double action.

Forehand & Wadsworth British Bulldog (II) . . **$135**
Caliber: 44 S&W. Five-shot cylinder. Double action.

Forehand & Wadsworth Bulldog (I) **$165**
Caliber: 38 Long RF. Five-shot cylinder. Barrel: 2 inches. Double action. Blued finish.

Forehand & Wadsworth Bulldog (II) **$135**
Caliber: 44 S&W. Five-shot cylinder. Double action.
Barrel: 2 inches.

**Forehand & Wadsworth New Model Army
Revolver** **$575**
Caliber: 38 Long RF. Six-shot cylinder. Single action.
Barrel: 6½ inches, round. Walnut grips. Blued finish.
Made late 1870s to 1880s.

Forehand & Wadsworth New Navy **$560**
Caliber: 44 Russian. Six-shot cylinder. Double action.
Barrel: 6 inches.

Forehand & Wadsworth Old Model Army **$625**
Caliber: 44 Russian. Six-shot cylinder. Single action.
Barrel: 7 inches, round. Walnut grips. Blued finish.
Made in the mid-1870s.

Forehand& Wadsworth Pocket Model **$105**
Caliber: 32 S&W Long. Six-shot cylinder. Double Action. Top break.

Forehand & Wadsworth Russian Model **$215**
Caliber: 32, 32 Short RF. Five-shot. Single action. Spur
trigger.

**Forehand & Wadsworth Single Action
Revolver (I)** **$210**
Caliber: 22 Short RF. Seven-shot cylinder. Barrel: 2¼
inches to 4 inches, octagonal. Side hammer. Spur trigger. Walnut grips. Bird's-head butt. Blued or nickel finish. Made in the early 1870s.

**Forehand & Wadsworth Single Action
Revolver (II)** **$210**
Caliber: 32 Short RF. Six-shot cylinder. Barrel: 3⅜
inches, octagonal. Rosewood or walnut grips. Bird's-
head butt. Blued or nickel finish frame. Made in the
early 1870s.

Forehand & Wadsworth Single Shot (I) **$290**
Caliber: 22 Short RF. Spur trigger. Barrel: 2 inches;
side-swing, part round/part octagonal. Iron frame with
nickel or silver-plated finish. Blued or plated barrel.
Bird's-head butt. Walnut grips.

Forehand & Wadsworth Single Shot (II) **$400**
Caliber: 41 Short RF. Spur trigger. Barrel: 2½ inches,
side-swing. Walnut grips. Bird's-head butt. Blued finish.

Forehand & Wadsworth Swamp Angel **$220**
Caliber: 41 Short RF. Five-shot cylinder. Single action.
Spur trigger.

Forehand & Wadsworth Terror **$185**
Caliber: 32 Short RF. Five-shot cylinder. Single action.
Spur trigger.

AUSTIN FREEMAN
Watertown, New York

Freeman 44 Cal. Percussion
Revolver

Freeman Percussion Revolver **$1350**
Caliber: 44. Six-shot cylinder. Barrel: 7½ inches, rifled.
Overall length: 12½ inches. Weight: 2 lbs. 13 oz. Produced at Hoard's Armory in Watertown, N.Y., this arm
was patented in 1862 by Austin Freeman. It is considered a rare Civil-War-period piece, although ordnance
records cannot substantiate its official use by the U.S.
military. It was the precursor to the Rogers and Spencer Revolver, which was purchased by the U.S. Government during the Civil War (*see* also U.S. Military
Revolvers).

FRENCH HANDGUNS
Various Manufacturers

French Charleville Flintlock Pistol **$1550**
Caliber: 69. Barrel: 7¾ inches, round; marked "MRE
RE de CHARLEVILLE." Overall length: 13½ inches.
Lockplate is 5 inches long. Brass side plate, single
brass band. Brass trigger guard, flash pan and butt.
Ring for lanyard. Made from 1777 to about 1800.

French 60 Cal. Coat Pistol

French Coat Pistol **$250**
Caliber: 60 percussion. Octagonal, Damascus barrel.
Engraved box lock. Large, round trigger guard. Finely
carved panel around butt of leaves. Made circa 1850.

French Coup de Poing Pepperbox

French Coup de Poing Pepperbox **$175**
Caliber: 7mm. Engraved checkered grips with ejector screwed into butt. "Coup de Poing" means simply a fist pistol.

French Flintlock Pistol
with Silver Embossing

French Flintlock Pistol (I) **$385**
Calibers: various. Barrel: various lengths, usually round. Brass furniture with highly embossed silver overlay from muzzle to butt. The model shown has ½-inch turquoise stone on wrist.

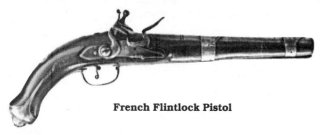

French Flintlock Pistol

French Flintlock Pistol (II) **$350**
Calibers: various. Similar to French Flintlock Pistol (I) with brass furniture, but with less embellishment.

French Flintlock Pistol (III) **$435**
Calibers: various, but 11/16-inch bore common. Barrel: 11½ inches, round. Overall length: 19 inches. Silvered butt fittings.

French Howdah Pistol **$360**
Caliber: 16mm pinfire. Barrel: engraved, marked "ST. ETIENNE 16.0." Fitting at butt made to accept shoulder stock. Made from 1860 to 1870.

French Military Flintlock Pistol **$965**
Caliber: 65. Typical of those made by Frappier of Paris with a turn-off barrel. Octagonal section of barrel designed for wrench. Copper fittings. Made circa 1793–94 during French Revolutionary period.

Louis XIV Flintlock Pistol, Pair **$2800**
Caliber: 69. Barrel: 4 inches, octagonal; etched with gold-plated designs. Overall length: 8¼ inches. Locks 3½ inches long. Silver wire inlaid grips. Round butts with plates.

GEM PISTOLS
Chicopee Falls, Massachusetts

See Stevens Arms & Tool Co.

GEM REVOLVERS
Norwich, Connecticut

See Bacon Arms Co.

GERMAN HANDGUNS
Various Manufacturers

German Cavalry Pistol **$250**
Calibers: various. Most were marked with the Regiment. Made circa 1851 to 1860.

German-Proofed 5-Shot
Pepperbox

German Pepperbox **$350**
Caliber: 45. Five-shot cylinder. Nickel-plated. Made circa 1890.

GOVERNOR REVOLVERS
Various Manufacturers

See also Bacon Arms Co.

Governor Double Action Revolver **$100**
Caliber: 32 S&W. Five-shot cylinder. Top break. Barrel: 3 inches, round.

Governor Double Action Revolver **$105**
Caliber: 38 S&W. Five-shot cylinder. Top break. Barrel: 3 inches, round.

W. L. GRANT
Philadelphia, Pennsylvania

W. L. Grant was supposedly one of the trade names used by William Uhlinger on revolvers he produced in the 1860s. His intention, presumably, was to avert attention from himself as the manufacturer since his designs were in violation of the S&W-owned/Rollin White patent in force at the time.

W. L. Grant Revolver (I) **$250**
Caliber: 22 Long RF. Six-shot cylinder. Barrels: 2³/₄ or 3 inches, octagonal. Spur trigger. Solid iron frame. Square butt. Blued finish. Rosewood or walnut grips. Made circa 1861 to 1865.

W. L. Grant Revolver (II) **$275**
Caliber: 32 Long RF. Six-shot cylinder. Barrels: 5, 6 or 7 inches; octagonal. Spur trigger. Solid iron frame. Plated or blued finish. Walnut or rosewood grips. Made circa 1861 to 1865.

GROSS ARMS CO.
Tiffin, Ohio

Henry Gross operated out of Tiffin from 1841 to 1852, when his son, Charles B., joined the business. Together they operated the firm until Henry's death in 1875. The business was carried on under the name of Charles B. Gross from 1875 to 1886.

Gross Arms Co. Pocket Revolver (I) **$680**
Caliber: 22 Short RF. Seven-shot cylinder. Barrel: 6 inches. Spur trigger. Tip-up. Blued finish. Walnut grips.

Gross Arms Co. Pocket Revolver (II) **$705**
Caliber: 25 Short RF. Six-shot cylinder. Barrel: 6 inches. Spur trigger. Tip-up. Blued finish. Walnut grips.

Gross Arms Co. Pocket Revolver (III) **$680**
Caliber: 32 Short RF. Five-shot cylinder. Barrel: 6 inches. Spur trigger. Tip-up. Blued finish. Walnut grips.

JAMES HARDING
Address unknown

James Harding Coat Pistol

James Harding Coat Pistol (Conversion) **$275**
Caliber: 69. Original flintlock converted to percussion. Brass furniture. Crudely checkered rounded grip. Made circa 1750 to 1815.

HARRINGTON AND RICHARDSON
Worcester, Massachusetts

Gilbert H. Harrington and William A. Richardson established the original H & R plant on Herman Street in Worcester, Mass., in 1874. Their initial enterprise consisted of producing shotguns and metallic cartridge revolvers.

H & R Model No. 1 Revolver (I) **$150**
Caliber: 32. Seven-shot cylinder. Barrel: 3 inches, octagonal. Iron frame. Spur trigger. Bird's-head butt. Checkered hard rubber grips. Full nickel finish only.

H & R Model No. 1 Revolver (II) **$160**
Caliber: 38. Five-shot cylinder. Barrel: 3 inches, octagonal. Iron frame. Spur trigger. Bird's-head butt. Checkered hard rubber grips. Full nickel finish only.

H & R Saw-Handled Frame Spur Trigger (I) **$75**
Caliber: 32 RF. Five-shot cylinder. Barrel: 2¹/₂ inches, octagonal. Nickel finish. Checkered hard rubber grips. Made from 1878 to 1883.

H & R Saw-Handled Frame Spur Trigger (II) . . .**$90**
Caliber: 32 RF. Seven-shot cylinder. Barrel: 3¹/₄ inches, octagonal. Nickel finish. Checkered hard rubber grips. Made from 1878 to 1883.

**H & R Saw-Handled Frame Spur Trigger
(III)** **$110**
Caliber: 38 RF. Five-shot cylinder. Barrel: 3¹/₂ inches,
octagonal. Nickel finish. Checkered hard rubber grips.
Made from 1878 to 1883.

**H & R Saw-Handled Frame Spur Trigger
(IV)**. **$150**
Caliber: 41 RF. Five-shot cylinder. Barrel: 2¹/₂ inches,
octagonal. Nickel finish. Checkered hard rubber grips.
Made from 1878 to 1883.

HILL'S PATENT HANDGUNS
Great Britain

Hill's Patent Bull Dog

Hill's Patent Bulldog. **$200**
Caliber: 44 Bulldog. Five-shot cylinder. Tip-up barrel.
Auto ejectors. Made circa 1880.

HENRY HOLMES
Liverpool, England

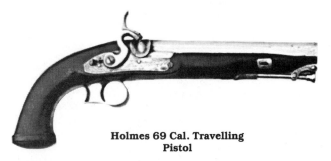

**Holmes 69 Cal. Travelling
Pistol**

Holmes Travelling Pistol **$385**
Caliber: 69 percussion. Sliding safety on lock. Finely
engraved iron furniture. Silver escutcheons on stock
and silver band at breech. Made circa 1800 to 1850.

HOOD FIREARMS COMPANY
Norwich, Connecticut

Freeman W. Hood patented a metallic cartridge revolver in February 1875, a description of which follows.

Hood Firearms Co. Single Action Revolver . . . **$175**
Calibers: 22 short, 32 short and 41, all rimfire. Five-
shot cylinder. Barrel: various lengths, but 3¹/₂ inches
common. Spur trigger. Solid frame. Walnut grips.
Blued or nickel-plated finish. Made from 1875 to 1880.

HOPKINS & ALLEN
Norwich, Connecticut

The Hopkins and Allen plant was in operation from
1868 to 1915, and turned out numerous handguns, rifles and shotguns. Many of their firearms were distributed under different names, including the revolvers
made under the Merwin and Hulbert patents (*see* separate listing). The business was sold in 1915 to Marlin-
Rockwell.

Allen Pocket Revolver. **$125**
Caliber: 22 Short RF. Seven-shot cylinder. Single ac-
tion. Solid frame. Spur trigger. Made between 1880 and
1917.

Hopkins & Allen Model 1876 Revolver. **$625**
Caliber: 44 - 40. Six-shot cylinder. Barrel: 4¹/₂, 6 or 7¹/₂
inches, round. Walnut grips with square butt. Blued or
nickel finish. Made in the late 1870s to early 1880s.

Hopkins & Allen Ladies Garter Pistol **$155**
Caliber: 22 Short RF. Single shot. Barrel: 1³/₄ inches.
Folding trigger; hammerless. Wooden, ivory or pearl
grips. Decorative scroll engraving standard. Plated or
full blued finish. Made from 1888 to 1893.

Hopkins & Allen New Model Target Pistol. . . . **$375**
Caliber: 22 RF. Top break. Barrel: 10 inches. Adjustable
sights. Target grips.

**Hopkins & Allen Ranger No. 1
Nickel Finish**

Hopkins & Allen Ranger No. 1 . . . . **$170**
Caliber: 22 Long. Seven-shot cylinder. Nickel-plated
with bluing that highlights the engraved frame and barrel. Made circa 1900.

Hopkins & Allen Ranger No. 2

Hopkins & Allen Ranger No. 2 . . . . **$165**
Caliber: 32 long or short RF. Single Action. Round or octagonal barrel. Spur trigger. Blued finish.

Hopkins & Allen Safety Police DA
Revolver (I) **$140**
Caliber: 22 RF. Barrel: various lengths. Double action.

Hopkins & Allen Safety Police DA
Revolver (II) **$135**
Caliber: 32 S&W or 38 S&W. Barrel: various lengths. Double action.

Hopkins & Allen XL 1 DA Revolver **$110**
Caliber: 22 Short RF. Double action. Folding hammer.

Hopkins & Allen XL 3 DA Revolver **$110**
Caliber: 32 S&W. Double action. Folding hammer.

Hopkins & Allen XL .30 Long Revolver **$180**
Caliber: 30 Long RF. Five-shot cylinder. Single action. Spur trigger.

Hopkins & Allen XL Bulldog Revolver (I) **$110**
Calibers: 32 S&W, 38 S&W. Folding hammer.

Hopkins & Allen XL Bulldog Revolver (II) **$100**
Caliber: 32 Short RF. Folding hammer.

Hopkins & Allen XL CR .22 Short RF
Revolver **$170**
Caliber: 22 Short RF. Seven-shot. Single action. Spur trigger.

Hopkins & Allen XL Derringer **$630**
Caliber: 41 Short RF. Single action. Spur trigger.

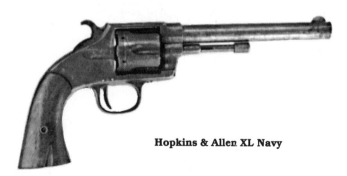

Hopkins & Allen XL Navy

Hopkins & Allen XL Navy Revolver **$500**
Caliber: 38 Short RF. Six-shot cylinder. Single action.

WILLIAM IRVING
New York, New York

William Irving manufactured percussion revolvers, James Reid patent (*see* separate listing) metallic cartridge revolvers, and single-shot derringers between 1861 and 1870.

W. Irving Derringer **$250**
Calibers: 22 or 32 RF. Single shot. Barrel: $2^3/4$ or 3 inches; part octagonal/part round. Spur trigger. Brass frame. Wood grips. Made in the 1860s.

W. Irving SA Knuckle-Duster Revolver (I) **$450**
Caliber: 22 RF. Seven-shot cylinder. Single action. Barrel: integral part of cylinder. Silver-plated brass frame, which could be used as "knuckles" for fist fighting. Based on the Jame Reid design, this gun was made from 1869 to 1870 by Irving; from 1871 to 1884 by Reid.

W. Irving SA Knuckle-Duster Revolver (II) . . . **$450**
Caliber: 32 RF. Five-shot cylinder. Silver-plated brass frame, slightly larger than the 22 cal. version; also used as "knuckles" for self-defense. Made from 1869 to 1870 by Irving; from 1871 to 1884 by Reid.

W. Irving SA Pocket Revolver (I) **$300**
Caliber: 31 RF. Seven-shot cylinder. Single action. Barrel: 3 inches, octagonal. Solid frame. Spur trigger.

W. Irving SA Pocket Revolver (II) **$390**
Caliber: 31 RF. Seven-shot cylinder. Single action. Barrel: about $4^1/2$ inches; round or octagonal. Brass or iron frame; iron frame apparently more plentiful, but commands less. Trigger guard.

IVER JOHNSON'S ARMS & CYCLE WORKS
Massachusetts and Arkansas

This manufacturer of metallic cartridge revolvers, shotguns and rifles was founded in 1871 in Worcester, Mass., as a partnership between Iver Johnson and Martin Bye. Twelve years later Johnson became the sole owner, moved the operation to Fitchburg and renamed the company by the above designation, an identity the firm enjoyed for almost 100 years. Modern management has abbreviated the name to Iver Johnson's Arms, and after several changing of hands, the company relocated to Jacksonville, Arkansas, where today it markets primarily shotguns and rifles.

Most Iver Johnson revolvers are distinguished by the owl-head design on the upper part of the grip and the company name imprint. Many handguns of early Iver Johnson manufacture, however, did not bear the company name. Now collector's items, these carried a spur trigger and were marketed under trade names such as "Eclipse," "Tycoon," etc.

**Iver Johnson Safety Hammer Model
with "Perfect" Rubber Grips**

**Iver Johnson Safety Hammer Model
with Western Walnut Grips**

**Iver Johnson DA Revolver—Safety Hammer
Model** **$105**
Calibers: 22 Long Rifle, 32 S&W, 32 S&W Long, 38 S&W. Seven-shot cylinder (22 LR.); 6-shot cylinder (32 S&W Long); 5-shot cylinder (32 S&W, 38 S&W). Barrel lengths: 2 to 6 inches. Weight: 15 to 19 oz. w/4-inch bbl., depending on caliber. Hinged frame. Fixed sights. Checkered hard rubber stocks. Round butt. Square butt and walnut stocks on some. 32 S&W Long and 38 S&W models built on heavy frame. Blued or nickel finish. Made 1892 to 1950.

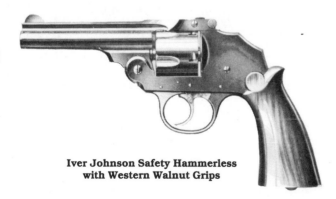

**Iver Johnson Safety Hammerless
with Western Walnut Grips**

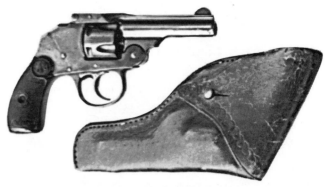

**Iver Johnson Safety Hammerless
with Holster**

**Iver Johnson DA Revolver—Safety
Hammerless**. **$125**
Same basic specifications as the Safety Hammer Model, except in a hammerless version, with weight ranging from 15 to 20½ oz., depending on caliber. Made 1895 to 1950.

**Iver Johnson "Eclipse" Single Shot
Derringer**. **$150**
Caliber: 25 Short RF. Typical derringer design. Spur trigger. Made from 1871 to 1875.

Iver Johnson "Favorite" Revolver **$325**
Caliber: 44 Short RF. Five-shot cylinder. Single action. Spur trigger. Solid frame. Made from 1873 to 1884.

Iver Johnson "Prince" Percussion Pistol **$360**
Caliber: 60. Single shot. Spur trigger. Barrel: various lengths. Made in the 1870s.

Iver Johnson "Tycoon" No. 1 Revolver. **$180**
Caliber: 22 Short RF. Seven-shot cylinder. Barrel: various lengths. Single action. Made from 1872 to 1887.

Iver Johnson "Tycoon" No. 2 Revolver. **$180**
Caliber: 32 Short RF. Five-shot cylinder. Barrel: various lengths. Single action. Made from 1872 to 1887.

Iver Johnson "Tycoon" No. 3 Revolver. **$180**
Caliber: 22 Short RF. Five-shot cylinder. Barrel: various lengths. Single action. Made from 1872 to 1887.

Iver Johnson "Tycoon" No. 4 Revolver. **$180**
Caliber: 41 Short RF. Five-shot cylinder. Barrel: various lengths. Single action. Made from 1872 to 1887.

Iver Johnson "Tycoon" No. 5 Revolver. **$180**
Caliber: 44 Short RF. Five-shot cylinder. Barrel: various lengths. Single action. Made from 1872 to 1887.

WILLIAM JOVER
London, England

Jover 61 Cal. Duelling Pistols

Jover Duelling Pistols (Pair) **$3500**
Caliber: 61 flintlock. Barrel: about 7 inches, octagonal; blued with Damascus pattern; top flat engraved "JOVER LONDON." Lockplate also engraved with "JOVER." Sliding safety on lockplate. Single set triggers. Gold touch holes. Weatherproof pans. Roller on frizzen spring. Iron furniture with engraving. Coarse checkering on grips. Made the last half of the 18th century.

B. KITTREDGE & CO.
Cincinnati, Ohio

The Sharps Pepperbox Pistol, upon which the following handgun is patterned, was designed by Christian Sharps in 22 and 30 caliber (*see* C. Sharps & Co.). According to the Kittredge catalog of the late 1800s, he reworked it, however, by producing a more compact gun, yet in a larger caliber. After Sharps died in 1874, Kittredge bought the entire stock of this pistol and sold it as the "Sharps Triumph." Kittredge was also an agent for Sharps rifles, Colt pistols, English and Belgian shotguns.

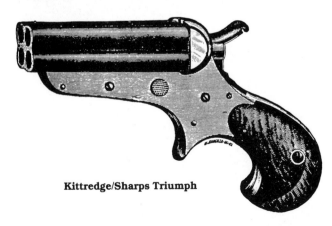

Kittredge/Sharps Triumph

Kittredge/Sharps "Triumph" **$295**
Caliber: 32 RF. Barrel: 2¹/₂ inches; four round barrels. Overall length: about 4³/₄ inches. Spur trigger. Bird's-head butt. Plated iron frame. Walnut grips. Some made in full plate; some with ivory grips.

HENRY LEECH
Sligo, Ireland

Henry Leech Pocket Pistol

H. Leech Pocket Pistol **$625**
Caliber: 45 percussion. Octagonal barrel. Sliding safety on lock. "LEECH" engraved on lockplate. German silver fittings with patchbox in butt. Silver escutcheon on wrist with Irish wolfhound engraved over initials "AC." Made circa 1820 to 1846.

EUGÈNE LEFAUCHEUX
Paris, France

Eugène Lefaucheux was the son of French gunmaker Casimir Lefaucheux, who invented the pinfire cartridge introduced in the 1840s. The first revolving pistols to use these cartridges were the popular pepperbox arms first exhibited at London's Great Exhibition of 1851. Three years later, Eugène applied for a patent using the pinfire cartridge in a breechloading revolver. The three firearms detailed below are variations of the single-shot, six-chambered pinfire revolvers bearing the Lefaucheux name.

Lefaucheux Brevete Pinfire
Military Revolver

Lefaucheux Brevete Military Revolver (I) **$200**
Caliber: 11mm pinfire. Six-shot cylinder. Octagonal barrel. Lanyard ring. Rod ejector on the right.

Lefaucheux Brevete Military Revolver (II) **$295**
Caliber: 11mm. Some converted from pinfire to rimfire. Six-shot cylinder. Round barrel. Finger spur trigger guard. Smooth grips.

Lefaucheux Brevete 7 mm
Military Pinfire Revolver

Lefaucheux Pinfire Revolver **$75**
Caliber: 7mm pinfire. Octagonal barrel. Cylinder stamped "SYSTEME LEFAUCHEUX PERFECTIONNE." Checkered grips.

JEAN A. LᴇMAT
New Orleans, Louisiana

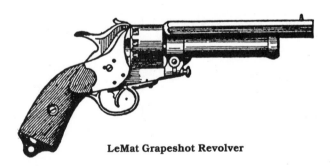

LeMat Grapeshot Revolver

LeMat Grapeshot Revolver **$3500**
Caliber: 40. Nine-shot cylinder surrounding a central bore that used 16 gauge buckshot. Single action. Barrel: about 7 inches. Finger spur trigger guard model consigned to the C.S. Army; those with plain round guards used by the Navy. Patented in 1856 by Jean Alexander Francois LeMat, a New Orleans doctor and Confederate Colonel; he received four British patents for revised models. Manufactured by partner C. Girard

in France and proofed in England. Early models have half-round, half-octagonal barrels and fragile swivel loop fitted into buttframe. Later models have full octagonal barrel and heavy lanyard loop cast into buttframe. Loading lever is on the right side of early models, on the left on later models. Barrels marked, "LeMat's Patent," "Col. LeMat's Patent," "Col. LeMat Bte.s.g.d.g. Paris," or "Systeme LeMat Bte.s.g.d.g. Paris." Some with Birmingham proof marks. "LM" also marked on some.

LEWIS AND TOMES
London, England

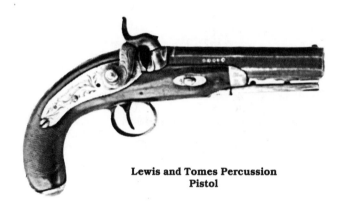

Lewis and Tomes Percussion
Pistol

Lewis & Tomes Percussion Pistol **$275**
Caliber: 54 percussion. Octagonal barrel. German silver lock and fittings. Cap box in butt. One gold, one silver band at breech.

Lewis and Tomes Sawhandle
Pistol

Lewis & Tomes Sawhandle Pistol **$350**
Caliber: 41 percussion. Barrel: octagonal, Damascus; engraved "LEWIS & TOMES LONDON." German silver frame and fittings. Belt hook on left side. Patchbox in butt.

LIDDLE & KAEDING
San Francisco, California

Robert Liddle was a general gunsmith and arms dealer in San Francisco from about 1857 to 1872. After that time until about 1889, the firm name was changed to Liddle & Kaeding. It was subsequently known as the Liddle Gun Company until 1894.

Liddle & Kaeding Pocket Revolver **$125**
Caliber: 32 rimfire. Five-shot cylinder. Barrel: 3¼ inches, octagonal. Blued finish on metal; oil finish on walnut grips. Made for Liddle by Forehand & Wadsworth (*see* separate listing) between 1872 and 1889.

H. C. LOMBARD & CO.
Springfield, Massachusetts

H. C. Lombard made single-shot metallic cartridge pistols between 1859 and 1870.

Lombard Single Shot Pocket Pistol **$145**
Caliber: 22 rimfire. Barrel: 3½ inches, octagonal; blued; pivots to load. Brass frame, silver-plated. Spur trigger. Walnut or rosewood grips, square butt on either. Made from 1859 to 1870.

T. LOVAT
Whitby, No. Yorkshire, England

T. Lovat Flintlock Pocket Pistol

T. Lovat Flintlock Pocket Pistol **$375**
Caliber: 43 flintlock. Sliding safety to lock pan. Lock engraved "LOVAT WHITBY." Walnut grip with diamond-shaped silver escutcheon. Made circa 1820.

LOWELL ARMS COMPANY
Lowell, Massachusetts

The Lowell Arms Company operated between 1864 and 1880, producing percussion and metallic cartridge revolvers. The firm was previously known as the Rollin White Arms Co., named after the owner of the same name (*see* separate listing), which made Smith & Wesson-marketed arms during the Civil War.

Lowell Pocket Revolver (I) **$375**
Caliber: 22 Short RF. Seven-shot cylinder. Spur trigger. Made from 1864 to 1880.

Lowell Pocket Revolver (II) **$390**
Caliber: 32 Long RF. Six-shot cylinder. Spur trigger. Made from 1864 to 1880.

Lowell Pocket Revolver (III) **$410**
Caliber: 38 Long RF. Six-shot cylinder. Spur trigger. Made from 1864 to 1880.

JOHN P. LOWER
Denver, Colorado

John P. Lower was a general gunsmith in Philadelphia from about 1850 to the mid-1870s. At that time he moved to Denver, where he established his own business. Supposedly, his name was used on derringer pistols produced by Slotter & Co. and on revolvers made by William Uhlinger, both Philadelphia gun firms active in the 1860s.

**J. P. Lower Single Action Pocket
Revolver (I)** **$200**
Caliber: 22 Long RF. Six-shot cylinder. Barrel: various lengths. Solid iron frame. Spur trigger. Made from 1861 to 1865.

**J. P. Lower Single Action Pocket
Revolver (II)** **$220**
Caliber: 32 long RF. Six-shot cylinder. Barrel: various lengths. Solid iron frame. Spur trigger. Made from 1861 to 1865.

MALTBY, HENLEY & CO.
New York, New York

From 1878 to 1890 this firm manufactured metallic cartridge revolvers, which were issued to the Metroplitan Police Force in New York City.

Maltby, Henley & Co. 22 Revolver **$105**
Caliber: 22 RF. Seven-shot cylinder. Double-action. Hammerless. Top-break loading.

Maltby, Henley & Co. 32 Revolver **$110**
Caliber: 32 S&W. Five-shot cylinder. Double-action.
Hammerless. Top-break loading.

Maltby, Henley & Co. 38 Revolver **$115**
Caliber: 38 S&W. Five-shot cylinder. Double-action.
Hammerless. Top-break loading.

MANHATTAN FIREARMS COMPANY
New York, New York

This firm initially made percussion pistols and pepperboxes, but in 1864, the firm opened offices in New
York and started producing percussion revolvers similar to the Colt Navy models. They were soon forced out
of business by a Colt lawsuit for infringement of patents.

**Manhattan "Bar Hammer" Double Screw
Barrel** **$255**
Calibers: various. Single shot.

Manhattan "Hero" Percussion Derringer **$230**
Calibers: various. Single-shot. Made from 1840 to
1864.

**Manhattan Navy Percussion
Revolver**

Manhattan Navy Percussion Revolver **$600**
Series II. Caliber: 36. Single action. Barrel length: 6¹⁄₂
inches.

Manhattan Percussion Pocket Revolver **$375**
Caliber: 36. Single action.

Manhattan Six-Shot Pepperbox **$375**
Caliber 28. Six-shot. Double action.

Manhattan Three-Shot Pepperbox **$535**
Caliber: 28. Three-shot. Double action.

JOHN MANTON
London, England

Manton 52 Cal. Coat Pistols

Manton Coat Pistol **$350**
Caliber: 52. Barrel: iron, octagonal; engraved, "MAN-
TON LONDON." Silver band around butt and silver escutcheon on butt and grips. Checkered grips. Often
found in pairs worth about $750 for the pair. Made
circa 1820.

MARLIN FIRE ARMS CO.
New Haven, Connecticut

During the 19th century, John Mahlon Marlin manufactured rifles and metallic cartridge revolvers in New
Haven, Conn., under the names J.M. Marlin, from 1870
to 1880, and the Marlin Fire Arms Co., from 1880 to
1915. The name was again changed to the Marlin Arms
Corp., 1915 to 1916; Marlin Rockwell Corp., 1916 to
1921; and finally the Marlin Firearms Co. from 1921 to
date.

Marlin Model 1872 XXX Standard Revolver . . **$225**
Caliber: 30 RF. Tip-up barrel. Spur trigger.

Marlin Model 1872 XXX Standard Revolver . . **$235**
Caliber: 30 RF. Tip-up octagonal barrel. Spur trigger.

Marlin Model 1873 XX Standard Revolver . . . **$210**
Caliber: 22 RF. Tip-up barrel. Spur trigger.

Marlin Model 1873 XX Standard Revolver . . . **$220**
Caliber: 22 RF. Tip-up. Octagonal barrel. Spur trigger.

Marlin Model 1875 Standard Revolver **$205**
Caliber: 30 RF. Tip-up barrel. Spur trigger.

**Marlin Model 1887
Double Action Revolver**

Marlin Model 1887 Double Action Revolver.. $200
Calibers: 32 S&W and 38 S&W. Five-shot cylinder. Top
break. Auto ejecting. Self-cocking. Barrel: 3¼ inches.
Steel frame. Rubber stock; ivory or pearl also available.
Nickel-plated or blued most common; some custom
made with engraved, full silver plating and gold trimmings.

WILLIAM W. MARSTON
New York, New York

Patentee and maker of the sling breech lock, William
Marston also made percussion pepperboxes, pistols
and revolvers. Three-barrel pepperboxes were also
made by this firm from 1850 to about 1863. While the
firm name was changed in 1862 to Marston & Knox, it
also used the trade names of Western Arms Co. and
The Union/Arms Co. (*see* separate listing).

Marston Breech Loader Handgun $1455
Caliber: 36. Barrel: half-octagonal. Single shot. Iron or
brass frame. Blued or silver-plated finish. Engraved.

Marston Pepperbox Handgun. $440
Caliber: 31. Double action. Six-shot. Bat hammer.

Marston Single Shot DA Handgun. $255
Caliber: 36. Bar hammer. Double action. Screw barrel.

Marston Single Shot SA Handgun. $265
Caliber: 36. Bar hammer. Single action. Screw barrel.

MASSACHUSETTS ARMS COMPANY
Chicopee Falls, Massachusetts

See Adams Revolving Arms Company under Handguns.

MAUSER PISTOL
Oberndorf, Germany

Manufactured by Waffenfabrik Mauser of Mauser-
Werke A.G.

**Mauser Model 1898 Military Automatic
Pistol. $1400**
Calibers: 7.63mm Mauser, 9mm Mauser and 9mm Lu-
ger. Ten-shot box magazine. Barrel: 5¼ inches. Overall
length: 12 inches. Weight: 45 ounces. Adjustable rear
sight. Walnut stocks. Blued finish. A number of variations exist at correspondingly higher prices; value
listed is for standard model. Made from 1898 to 1945.

MERRIMACK ARMS MFG. CO.
Newburyport, Massachusetts

For a few years beginning about 1870, the Brown
Manufacturing Co. (*see* separate listing) produced
these derringers, originally made by Merrimack in the
late 1860s.

Merrimack Southerner Handgun. $500
Caliber: 41 short RF. Single-shot derringer. Barrel:
short, octagonal, side swing. Brass frame. Light engraving. Stamped "SOUTHERNER."

MERWIN & BRAY
New York, New York

Joseph Merwin and Edward Bray apparently began
their partnership in Worcester, Mass., in the early
1860s. After relocating to New York City, they continued as primarily dealers and sales agents for a variety
of popular arms of the day. Known also as Merwin &
Simpkins and Merwin, Taylor & Simpkins toward the
end of the decade, they finally reorganized as Merwin
Hulbert & Co., with its own reputation as firearms dis-
tributors (*see* separate listing).

Merwin & Bray 22 Revolver. $205
Caliber: 22 short RF. Seven-shot. Single action. Spur
trigger. Solid frame.

Merwin & Bray 28 Revolver. $210
Caliber: 28 cup primed cartridge. Six-shot. Single action. Spur trigger. Solid frame.

Merwin & Bray 30 Cal. Revolver. $220
Caliber: 30 cup primed cartridge. Six-shot. Single action. Spur trigger. Solid frame.

Merwin & Bray 31 Cal. Revolver $180
Caliber: 31 RF. Six-shot. Single action. Solid frame. Spur trigger.

Merwin & Bray 32 Cal. Revolver $200
Caliber: 32 short RF. Six-shot. Single action. Solid frame. Spur trigger.

Merwin & Bray 42 Cal. Revolver (I) $260
Caliber: 42 cup primed cartridge. Six-shot. Single action. Spur trigger. Solid frame.

Merwin & Bray Handgun 42 Cal. Revolver (II) $440
Caliber: 42 cup primed cartridge. Six-shot. Single action. Barrel: 6 inches. Spur trigger. Solid frame.

Merwin & Bray Navy Revolver $500
Caliber: 38 short RF. Six-shot. Single action. Solid frame. Finger rest trigger guard.

Merwin & Bray "Original" 28 Cal. Revolver . . $725
Caliber: 28 cup primed cartridge. Six-shot. Single action. Spur trigger. Tip-up.

Merwin & Bray "Original" 30 Cal. Revolver . . $770
Caliber: 30 cup primed cartridge. Six-shot. Single action. Spur trigger. Tip-up.

Merwin & Bray "Original" 42 Cal. Revolver . . $745
Caliber: 42 cup primed cartridge. Six-shot. Single action. Spur trigger. Tip-up.

Merwin & Bray "Original" Revolver $850
Calibers: various, cup primed. Extra cylinder. Percussion.

Merwin & Bray Reynolds Revolver $205
Caliber: 25 short RF. Five-shot. Single action. Barrel: 3 inches. Spur trigger.

Merwin & Bray Single Shot Handgun $200
Caliber: 32 RF. Barrel: 3 1/2 inches; octagonal, side swing. Silver-plated brass frame. Blued finish. Spur trigger. Walnut grips. Square butt.

MERWIN, HULBERT & CO.
New York, New York

In 1874, this company, previously named Merwin, Taylor & Simpkins (*see* Merwin & Bray), patented an Army Model 1876 metallic cartridge revolver. These were made under United States Government contract at the Hopkins and Allen plant in Norwich, Conn. They were also sold to foreign governments and are usually stamped "MERWIN HULBERT & CO."

Merwin, Hulbert & Co. Army Model DA Pocket Pistol $595
Caliber: 44 - 40 WCF. Barrel: 3 1/2 inches. Six-shot. Double action. Round butt.

Merwin, Hulbert & Co. Army Model DA Revolver $645
Belt pistol. Caliber: 44 - 40 WCF. Barrel: 7 inches. Double action. Six-shot. Nickel-plated finish standard. Walnut or hard rubber grips. Round butt. With extra barrel, add **$145 to $200**. With safety hammer, add **$40 to $65.**

Merwin, Hulbert & Co. Army Model SA Pocket Pistol $615
Caliber: 44 - 40 WCF. Barrel: 3 1/2 inches. Six-shot. Single action. Square butt.

Merwin, Hulbert & Co. Army Model SA Revolver $735
Belt pistol. Caliber: 44 - 40 WCF. Barrel: 7 inches. Single action. Six-shot. Nickel-plated finish standard. Walnut or hard rubber grips. Square butt.

Merwin, Hulbert & Co. Pocket Model $295
Caliber: 32 S&W. Five-shot. Double action.

Merwin, Hulbert & Co. Revolver (32 Cal.) $295
Caliber: 32 S&W. Seven-shot. Double action. Barrel lengths: 3, 3 1/2, 5 and 5 1/2 inches. Automatic shell ejecting.

Merwin, Hulbert & Co.
Automatic Shell Ejecting Revolver

Merwin, Hulbert & Co. Revolver (38 Cal.) $365
Caliber: 38 S&W. Seven-shot. Double action. Barrel lengths: 3 1/2, 5 1/2 inches. Automatic shell ejecting. Folding hammer or "old style." Adopted by the police in cities such as Cleveland and Cincinnati, Ohio.

MINNEAPOLIS FIREARMS CO.
Minneapolis, Minnesota

Starting in 1875, this plant made the so-called Protector Palm Metallic Cartridge Revolver. This gun was fired by holding the barrel between the index and second fingers while squeezing a lever against the frame holding the cylinder.

Minneapolis Firearms Co. "The Protector"
Handgun. **$660**
Caliber: 32 extra short RF. Nickel-plated finish.

MONARCH REVOLVER
Maker Unknown

Monarch Handgun Revolver **$185**
Caliber: 32 short RF. Five-shot. Single action. Spur trigger. Solid frame.

MOORE'S PATENT FIRE ARMS CO.
Brooklyn, New York

Operating from 1862 to 1865, the Moore's Patent Fire Arms Co. made Daniel Moore-patent teat cartridge single-action revolvers. They later made the David Williamson-patent metallic cartridge revolvers and also all-metal derringer-type cartridge pistols. In 1865 the firm became the National Arms Company (*see* separate listing).

Moore's Front-loading Revolver. **$325**
Caliber: 32 TF. Barrel: 3¼ inches. Six-shot blued cylinder. Brass frame with silver-plated finish. Walnut or gutta percha grips. Bird's-head butt. Spur trigger. Single action.

Moore's Handgun Revolver **$320**
Caliber: 32 TF. Barrel: 3¼ inches. Six-shot blued cylinder. Single action. Brass frame with silver-plated finish. Walnut or gutta percha grips. Bird's-head butt. No extractor. Spur trigger.

Moore's Single Action Revolver

Moore's Single Action Revolver **$330**
Caliber: 32 RF. Seven-shot cylinder. Brass frame. With holster. Made circa 1860.

Moore's No. 1 Deringer

Moore's Single Shot No. 1 Derringer. **$500**
Caliber: 41 short RF. Barrel: 2½ inches. Brass frame with silver-plated finish. Barrel either plated or blued finish.

Moore's Williamson's Patent. **$270**
Caliber: 32 TF. Barrel: 3¼ inches. Six-shot blued cylinder. Brass frame with silver-plated finish. Walnut or gutta percha grips. Bird's-head butt. Hook extractor.

MORGAN & CLAPP
New Haven, Connecticut

In operation from 1864 to 1877, Morgan & Clapp made Lucius Morgan-patent metallic cartridge revolvers.

Morgan & Clapp Single Shot Pocket Pistol. . . **$195**
Calibers: 22 and 32 RF. Barrel: 3½ inches; octagonal, side swing. Spur trigger. Blued barrel. Silver-plated brass frame. Square butt with walnut grips.

NATIONAL ARMS COMPANY
Brooklyn, New York

The National Arms Company took over the Moore Patent Fire Arms Co. and continued to manufacture Daniel Moore-patent teat cartridge revolvers as well as other types of handguns from about 1863 to 1870.

National Arms/Moore's
Front-Loading Revolver

**National Arms/Moore's Front-loading
Revolver** **$305**
Caliber: 32 TF. Barrel: 3¼ inches. Six-shot blued cyl-
inder. Brass frame with silver-plated finish. Walnut or
gutta percha grips. Bird's-head butt. Spur trigger. Single action. Made by National Arms Co. about 1865 to
1870.

National Arms/Moore's
No. 2 Derringer

**National Arms/Moore's Single Shot No. 2
Derringer** **$425**
Caliber: 41 RF. Single-shot. Barrel: 2 or 2½ inches.
Decorative scroll engraving was standard on frame and
breech of barrel. Walnut grips. Patent purchased by
Colt who continued manufacturing this model under
its own name. Made from 1864 to 1870 by National
Arms.

National Arms Teat-Fire Revolver **$1495**
Caliber: 42 teat fire. Six-shot cylinder. Barrel: 7½
inches, half-octagonal. Silver-plated brass frame; barrel and cylinder blued. Walnut grips. Made from 1863
to 1868.

NEWBURY ARMS CO.
Albany, New York

Frederick D. Newbury patented percussion revolvers
that were manufactured between 1855 and 1860.

Newbury Single Shot Pistol **$395**
Caliber: 25 RF. Barrel: 4 inches, octagonal. Silver-
plated brass frame. Blued barrel. Walnut grips. Spur
trigger. Made from 1856 to 1860.

HENRY NOCK
London, England

Henry Nock (1741–1804) was a well-known and in-
ventive English gunmaker. He produced arms for the
royal families of Britain, made multi-barreled pepperbox handguns and long arms, and in 1785 devised a
type of screwless lock that was used on flintlock arms
of the day. This was adopted for limited use by the British Ordnance. He was also responsible for the introduction of early breechloaders in England.

Henry Nock British Trade Pistol

Henry Nock Flintlock Trade Pistol **$440**
Caliber: 60 flintlock. Octagonal barrel stamped "H.N."
Lockplate engraved "LONDON WARRANTED." Brass
furniture. Made circa 1800.

OSGOOD GUN WORKS
Norwich, Connecticut

This firm manufactured metallic cartridge revolvers
between 1870 and 1880.

Osgood Duplex Revolver **$380**
Calibers: 22 RF and 32 RF. Eight-shot 22 RF cylinder
with 32 RF single-shot center barrel. Barrels: 2½
inches, round over/under. Blued or nickel-plated finish. Walnut grips. Made late 1870s to 1880.

JAMES PARR
Liverpool, England

Parr English Flintlock

Parr Flintlock Pistol **$675**
Caliber: 64. Barrel: brass, engraved. Brass furniture.
"PARR" engraved on lockplate. Made circa 1795.

CHARLES S. PETTENGILL
New Haven, Connecticut

See also U.S. Military Revolvers.

**Pettengill 36 Cal. Hammerless
Revolver**

Pettengill Hammerless Revolvers
Double action. Hammerless-type frames of iron or
brass. Calibers: 31, 34–36, 44. Six-shot round cylinder.
Barrel: 4, 4½, 7 inches. Two-piece walnut grips. Blued
finish. Made by Rogers, Spencer & Co. for Pettengill
late 1850s to early 1860s.
Army Model, 7½-inch bbl., 44 cal. **$725**
Belt or Navy Model, 4½-inch bbl. **725**
Pocket Model, 4-inch bbl., 31 cal. **495**

PLANT MANUFACTURING CO.
New Haven, Connecticut

E. H. and A. H. Plant manufactured metallic cartridge
revolvers under the Ellis patents and the N. White patents assigned to the Plant Manufacturing Co. between
1860 and 1866. They also had a U.S. Government contract to manufacture Army revolvers.

Plant's Cup Primed Cartridge Revolver (I). . . . **$245**
Caliber: 28. Six-shot. Single action. Spur trigger. Solid
frame.

**Plant's Front-Loading Cup Primed
Pocket Revolver**

Plant's Cup Primed Cartridge Revolver (II). . . **$250**
Caliber: 30. Six-shot. Single action. Spur trigger. Solid
frame. Front loading. Made circa 1865.

Plant's "Original" Revolver (I) **$735**
Caliber: 28 cup primed cartridge. Six-shot. Single action. Spur trigger. Tip-up.

Plant's "Original" Revolver (II) **$755**
Caliber: 30 cup primed cartridge. Six-shot. Single action. Spur trigger. Tip-up.

Plant's "Original" Revolver (III). **$800**
Caliber: 42 cup primed cartridge. Six-shot. Single action. Spur trigger. Tip-up.

Plant's Revolver (I). **$220**
Caliber: 31 RF. Six-shot. Single action. Solid frame.
Spur trigger.

Plant's Revolver (II). **$220**
Caliber: 32 short RF. Six-shot. Single action. Solid
frame. Spur trigger.

Plant's Revolver (III). **$285**
Caliber: 42 cup primed cartridge. Six-shot. Single ac-
tion. Spur trigger. Solid frame. Walnut or rosewood
grips.

Plant's Revolver (IV) **$465**
Caliber: 42 cup primed cartridge. Six-shot. Single ac-
tion. Barrel: 6 inches. Spur trigger. Solid frame.

Plant's Reynold's Revolver. **$210**
Caliber: 25 short RF. Five-shot. Single action. Barrel: 3
inches. Spur trigger.

LUCIUS W. POND
Worcester, Massachusetts

Lucius W. Pond produced top-break metallic cartridge revolvers that were declared an infringement on
Smith & Wesson patents. He later made a front-loading
cylinder revolver with removable steel shells.

L.W. Pond Revolver **$350**
Caliber: 22. Seven-shot cylinder; front loading. Brass
frame. Rosewood grips. Made from 1863 to 1870.

EDWIN A. PRESCOTT
Worcester, Massachusetts

In operation from 1860 to 1864, E. A. Prescott made
metallic cartridge revolvers and had a U.S. Government
contract for Navy revolvers. He was later sued by Smith
and Wesson for patent infringement.

Prescott Revolver (I) **$180**
Caliber: 22 short RF. Seven-shot. Single action. Solid
frame. Spur trigger.

Prescott Revolver (II) **$185**
Caliber: 30 RF or 32 short RF. Six-shot. Single action.
Solid frame. Spur trigger.

Prescott Navy Revolver (I) **$355**
Caliber: 32 short RF. Six-shot. Single action. Solid
frame. Finger rest trigger guard.

Prescott Navy Revolver

Prescott Navy Revolver (II) **$675**
Caliber: 36 RF. Six-shot cylinder. Single action. Barrel:
about 7 inches, octagonal. Solid frame. Finger rest trigger guard. Patented in 1860. Possibly used during the
Civil War as perhaps a "trial" model, but no U.S. Government records substantiate its being officially purchased.

JAMES REID
Catskill, New York

James Reid patented a metallic cartridge revolver on
April 28, 1863, which was initially manufactured by
William Irving of New York City (*see* separate listing).
Originally located in the same city, he moved his business in the mid- to late 1860s to Catskill, N.Y., where
he operated until about 1884, making both percussion
and metallic cartridge revolvers and derringer-type pistols. His "Knuckle-Duster" is considered to be a
unique American revolver.

**James Reid Single Action "Knuckle-Duster"
Revolver** **$450**
Calibers: 22 RF and 32 RF. Seven-shot cylinder. Barrel:
integral part of cylinder. Silver-plated brass frame (also
some blued with iron frame), which also acts as a set
of knuckles for fist fighting. Made from 1869 to 1870 by
Irving; from 1871 to 1884 by Reid.

James Reid Single Action Revolver (I) **$300**
Caliber: 22 short RF. Seven-shot cylinder. Spur trigger.
Solid frame.

James Reid Single Action Revolver (II) **$390**
Caliber: 32 short RF. Seven-shot cylinder. Spur trigger.
Solid frame.

James Reid Single Action Revolver (III). **$625**
Caliber: 41 short RF. Five-shot cylinder. Spur trigger.
Solid frame.

REMINGTON ARMS CO.
Ilion, New York

Eliphalet Remington Jr. made his first rifle in 1816,
and was actively engaged in the manufacture of firearms and gun parts for the next 45 years. The partnership of E. Remington & Sons was formed in 1856 and
continued as a family-run business until the organi-
zation was taken over by Hartley & Graham in 1886. At
this time, the firm name was changed to Remington
Arms Co. and many of the handguns were dropped
from the line.

For further information, *see* U.S. Military Revolvers
and also Remington Arms Co. in the Rifle Section.

Remington Model 1861 Army Revolver **$710**
Old Model Army. Caliber: 44 percussion; converted to
46 RF. Six-shot plain cylinder. Barrel: 8 inches, octagonal. Weight: 46 ounces. Brass trigger guard. Conversion was achieved in either of two ways: new cartridge
cylinder fitted, and a metal spacer attached to standing
breech, no loading gate, no ejector rod; or similar to
above, except metal spacer fitted with loading gate, and
ejector rod added. Smooth walnut grips. Blued finish.
Made from the early 1860s to late 1870s; later factory
conversions command less.

Remington Model 1861 Navy Revolver. **$750**
Old Model Navy. Caliber: 36 percussion; converted to
38 RF or CF. Six-shot round cylinder. Barrel: 7$\frac{1}{2}$
inches, octagonal. Single action. Overall length: 13$\frac{1}{4}$
inches. Weight: 42 ounces. Blued or nickel-plated finish. Brass trigger guard. Conversion same as Remington Model 1861 Army Revolver.

**Remington Model 1865 Navy Single Shot
Pistol**. **$1450**
First of the rolling block pistols. Caliber: 50 CF. Barrel:
8$\frac{1}{2}$ inches, round; blued. Casehardened frame. Spur
trigger. Smooth walnut grips. Uses "Remington System" rolling block action of breechblock and hammer.
Remington made a small quantity of these under contract for the Navy in 1866 and the model was soon
superseded by the Model 1867 Navy, below.

**Remington Model 1867 Navy Single Shot
Pistol**. **$795**
Rolling block action. Caliber: 50 CF. Barrel: 7 inches,
round; blued. Casehardened frame. Oval trigger guard.
Smooth walnut stock. Made under contract with the
Navy.

**Remington Model 1875 Improved
Army Revolver**

**Remington Model 1875 Single Action Army
Revolver** **$1200**
Improved or New Model Army. Calibers: 44 Rem. CF,
44-40, 45 Colt CF. Six-shot, half-fluted cylinder. Barrel: 7¹/₂ or 8 inches, round. Weight: about 32 ounces.
Overall length: 13³/₄ inches. Web underneath ejector
housing. Smooth walnut grips; offered with ivory or
pearl grips. With or without lanyard ring in butt. Blued
or nickel-plated finish. Made from 1875 to 1889.

**Remington Model 1890 Single Action Army
Revolver** **$1850**
Closely resembles the Colt Single Action Army. Caliber: 44-40 CF. Six-shot, half-fluted cylinder. Barrel: 5¹/₂ or 7¹/₂ inches, round. Unlike the Remington Model
1875, the web underneath the ejector housing is cut
away. Checkered hard rubber grips. Lanyard ring in
butt. Nickel-plated or blued finish. Made from 1891 to
1894.

**Remington Model 1891 Single Shot Target
Pistol**. **$1225**
Rolling block action. Calibers: 22, 25 or 32 RF; 32 S&W
CF or 32-20. Barrels: 8 to 12 inches; half-octagonal and
round. Blade front sight in slot and adjustable V-notch
rear sight. Smooth walnut grips. Blued finish. Introduced in 1891 and discontinued about 1900.

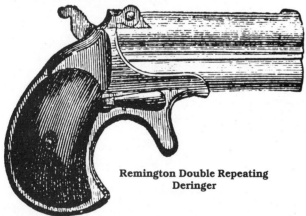

**Remington Double Repeating
Deringer**

NOTE

Numbers on Remington over/under deringers were used
solely for assembly purposes. The only way these pistols can
be dated is by the barrel markings, and this method is approximate.

Remington Double Repeating Deringer **$710**
Caliber: 41 RF. Two-shot. Single action. Barrel: 3
inches, superposed. Overall length: 4⁷/₈ inches.
Weight: 11 ounces. Sheath trigger. Walnut or checkered hard rubber grips. Finished in blue or nickel.
Made from 1866 to 1935.

Remington Navy Revolver

Remington Improved Navy Revolver . . . . **$*****
Caliber: 38 RF or CF. Six-shot plain cylinder. Barrel:
7¹/₂ inches, octagonal. Overall length: 13¹/₄ inches.
Weight: 2⁵/₈ pounds. Web underneath ejector housing.
Walnut grips; ivory and pearl also offered. Blued or
nickel-plated finish. Made about 1873 to 1888.

Remington Iroquois Revolver **$345**
Caliber: 22 RF. Seven-shot cylinder, plain or fluted.
Single action. Barrel: 2¹/₄ inches, round. Top of barrel
marked "IROQUOIS." Sheath trigger. No ejector.
Checkered hard rubber bird's-head grip. Blued or
nickel finish. Made from 1878 to 1888.

**Remington New Model No. 1
Revolver (Smoot)**

Remington New Model No. 1 Revolver. **$250**
Based on Smoot's patent of 1873 (also referred to as
New Line). Caliber: 30 RF. Five-shot cylinder. Single action. Barrel: 2³/₄ inches; octagonal, integral with one-piece frame and ejector housing. Sheath trigger.
Bird's-head grip of checkered hard rubber or smooth
walnut. Nickel-plated or blued (less common) finish.
Made from 1873 to 1888.

Remington New Model No. 2 Revolver. **$245**
Same general specifications as No. 1 Smoot-Patent Revolver, except chambered for 32 short.

The Remington Armory in Ilion, New York, as it was reproduced in Remington's "Reduced Price List" of 1877. E. Remington & Sons at that time manufactured "military, sporting, hunting and target breech-loading rifles, shot-guns and pistols, also cartridges, primers, bullets, shot-shells, loading implements, rifle canes, etc., etc."—everything to meet the shooter's needs.

Remington New Model No. 3 Revolver **$325**
Based on Smoot's patent. Caliber: 38 short RF or CF (less common). Five-shot cylinder. Single action. Barrel: 3³/₄ inches; octagonal, some ribbed. Barrel and ejector made separately from, and screwed into, two-piece frame. Sheath trigger. Checkered hard rubber grips, bird's-head or saw-handle style. Nickel-plated or blued finish. Made from 1875 to 1888.

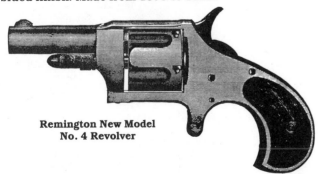

**Remington New Model
No. 4 Revolver**

Remington New Model No. 4 Revolver **$245**
Caliber: 38 short or 41 short RF or CF. Five-shot cylinder. Single action. Barrel: 2¹/₂ inches; round, screwed

into frame. Overall length: 6¹/₂ inches. Spur trigger. No ejector. Bird's-head-style grip of checkered, hard rubber; pearl and ivory also offered. Nickel-plated or blued finish. Made from 1877 to 1888.

**Remington New Model Police
Revolver**

Remington New Model Police Revolver **$600**
Caliber: 36 percussion; after 1873 made in 38 RF cartridge. Five-shot plain cylinder. Barrel: 3¹/₂, 4¹/₂, 5¹/₂ or 6¹/₂ inches; octagonal. Weight: 21 to 24 ounces. Overall length: 8¹/₂ to 11¹/₂ inches. Walnut grips; also offered with ivory or pearl. Finished in either blue or nickel plate. Brass trigger guard optional. Made from the early 1860s to the late 1800s.

Remington New Pocket Revolver

Remington New Pocket Revolver **$595**
Caliber: 31 percussion; later made in 32 RF cartridge version. Five-shot plain cylinder. Single action. Barrels: 3¹/₂ and 4¹/₂ inches; octagonal. Weight: 14 to 16 ounces. Finished in either blue or nickel plate. Spur trigger with optional brass trigger guard. Made early 1860s to late 1800s.

**Remington Single Action
Belt Revolver**

Remington Single Action Belt Revolver **$625**
Caliber: 36 percussion; production after 1873 in 38 RF cartridge. Six-shot plain cylinder. Barrel: 6 inches, octagonal. Overall length: 11³/₄ inches. Weight: 2⁷/₈ pounds. Some made in double action. Brass trigger guard. Web under ejector housing. Walnut grips; ivory and pearl also offered. Finished in either blue or nickel plate.

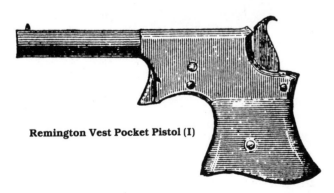

Remington Vest Pocket Pistol (I)

Remington Vest Pocket Pistol (I) **$495**
Caliber: 22 RF. Single shot. Barrel: 3 inches, round. Overall length: 4 inches. Weight: 3¹/₂ ounces. Trigger

Remington Vest Pocket Pistol (I)
projects from forward edge of frame. Hammer also serves as breechblock, which is one-piece with frame. Smooth walnut saw-handle grips. Finished in blue or nickel plate. Also known as "Saw-handle Deringer." Made 1865 to 1888.

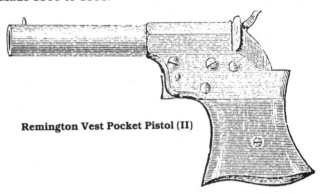

Remington Vest Pocket Pistol (II)

Remington Vest Pocket Pistol (II) **$495**
Calibers: 22, 32, 41 RF. Single shot. Barrel: 4 inches; part round, part octagonal. Separate split breechblock. Trigger projects from forward edge of frame. Blued or nickel finish. Smooth walnut saw-handle grips. Made 1865 to 1888.

Remington-Elliot Pepperbox Deringer **$450**
Calibers: 22 RF (5-shot) and 32 RF (4-shot). Double action. Barrels: 3 inches, fluted (22 cal.); 3³/₈ inches, ribbed (32 cal.). Barrels are stationary and firing pin revolves. Large ring trigger. Smooth walnut or hard rubber grips with saw handle. Finished in blue or nickel. Based on W.H. Elliot's patents of the early 1860s, these were made from about 1863 to 1888.

**Remington-Elliot Single Shot
Deringer**

Remington-Elliot Single Shot Deringer **$645**
Caliber: 41 RF. Single action. Barrel: 2¹/₂ inches, round. Overall length: 4⁷/₈ inches. Sheath trigger. Hammer also serves as breechblock. Smooth walnut bird's-head grips. Blued or nickel-plated finish or combination of both. Made late 1860s to about 1888.

Remington-Elliot "Zig-Zag" Deringer **$1450**
Double action. Caliber: 22 RF. Six-shot pepperbox. Barrels: 3³/₁₆ inches; they rotate by means of zig-zag grooves at end of breech. Large ring trigger. Smooth hard rubber grips with saw handle. Based on W.H. Elliot patents, this unique pepperbox was produced only one year, from 1861 to 1862.

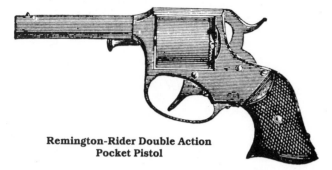

**Remington-Rider Double Action
Pocket Pistol**

Remington-Rider DA Pocket Pistol **$525**
Double action; probably one of the first of its kind produced in the U.S. and based on the Joseph Rider patents of the late 1850s. Caliber: 31 percussion; later converted to 32 RF metallic cartridge in the 1870s. Five-shot plain cylinder. Barrel: 3 inches, octagonal. Overall length: 6¹/₂ inches. Weight: 10 ounces. Self-cocking. Brass trigger guard optional. Checkered hard rubber, saw-handle grips; also ivory and pearl offered. Finished in either blue or nickel plate. Made 1860s until the late 1800s.

**Remington-Rider New Model
Magazine Pistol**

**Remington-Rider New Model Magazine
Pistol** **$1900**
Caliber: 32 extra short RF. Five-shot. Single action. Barrel: 3 inches, octagonal. Overall length: 5³/₄ inches. Weight: 9 ounces. Trigger projected from forward edge of frame. Based on the 1871 patent of Joseph Rider, a tubular magazine under the barrel held five cartridges. Projection on the breechblock is pressed down, pulled back, and then released. This process must be repeated for successive shots. Smooth walnut grips; ivory or pearl also offered. Full nickel or casehardened finish. Made from 1871 to 1888.

NOTE
*** after a dollar sign indicates that there was not enough trading at press time to establish a valid selling price.

RICHARDSON
Address Unknown

Richardson Flintlock Pistol **$435**
Calibers: various, but ⁵/₈-inch common. Barrel: 4 inches, octagonal. Overall length: 9 inches. Checkered stock. Steel trim.

JOHN RIGBY
Dublin, Ireland

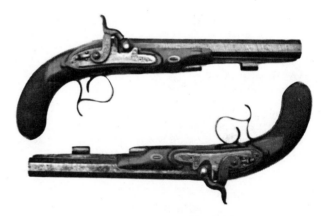

Rigby 67 Cal. Dueling Pistols

Rigby Dueling Pistols (Pair) **$2000**
Caliber: 67. Gold band at breech with gold blow plugs. Engraved iron furniture. Checkered grips with silver escutcheons. Made from 1781 to 1819.

JACOB RUPERTUS
Philadelphia, Pennsylvania

Founded in 1858 and in operation until 1888, the Jacob Rupertus company started as a manufacturer of percussion pepperboxes, patented July 19, 1864. The firm later manufactured small caliber metallic cartridge revolvers.

Rupertus Double Barrel Derringer **$465**
Caliber: 22 short RF. Barrel: 3¹/₈ inches; side by side, round. Iron frame. Spur trigger. Walnut grips. Squared butt. Overall blued finish.

Rupertus Eight-Shot Pepperbox **$425**
Caliber: 22 short RF. Eight shots. Barrel: 2¹/₂ to 3 inches; tapered, blued finish. Spur trigger. Walnut grips.

Rupertus Revolver (I) **$425**
Caliber: 22 short RF. Single action. Seven-shot. Barrel:
2³/₄ inches, round. Spur trigger.

Rupertus Revolver (II). **$215**
Calibers: 32 short or 38 short RF. Five-shot cylinder.
Single action. Spur trigger. Solid frame.

Rupertus Revolver (III). **$240**
Caliber: 41 short RF. Single action. Barrel: 2⁷/₈ inches,
round. Semi-fluted cylinder. Spur trigger. Solid frame.
Plated or blued finish.

Rupertus Singleshot Derringer (I) **$250**
Caliber: 22 short RF. Barrel: 3 inches; part-round, part-
octagonal, side-swing. Iron frame. Spur trigger. Walnut
grips. Squared butt. Blued finish.

Rupertus Singleshot Derringer (II) **$210**
Caliber: 32 short RF. Barrel: 4 or 5 inches; part-round,
part-octagonal, side-swing. Iron frame. Spur trigger.
Walnut grips. Squared butt.

Rupertus Singleshot Derringer (III) **$215**
Caliber: 38 short RF. Barrel: 5 inches; part-round, part-
octagonal, side-swing. Iron frame. Spur trigger. Walnut
grips. Squared butt. Blued finish.

SEGALLAS
London, England

"Segallas" was a common alias of gunmakers of the
18th century who, for sales purposes, wished to dis-
guise their true identity. Pistols stamped with this
name (spelled a variety of ways) often bore markings of
"PARIS" and "DUBLIN" in addition to "LONDON." The
guns were made exclusively of metal and were inex-
pensively produced, although to the inexperienced
eye, they did appear well done on the surface. They
could carry any number of barrels of the turn-off type,
which allowed the shooter to screw them off for easy
loading from the breech. The ball was held firmly in its
breech cup when the barrel was screwed back in, thus
eliminating the need for a patch. These guns were quite
accurate and a good examples of early breechloaders.

Segallas Flintlock
Pocket Pistol

Segallas Flintlock Pocket Pistol **$800**
Caliber: 31 flintlock. Double turn-off barrels. All-steel
construction. Double triggers. Oversized trigger guard.
Scroll engraved. "LONDON" engraved on both sides.
Made circa 1730 to 1750.

C. SHARPS & COMPANY
Philadelphia, Pennsylvania

Christian Sharps filed for his first patent in 1848
while living in Cincinnati, Ohio. This patent was for his
famous falling breechblock used in breechloading rifles. His first plant was in Mill Creek, Penn., where his
early rifles were made. In 1851 he moved to Hartford,
Conn., forming the Sharps Rifle Mfg. Co., from which he
received royalties on the rifles produced. After a few,
short tumultuous years, he left the company in 1853
and broke relations completely.

The Hartford-based company continued to manufacture rifles and received many government contracts
during the Civil War. In 1876 the operation moved to
Bridgeport, Conn., where it carried on until the firm
went out of business in 1881.

Meanwhile, Christian Sharps returned to Philadelphia and in 1854 formed C. Sharps & Company, which
manufactured pistols only. In 1862, he formed the partnership of Sharps and Hankins, producing pepperboxes based on Sharps' patent of 1859 (see below) and
military rifles and carbines for Civil War use. In 1866
the partnership was dissolved and Sharps went back to
his former firm name, C. Sharps & Company, which it
remained until his death in 1874.

Sharps Breech-Loading Single Shot Pistol. . **$2000**
Calibers: 31, 34 and 36. Dropping block action. Various
barrel lengths. Fixed front sight. Smooth walnut grips.
Made by C. Sharps & Co. 1853 to 1857.

Sharps Bryce Revolver **$1065**
Same general specifications as Sharps Percussion Re-
volver, but marked "WM BRYCE & CO."

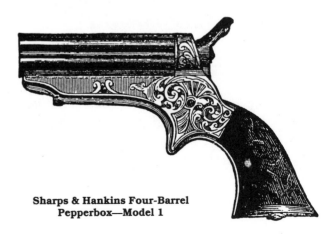

Sharps & Hankins Four-Barrel
Pepperbox—Model 1

**Sharps Model 1 Four-Barrel Pepperbox
Pistol**. **$440**
Caliber: 22 RF. Barrel: 2$\frac{1}{2}$ inches. Rotating firing pins.
Walnut grips were used most often, although gutta-
percha grips also found. Silver-plated frame and blued
barrel were standard finishes. Variations exist. Made
by C. Sharps & Co. and Sharps & Hankins.

**Sharps Model 2 Four-Barrel Pepperbox
Pistol**. **$395**
Caliber: 30 RF. Barrel: 2$\frac{1}{2}$ inches. Rotating firing pins.
Walnut grips were used most often, but variations exist
with gutta-percha grips. Silver-plated frame and blued
barrel were standard finishes.

Sharps & Hankins Four-Barrel
Pepperbox—Model 3

**Sharps Model 3 Four-Barrel Pepperbox
Pistol**. **$550**
Caliber: 32 RF. Barrel: 3$\frac{1}{2}$ inches. Rotating firing pins.
Smooth or checkered gutta-percha or walnut grips. Sil-
ver-plated frame and blued barrel were standard fin-
ishes. Variations exist. Sharps & Hankins.

**Sharps Model 4 Four-Barrel Pepperbox
Pistol**. . . . . **$*****
Caliber: 32 RF. Barrel: 2$\frac{1}{2}$, 3 or 3$\frac{1}{2}$ inches. Smooth
walnut bird's-head-style grips.

Sharps Percussion Revolver. **$925**
Caliber: 25. Six-shot engraved cylinder. Barrel: 3
inches; octagonal, tip-up type. Two-piece walnut grips.
Blued and plated finishes. Made by C. Sharps & Co.
from about 1856 to 1858.

Sharps Pistol Rifle. **$2400**
Calibers: 31 and 38. Barrel: various lengths, but 28
inches standard. Silver ornamentation on walnut
stock. Made by C. Sharps & Co. in the 1850s.

SHARPS & HANKINS
Philadelphia, Pennsylvania

See C. Sharps & Co.

C. S. SHATTUCK
Hatfield, Massachusetts

C. S. Shattuck made metallic cartridge shotguns, pistols and revolvers from about 1880 to 1890.

Shattuck Pocket Revolver
Calibers: 22, 32, 38, 41 rimfire. Single action. Five-shot,
swing-out cylinder. Barrel: 3$\frac{1}{2}$ inches, octagonal. Spur
trigger. Nickel finish. Slender black rubber grips with
square butt. Made from about 1880 to 1890.
22 Caliber. **$325**
32 Caliber. 340
38 Caliber. 375
41 Caliber. 425

SMITH ARMS COMPANY
New York, New York

See Silas Crispin

OTIS A. SMITH
Brook Falls, Connecticut

This firm manufactured metallic cartridge revolvers
from about 1873 to 1890.

Smith Single Action Revolver (I). **$180**
Caliber: 22 RF. Seven-shot cylinder. Barrel: various
lengths. Solid frame. Spur trigger.

Smith Single Action Revolver (II)
Calibers: 32 Short, 32 S&W, 38 Short, 41 Short RF.
Five-shot cylinder. Barrel: various lengths. Solid frame.
Spur trigger.
32 Short. **$180**
32 S&W. 180
38 Short. 200
41 Short. 225

WILLIAM SMITH
Bath, England

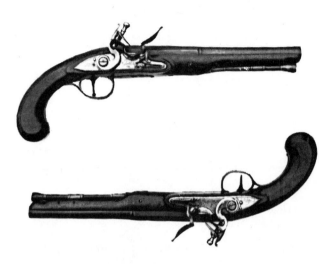

Smith 59 Caliber Flintlock
Duelling Pistols

Smith Duelling Pistols (Pair) **$3500**
Caliber: 59 flintlock. Lock engraved "SMITH." "BATH"
engraved on the top of the Spanish-style half-round,
half-octagonal barrels. Flat-sided butts. Brass furniture. Made circa 1791 to 1817.

Smith Flintlock Pocket Pistol

Smith Flintlock Pocket Pistol **$400**
Caliber: 45 flintlock. Engraved lock. Large trigger
guard. Made circa 1800.

SMITH & WESSON, INC.
Springfield, Massachusetts

Daniel Baird Wesson and Horace Smith began manufacture of the famous Volcanic Action Repeating Pistol in Norwich, Conn.,in 1854. In 1856 the Smith &
Wesson patents were released to Oliver Winchester
and others, resulting in the eventual formation of the
Winchester Repeating Arms Co. (*See* separate history).

Manufacture of the first revolver to use self-contained ammunition began in a Market Street delivery
stable in Springfield, Mass., with 25 employees. In
1859 the first building in the present location was
erected. With the advent of the Civil War, Government
orders expanded the business to 600 employees, and
hundreds of thousands of arms were produced.

In 1870 Smith & Wesson designed the .44 Russian
Model for the Russian Imperial Army and delivered
huge numbers of them. Five years later, the .45 Schofield Model was adopted by the U.S., and it is reliably
reported that General Custer used this model in his
historical "Last Stand" at the Battle of Little Bighorn.

The year 1880 saw the introduction of the double-action type of revolver and the .44 caliber became immensely popular with Western peace officers. Near the
end of that decade the Safety Hammerless revolver was
brought out, making a much safer revolver that lowered the chances of accidental discharge.   The firm of
Smith & Wesson successfully produced firearms well
into the 20th century and is still in business today.

PISTOLS

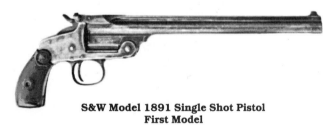

S&W Model 1891 Single Shot Pistol
First Model

**Smith & Wesson Model 1891 Single Shot Target
Pistol—First Model**
Calibers: 22 Long Rifle, 32 S&W, 38 S&W. Barrel: 6, 8
or 10 inches. Overall length: approx. 11¹/₂ inches with
8-inch bbl. Weight: about 1¹/₂ pounds. Hinged frame.
Target sights, barrel catch adjustable rear sight.
Squared butt. Checkered hard rubber grips. Blued fin-
ish. Offered as a combination gun with 38 caliber re-
volver barrel/cylinder that converts the pistol into a
revolver. Made 1893 to 1905.
Single-shot pistol (22 Long Rifle)............ **$ 345**
Single-shot pistol (32 S&W or 38 S&W) **1050**
Combination set w/revolver cylinder/bbl. **1000**

REVOLVERS

S&W Model No. 1
Second Issue

Smith & Wesson Model No. 1 Revolver
A "tip-up" revolver, this was Smith & Wesson's first metallic cartridge gun. Caliber: 22 Short RF. Seven-shot non-fluted cylinder. Barrel: 3³/₁₆ inches; octagonal, blued. Bayonet-type barrel catch. Square butt. Rosewood grips. Silver-plated brass frame.
First Issue, made 1857-1860 . . . . $1750
Second Issue, made 1860-1868 300
  (Frame had flat sides; sideplates were different shape from First Issue.)

**Smith & Wesson Model No. 1 Revolver—
Third Issue** $250
Improved version of the First and Second issues. Caliber: 22 Short RF. Seven-shot fluted cylinder. Barrel lengths: 2¹¹/₁₆ and 3³/₁₆ inches; round ribbed. Rounded butt. Rosewood grips. Nickel-plated frame with blued barrel and cylinder, or full nickel-plating or full blued finish. Made 1868 to 1881.

**Smith & Wesson Model 1 Hand Ejector
Revolver—First Model** $525
Double action. This was the first solid-frame, swing-out cylinder S&W revolver, the precursor to the current 32 Hand Ejector and Regulation Police models. Caliber: 32 S&W Long. Barrel: 3¹/₄, 4¹/₄, 6 inches. Fixed sights. No cylinder latch, and has longer top strap than that of later models. Rounded butt. Checkered hard rubber grips. Blued or nickel finish. Made 1896 to 1903.

S&W Model No. 1¹/₂
First Issue

**Smith & Wesson Model No. 1¹/₂—First
Issue** $350
Improved version of Model No. 1. Caliber: 32 RF. Five-shot non-fluted cylinder. Barrel: 3¹/₂, 4 inches; octagonal. Rosewood grips. Squared butt. Blued or nickel-plated finish. Made 1865 to 1868.

**Smith & Wesson Model No. 1¹/₂—Second
Issue** $400
Improved version of First Issue Model No. 1¹/₂ with more sleek appearance, cylinder stop in topstrap. Caliber: 32 Long RF. Five-shot fluted cylinder. Barrel: 2¹/₂, 3¹/₂ inches; round. Rosewood grips. Rounded butt. Blued or nickel-plated finish. Made 1868 to 1875.

S&W Model No. 2 Army

**Smith & Wesson Model No. 2 Army (Old
Model)** $450
Popular Civil War arm. Caliber: 32 Long RF. Six-shot non-fluted cylinder. Barrel: 4, 5, 6 inches; octagonal. Rosewood grips. Square butt. Blued or nickel-plated finish. Made 1861 to 1874.

**Smith & Wesson No. 3 Single Action Frontier
Revolver** $1250
Caliber: 44-40 Win. Barrel: 4, 5 or 6¹/₂ inches. Fixed or target sights. Rounded butt. Checkered hard rubber or walnut grips. Blued or nickel-plated finish. Made 1885 to 1908.

S&W No. 3 SA American Revolver
Second Model

Smith & Wesson No. 3 Single Action Revolver
Also known as the American, this is S&W's first top-break revolver. Caliber: 44 S&W American, 44 RF Henry (rare). Six-shot fluted cylinder. Barrel: 8 inches, round. Squared butt. Walnut grips. Blued or nickel-plated finish. A number of variations exist, including shorter barreled versions, with correspondingly higher prices.
First Model American (1870–72) $1950
Second Model American
  (1872–74 w/steel blade front sight) 2700

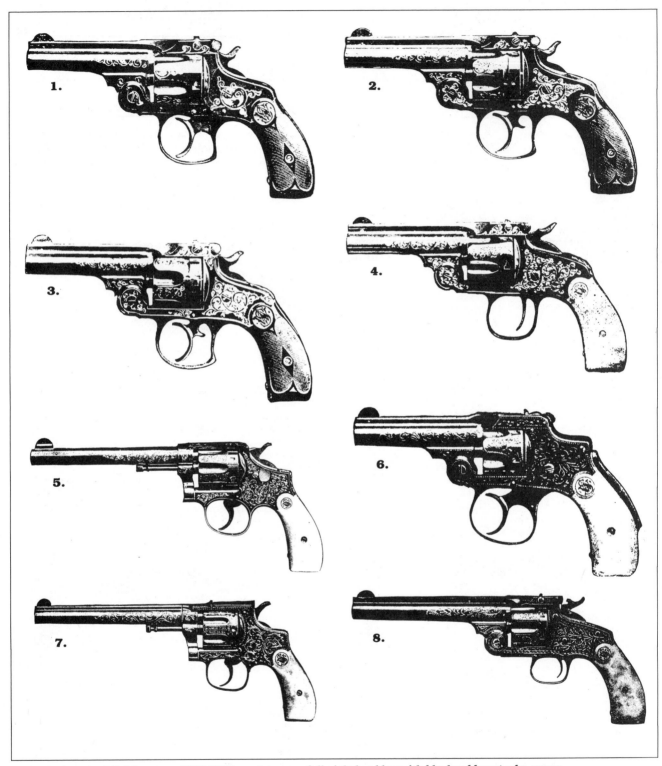

While the standard finish on pre-1900 S&W revolvers was full nickel or blue with black rubber stocks, many custom engravings, inlays and fancy pearl or ivory stocks were available. The above eight styles are examples of some of the variations that existed, which the collector may encounter. Oftentimes, guns were purchased and customized later; note that on true S&W factory-fitted pearl grips, the S&W monogram trademark would have been inserted in gold or silver as "a guarantee of quality."

Smith & Wesson No. 3 Single Action Revolver—New Model **$1430**
Caliber: 44 S&W Russian. Six-shot cylinder. Barrel: 4 to 8 inches. Hinged frame. Fixed or target sights. Rounded butt. Checkered hard rubber or walnut grips. Blued or nickel-plated finish. A number of variations exist over the standard model listed, with correspondingly higher values. Made 1878 to 1908.

Smith & Wesson No. 3 Single Action Russian—First Model
The Old, Old Model Russian. Basically the same as the No. 3 American, but in caliber 44 S&W Russian. Made 1871 to 1874.
Standard Commercial Model
  (6-, 7-, 8-inch bbl.) **$1450**
Russian Contract Model (8-inch bbl. w/Imp.
  Russian Eagle and Cyrillic markings **2450**

Smith & Wesson No. 3 Single Action Russian—Second Model
The Old Model Russian. Same as the First Model Russian, except in calibers 44 S&W Russian and 44 RF Henry with 7-inch barrels, rounded butt and spurred trigger guard. Made 1873 to 1878.
Standard Commercial Model
  (44 S&W Russian) **$1425**
Standard Commercial Model (44 Henry) **2700**
Japanese Issue (44 S&W Russian) **1100**
Russian Contract Model (44 S&W Russian w/Imp.
  Russian Eagle and Cyrillic markings) **1265**
Turkish Issue (44 Henry) **1100**

Smith & Wesson No. 3 Single Action Russian—Third Model
New Model Russian. Basically the same as the Second Model, except with 6¹/₂-inch barrel, integral front sight, shorter extractor housing. Made 1874 to 1878.
Standard Commercial Model
  (44 S&W Russian) **$1265**
Standard Commercial Model (44 Henry) **1800**
Japanese Issue (44 S&W Russian) **1650**
Russian Contract Model (44 S&W Russian w/Imp.
  Russian Eagle and Cyrillic markings) **1265**
Turkish Issue (44 Henry) **1470**

Smith & Wesson No. 3 Single Action Target Revolver **$825**
Calibers: 32/44 S&W, 38/44 S&W Gallery & Target. Six-shot cylinder. Barrel: 6¹/₂ inches only. Hinged frame. Fixed or target sights. Rounded butt. Checkered hard rubber or walnut grips. Blued or nickel-plated finish. Made 1887 to 1910.

S&W 32 Double Action Revolver

Smith & Wesson 32 Double Action Revolver
Caliber: 32 S&W. Five-shot fluted cylinder. Barrel: 3, 3¹/₂ or 6 inches. Hinged frame. Fixed sights. Rounded butt. Checkered hard rubber grips. Blued or nickel-plated finish. Made 1880 to 1919.
First Issue of 1880 (rare; square sideplate, serial
nos. 1–30) **$1625**
Standard Model **225**

Smith & Wesson 32 Single Action Revolver . . **$480**
Smith & Wesson's first 32 caliber, automatic ejecting, break-open model. Caliber: 32 S&W. Five-shot fluted cylinder. Barrel: 3, 3¹/₂, 6, 8, 10 inches; round. Plain wood or chekered hard rubber grips. Rounded butt. Blued or nickel-plated finish. Made 1878 to 1892.

S&W 38 Double Action Revolver

Smith & Wesson 38 Double Action Revolver
Caliber: 38 S&W. Five-shot fluted cylinder. Barrel: 3¹/₄ to 10 inches. Weight: 17 to 19 ounces. Hinged frame. Fixed sights. Hard black rubber grips. Blued or nickel-plated finish. Made 1880 to 1911.
First Issue of 1880 (squared sideplate,
  serial nos. 1 to 4000) **$685**
Third Issue (1884–5 w/8- or 10-inch bbl.) **200**
Standard Model (incl. 1st thru 4th issues) **480**

S&W 38 Cal. Military & Police
R.A.F. Issue

Smith & Wesson Model 38 Military & Police—First Model **$375**
Also known as Model 38 Hand Ejector Double Action Revolver or Model 1899 Army or Navy Revolver. One of the first S&W swingout-cylinder models that resembles the Colt New Navy, minus the barrel lug and locking bolt that later S&W hand ejector models had. Caliber: 38 Long Colt. Six-shot cylinder. Barrel: 4, 5, 6 or 6¹/₂ inches. Overall length: 9 inches with 4-inch bbl. Fixed sights. Checkered walnut or hard rubber stocks. Round butt. Blued or nickel-plated finish. Made 1899 to 1902.

Smith & Wesson 38 Military & Police—Target Model **$895**
Same general specifications as the 38 Military & Police, except in target version with adjustable target sights. Caliber: 38 Special. Barrel: 6 inches. Weight: 32 ounces. Checkered walnut grips. Blued finish. Made 1899 to 1940.

S&W Baby Russian
First Model

Smith & Wesson 38 Single Action Revolver
Single Action Model No. 2 or Baby Russian. Caliber: 38 S&W. Five-shot fluted cylinder. Top-break action. Spur trigger. Barrels: 3¹/₄, 4 inches, round (First Model); 3¹/₄ to 10 inches, round (Second Model). Checkered hard rubber or wood grips. Blued or nickel-plated finish. Second Model has improved ejection with shorter extractor housing.
First Model (1876–77) **$425**
Second Model (1877–1981) **925**

S&W 38 Cal. Single Action
Revolver—Third Model

Smith & Wesson 38 Single Action Revolver—Third Model, or Model 1891
Caliber: 38 S&W. Five-shot fluted cylinder. Barrel: 3¹/₄, 4, 5 or 6 inches. Weight: 17¹/₂ to about 20 ounces. Hinged frame. Fixed sights. Automatic shell extractor. Hard black rubber grips. Blued or nickel-plated finish. Available with single shot pistol barrels of 6, 8 or 10 inches in 22, 32 or 38 caliber. Made 1891 to 1911.
Revolver only . . . . **$ 925**
Set with single-shot barrel **1400**

Smith & Wesson 38 Single Action Mexican Model **$1750**
Same as S&W Model 1891 above, except has flat-sided hammer, spur trigger assembly not integral to the frame; lacks half-cock notch on hammer.

S&W 44 Double Action
Frontier Model

Smith & Wesson 44 Double Action Revolver

Lightweight. Calibers: 44 S&W Russian, 38-40, 44-40 Win. Six-shot fluted cylinder. Barrel: 4, 5, 6 or 6¹/₂ inches. Weight: 34¹/₄ to 37¹/₂ ounces depending on barrel length. Hinged frame. Fixed sights. Checkered hard rubber or walnut grips. Blued or nickel-plated finish. Made 1881 to 1913; Frontier Model discontinued 1910.

DA Frontier (44-40 Win.)	**$ 725**
Standard Model (38-40)	**700**
Standard Model (44 S&W Russian)	**675**
Wesson Favorite (1882–3, 5-inch bbl.)	**1750**

S&W 44 Single Action Russian

Smith & Wesson 44 Single Action Russian Model $675

Calibers: 32-44, 38-44, 38 Win., 44 Russian, 44 Win., 450. Six-shot cylinder. Barrel: 4, 5, 6, 6¹/₂ or 8 inches (only cal. 44 Russian avail. in 8-inch). Weight: about 36 to 43 ounces. Automatic shell extractors. Checkered black rubber or wood grips.

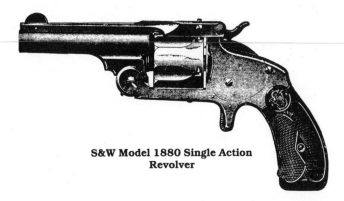

S&W Model 1880 Single Action Revolver

Smith & Wesson Model 1880 Single Action Revolver $480

Caliber: 38 S&W. Five-shot cylinder. Barrel: 3¹/₄, 4, 5 or 6 inches. Weight: 17¹/₄ to 19³/₄ ounces. Automatic shell extractor. Black rubber stocks. Special target sights and stocks were avail. Blued or nickel-plated finish. Introduced in 1880.

Smith & Wesson Model 1891 Single Action Revolver

See Smith & Wesson 38 Single Action Revolver—Third Model.

S&W Bicycle Revolver

Smith & Wesson Bicycle Revolver $265

Safety hammerless. Caliber: 32 S&W. Five-shot cylinder. Barrel length: 2 inches. Weight: 14 ounces. Black rubber stocks. Blued or nickel-plated finish. Made late 1800s.

S&W Safety Hammerless Revolver

Smith & Wesson Safety Hammerless Revolver—New Departure Double Action. $200

Calibers: 32 S&W, 38 S&W. Five-shot cylinder. Barrel: 2, 3 or 3¹/₂ inches (32 cal.); 2, 3¹/₄, 4, 5 or 6 inches (38 cal.). Overall length: 6³/₄ inches (32 cal. with 3-inch bbl.); 7¹/₂ inches (38 cal. with 3¹/₄-inch bbl.). Weight: 14¹/₄ to 18¹/₄ ounces. Hinged frame. Fixed sights. Hard rubber stocks. Blued or nickel-plated finish. Minor variations. Made 1888 to 1937 (32 cal.); 1887 to 1941 (38 cal.).

Smith & Wesson-Schofield Single Action Revolver

Modification of S&W No. 3 by Col. G.W. Schofield's patents of 1871 and 1873. Caliber: 45 S&W. Six-shot fluted cylinder. Barrel: 5 inches; 7 inches standard. Squared butt. Walnut grips. Blued or nickel (rare) finish. Two models made; the Second Model was an improved version of the First Model with no recoil plate in frame. Both models made in the 1870s.

Commercial Issue (rare)	**$2650**
Standard Military Issue	**2100**
Wells Fargo & Co. Issue (w/5-inch bbl.)	**1900**

SPANISH HANDGUNS
Various Manufacturers

Spanish Percussion Pistol
(Pedro José Cibar)

Pedro José Cibar Percussion Pistol **$200**
Caliber: 68. Belt hook on left side.

Spanish 65 Cal. Miquelet Pistol **$350**
Caliber: 65 percussion. Barrel: 3¹/₂ inches, half-octagonal. Engraved brass furniture.

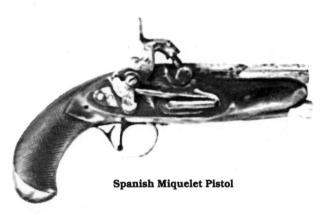

Spanish Miquelet Pistol

Spanish 69 Cal. Miquelet Pistol **$300**
Caliber: 69 percussion. Iron furniture with little or no engraving. Made circa 1850.

Spanish Flintlock Trade Pistol

Spanish Flintlock Trade Pistol **$350**
Calibers: various. Round barrel. Brass furniture. Typical of those manufactured for import to the East.

STARR ARMS COMPANY
New York, New York

Ebenezer Townsend Starr obtained Patent No. 14118 in January 1856 for a single-action percussion revolver. In December 1861, he received a second patent for a double-action revolver of the same type. Both single and double action revolvers were purchased under U.S. Government contracts during the Civil War and played a major part of the conflict (*see* U.S. Military Revolvers). Although New York City was home base for their offices, Starr firearms were produced at two plants, one in Yonkers and the other in Binghamton, N.Y. The firm closed in 1868.

Starr Model 1858 DA Army Revolver **$600**
Caliber: 44. Six-shot round, plain cylinder. Barrel: 6 inches. Double action. Blued finish. Smooth walnut grips. Made late 1850s to early 1860s.

Starr Model 1863 Single Action
Army Revolver

**Starr Model 1863 Single Action Army
Revolver** **$700**
Caliber: 44. Six-shot round, plain cylinder. Barrel: 8 inches. Blued finish. Smooth walnut grips. Made mid-1860s.

J. STEVENS ARMS & TOOL CO.
Chicopee Falls, Massachusetts

Although this company is known primarily for its long arms, it did produce handguns in the early days of operation. For further background information, please turn to J. Stevens Arms & Tool Co. under Rifles.

Stevens Diamond No. 43 Target
Pistol—First Issue

Stevens Diamond No. 43 Pistol—First Issue **$390**
Calibers: 22 Short, 22 LR. Single shot. Barrel: 6 or 10 inches; half-octagonal, rust blued. Spur trigger. Nickel-plated brass frame with or without sideplates. Globe or bead front sight; peep or open adjustable rear sight. Plain walnut grips with square butt. Although this model was very lightweight, it proved to be an accurate target pistol. Made 1886 to 1896.

Stevens Diamond No. 43 Pistol—Second Issue **$140**
Calibers: 22 Short, 22 LR, 22 Stevens-Pope. Single shot. Barrel: 6 or 10 inches; half-octagonal, rust blued. Spur trigger. Iron frame. Globe or bead front sight; peep or open adjustable rear sight. Full blued finish or nickel-plated frame with blued barrel. Plain walnut grips with square butt. Made from 1896 to 1916.

Stevens GEM Pocket Pistol **$205**
Calibers: 22 and 30 Short RF. Barrel: 3 inches; round, octagonal toward the breech, with side swing. Brass frame. Spur trigger. Blade front sight. Walnut or rosewood grips. Bird's-head butt. Full nickel-plated finish or nickel-plated frame with blued barrel. This is the only Stevens pistol (a derringer) without a tip-up action for loading and extraction. Made 1872 to 1890.

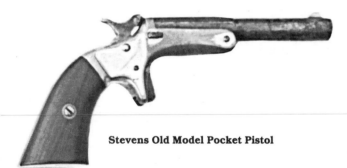

Stevens Old Model Pocket Pistol

Stevens Old Model Pocket Pistol **$160**
Caliber: 22 or 30 short RF. Barrel: 3½ inches; half-octagonal. Brass frame with sideplate. Blade front sight; rear notch in hammer. Spur trigger. Rosewood grips. Full nickel-plated finish, or nickel- or silver-plated frame with blued barrel. This is one of the two original models that Joshua Stevens' 1864 patent was based on, and prior to the introduction of the GEM Pocket Pistol, this gun was known as "The Pocket Pistol." Made 1864 to 1886.

Stevens "Tip-Up No. 41" Pistol **$116**
Calibers: 22 and 30 Short RF. Single shot. Barrel: 3½ inches, half-octagonal. Iron frame. Spur trigger. Blade front sight; rear groove in frame. Plain walnut grips. All blued finish or nickel-plated frame with blued barrel. Made from 1896 to 1916.

— NOTE —
*** after a dollar sign indicates that there was not enough trading at press time to establish a valid selling price.

STOCKING & COMPANY
Worcester, Massachusetts

Alexander Stocking made percussion pepperboxes and single-shot pistols. He was particularly noted for his fine-cased presentation models.

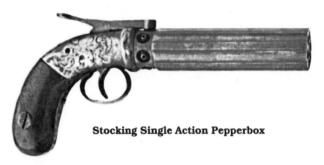

Stocking Single Action Pepperbox

Stocking Single Action Pepperbox **$275**
Caliber: 28. Barrel: 5 inches. Engraved frame. Made from 1847 to 1865.

C. D. TANNER
Hanover, Germany

C.D. Tanner Double Barrel Percussion Pistol

Tanner Double Barrel Percussion Pistol **$450**
Calibers: various. Rifled octagonal barrels. Double triggers. Light engraving. Iron fittings. Silver escutcheon on wrist. Made from 1846 to 1854.

WILLIAM TRANTER
Birmingham, England

William Tranter was a major manufacturer of early model percussion revolvers, some of which were based on the Robert Adams patent of 1851 (*see* separate listing). He added his own variation with a double-trigger mechanism, which he patented in 1853, and which proved quite successful with English shooters.

Tranter Percussion Revolver with Case **$1000**
Calibers: varied. Removable rammer. Checkered grips with square butt. Mahogany case came complete with all accessories, including an ebony-handled nipple wrench and screwdriver, wooden cleaning rod with two brass attachments, Dixon oil bottle, Dixon brass bag flask, brass mould with Tranter's stamp, round tin containing percussion caps, etc. Made circa 1850 to 1862.

TURKISH FLINTLOCKS
Various Manufacturers

Turkish Flintlock Pistol **$475**
Calibers: various, but 5/8-inch bore common. Barrel: 9 1/2 inches, round. Overall length: 16 inches. Brass butt, ramrod and ornamented barrel.

JOHN TWIGG
London, England

London gunmaker John Twigg (1732–1790) produced hand-rotated pepperboxes in the latter half of the 18th century.

Twigg Revolving Flintlock Pistol **$7500**
Caliber: about 32. Flintlock ignition. Barrels: 3 inches, round. Six barrels were grouped around a seventh, revolved by hand and all were numbered with proof marks. Overall length: 9 1/2 inches. Center hammer. Engraved frame and trigger guard.

UNION ARMS COMPANY
Hartford, Connecticut

While the plant of this firm was located in Hartford, the main office was in New York City. Union Arms made percussion pepperboxes and had U.S. Government contracts for percussion revolvers and rifles.

Union 31 Cal. Pocket Revolver

Union Arms Co. Pocket Revolver **$350**
Caliber: 31. Barrel: 3 1/4 inches, octagonal. Engraved frame. Made from about 1858 to 1865.

UNWIN & RODGERS
Sheffield, England

Of the unique and unusual arms that emerged in the 19th century, the knife pistol was perhaps most well known. The cutlery firm of Unwin & Rodgers, in business from about 1827 to 1868, advertised their version as early as 1839.

Unwin & Rogers Knife Pistol

Unwin & Rodgers Pocket Knife Pistol **$625**
Caliber: 31 percussion. Horn sides. Two blades. "JAMES RODGERS" marked on blades. Made circa 1845.

Unwin & Rodgers Pocket Knife Pistol **$325**
Caliber: 30 percussion. Two blades: one clip point, one spear point. Walnut sides. Cartridge compartment in handle. Made circa 1860s.

U.S. REVOLVER CO.
Address Unknown

U.S. Revolver Co. 32 Cal. Revolver
Nickel Finish

U.S. Revolver Co. Revolver **$95**
Caliber: 32. Nickel plated. Made circa 1890.

JAMES WARNER
Springfield, Massachusetts

Warner Percussion Revolver

Warner Percussion Revolver. **$1540**
Caliber: 36. Patented in June 1856 by James Warner, who was a designer and manager of the Springfield Arms Co. of Springfield, Mass., which produced the gun. Engraved rolled cylinder. Double triggers, the front one revolves the cylinder and as it is drawn back, it strikes the rear trigger, which fires the gun.

WEBLEY & SCOTT LTD.
London and Birmingham, England

Webley Model 1883 R.I.C. Revolver

Webley Model 1883 Revolver **$250**
Caliber: 450. Five-shot cylinder. Barrel: 2½ inches. Marked "R.I.C." for Royal Irish Constabulary. Made circa 1880.

**Webley Mark III 38 Military and Police
Revolver** **$225**
Caliber: 38 S&W. Six-shot half-fluted cylinder. Double action. Hinged frame. Barrel: 3 or 4 inches. Overall length: 9½ inches with 4-inch barrel. Weight: about 1¼ pounds. Fixed sights. Checkered walnut or vulcanite grips. Blued finish. Made 1897 to 1945.

Webley Self-cocking Percussion
Revolver

Webley Self-cocking Percussion Revolver **$300**
Caliber: 36 percussion. Five-shot cylinder. Octagonal barrel. Self-cocking. Open, engraved frame with "LONDON NO. 40406." Checkered grips.

Webley "Senior" Air Pistol **$75**
Caliber: 22. Plastic grips with Webley in cartouche. "WEBLEY & SCOTT LTD. BIRMINGHAM 4, WEBLEY PATENTS" stamped on right side. "THE WEBLEY SENIOR MADE IN ENGLAND" stamped on left.

Webley Wedge Frame Double Action
Revolver

Webley Wedge Frame Revolver **$400**
Caliber: 44. Double action. Octagonal barrel. "BUCK. EDGEWARD ROAD LONDON" engraved on top strap.

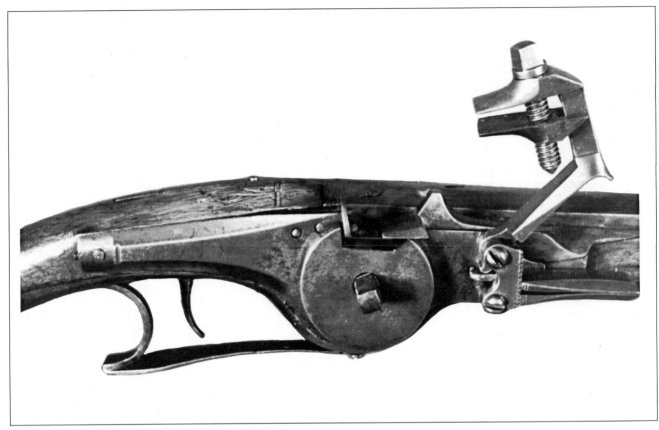

Close up of a prototype wheel lock: a French-made, 69-caliber version found at Yorktown, Virginia. It is believed that this was used by early American settlers.

WHEELLOCK PISTOLS
Various Manufacturers

The wheel lock was invented in Nuremberg about 1517 and was used on firearms at the siege of Parma in 1521 before being taken to England circa 1530. An improvement over the earlier match lock, the mechanism consisted of a steel wheel rasped at the edge, which protruded into a priming pan, a strong spring, and a cock into which was fixed a piece of pyrite. The wheel fit on the square end of an axle or a spindle, to which the spring was connected by a chain swivel. The cock was so fitted that it could be moved backwards or forwards at will. A strong spring was connected with it to keep it in a secure position.

When the gun was to be discharged, the lock was wound up by means of a key or spanner that fit on the axle or spindle, and the cock was let down to the priming pan with the pyrite resting on the wheel. When the trigger was pressed, the wheel was released and put in motion, causing sparks to be emitted, which ignited the powder in the priming pan. The wheel lock frequently misfired, as the pyrites were of a friable nature and would sometimes break in the pan—impeding the free action of the wheel. Therefore, the old match was kept handy for use when required.

Italian Wheellock Pistol.....................$***
Fancy, engraved wheellock pistol with gold plating made in the Gardone area of Italy. Stamped "BORTOLO CHINELLI." This is an excellent specimen of the European wheellock and is pictured in color on the front cover. Note the Eastern Mediterranean influence on the style of the grip and engraved butt.

Typical Wheellock Pistol **$1550**
Calibers: various, but 69 common. Barrel: 17³/₄ inches, octagonal. Overall length: 23 inches. Seven-inch lockplate with sliding pan cover. One model marked with letter "Z" in shield. Full stock, pin fastened, straight butt with metal cap. Iron guard and iron tipped rod.

Typical Wheellock Pistol **$1550**
Calibers: various, but 69 common. Barrel: 15¹/₄ inches with makers mark. Overall length: 23 inches. Lockplate: 6¹/₄ inches with sliding pan. Full stock, pin fastened, curved butt with iron plate. Iron trigger guard.

ROLLIN WHITE ARMS CO.
Lowell, Massachusetts

Rollin White was the patentee in 1855 of a revolver made with the cylinder bored end-to-end with a special cartridge. It was this patent that Smith & Wesson later purchased, which many firearms companies tried to duplicate or adapt, often with legal consequences. During the Civil War, however, when S&W had difficulty fulfilling government contracts for military arms because of heavy demand, Rollin White Arms was commissioned by S&W to manufacture guns. The company operated from 1861 to 1864, after which time under new management sans White, it became the Lowell Arms Company (*see* separate listing).

Rollin White 22 Cal. Revolver

Rollin White Arms Co. Revolver **$225**
Caliber: 22 RF. Seven-shot plain, round cylinder. Barrel: about 3 inches, octagonal. Spur trigger. Brass frame. With or without ejector (this version without). Walnut grips with square butt. Some marked "MADE FOR SMITH & WESSON BY ROLLIN WHITE ARMS CO. LOWELL, MASS." Made in the 1860s by both Rollin White Arms and Lowell Arms companies.

WHITNEY ARMS COMPANY
New Haven, Connecticut

Although he did not possess the inventiveness or shrewd business sense of his father, Eli Whitney Jr. ran the Whitney Arms Company from the early 1840s to 1888, when it was purchased by Winchester Repeating Arms. During that period the firm flourished, producing handguns and long arms under government contracts, and later for the sporting market.

For further background information, *see* also Whitney Arms Company under Rifles.

Whitney Pocket Revolver
Second Model

Whitney Pocket Percussion Revolver—Second Model **$395**
Caliber: 31 percussion. Five-shot cylinder. Barrel: 3 to 6 inches, octagonal. Five-groove rifling. Walnut grips. Blued finish. Somewhat similar to the Whitney Navy Revolver (*see* U.S. Military Revolvers). Made late 1850s to early 1860s.

WILLIAMS & POWELL
Liverpool, England

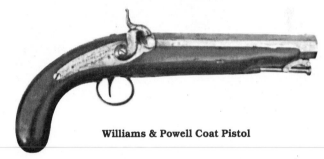

Williams & Powell Coat Pistol

Williams & Powell Coat Pistol. **$300**
Caliber: 68 percussion. Octagonal barrel. Brass furniture. Lockplate engraved "WILLIAMS & POWELL." Made circa 1840.

Williams & Powell Double Barrel
Percussion Pistol

Williams & Powell Double Barrel Pistol **$750**
Caliber: 50 percussion. Engraved with belt hook on left side. Swivel ramrod. Checkered grip with silver tacks in hatching. Minute silver floral design around butt. Cap-box in butt.

WINCHESTER REPEATING ARMS CO.
New Haven, Connecticut

In the mid-1850s, Horace Smith and Daniel Wesson manufactured the first "Volcanic," an iron-frame, lever-action repeating pistol. When the firm was incorporated as the Volcanic Repeating Arms Company of Norwich, Conn., Oliver Winchester became a major investor. By 1857 production of a brass-frame Volcanic had been well under way. Unfortunately, the company met with dim financial success and Smith & Wesson sold their assests and patents to the Volcanic firm, which were, in turn, acquired by the clothing manufacturer-turned-gunmaker Winchester. Production was moved to New Haven and Volcanic Arms became New Haven Arms Company. Manufacture of the brass-frame Volcanic continued, with B. Tyler Henry at the helm. (*See* Winchester Repeating Arms Co. under Rifles for further background information.)

**Winchester/S&W Lever Action
Volcanic Repeating Pistol**

Winchester Volcanic Repeating Pistol
Lever action. Caliber: 38. Barrel: 6, 8 or 16 inches; blued. Unfinished brass frame. Walnut grips. A few scroll engraved examples priced higher. Made by Volcanic Repeating Arms Co. 1855 to 1857.
6- or 8-inch barreled models **$2250**
16-inch barrel w/o shoulder stock (rare) **3500**
16-inch barrel with shoulder stock (rare) **5950**

**Winchester Volcanic/New Haven
Repeating Pistol**

Winchester Volcanic New Haven Repeating Pistol
Lever action. Caliber: 30. Smaller brass frame than the 38 caliber model. Barrel: 3½ or 6 inches; octagonal, blued. Walnut grips. A few scroll engraved examples, although most are "unfinished." Made by New Haven Arms Co. 1857 to 1860.
3½-inch barreled model **$1750**
6-inch barreled model **2650**

AMERICAN KENTUCKY FLINTLOCK PISTOLS

The "Kentucky" pistol was the shorter counterpart of the famed Kentucky rifles and, like the rifle, the majority of the Kentucky pistols were manufactured in Pennsylvania. Some may be unmarked; others will have initials of the makers, while still others will have the complete name and address—although the spelling has been known to vary in some cases. Specifications for "typical" Kentucky pistols are detailed below, followed by a listing of gunmakers who were known to have produced Kentucky pistols of varying quality; approximate dates of production are indicated. Separate, additional listings appear at the end of this section, which reflect more definitive information and values about particular manufacturers' pistols.

Kentucky Flintlock Pistol **$3800**
Calibers: 34 to 48. Barrel: 9 inches; octagonal, smoothbore. Overall length: 14½ inches. Kentucky-type front sight, usually no rear sight. Full maple stock with brass furniture.

Kentucky Flintlock High-Grade Pistol **$7800**
Same general specifications as "standard" pistol, except with fancy decoration.

Kentucky Converted Pistol **$1650**
Same general specifications as the original flintlock pistol, except it has been converted from flintlock to percussion.

James Angush
Lancaster, Pennsylvania, 1774–1775

Edward and Thomas Annely
New Jersey, 1748–1777

Jacob Anstadt
Kutztown, Pennsylvania, 1814–1815

A. and J. Ansted
Pennsylvania, circa 1810

William Antis
Frederickstown, Pennsylvania, 1775–1782

John Armstrong
Emmetsburg, Maryland, 1790–1855

R. Ashmore & Son
Lancaster County, Pennsylvania, circa 1800

Thomas Austin
Charlestown, Massachusetts, 1774–1778

Nathan Bailey
New London, Connecticut, 1776–1779

Jacob Baker
Philadelphia, Pennsylvania, 1820–1833

Samuel Baum
Mahoning Township, Columbia County, PA., circa 1820

Russell Bean
Jonesboro, Tennessee, circa 1770

Christopher Bechtler
Rutherford, North Carolina, 1829–1874

Elias Beckley
Berlin, Connecticut, 1807–1828

Edmund Bemis
Boston, Massachusetts, 1746–1785

Amos Benfer
Beaverstown, Pennsylvania, circa 1830

Peter Berry
Dauphin, Pennsylvania, circa 1800

Thomas Bicknell
Philadelphia, Pennsylvania, 1799–1803

Oliver Bidwell
Hartford, Connecticut, 1756–1812

Marmaduke Blackwood
Philadelphia, Pennsylvania, 1775–1777

Jonathan Blaisdel
Amesbury, Massachusetts, circa 1775

P. & E.W. Blake
New Haven, Connecticut, circa 1825

Samuel Boardlear
Boston, Massachusetts, circa 1795

Anthony Bobb
Reading, Pennsylvania, 1778–1781

Samuel Boone
Berks County, Pennsylvania, circa 1770

William Booth
Philadelphia, Pennsylvania, circa 1797–1820

Robert Boyd
New Windsor, New York, 1772–1778

Peter Brong
Lancaster, Pennsylvania, 1795–1816

John Brooke
St.Louis, Missouri, circa 1845

John Buckwalter
Lancaster County, Pennsylvania, 1771–1780

Elisha Buell
Marlborough, Connecticut, 1797–1850

Elisha Burnham
Hartford, Connecticut, 1776–1781

John Butler
Lancaster, Pennsylvania, 1775–1778

William Calderwood
Philadelphia, Pennsylvania, 1807–1819

George Call
Lancaster, Pennsylvania, 1775–1780

William Campbell
Annapolis, Maryland, circa 1780

Adam Carruth
Philadelphia, Pennsylvania, 1809–1821

John Carpenter
Lancaster, Pennsylvania, 1771–1790

Stephen Chandler
Connecticut, circa 1775

Darius Chipman
Rutland, Vermont, 1799–1816

Lewis Chriskey
Philadelphia, Pennsylvania, circa 1815

Jacob Christ
Lancaster, Pennsylvaina, 1772–1780

Alexander Clagett
Hagerstown, Maryland, circa 1800

Joseph Clark
Danbury, Connecticut, circa 1800

Henry Clause
Heidelberg, Pennsylvania, circa 1820

Henry and Nathan Cobb
Norwich, Connecticut, 1795–1801

S. Cogswell
Albany, New York, circa 1810

Levi Coon
Ithaca, New York, 1776–1821

Abraham Coster
Philadelphia, Pennsylvania, 1810–1814

Samuel Coutty
Philadelphia, Pennsylvania, 1783–1795

Joseph Cowell
Boston, Massachusetts, 1745–1775

Thomas Crabb
Frederick Town, Maryland, 1799–1805

Royal Craft
Rutland, Vermont, 1799–1810

John Cryth
Lancaster, Pennsylvania, circa 1800

Jesse Curtis
Waterbury, Connecticut, 1776–1780

Richard Dalam
Hartford County, Maryland, 1775–1778

Jacob Dechert
Philadelphia, Pennsylvania, 1732–1782

Peter DeHaven
Philadelphia and Valley Forge, Penn., 1769–1778

Henry DeHuff
Lancaster, Pennsylvania, 1801–1807

Michael DeReiner
Lancaster, Pennsylvania, 1773–1777

John Derr
Lancaster, Pennsylvania, 1810–1844

John Devane
Wilmington, North Carolina, 1776–1832

Samuel Dewey
Hebron, Connecticut, 1775–1778

Jacob Dickert
Lancaster, Pennsylvania, 1762–1822

Jacob Doll
York, Pennsylvania, 1780–1805

John Douglas
Huntington, Pennsylvania, circa 1840

Christian Durr
Lancaster, Pennsylvania, circa 1840

George Dunkle
Sheppensburg, Pennsylvania, circa 1825

William Dunwicke
Chester County, Pennsylvania, 1770–1776

Elias Earle
Centerville, North Carolina, 1811–1816

Thomas Earle
Leicester, Massachusetts, 1848–1857

Jacob Early
Atcheson, Kansas, 1864–1886

John Eberly
Lancaster, Pennsylvania, 1774–1777

Matthew and Nathan Elliott
Kent, Connecticut, circa 1800

Henry Elwell
Liverpool, Pennsylvania, circa 1770

Martin Ely
Springfield, Massachusetts, 1770–1776

Jacob Ernst
Frederick, Maryland, 1780–1820

Brooke Evans
Evansburg, Pennsylvania, 1821–1825

Edward and James Evans
Evansburg, Pennsylvania, 1801–1818

Owen and Edward Evans
Evansburg, Pennsylvania, 1790–1815

Stephen Evans
Mt. Joy Forge, Pennsylvania, 1741–1797

William L. Evans
Evansburg, Pennsylvania, 1823–1833

Edward Evatt
Baltimore, Maryland, 1804–1818

Richard Falley
Westfield, Massachusetts, 1761–1808

Thomas Fancher
Waterbury, Connecticut, 1770–1779

Frank and Jacob Farnot
Lancaster, Pennsylvania, 1775–1783

William Farver
Brown County, Ohio, 1848–1854

Adam Faulk
Lancaster, Pennsylvania, 1830–1835

J. Fehr
Nazareth, Pennsylvania, 1830–1835

Jacob Ferree
Lancaster, Pennsylvania, 1774–1807

Conrad Fesig
Reading, Pennsylvania, 1779–1790

I. Field
Philadelphia, Pennsylvania, circa 1790

John Fitch
Bucks County, Pennsylvania, 1769–1796

Heinrich Fogle
Lancaster, Pennsylvania, circa 1855

Ludwig Foher
Philadelphia, Pennsylvania, circa 1775

Follecht
Lancaster, Pennsylvania, 1740–1770

John Ford
Harrisburg, Pennsylvania, 1800–1817

Jacob Fordney
Lancaster, Pennsylvania, 1837–1857

Melchior Fordney
Lancaster, Pennsylvania, 1823–1843

Franck
Lancaster, Pennsylvania, circa 1775

John Frazier
Lancaster, Pennsylvania, 1740–1756

Gideon Frost
Massachusetts, circa 1775

John Gall
Lancaster, Pennsylvania, circa 1850

Albert Gallatin
Fayette County, Pennsylvania, 1796–1808

Peter Gander
Lancaster, Pennsylvania, circa 1780

G. Gardner
Lima, Ohio, 1859–1865

Gaspard
Lancaster, Pennsylvania, circa 1775

Jacob George
Greenwich, Pennsylvania, circa 1800

John Gerrish
Boston, Massachusetts, circa 1710

Lewis Ghriskey
Philadelphia, Pennsylvania, 1812–1816

Henry Gibbs
Lancaster, Pennsylvania, 1824–1857

Daniel Gilbert
Brookfield, Massachusetts, 1782–1813

Benjamin Gill
Lancaster, Pennsylvania, 1830–1850

Glaze & Co.
Columbia, South Carolina, 1852–1865

Frederick Goetz
Philadelphia, Pennsylvania, 1806–1812

James Golcher
Philadelphia, Pennsylvania, 1820–1833

Joseph Golcher
Philadelphia, Pennsylvania, circa 1800

Peter Gonter
Lancaster, Pennsylvania, 1750–1818

Jonathan Goodwin
Lebanon, Connecticut, circa 1778

William Graeff
Reading, Pennsylvania, 1751–1784

Samuel Grant
Walpole, New Hampshire, circa 1800

J. Gresheim
Lancaster, Pennsylvania, 1775–1783

Samuel Grove
York, Pennsylvania, 1779–1783

Christopher Gumpf
Lancaster, Pennsylvania, 1791–1842

Nicholas Hawk
Gilbert, Pennsylvania, 1805–1835

J. Hillegas
Pottesville, Virginia, 1810–1830

Thomas Hooker
Rutland, Vermont, 1798–1802

James Hunter
Falmouth, Virginia, 1760–1775

Benjamin Hutz
Lancaster, Pennsylvania, circa 1800

Benedick Inhoff
Heidelberg, Pennsylvania, circa 1785

Christian Isch
Lancaster, Pennsylvania, 1774–1782

Robert James
Baltimore, Maryland, circa 1795

Stephen Jenks
Pawtucket, Rhode Island, 1795–1814

Robert Johnson
Middletown, Connecticut, 1822–1854

Charles and Robert Jones
Lancaster, Pennsylvania, 1775–1783

Peter Kascheline
Northampton County, Pennsylvania, circa 1775

Samuel Kearling
Bucks County, Pennsylvania, circa 1780

Sebastian and Mathias Keeley
Philadelphia, Pennsylvania, circa 1775

Jacob Keffer
Lancaster, Pennsylvania, circa 1800

David Kemmerer
Lehighton, Pennsylvania, circa 1850

Nathan Kile
Jackson County, Ohio, circa 1815

Samuel Kinder
Philadelphia, Pennsylvania, circa 1775

Adam Kinsley
Bridgewater, Massachusetts, 1795–1812

Daniel Kleist
Easton, Pennsylvania, 1780–1792

Conrad Kline
Lancaster, Pennsylvania, circa 1780

John Krider
Philadelphia, Pennsylvania, 1839–1870

Kunkle
Philadelphia, Pennsylvania, 1810–1814

Jacob Kunz
Philadelphia, Pennsylvania, 1770–1817

W. Larson
Harrisburg, Pennsylvania, circa 1830

George Laydendecker
Allentown, Pennsylvania, 1774–1783

H. Lechler
Lancaster, Pennsylvania, 1848–1857

Philip Lefever
Beaver Valley, Pennsylvania, 1731–1766

Adam and Ignatius Leitner
York, Pennsylvania, 1779–1810

Michael Lenz
Baltimore, Maryland, circa 1805

Eliphalet Leonard
Boston, Massachusetts, 1775–1780

Jacob Lether
York, Pennsylvania, 1777–1820

Peter Light
Berkeley County, Virginia, circa 1775

John Livingston
Walpole, New Hampshire, 1795–1801

Matthew Llewelyn
Lancaster, Pennsylvania, circa 1740

Loder
Lancaster, Pennsylvania, circa 1770

Longstretch & Cook
Philadelphia, Pennsylvania, circa 1770

Earl Loomis
Hamilton, New York, circa 1850

M. Lorney
Boalsburg, Pennsylvania, circa 1810

Peter Lydick
Baltimore, Maryland, 1773–1779

Simeon Marble
Sunderland, Vermont, circa 1850

Robert McCormick
Philadelphia, Pennsylvania, 1796–1802

Kester McCoy
Lancaster, Pennsylvania, circa 1770

Alexander McRae
Richmond, Virginia, 1815–1821

Silas Merriman
Connecticut, circa 1775

Jacob Messersmith
Lancaster, Pennsylvania, 1779–1802

Samuel Messersmith
Baltimore, Maryland, 1775–1778

Jacob Metzger
Lancaster, Pennsylvania, 1849–1857

Henry Meyer
Pennsylvania, 1771–1778

Martin Meylin
Lancaster, Pennsylvania, 1710–1749

Simon Miller
Hamburg, Pennsylvania, 1790–1820

Isaac Milnor
Philadelphia, Pennsylvania, circa 1760

Peter Moll
Hellerstown, Pennsylvania, 1791–1835

George Moore
Mt. Vernon, Ohio, 1885–1894

Joseph Morgan
Philadelphia, Pennsylvania, circa 1810

Abraham Morrow
Philadelphia, Pennsylvania, 1781–1798

Peter Neihart
Lehigh County, Pennsylvania, circa 1770–1810

Alexander Nelson
Philadelphia, Pennsylvania, circa 1775

John Newcomer
Lancaster, Pennsylvania, circa 1770

John Nicholson
Philadelphia, Pennsylvania, 1774–1792

Daniel Nippes
Philadelphia, Pennsylvania, 1808–1848

Simeon North
North Berlin, Connecticut, 1794–1852

Ebenezer Nutting
Falmouth, Maine, 1722–1745

Samuel Oakes
Philadelphia, Pennsylvania, circa 1800

Christian Oberholzer
Lancaster, Pennsylvania, 1775–1778

S. Odell
Natchez, Mississippi, circa 1855

John Odlin
Boston, Massachusetts, 1671–1685

E. Ong
Philadelphia, Pennsylvania, 1773–1777

Hugh Orr
Springfield, Massachusetts, 1737–1798

H. Osborn
Springfield, Massachusetts, 1815–1830

John Page
Preston, Connecticut, 1770–1777

Jacob Palm
Lancaster, Pennsylvania, 1759–1777

Jefferson Pannabecker
Lancaster, Pennsylvania, 1790–1810

Samuel Pannabecker
Allentown, Pennsylvania, 1780–1825

William Pannabecker, Jr. and Sr.
Mohnton, Pennsylvania, 1800–1880

James Pearson
Philadelphia, Pennsylvania, circa 1775

A. Peck
Hartford, Connecticut, circa 1800

James and Rufus Perkins
Bridgewater, Massachusetts, 1800–1813

Silas Phelps
Lebanaon, Connecticut, 1770–1777

Henry Pickel
York, Pennsylvania, 1800–1811

Samuel Pike
Brattleboro, Vermont, circa 1845

Lewis Prahl
Philadelphia, Pennsylvania, 1775–1790

Frederick Rathfong
Conestoga, Pennsylvania, 1770–1772

George Rathfong
Lancaster, Pennsylvania, 1774–1819

Reddick
Baltimore, Maryland, circa 1775

Robert Read
Chesterton, Maryland, 1775–1802

Francis Reynolds
New York, New York, 1844–1865

William Robertson
Rochester, New York, circa 1840

Peter Roesser
Lancaster, Pennsylvania, 1739–1782

John Roop
Allentown, Pennsylvania, 1770–1775

William Ruppert
Lancaster, Pennsylvania, circa 1775

Michael Rynes
Lancaster, Pennsylvania, circa 1770

Gordon Saltonstall
Connecticut, 1762–1775

Jacob Saylor
Bedford County, Pennsylvania, 1779–1790

Jacob Schley
Frederick Town, Maryland, circa 1775

Mathias Schroyer
Taney Town, Maryland, circa 1800

James Teaff
Steubenville, Ohio, 1849–1861

P. Valle
Philadelphia, Pennsylvania, 1826–1840

Peter White
Bedford County, Pennsylvania, circa 1810–1820

Casper Yost
Lancaster, Pennsylvania, 1773–1778

Frederick and George Zorger
York, Pennsylvania, 1770–1802

HENRY ALBRIGHT
Lancaster, Pennsylvania

Albright Kentucky Flintlock Pistol........ **$4300**
Calibers: various, but 48 smoothbore. Barrel: 7½ inches; half-octogonal, brass. Overall length: 13½ inches. Weight: 1 lb. 12 oz. Full curly maple stock. Brass ramrod thimbles. No muzzle cap. Made from 1740 to 1792.

PETER ANGSTADT
Lancaster, Pennsylvania

Angstadt Kentucky Flintlock Pistol....... **$3825**
Calibers: various, but 44 smoothbore common. Barrel: about 9 inches, half-octagonal. Overall length: 13½ inches. Weight: 1 lb. 11 oz. Full curly maple stock. Brass butt cap, trigger guard, side plate, ramrod thimbles and muzzle cap. Made from 1770 to 1777.

JOHN & PATRICK BALLANTINE
Charleston, South Carolina

Ballantine Kentucky Flintlock Pistol....... **$4150**
Calibers: various, but 48 smoothbore common. Barrel: 7½ inches; half-octagoal, brass. Overall length: about 13½ inches. Weight: 1 lb. 12 oz. Full curly maple stock, brass ramrod thimbles. No muzzle cap. Made from 1720 to 1740.

BIELRY
Philadelphia, Pennsylvania

Bielry Kentucky Flintlock Pistol.......... **$4200**
Calibers: various, but 44 smoothbore common. Barrel: about 9 inches, half-octagonal. Overall length: 13½ inches. Weight: 1 lb. 11 oz. Full curly maple stock. Brass butt cap, trigger guard, side plate, ramrod thimbles and muzzle cap. Made from 1769 to 1770.

THOMAS P. CHERRINGTON
Cattawissa, Pennsylvania

Cherrington Kentucky Flintlock Pistol **$4125**
Calibers: various, but 44 smoothbore common. Barrel: about 9 inches, half-octagonal. Overall length: 13½ inches. Weight: 1 lb. 11 oz. Full curly maple stock. Brass butt cap, trigger guard, side plate, ramrod thimbles and muzzle cap. Made from 1765 to 1805.

JOHN DODD
Charleston, South Carolina

Dodd Kentucky Flintlock Pistol........... **$4800**
Calibers: various, but 48 smoothbore common. Barrel: 7½ inches; half-octagonal, brass. Overall length: 13½ inches. Weight: 1 lb. 12 oz. Full curly maple stock. Brass ramrod thimbles. No muzzle cap. Made from 1755 to 1762.

GILBERT FORBES
New York, New York

Forbes Kentucky Flintlock Pistol.......... **$4135**
Calibers: various, but 44 smoothbore common. Barrel: about 9 inches, half-octagonal. Overall length: 13½ inches. Weight: 1 lb. 11 oz. Full curly maple stock. Brass butt cap, trigger guard, side plate, ramrod thimbles and muzzle cap. Made from 1767 to 1776.

ADAM FOULKE
Allentown, Pennsylvania

Foulke Kentucky Flintlock Pistol **$3995**
Calibers: various, but 44 smoothbore common. Barrel: about 9 inches, half-octagonal. Overall length: 13½ inches. Weight: 1 lb. 11 oz. Full curly maple stock. Brass butt cap, trigger guard, side plate, ramrod thimbles and muzzle cap. Made from 1773 to 1794.

DAVIE & WILLIAM GEDDY
Williamsburg, Virginia

Geddy Kentucky Flintlock Pistol.......... **$5200**
Calibers: various, but 48 smoothbore common. Barrel: 7½ inches; half-octagonal, brass. Overall length: about 12 inches. Weight: 1 lb. 10 oz. Full curly maple stock. Brass ramrod thimbles. No muzzle cap. Made from 1748 to 1752.

JAMES & JOHN WALSH
Allentown, Pennsylvania

Walsh Kentucky Flintlock Pistol.......... **$4230**
Calibers: various, but 44 smoothbore common. Barrel: about 9 inches, half-octagonal. Overall length: 13½ inches. Weight: 1 lb. 11 oz. Full curly maple stock. Brass butt cap, trigger guard, side plate, ramrod thimbles and muzzle cap. Made from 1760 to 1779.

CONFEDERATE HANDGUNS

The following Civil War-period handguns include only those manufactured in the South. Other guns were of course used by the Confederate States but produced elsewhere; those firearms are detailed in separate listings throughout the Handgun Section. *See*, for example, the LeMat "Grapeshot" Revolver and the U.S. Model 1842 Percussion Pistol.

Cofer Revolver **$20,500**
Caliber: 36 percussion. Six-shot cylinder. Barrel: 7+ inches, octagonal; marked "T.W. Cofer's Patent, Portsmouth, VA." Brass frame. Square trigger guard. Colt-type loading lever. Made in 1861.

Columbus Revolver **$10,500**
Caliber: 36 percussion. Six-shot cylinder. Barrel: 7½ inches, round; marked "Columbus Fire Arms Manuf. Col, Georgia." Octagonal breech. Brass trigger guard, front sight, handle strap.

Dance Navy Revolver **$5400**
Caliber: 36 percussion. Six-shot cylinder. Barrel: 7⅜ inches, half-octagonal. Iron frame. Made 1863–64 by the Dance Brothers —David, George and James —near Galveston, Texas.

Dance Revolver **$5400**
Caliber: 44 percussion. Six-shot cylinder. Barrel: 8 inches, round or octagonal. Iron "milled flat" frame. Brass trigger guard, backstrap, blade front sight. Made 1863–64 by the Dance Brothers; about only 300 or so total Dance revolvers were supposedly produced by the time the war ended.

Fayetteville Model 1855 Pistol-Carbine **$3000**
Caliber: 58. Single shot. Barrel: 12 inches. Detachable shoulder stock. Lockplate marked "Fayetteville" with spread eagle over "C.S.A." Made at the Fayetteville, N.C., armory 1861 to about 1863.

Griswold & Grier Revolver **$4500**
Also known as the Griswold & Gunnison Revolver, after Samuel Griswold and A.W. Gunnison, one of the most reliable producers of CSA guns. Caliber: 36 percussion. Six-shot cylinder. Barrel: 7½ inches, round. Later models have octagonal breech. Brass frame. Squarish trigger guard. Often called the "Brass-frame Confederate Colt." Made 1862–64 in Griswoldville, Ga.

Leech & Rigdon Revolver **$4800**
Caliber: 36 percussion. Six-shot cylinder. Barrel: 7½ inches; marked "Leech & Rigdon" or "Leech & Rigdon, C.S.A." Brass front sight, trigger guard, handle strap. Made by C.H. Rigdon and Thomas Leech in Greensboro, Ga., 1862–63.

Richmond Pistol **$2700**
Caliber: 54. Single shot. Barrel: 10 inches, round. Brass band and butt plate. Swivel ramrod. Lockplate marked "C.S. Richmond, Va." Made at the Richmond Armory about 1861.

Rigdon & Ansley Revolver **$4285**
Caliber: 36 percussion. Six-shot cylinder. Barrel: 7½ inches, round; marked "Augusta, Ga. C.S.A." plus serial number. Twelve cylinder stops. Brass front sight, handle strap and trigger guard. Trigger guard machined and distinctly shaped—not round or square —same as on Leech & Rigdon Revolver. Made 1864–65.

Schneider & Glassick Revolver **$4500**
Caliber: 36 percussion. Six-shot cylinder. Barrel: 7½ inches; marked "Schneider & Glassick, Memphis, Tenn." Brass trigger guard, front sight and backstrap. Made by William S. Schneider and Frederick G. Glassick, both of Memphis. Extremely rare.

Sherrard & Taylor Revolver **$9600**
Caliber: 44 percussion. Six-shot cylinder. Barrel: 7½ inches, octagonal. Close copy of the Colt. Made by Sherrard, Taylor & Co. (Joseph Sherrard and Pleasant Taylor) of Lancaster, Texas, 1862–63.

Spiller & Burr Revolver **$4285**
Caliber: 36 percussion. Six-shot cylinder. Barrel: 7½ inches, octagonal; marked "Spiller & Burr" (later models stamped with "C.S."). Brass frame. In Nov. 1861, the C.S. War Department contracted for 15,000 S & B Navy revolvers based on Colt Navy design; problems, however, led to the manufacture of a Colt Whitney-styled gun, many of which had iron barrels because steel was not available; total production was not met. Made by Edward N. Spiller of Baltimore and David J. Burr of Richmond, Va., in Atlanta and the C.S. Armory at Macon, Ga., 1862–64.

Sutherland Pistol **$1050**
Caliber: 60 percussion. Single shot. Barrel: 6¼ inches, octagonal. Lockplate marked "Sutherland, Richmond." Made by master gunmaker Samuel Sutherland in Virginia.

U.S. MILITARY HANDGUNS

Most of the handguns featured in the following section were contracted by the federal government for use by the military services. The Rappahannock Forge Flintlock Pistol, however, dates back to about 1775, even before the United States was officially a recognized nation; it is considered a military arm since it was used by the State of Virginia during the Revolutionary War. During the 19th century, Colt handguns were particularly popular, and a separate grouping details the pistols and revolvers of Colt manufacture that were issued to the military. The other two groupings contain U.S. Military pistols and revolvers that were produced by various manufacturers.

U.S. MILITARY HANDGUNS
Of Colt Manufacture

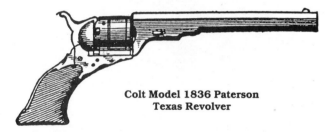

**Colt Model 1836 Paterson
Texas Revolver**

Colt Model 1836 Paterson Texas Revolver .. **$1200**
Calibers: 28, 31, 36. Five-shot round cylinder. Barrels: 4¹/₂ to 12 inches, octagonal. All had folding triggers with no trigger guard. Cylinder pin had a cup-shaped end that was used as a ramrod. Square-cornered butt. Made in Paterson, N.J., from 1836 to 1841.

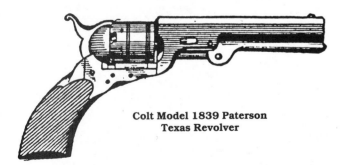

**Colt Model 1839 Paterson
Texas Revolver**

Colt Model 1839 Paterson Texas Revolver .. **$1000**
Caliber: 28. Later model of the 1836 Paterson. Changes were made in the shape of the handle, and was equipped with a loading lever. Made in Paterson from 1839 to 1841.

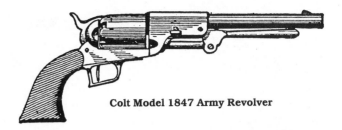

Colt Model 1847 Army Revolver

Colt Model 1847 Army Revolver **$30,000**
Caliber: 44. Six-shot cylinder. Barrel: 9 inches, round with octagonal breech. Overall length: 15¹/₂ inches. Weight: 4 lbs. 9 oz. Straight, round cylinder that revolves to the right. Squareback trigger guard. One thousand were made in 1847 by Colt at the Eli Whitney (of cotton gin fame) Armory in Whitneyville, Conn. They had been commissioned by Captain Samuel Walker for use by the U.S. Government and were subsequently known as the "Whitneyville Walkers."

Colt Model 1848 Army Revolver **$3000**
Also known as the No. 1 Dragoon or Model of 1848 Holster Pistol. Caliber: 44. Six-shot fluted cylinder. Barrel: 7¹/₂ inches, round. Overall length: 14 inches. Weight: 4 pounds. Squareback trigger guard. Made in Hartford, Conn., from 1848 to 1849.

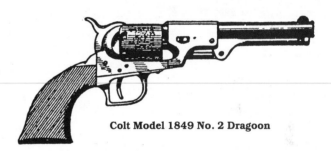

Colt Model 1849 No. 2 Dragoon

Colt Dragoon, 2nd Model **$5000**
Known as No. 2 Dragoon or Old Model Army Pistol. Caliber: 44. Six-shot round, straight cylinder. Barrel: 8 inches. Overall length: 14¹/₂ inches. Weight: 4 lbs. 2 oz. Brass backstrap and squareback trigger guard. Hinged lever ramrod. Made in Hartford 1850 to 1851.

Colt Dragoon, 3rd Model **$4000**
Caliber: 44. Six-shot round, straight cylinder. Barrel: 7¹/₂ inches; round with octagonal breech. Overall length: 14 inches. Hinged lever ramrod. Brass backstrap and oval trigger guard. Cut and fitted for shoulder stocks. Made in Hartford 1851 to 1860.

NOTE

The rarest of the Colt Second Model Dragoons have "V" hammer springs and no bearing wheel, and were numbered between 8,000 and 10,000.

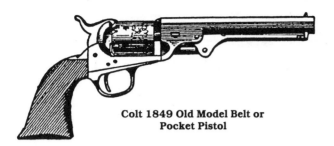

Colt 1849 Old Model Belt or
Pocket Pistol

Colt Model 1851 Navy Revolver

Colt 1849 Old Model Belt or Pocket Pistol . . **$5000**
Pattern of 1849. Caliber: 31. Six-shot straight, round
cylinder. Barrels: 3, 4, 5, 6 inches; octagonal. Smaller
sizes were known as "Pocket" pistols. Hinged loading
lever. Oval brass trigger guard. Made from 1849 to
1873.

Colt Model 1849 Wells Fargo Revolver **$2950**
This is the same as the Model of 1849 Pocket Pistol
without the rammer, and is often confused with the
Model of 1848. Also known as the Old Model Police Pistol. Caliber: 31. Five-shot cylinder. Barrels: 3, 4, 5, 6
inches; octagonal. Made without loading lever or ramrod. Nickel-plated backstrap and oval trigger guard.
Made during the 1850s.

Colt Model 1851 Navy Revolver **$1500**
Called the Old Model Belt Pistol. Caliber: 36. Six-shot
cylinder. Barrel: 7 inches, octagonal. Overall length: 13
inches. Weight: 2 lbs. 10 oz. Straight, round cylinder
with rectangular slots and safety pins to keep the
capped nipples away from the hammer. Oval, iron trigger guard. For military purposes, this arm was
equipped with a Dragoon-type canteen shoulder stock
and sling swivel. Introduced in 1851.

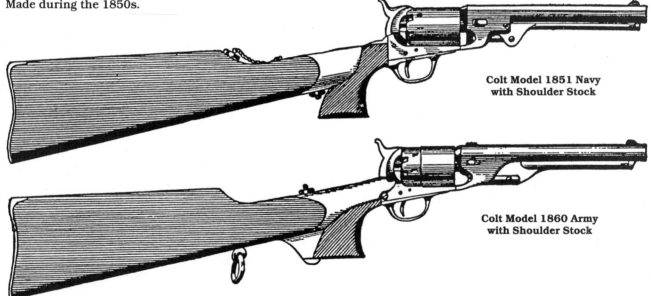

Colt Model 1851 Navy
with Shoulder Stock

Colt Model 1860 Army
with Shoulder Stock

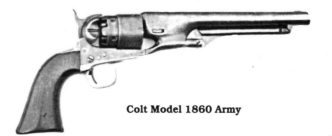

Colt Model 1860 Army

Colt Model 1860 Army Revolver **$4000**
Caliber: 44. Six-shot cylinder. Barrel: 8 inches, round.
Overall length: 14 inches. Weight: 2 lbs. 11 oz. Round
or oval brass trigger guard. Frame and backstrap are
notched for attaching a shoulder stock, for a total
length of 26$^{1}/_{2}$ inches and weight of 5 pounds. This arm
was the principal revolver of the Civil War, since about
130,000 were purchased by the U. S. Government.
Made from about 1860 to 1873.

Colt Model 1860 Army
45 Revolver

Colt Model 1860 Army 45 Revolver $2800

Altered version of Model 1860 Army for use with metallic cartridges. Caliber: 45. Six-shot cylinder. Barrel: 8 inches, round. Overall length: 14 inches. Weight: 2 lbs. 11 oz. Ramrod and lever were removed and an ejector added to the right side of the barrel. A gate was added to facilitate loading and ejecting.

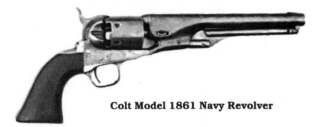

Colt Model 1861 Navy Revolver

Colt Model 1861 Navy Revolver $5200

Also called New Model Belt or Pocket Pistol. Caliber: 36. Six-shot round, straight cylinder, some fluted. Barrels: 7½ inches; (also made in 4½, 5½, 6½ inches for civilian use). Weight: 2 lbs. 9 oz. Creeping lever ramrod. Brass backstrap. Oval brass trigger guard. Made from 1861 to 1873.

Colt Model 1873 Single Action
Army Revolver

Colt Model 1873 Single Action Army Revolver $1200

Caliber: 45 centerfire. Barrels: 5½, 7½ inches, round. Overall length: 11, 12½ inches, respectively. Weight: 2 lbs. 5 oz. Large steel blade front sight; V-notch rear sight. Steel frame and trigger guard. Blued barrel and cylinder. Casehardened hammer and frame. Introduced in 1873.

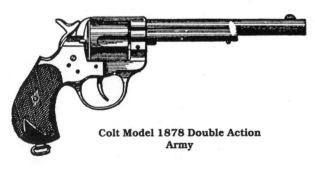

Colt Model 1878 Double Action
Army

Colt Model 1878 Double Action Army Revolver $1000

Caliber: 45 centerfire. Six-shot, two-thirds fluted cylinder. Barrel: 7½ inches, round. Overall length: 12½ inches. Weight: 2 lbs. 7 oz. Side rod ejector. Hard rubber bird's-head grips. This is the first heavy double-action revolver made by Colt. Last patent date is 1880. Made in Hartford from 1878 to 1905.

Colt Model 1892 Army
(Government) Revolver

Colt Model 1892 Army (Government) Revolver $250

Double action. Caliber: 38. Six-shot, swing-out cylinder, the first of its type. Solid frame. Barrel: 7½ inches (Army); also 3, 4½, 6 inches; round. Overall length: 11¼ inches with 4½-inch bbl. Weight: 2 pounds. Used by the Army and Marines, whose model had plain walnut grips; the Navy's had black rubber handles. Made 1892 to about 1907.

Colt Model 1902 Military Auto

Colt Model 1902 Military Automatic Pistol . . **$800**
Caliber: 38. Eight-shot magazine. Barrel: 6 inches.
Overall length: 9 inches. Weight: 37 ounces. Fixed
sights, knife-blade and V-notch. Blued finish. Checkered hard rubber stocks. Round-back hammer and
later spur-type hammer. No safety. Used by the U.S.
Navy until the larger caliber 45 Model 1911 superseded
it. Made from 1902 to 1929.

Colt Model 1902 Philippine
Revolver

Colt Model 1902 Philippine Revolver **$900**
Enhanced version of the Double Action Army with extremely large trigger guard and long trigger to allow for
use with gloves. This arm was originally planned for
U.S. troops in Alaska, but was sent instead to the Phil-
ippines where 45-caliber firepower was needed. Caliber: 45 centerfire. Six-shot fluted cylinder. Barrel: 6
inches, round. Overall length: 11 inches. Blued iron
frame. Iron backstrap. Bird's-head grips. Made 1902.

U.S. MILITARY PISTOLS
Various Manufacturers

Henry Deringer Flintlock Pistol

Henry Deringer Flintlock Pistol **$3500**
Single shot. Caliber: 52. Barrel: 10 inches, round. Overall length: 16½ inches. Weight: 2 lbs. 10 oz. Walnut
stock with brass trigger guard, butt cap and thimbles.
Made circa 1807 by Henry Deringer Sr.

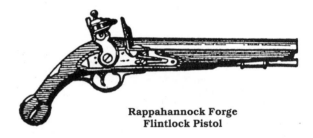

Rappahannock Forge
Flintlock Pistol

Rappahannock Forge Flintlock Pistol **$2550**
Single shot. Calibers: 66 to 69. Barrel: 9 inches, average; smoothbore. Overall length: 15 inches, average.
Brass mountings. Patterned after the British Light
Dragoon of the period. Made circa 1775 at Rappahannock Forge, Virginia. Although contracted by the State
of Virginia during the Revolutionary War, these pistols
(only a few authentic ones survive) are considered by
experts as the earliest "true" American military arms.

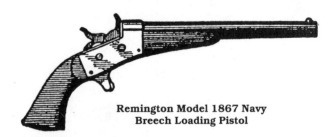

Remington Model 1867 Navy
Breech Loading Pistol

**Remington Model 1867 Navy Breech Loading
Pistol**. **$825**
Single-shot rolling block pistol. Caliber: 50 centerfire.
Barrel: 7, 8½ inches. Similar to 1865 Navy Rolling
Block, but with trigger guard. Walnut grips and forend.
Made late 1860s to early 1870s.

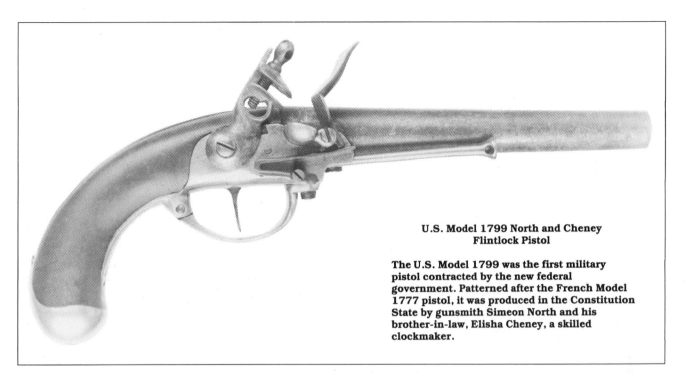

**U.S. Model 1799 North and Cheney
Flintlock Pistol**

The U.S. Model 1799 was the first military
pistol contracted by the new federal
government. Patterned after the French Model
1777 pistol, it was produced in the Constitution
State by gunsmith Simeon North and his
brother-in-law, Elisha Cheney, a skilled
clockmaker.

Remington Model 1871 Army
Breech Loading Pistol

U.S. Model 1805 Harpers Ferry
Flintlock Pistol

**Remington Model 1871 Army Breech Loading
Pistol** **$595**
Single shot. Caliber: 50 centerfire. Barrel: 8 inches.
Walnut grips and forend. Has a slight peak above the
grip at rear of the frame. Made 1870s through 1880s.

**U.S. Model 1799 North and Cheney Flintlock
Pistol** **$25,000**
Single shot. Caliber: 69. Barrel: 8 1/2 inches; iron,
smoothbore. Overall length: 14 1/2 inches. Weight: 3 lbs.
4 oz. Brass frame, trigger guard and butt cap. Steel ramrod. One-piece walnut stock. Patterned after the
French Model 1777 pistol used during the Revolutionary War. First U.S. Government pistol produced under
contract. Total of 2,000 manufactured between 1799
and 1802 by Simeon North in Berlin, Conn. *See* photo,
above.

**U.S. Model 1805 Harpers Ferry Flintlock
Pistol** **$2250**
Single shot. Caliber: 54. Barrel: 10 1/2 inches; round, ri-
fled. Overall length: 16 inches. Weight: 2 lbs. 9 oz. Walnut half-stock with brass mountings. Made 1806 to
1808 at Harpers Ferry Armory, W. Virginia. Earliest military pistol manufactured by a government armory.

U.S. Model 1808 Navy Flintlock Pistol **$4500**
Caliber: 64. Barrel: 10 1/8 inches; round, iron, smoothbore. Overall length: 16 1/4 inches. Full walnut stock fitted with belt hook. 3,000 made between 1808 and 1810
by Simeon North. Used during the War of 1812. *See*
photo next page.

U.S. Model 1811 Flintlock Pistol **$750**
Caliber: 69. Barrel: 8 5/8 inches; round, smoothbore.
Overall length: 15 inches. Brass mountings, including
butt cap, trigger guard, sideplate. Manufactured by
Simeon North about 1811 to 1813. Value shown is for
percussion conversion; original flintlock should bring
twice as much or better.

19th-CENTURY U.S. MILITARY FLINTLOCKS MANUFACTURED BY SIMEON NORTH

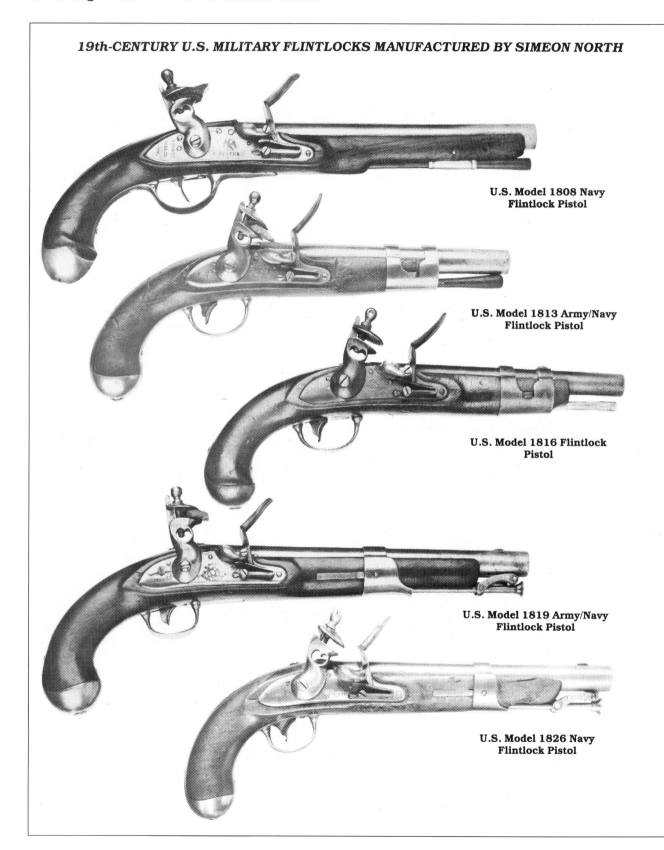

U.S. Model 1808 Navy
Flintlock Pistol

U.S. Model 1813 Army/Navy
Flintlock Pistol

U.S. Model 1816 Flintlock
Pistol

U.S. Model 1819 Army/Navy
Flintlock Pistol

U.S. Model 1826 Navy
Flintlock Pistol

U.S. Model 1811 Transition Flintlock Pistol **$800**
Same general specifications as U.S. Model 1811, except for iron double-strap barrel bands that secured the barrel to the stock. Value shown is for percussion conversion models.

U.S. Model 1813 Army/Navy Flintlock Pistol **$2500**
Caliber: 69. Barrel: 9¹/₁₆ inches; round, iron, smoothbore; fitted with "Wickham" double-barrel band. Overall length: 15¹/₄ inches. Made 1813 to 1815 by Simeon North in Middletown, Conn., under the first government arms contract specifying interchageable parts. *See* photo, opposite.

U.S. Model 1816 Flintlock Pistol **$975**
Calibers: 54 and 69. Single shot. Barrel: 9¹/₁₆ inches; iron, round, smoothbore. Overall length: 15¹/₄ inches. Made by Simeon North 1817 to 1820. *See* photo, opposite.

U.S. Model 1817 or 1818
Springfield Flintlock Pistol

U.S. Model 1817 or 1818 Springfield Flintolck Pistol **$2700**
Single shot. Caliber: 69. Barrel: about 11 inches; round, smoothbore. Overall length: 17¹/₂ inches. Iron mountings. Double-strap barrel bands. Manufactured at Springfield Armory, Mass., some in 1807–1808 (hence the additional designation of Model 1808), but most made in and stamped 1818.

U.S. Model 1819 Army/Navy Flintlock Pistol **$1050**
Caliber: 54. Single Shot. Barrels: 10 inches (Army); 8¹/₂ inches (Navy); round, iron, browned, smoothbore. Weight: 2 lbs. 10 oz. Sliding safety lock. Manufactured by Simeon North 1819 to 1823. *See* photo, opposite.

U.S. Model 1826 Navy Flintlock Pistol **$975**
Caliber: 54. Barrel: 8⁵/₈ inches; round, iron, smoothbore. Overall length: 13¹/₄ inches. Made by Simeon North from 1826 to 1829. Value shown is for percussion conversion specimens; original flintlock commands more. *See* photo, opposite.

U.S. Model 1826 Navy Flintlock Pistol (Evans) **$875**
Same general specifications as the North-manufactured model, above, except for markings. Made by W.L. Evans of Valley Forge, Penn., about 1830.

U.S. Model 1836 Flintlock
Pistol

U.S. Model 1836 Flintlock Pistol **$850**
Single shot. Caliber: 54. Barrel: 8¹/₂ inches; round, smoothbore. Overall length: 14¹/₄ inches. Weight: 2 lbs. 10 oz. Made from 1836 to 1844 by A. Waters and A. H. Waters & Co., Millbury, Mass., and Robert Johnson, Middlebury, Conn. This is the last military flintlock commissioned by the government.

U.S. Model 1842 Percussion
Pistol

U.S. Model 1842 Percussion Pistol **$625**
Single shot. Caliber: 54. Barrel: 8¹/₂ inches; round, smoothbore. Overall length: 14 inches. Weight: 2 lbs. 12 oz. Brass mountings. Blued trigger. Made from about 1845 to 1855 by Henry Aston and Ira Johnson of Middletown, Conn. Those made by the Palmetto Armory of Columbia, S.C., were for use by the South Carolina militia and are considered Confederate arms.

U.S. Model 1843 Navy Pistol

U.S. Model 1843 Navy Pistol **$925**
Single shot. Caliber: 54. Barrel: 6 inches; round, smoothbore, browned. Overall length: 11½ inches. Brass mountings. Casehardened box lock. Made by N.P. Ames, Springfield, Mass., and by Henry Deringer Jr., Philadelphia, between 1842 and 1847.

U.S. Model 1855 Springfield Pistol Carbine. **$2150**
Single shot. Caliber: 58. Barrel: 12 inches; round, rifled. Overall length: 17¾ inches (pistol); 28¼ inches (with detachable stock). Weight: 3 lbs. 13 oz. (pistol); about 5½ pounds (with stock). Walnut stock. Made by Springfield Armory, Springfield, Mass., about 1855 to 1857.

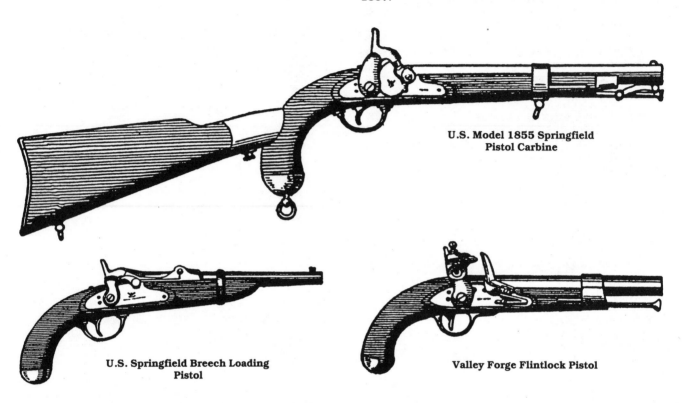

U.S. Model 1855 Springfield
Pistol Carbine

U.S. Springfield Breech Loading
Pistol

Valley Forge Flintlock Pistol

U.S. Springfield Breech Loading Pistol. **$1200**
Single shot. Caliber: 50. Overall length: 18½ inches. Weight: 5 pounds. Has regulation musket lock of 1868. Perhaps because of the difficulty of holding this gun in one hand, none were actually issued.

Valley Forge Flintlock Pistol. **$1900**
Single shot. Caliber: 69. Brass mounted. Patterned after the French Model 1805. Made circa 1809. Very rare.

U.S. MILITARY REVOLVERS
Various Manufacturers

The following revolvers were employed by the U.S. military services during the 19th century. While other revolvers can be sited as U.S. Government weapons, these are known to have been officially contracted, most often bear government markings and can be substantiated in ordnance records. (*See* also U.S. Military Handguns of Colt Manufacture and individual listings.)

Adams Army Revolver

Allen and Wheelock Army Revolver

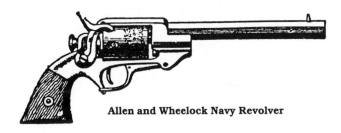

Allen and Wheelock Navy Revolver

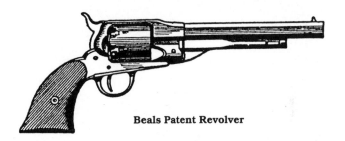

Beals Patent Revolver

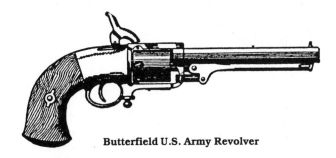

Butterfield U.S. Army Revolver

Adams Army Revolver **$2100**
Caliber: 44. Five-shot. Solid frame. Sliding safety. Patented in England in 1854 by Robert Adams (*see* separate listing). A small quantity were purchased by government agents for use during the Civil War. Probably manufactured by London Armoury Company. Very few Adams revolvers were made in 44 caliber.

Allen and Wheelock Army Revolver **$990**
Caliber: 44. Six-shot cylinder. Barrel: 7¹/₂ inches, part octagonal. Overall length: 13¹/₄ inches. Weight: 2 pounds. Brass front sight, V-notch in center hammer serves as rear sight. Patent date 1857. About 500 purchased during the Civil War.

Allen and Wheelock Navy Revolver **$1050**
Caliber: 36. Barrel: 8 inches, octagonal. Overall length: 13¹/₂ inches. Weight: 2 pounds. Cylinder engraved with animal scene. German silver blade front sight; V-notch rear sight grooved in frame. Casehardened side hammer and trigger guard. Patented in 1857.

Beals Patent Revolver. **$1100**
Single-action Army revolver. Caliber: 44. Six-shot cylinder. Barrel: 8 inches, octagonal. Overall length: 13³/₄ inches. Weight: 2 lbs. 14 oz. Brass front sight; rear sight grooved in frame. Patented in 1858 by Fordyce Beals, inventor with the E. Remington & Sons Co., which manufactured the handgun. Together with the 36-caliber Navy version, about 2,800 were purchased by the U.S government for use during the Civil War.

Butterfield U.S. Army. **$2470**
Caliber: about 36. Five-shot. Barrel: 7 inches. Overall length: about 14 inches. Bronze frame. Stamped "Butterfield Patent Dec. 11, 1855." A limited number were produced by Jesse Butterfield of Philadelphia in the early part of the Civil War. Rare, since the Government canceled the contract.

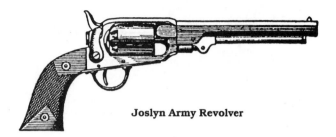

Joslyn Army Revolver

Joslyn Army Revolver **$1600**
Caliber: 44. Five-shot round cylinder. Barrel: 8 inches; octagonal, rifled. Weight: 3 pounds. Side hammer. Patented in 1858 by Benjamin Joslyn of the Joslyn Firearms Co., Stonington, Conn. The U.S. Government purchased over 1,000 during the Civil War.

Lefaucheux Army Pinfire Revolver

Lefaucheux Army Pinfire Revolver **$425**
Caliber: about 44 (12mm). Single action. The metallic shell for the cartridge had a small pin attached at a right angle to the length and the shell could only be inserted one way. Based on the 1854 patent owned by French gunmaker Eugène Lefaucheux. Made in France and Belgium and used for a brief time in the early Civil War, but eventually discarded for American weapons; more than 12,000 were purchased, including a smaller caliber Navy revolver of the same design.

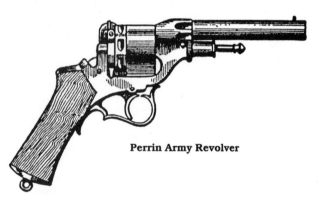

Perrin Army Revolver

Perrin Army Revolver **$695**
Caliber: about 44 (12mm). Double action. Six-shot cylinder. Made in France, about 2,000 were purchased for use during the Civil War.

Pettingill Army Revolver

Pettingill Army Revolver **$1050**
Caliber: 44. Six-shot cylinder. Double action. Hammerless. Barrel: 7¹/₂ inches. Overall length: 14 inches. Weight: about 3 pounds. Brass cone front sight, rear sight grooved in frame. Blued barrel and either blued or browned frame. Patented in 1856. About 2,000 were purchased during the Civil War.

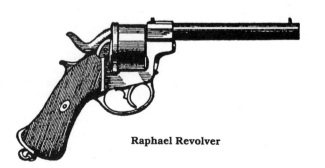

Raphael Revolver

Raphael Revolver **$700**
Caliber: about 41 centerfire. Six-shot cylinder. Double action. Barrel: 5¹/₂ inches. Made in France, about 2,000 were purchased during the Civil War.

Remington Army Revolver **$725**
Caliber: 44 paper cartridge. Six-shot cylinder. Barrel: 8 inches. Overall length: 13³/₄ inches. Weight: about 2³/₄ pounds. Patent dated 1858. Between 1861 and 1865 approximately 125,300 were purchased by the Army; second only to Colt in Civil War production.

Remington Army Revolver

Remington Navy Revolver **$725**
Same general specifications as Remington Army Revolver, except in 36 caliber paper cartridge with 7¹/₂-inch barrel. About 5,000 were purchased by the Navy for use in the Civil War.

Rogers and Spencer Revolver **$925**
Caliber: 44. Six-shot cylinder. Barrel: 7 inches. About 5,000 were purchased for the Army in the latter part of the Civil War. Apparently few saw heavy action, since these arms are frequently found in quite good condition. Based on the Freeman Revolver design (*see* separate listing).

Rogers and Spencer Revolver

Savage Navy Revolver **$800**
Caliber: 36. Overall length: 14¹/₄ inches. This arm has two triggers, the rear (ring) trigger to revolve the cylinder and cock the hammer, and the front one to fire. Patented in 1856 and made at the Savage Armory in Middletown, Conn. More than 14,000 were purchased for use by the Navy during the Civil War.

Savage Navy Revolver

Schofield/Smith and Wesson Revolver **$545**
Caliber: 45. Barrel: 7 inches. Weight: 2¹/₂ pounds. Modification of S&W No. 3 by Col. G.W. Schofield who, in 1871, patented an improved latch pivoted on the frame, rather than the barrel strap. Adopted by the military about 1873.

Schofield/Smith and Wesson Revolver

Smith and Wesson Revolver **$525**
Caliber: 38. Barrel: 6¹/₂ inches. Overall length: 11¹/₂ inches. Used by both the Army and the Navy. Last patent date is 1898.

**Smith & Wesson
38 Caliber Revolver**

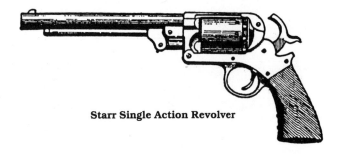

Starr Single Action Revolver

Starr Revolvers. **$925**
Caliber: 44. Six-shot cylinder. Barrel: 8 inches. Overall
length: 14 inches. Weight: 3 pounds. Also made in double action with 6-inch barrel in 36 and 44 calibers. This
is a major Civil War arm, since almost 48,000 were
bought between 1861 and 1865.

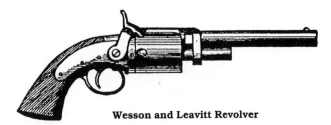

Wesson and Leavitt Revolver

Wesson and Leavitt Revolver **$2175**
Calibers: 31 and 40. Six-shot cylinder. Barrel: $6^3/_4$
inches, round. Overall length: $13^3/_4$ inches. Often referred to as a Dragoon, this was produced by the Massachusetts Arms Co. in the early 1850s. Patented in
1837 by Leavitt and in 1849 by Edwin Wesson.

Whitney Navy Revolver

Whitney Navy Revolver **$990**
Caliber: 36. Six-shot cylinder. Barrel: $7^1/_2$ inches; octagonal, rifled. Weight: 2 lbs. 9 oz. Brass front sight, V-
notch rear sight. Solid iron frame. Made under the ae-
gis of Eli Whitney Jr. in Connecticut. About 11,200
were purchased by the U. S. Government during the
Civil War. This was copied at Confederate armories and
made with a brass frame.

CHAPTER TWO
RIFLES

Until about 125 years ago, most long arms were muzzleloaders. They were loaded from the muzzle or mouth of the barrel with black powder and a lead projectile that was either a round ball or a conical bullet. The earliest long arms had smooth bores and, by name, were known as arquebuses and blunderbusses, muskets and fowling pieces.

Although loading from the breech or back of the barrel had been tried prior to this time, all such arms leaked powder gas at the breech, weakening the charge, and often burned the hand or face of the shooter. It was not until about 1860 that breechloaders first became practical because of fixed ammunition, that is, a cartridge with a metallic cartridge case that acted as a gas shield.

The earliest muzzleloaders were fired by a slow match applied to a "touch hole" that was located at the breech. Later the charge was set off by a shower of sparks from steel and flint, first by a wheellock wound up by a special key, and then by a more practical device called a flint lock. Thus, a gun was composed of "lock, stock, and barrel," an expression for completeness that is still frequently used today. Flintlock firearms were "primed" by fine black powder carried in a "pan" into which the sparks from the contact of flint and steel were showered. But sometimes the priming powder jarred away from the touch hole and went off with a flash that failed to set off the powder charge in the barrel. This was called a "flash in the pan."

Smoothbore muskets were far from accurate. "Don't fire until you see the whites of their eyes," was shouted at Bunker Hill for good reason. Hits beyond fifty yards became more and more unlikely as the range increased from shooter to target. Before the advent of Kentucky rifles, European gunmakers had discovered that grooves in a barrel enabled tighter fitting bullets to be rammed down the barrel easily. If the grooves were spiraled so the bullet spun, accuracy was immensely improved. This process of grooving the barrels was called "rifling," from which the word "rifle" developed.

About 1725, German gunsmiths in Pennsylvania were producing the famous "Kentucky" pattern flintlock rifles. These were light, very accurate, and being of smaller bore, were economical of lead and powder, which were scarce items along the frontier.

The next great improvement in firearms was the invention of the percussion cap in the early 1800s. The Civil War was fought mainly with percussion-cap, muzzleloading rifles using conical lead "Minie" balls. Today's primer is simply a refinement of the "cap" that fit over a "nipple" that extended into the breech. The hollow-faced hammer, on hitting the cap, exploded the fulminate compound in the cap, which shot a stream of flame through the hollow nipple into the powder charge. Bullets began to assume a conical shape, but most were of large caliber and were flatter and shorter compared to the slimmer, more elongated bullets of modern design.

Practical breechloaders began to appear at the end of the Civil War. Some were used in the Civil War, primarily by Union troops. Most notable among them were the Spencer and Henry carbines, both practical repeating rifles using the then recently invented metallic cartridge. These rifles used rimfire, coppercased cartridges of relatively low power by modern standards.

With sturdier, stronger brass cases and centerfire primers, heavier loads and the rifles to use them went hand in hand. Knockdown power was obtained by large caliber, heavy bullets propelled to the limit of black powder velocities, black powder being the only type of powder known at the time. Still, velocities were very low by present-day standards and the path of the bullet's flight was highly curved—limiting its range, for most shooters, to about 150 yards. If you've heard stories of the old buffalo hunters downing their game at ranges of 500 or even 1000 yards, remember, these were professional hunters who had fired hundreds of rounds through their Sharps' to be able to shoot this well.

The advent of smokeless powder brought far-reaching changes. Among these was a great increase in velocity. By reducing bullet diameter and weight, striking energy was amplified by increased velocities that were nearly double those obtained with black powder. This, in turn, meant a much flatter shooting rifle, as the force of gravity had less time to blow the bullet off its course. Also, the target was not obscured by smoke.

On the following pages you will see all types of muskets, musketoons, carbines and rifles that span the early days until about 1900. For your ease in locating specific firearms, the section is divided into groupings:

ARABIAN ARMS
Various Manufacturers

North African Arab Snaphaunce **$200**
Many different makers; some were made especially for the tourist trade and were not of high quality. Most were very decorative, but few were of high quality.

ARGENTINA MILITARY
Manufactured in Germany

Argentina Model 1891 Mauser Military Rifle **$115**
Bolt action. Caliber: 7.65 Belgian Mauser. Five-shot clip loaded box magazine. Barrel: 29 inches. Weight: about 8¾ pounds. Sights: inverted "V" front; open rear sight. Military-type full stock. Adopted in 1891 by Argentina and several other South American countries.

Argentina Model 1891 Mauser Carbine **$125**
Same general specifications as Model 1891 Rifle, except has 17½-inch barrel and stocked to muzzle.

R. ASHMORE & SON
Lancaster County, Pennsylvania

R. Ashmore Kentucky Caplock Rifle **$1200**
Caliber: 44. Barrel: various lengths. Striped maple stock, brass fittings with large patch box. Made circa early 1800s.

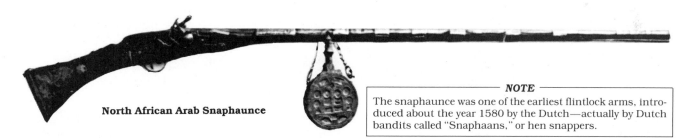

North African Arab Snaphaunce

> ── *NOTE* ──
> The snaphaunce was one of the earliest flintlock arms, introduced about the year 1580 by the Dutch—actually by Dutch bandits called "Snaphaans," or hen snappers.

**R. Ashmore 44 Caliber
Kentucky Caplock Rifle**

**Australian Cadet Martini B.S.A.
Second Pattern**

AUSTRALIAN MILITARY
Various Manufacturers

**Australian Cadet Martini B.S.A. 2nd
Pattern**. **$225**
Caliber: 310 Cadet. Barrel: 29 inches, round. Weight: 9
pounds. Receiver stamped "Commonwealth of Australia over VIC." Also same stamp on butt plate.

AUSTRIAN MILITARY
Steyr, Austria

Austrian Model 90 Mannlicher Carbine. **$125**
Same general specifications as Model 1895 Rifle, except has 19¹/₂-inch barrel. Weight: about 7 pounds.

Austrian Model 1867 M. Werndl Rifle **$350**
Caliber: 11.2mm. Regimentally marked on butt tang.
Made 1867.

**Austrian Model 1868 M. Werndl Cavalry
Carbine**. **$300**
Caliber: 11.2mm. Barrel: 22 inches, round. Regimentally marked on butt. Made 1868.

Austrian Model 1886 Military Rifle **$100**
Caliber: 8x50R. Military-type stock. Adjustable rear
sight, fixed blade front sight.

**Austrian Model 1895 Steyr-Mannlicher
Carbine**. **$130**
Same general specifications as Model 1895 Rifle, except has 19¹/₂-inch barrel. Weight: about 7 pounds.
Made by Steyr Armory, Steyr, Austria.

**Austrian Model 1895 Steyr-Mannlicher
Rifle**. **$120**
Also known as Model 95. Straight-pull bolt action. Caliber: 8x50R Mannlicher (.315 bore). Five-shot projecting box magazine. Barrel: about 31 inches, round; 4
groove, 1 turn in 9.84 inches. Overall length: 48 inches.
Weight: 8¹/₂ pounds with bayonet. Adjustable rear
sight, blade front sight. Military full stock. Introduced
in 1895. Manufactured by Steyr Armory.

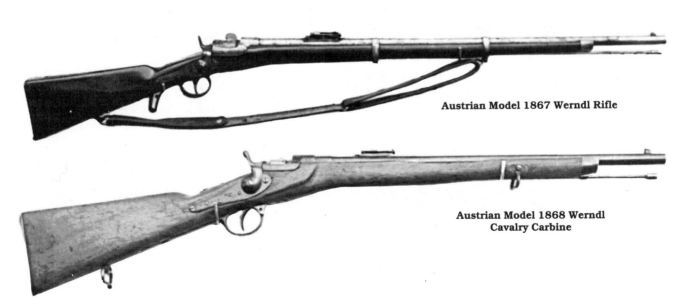

Austrian Model 1867 Werndl Rifle

**Austrian Model 1868 Werndl
Cavalry Carbine**

Balkan Miquelet

BALKAN MILITARY
Various Manufacturers

Balkan Miquelet.......................... **$500**
Iron stock with wood inlay at butt. Brass barrel bands.
Usually engraved.

BALLARD RIFLES
Massachusetts and Connecticut

The Ballard Rifle was patented by C. H. Ballard in
1861 and was used for military, sporting and target
purposes for nearly thirty years. It was originally manufactured by Ball & Williams of Worcester, Mass., but
by 1866, the firm was reorganized and was succeeded
by the Merrimack Arms Mfg. Co. of Newburyport, Mass.
(*see* separate listing). Merrimack manufactured various Ballard rifles and shotguns until they, too, went
through a reorganization; in 1869 they were succeeded
by the Brown Manufacturing Co. also of Newburyport.
On July 23, 1873, Brown Manufacturing was sold under foreclosure proceedings to a Mr. Daly of Schover-
ling & Daly. This firm then made arrangements with
John M. Marlin of Marlin Firearms in Connecticut to
manufacture the Ballard rifles beginning in 1875. Marlin continued to produce the Ballard rifle until 1888,
when the newer repeating rifles made the Ballard un-
practical for hunting purposes.
Although Ballard rifles were not manufactured after
1888, they were still used by many target shooters well
into the twentieth century and had the reputation of
being super-accurate target guns. These same fine
guns are highly coveted today by collectors all over the
world.

Ballard Model of 1861 Sporting Rifle **$795**
Single-shot falling block. Calibers: 32, 38 Long and 44
Long RF. Barrel: 24 inches. Weight: 7 pounds. Intro-
duced in 1861.

Ballard Model of 1862 Military Carbine **$875**
Single-shot falling block. Caliber: 54 RF (called No. 56
Ballard). Barrel: 22 inches, with markings "Merwin &
Bray, Agts., N.Y.," and also "Ballard's Patent November
5, 1861." Overall length: 38 inches. Made from 1862 to
1863.

Ballard Model of 1862 Military Rifle **$1000**
Same general specifications as Model of 1862 Carbine,
except has a 30-inch barrel.

Ballard Model of 1863 "Kentucky" Rifle.... **$1075**
Same general specifications as the Model of 1863 Military Carbine, except chambered for 46 RF, with 30-
inch barrel, 45$^{1}/_{4}$ inches overall length and weight of 8
pounds. Made from about 1863 to 1865.

Ballard Model of 1863 Military Carbine **$795**
Single-shot, falling block action. Caliber: 44 Long RF.
Barrel: 22 inches with markings, "Ball & Williams,
Worcester, Mass., Ballard's Patent November 5, 1861,
Merwin & Bray, Agts., N.Y." Overall length: 37$^{1}/_{4}$
inches. Weight: 6 lbs. 6 oz. Some of these rifles were
made with solid breech blocks. Made from 1863 to
about 1864.

Ballard Model 1864 Sporting Rifle.......... **$600**
Single-shot, Falling block action. Calibers: 32 Long, 38
Long, 44 Long RF. Dual ignition system, combination
rimfire and percussion. Swivel striker on hammer. Patented Jan. 5, 1864.

Ballard Model 1864 Sporting Rifle
44 Caliber

Ballard Model 1866 Carbine **$840**
Falling block, lever-operated, single-shot. Calibers: 44
Long RF and later for 56/52 Spencer. Barrel: 22 inches,
marked "Merrimack Arms & Mfg. Co., Newburyport,
Mass." and also "Ballard Patent Nov. 5 1861." Hammer
marked, "Patented Jan. 5, 1864." Overall length: 37½
inches. Weight: 6½ pounds. Made from 1866 to 1873.

Ballard Model 1866 Sporting Rifle. **$625**
Same general specifications as Model 1866 Carbine,
except provided with 24- and 28-inch barrels. Calibers:
22 Long RF, 32 Long, 44 Long, 46 Long and 50 RF. Made
from 1866 to 1873.

Ballard Model 1872 Military Rifle **$945**
Falling block, lever-operated. Single shot. Caliber: 56/
52 Spencer. Barrel: 30 inches. Overall length: 35
inches. Weight: about 9 pounds. Made from 1872 to
1873.

Ballard Hunter's Rifle. **$795**
Falling block, lever-operated. Single shot. Caliber: 44
Long rimfire or centerfire. Barrel: round. Weight: about
8 pounds. Features reversible firing pin for use with
either rimfire or centerfire ammunition. Made from
1875 to 1876.

Ballard Hunter's Rifle No. 1 . . . . **$825**
Falling block, lever-operated. Single shot. Caliber: 44
Long rimfire or centerfire. Barrel: 26, 28 or 30 inches.
Automatic extractor. Made from 1876 to 1880.

Ballard Hunter's Rifle No. 1½ **$840**
Falling block, lever-operated. Single shot. Caliber: 45-
70 or 40-65-2⅜". Barrel: 28, 30 or 32 inches. Weight:
about 10 pounds. Walnut stock with rifle butt. Made
from 1879 to 1883.

Ballard Mid-Range Target Model. **$1095**
Falling block, lever-operated. Single shot. Caliber: 44
Long RF. Barrel: 28 inches; extra-heavy, octagonal.
Overall length: 43½ inches. Weight: about 10 pounds.
Elevating peep sights. Made from 1869 to 1873.

Ballard Sporting Model No. 2. . . . . **$625**
Calibers: 32 and 38 RF or centerfire; 44 centerfire. Barrel: 26, 28 or 30 inches; octagonal. Reversible firing pin
for rimfire or centerfire cartridge use. Casehardened
frame. Made by J.M. Marlin and the Marlin Firearms
Company about 1876 to 1881.

BELGIAN MILITARY
Herstal, Belgium

Belgian Model 1889 Mauser Military Rifle. . . **$125**
Caliber: 7.65 Belgian Mauser. Five-shot projecting box
magazine. Barrel: 31 inches. Weight: 8½ pounds.
Straight-grip military stock. Made by Fabrique National
D'Armes de Guerre from 1889 to 1935.

Belgian Model 1889 Mauser Carbine. **$150**
Same general specifications as Model 1889 Rifle, except has 20¾-inch barrel. Weight: about 8 pounds.
Made by Fabrique National D'Armes de Guerre from
1889 to 1916.

BLAKE RIFLE COMPANY
Address Unknown

According to our reference, every catalog issued by
Blake was filled with elaborate promises and heavily
over-advertised with purely fictitious statements that
may have contributed more or less to the failure of the
firm. It is doubtful that all of the models listed in the
Blake catalog were actually manufactured. Be that as it
may, the Blake rifles were very strong and of excellent
design and balance. The superior workmanship on all
Blake rifles make them very attractive collectors'
items.

Blake Grade A Sporting Rifle **$25,000**
Calibers: 30-40 Army, 30-06, 400 Blake, and others.
Barrels: 18 to 30 inches long; round, octagonal, half-
octagonal; or round at breech, a change to octagonal
and then back to round. Weight: 6 pounds and up. Finest figured imported walnut stock with very high-grade
checkering. Metal engraved with excellent workmanship and finish. The magazine was of aluminum bronze
or solid silver, embossed and engraved if desired. This
was practically a custom rifle made to order. Magazine
hinged on left and opened on right to accept spool-type
packet that holds up to seven cartridges. Made from
1895 to 1903.

Ballard Sporting Rifle No. 2

Blake Grade B Hunting Rifle. **$20,000**
Calibers: 30-40 Army, 30-06, 400 Blake and others.
Barrels: 18 to 30 inches long; round, octagonal, half-
octagonal; or round at breech, a change to octagonal,
then back to round. Weight: 7½ pounds and up. Magazine made of aluminum bronze, either blackened or
plated. Fine figured imported walnut stock with
straight or pistol-grip design. High-grade checkering
on stock and engraving on metal parts, slightly less
elaborate than the A grade. Made from 1895 to 1903.

Blake Grade C Hunting Rifle. **$15,000**
Calibers: 30-40 Army, 30-06, 400 Blake, and others.
Barrels: 18 to 30 inches long; round, octagonal, half-
octagonal; or round at breech, a change to octagonal
then back to round. Weight: 7½ pounds and up. Magazine made of aluminum bronze, either blackened or
plated. American walnut stock with straight or pistol-
grip design. Made from 1895 to 1903.

Blake Grade D Hunting Rifle **$12,000**
Calibers: 30-40 Army, 30-06, 400 Blake, and others.
Barrels: 18 to 30 inches long; round or octagonal.
Weight: 7½ pounds and up. Magazine made of aluminum bronze, either blackened or plated. American walnut stock with straight or pistol-grip design. Made from
1895 to 1903.

BRITISH MILITARY
Various Manufacturers

The British long arms featured below are as varied
and interesting as their makers. They have played a
major role in the course of United States history because as Colonies of the British Crown, we purchased
many of them and fought with many of them in battle.
The Short Land Brown Bess Musket, for example, was
a particular favorite during the Revolutionary War.

British P. 1839 Rifle **$700**
Caliber: 76. Fitted with Lovell's bayonet catch. Made
circa 1840.

British P. 1841 Rifle **$700**
Caliber: 704. Barrels: Damascus pattern. Made circa
1845.

British P. 1844 Yeomanry Carbine. **$600**
Caliber: 66. Long side saddle ring bar with ring.

British P. 1853 Rifle **$400**
Caliber: 577. Dated 1861. Volunteer Pattern. Used by
both sides in the U.S. Civil War.

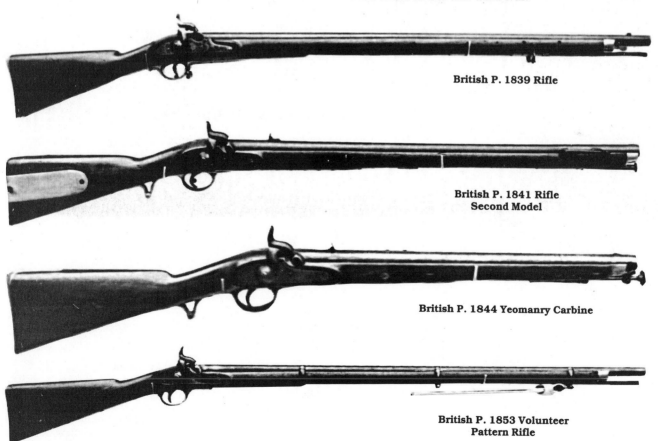

British P. 1839 Rifle

British P. 1841 Rifle
Second Model

British P. 1844 Yeomanry Carbine

British P. 1853 Volunteer
Pattern Rifle

British P. 1853 Rifle
Second Model

British P. 1856 Cavalry Carbine
East India Pattern

British P. 1853 Rifle, 2nd Model **$500**
Caliber: 577. Dated 1857. Rare.

British P. 1856 Cavalry Carbine **$650**
Caliber: 577. Made circa 1857.

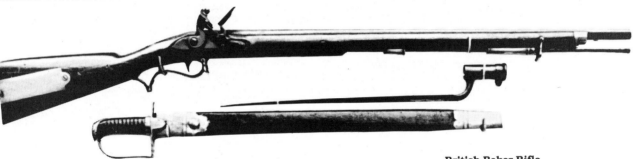

British Baker Rifle
with Socket Bayonet

British Baker Rifle, Socket Bayonet Model . . **$2400**
Caliber: 65. Originally made for sword bayonet. Made
1815 to 1823.

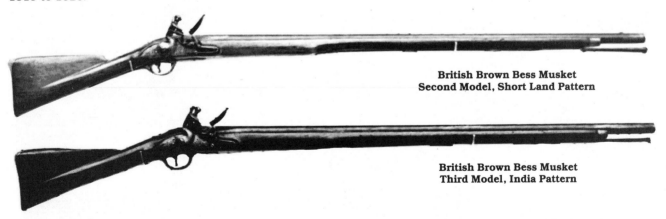

British Brown Bess Musket
Second Model, Short Land Pattern

British Brown Bess Musket
Third Model, India Pattern

**British Brown Bess Musket, Short Land
Pattern** **$1500**
Caliber: about 75. Barrel: 42 inches, round. Typical
Brown Bess pattern with brown stock. This model,
standardized in the 1760s with 42-inch barrel, was the
Second Model Brown Bess. The first was the Long Land
Musket, which had a 46-inch barrel. The Short Land
Pattern was a favorite during the Revolutionary War because it could be fired so rapidly. The Colonists could
usually do it about 4 times per minute, while the Hes-
sian troops were known to fire it about 6 times per minute. According to sources at Colonial Williamsburg,
they used a 71 caliber bullet in the 75 caliber barrel,
which facilitated loading.

**British Brown Bess Musket, India
Pattern** **$500**
Caliber: 75. Typical Brown Bess pattern, except con-
verted to percussion. The India Pattern was the third
Brown Bess model and was cheaply made in compari-
son to its predecessors. Barrel: 39 inches average.
Originally made 1800; converted around 1830.

British Eliott Carbine

British Eliott Carbine. **$1500**
Caliber: 65. Dublin Castle on lock plate. Made 1760 to 1798.

British Double Rifle **$900**
Caliber: 67 percussion. Seven-groove rifling, browned barrels. Walnut checkered stock. Iron furniture. Engraved.

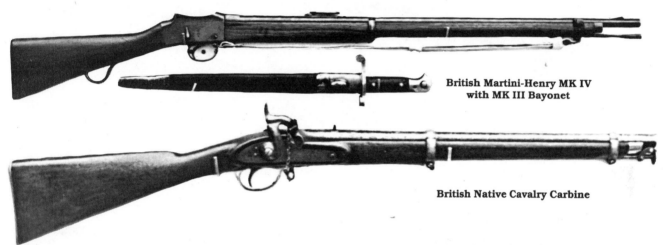

British Martini-Henry MK IV
with MK III Bayonet

British Native Cavalry Carbine

British Martini Enfield Conversion **$395**
Caliber: converted to 303 British. Made from 1874 to 1899. Conversion made in 1899.

British Martini-Henry MK IV **$275**
Caliber: 450-577. Made circa 1887.

British Native Cavalry Carbine **$525**
Caliber: 65. Barrel: smoothbore. Issued to Native Cavalry Regiments. The standard issue was 577 caliber, but the overbore ensured that the weapons could not be used against the British with their own ammunition as they would not be accurate. This proved quite useful during the Indian Mutiny. Made circa 1858.

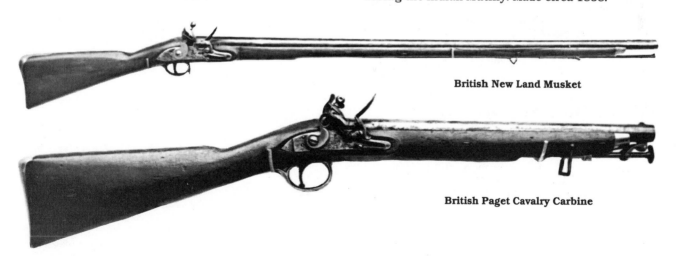

British New Land Musket

British Paget Cavalry Carbine

British New Land Musket **$900**
Caliber: 75. Regimentally marked on butt tang. Similar specifications as British Brown Bess. Made circa 1802.

British Paget Cavalry Carbine **$1000**
Caliber: 67. Made circa 1808.

British Snider MK II

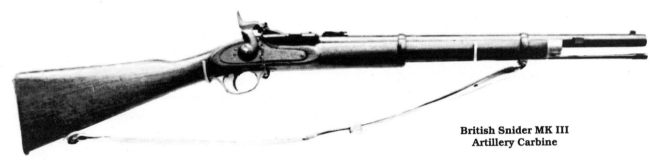

British Snider MK III
Artillery Carbine

British Snider MK II..................... **$1000**
Caliber: 577. Made circa 1861.

British Snider MK III Artillery Carbine...... **$500**
Caliber: 577. Made circa 1860.

British Snider MK III
Percussion Rifle

British Snider-type Breechloading
Target Rifle

British Snider MK III Percussion Rifle **$200**
Caliber: 577. Made circa 1871.

British Snider Target Rifle................. **$450**
Caliber: 45. Barrel: Damascus steel. Adjustable rear
sight on barrel tang; hooded front sight. Engraved action. High-grade walnut with checkered grips and forend.

--- *NOTE* ---
The Snider breech action was the invention of Jacob Snider
of Baltimore, Md. After the British authorities saw the repeated success of breechloaders during the U.S. Civil War,
they adopted it as a means to convert their own muzzleloaders to breechloaders. Interestingly, the Snider action was not
popular in the inventor's native country.

BULLARD REPEATING ARMS CO.
Springfield, Massachusetts

The Bullard Repeating Arms Co. is best known for its
development in the late 1880s of a lever-action repeating rifle, patented by former S&W mechanic and inventor, James H. Bullard. Although the gun had the
general external appearance of the Winchester, the
Bullard mechanism is entirely different. Before starting his own company, Bullard was responsible for inventing a simplified extractor mechanism used on the
S&W No. 3 Single Action New Model Revolver.

The Bullard company also manufactured single-shot rifles in all calibers from the .22 short to the big .50-115 Bullard—a special cartridge believed to have been adapted to no other rifle.

Bullard rifles were made of the finest forged steel of the day, utilizing the best in workmanship. Because of its excellence, it is believed that pressure was brought to bear by other manufacturers and the firm was purchased by Winchester in 1889 after being in business for only two years. The following rifles were made during that brief two-year period.

Bullard 40-90 Lever Action Sporting Rifle.................................... $3000
Caliber: 40-90. Seven-shot magazine. Barrel: 28 inches; round, octagonal or half-octagonal. Weight: 10½ pounds. Full-stocked, straight grip with checkering.

Bullard Express Rifle..................... $3500
Caliber: 50-95-300. Barrel: 28 inches, round. Full or half-magazine.

Bullard Heavy Frame Sporting Rifle........ $1250
Calibers: 40-75-258, 40-60-260, 45-85-290 and 45-70. Eleven-shot full-length magazine. Barrel: 28 inches; round, octagonal or half-octagonal. Weight: about 9½ pounds.

Bullard Lever Action Sporting Rifle (Standard)............................. $1100
Calibers: 32-40-150 and 38-45-190. 11-shot full magazine. Barrel: 26 inches; round, octagonal or half-octagonal. Weight: 8½ pounds. Stand open and bead front sights were used, but a variety of extras were available on all models.

Bullard Military Lever Action Carbine...... $3300
Same general specifications as the Military Lever Action Rifle, except it has a 22-inch carbine barrel and weighs 8½ pounds.

Bullard Military Lever Action Rifle......... $3200
Same general specifications as the Lever Action Sporting models, except full stocked with bayonet lug and open sights.

Bullard Rim Fire Hunting Rifle $1250
Caliber: 22 rimfire. Barrel: 26 inches. Weight: about 7½ pounds.

Bullard Schuetzen Rifle................... $2100
Calibers: various. Barrel: 30 inches most common; half-octagonal, but could be furnished in any length or weight. Weight: 12 pounds average.

Bullard Single Shot Military Carbine...... $1850
Same general specifications as the Single Shot Military Musket, except it had either a 24- or 26-inch round barrel, and weighed from 7 lbs. 8 oz. to 8 pounds.

Bullard Single Shot Military Musket $1795
Caliber: 45-70 Govt. Barrel: 32 inches with triangular bayonet lug. Weight: 8 lbs. 8 oz.

Bullard Target Rifle $1100
Calibers: various. Barrel: lengths of up to 28 inches in round, octagonal or half-octagonal. Regular sights included a Vernier peep rear on the tang and a wind gauge front sight.

Bullard Target and Hunting Rifle $1050
Calibers: various. Barrel: lengths of up to 28 inches in round, octagonal or half-octagonal style. Weight: 8 to 10 pounds.

CANADIAN RIFLES
Various Manufacturers

Lower Canada P. 1853 Artillery Carbine $800
Caliber: 577. Made circa 1856.

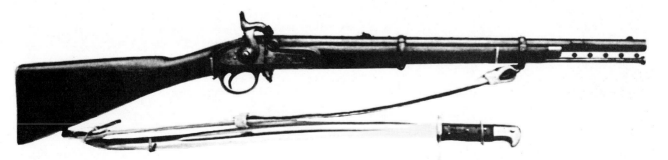

Lower Canada P. 1853 1st Model
Artillery Carbine

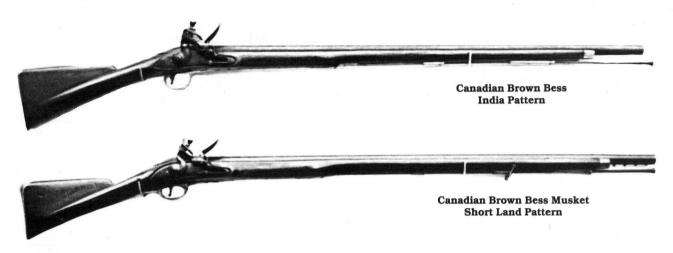

Canadian Brown Bess
India Pattern

Canadian Brown Bess Musket
Short Land Pattern

Canadian Brown Bess, India Pattern **$800**
Caliber: 75. Typical Brown Bess pattern.

**Canadian Brown Bess, Short Land
Pattern** **$1400**
Caliber: 78. Typical Brown Bess pattern. Made circa
1785.

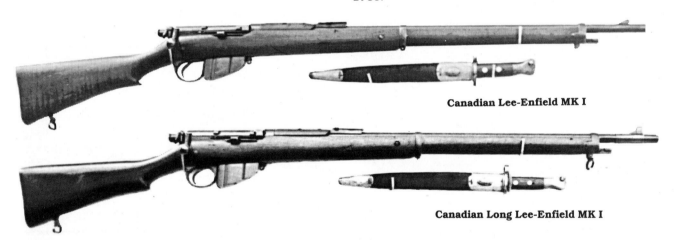

Canadian Lee-Enfield MK I

Canadian Long Lee-Enfield MK I

**Canadian Lee-Enfield MK 1, Bolt Action
Rifle.** **$375**
Caliber: 303 British. Barrel: 25¼ inches. Weight: 8½
pounds. Walnut military stock. Bayonet lug. Made
circa 1896.

**Canadian Long Lee-Enfield MK 1
Bolt Action Rifle.** **$375**
Same general specifications as Lee Enfield MK 1,
above, except has 31-inch barrel.

Canadian Martini-Henry MK I

Canadian Martini-Henry MK I Rifle **$425**
Caliber: 450-577. Same general specifications as the
standard Martini. Made circa 1873.

**Canadian Martini-Henry MK III
Presentation Rifle**

**Canadian Martini-Henry MK III
Presentation Rifle** **$400**
Caliber: 450-577. Same general specifications as the Martini Rifle, with Henry rifling system. Sterling silver plaque in butt engraved "ROYAL SCOTS of CANADA 5th GEORGE COOK, MONTREAL, 1885." With sling, bayonet and scabbard.

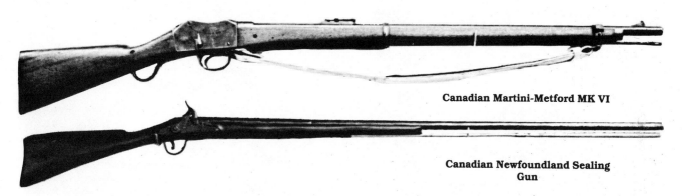

Canadian Martini-Metford MK VI

**Canadian Newfoundland Sealing
Gun**

Canadian Martini-Metford MK VI **$400**
Same general specifications as the Martini action. Caliber: 303. Action circa 1887, probably converted during 1890s to 303.

Canadian Newfoundland Sealing Gun **$200**
Barrel: 42 inches round. The gun pictured converted from flint to percussion.

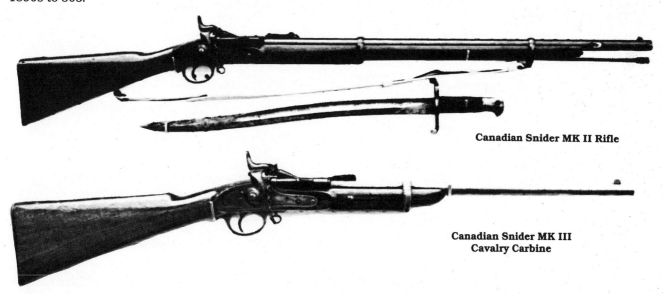

Canadian Snider MK II Rifle

**Canadian Snider MK III
Cavalry Carbine**

Canadian Snider MK II Rifle. **$450**
Caliber: 577. Walnut stock. Iron barrel bands. Made circa 1866.

Canadian Snider MK III Cavalry Carbine **$500**
Caliber: 577. Same specifications as Snider MK II Rifle, except has short carbine barrel. Made circa 1860.

A. H. CHAPIN
Earlville, New York

Chapin Percussion Rifle **$900**
Caliber: 45. Barrel: heavy octagonal, 1-inch across flats. Lock made by Warren & Steel of Albany, N.Y. American walnut stock. Iron trigger guard. Brass butt plate, ramrod thimbles, and nose cap. Made circa 1840.

CHINESE MILITARY
Various Manufacturers

Chinese Model 1888 Mauser **$100**
Bolt action. Caliber: 8mm. Four-shot magazine. Barrel: 29 inches. Weight: 8½ pounds. Military-type stock. Introduced in 1888.

COLOMBIAN MILITARY
Various Manufacturers

Colombian Model 1891 Mauser Military Rifle **$115**
Caliber: 7.65 Mauser. Five-shot box magazine. Barrel: 29 inches. Weight: about 8¾ pounds. Open rear sight, inverted "V" front sight. Military-type full stock.

COLT'S PATENT FIRE ARMS MFG. CO.
Hartford, Connecticut

The Colt's Patent Fire Arms Manufacturing Co. is known mainly for the invention and development of the first successful revolver, and therein lies Samuel Colt's personal claim to fame. However, the Colt firm also produced thousands of rifles, mostly of the revolving type, but lever-action and slide-action types as well.

It is not known exactly how many different variations of repeating rifles were turned out by the Colt factory, as researchers tend to disagree, but the following is an attempt at listing as many as could be found at this time.

For additional Colt information, *see* also the Colt sections under Handguns and Shotguns.

Colt Model 1850 Percussion Carbine **$4800**
Six-shot cylinder. Apparently a revision of the Paterson Model 1839 Carbine (*see* separate listing). Barrel marked "Address Sam'l Colt, New York City." Introduced in 1850.

Colt Model 1855 Percussion Revolving Rifle
Calibers: 36, 40, 44, 50, 56 percussion. Six-shot cylinder (56 cal. is five-shot). Barrels: 24, 27 or 30 inches. Overall length: 43 inches with 24-inch barrel. Weight: ranged from 8 lbs. 12 oz. to 10 lbs. 8 oz. Introduced in 1855.

36 Caliber	$3500
40 Caliber	3500
44 Caliber	3200
50 Caliber	2900
56 Caliber	3000

Colt Model 1855 Percussion Revolving Military Rifle
Calibers: 40, 44, 50, 56. Six-shot cylinder (56 cal. is five-shot). Barrel: 31⁵/₁₆ inches. Weight: 9 lbs. 6 oz. to 10 lbs. 4 oz. Included a full-stock barrel extending underneath the barrel itself. Introduced in 1855.

40 Caliber	$4500
44 Caliber	2800
50 Caliber	4500
56 Caliber	4500

Colt Model 1855 Revolving Carbine **$3000**
Calibers: 36, 44 and 56 percussion. Six-shot cylinder with side hammer. Barrel: 15, 18 and 21 inches. Weight: 8 lbs. 8 oz. to 9 lbs. 8 oz. Side hammers marked "Address Col Colt, Hartford, Conn." Made from 1855 to 1866.

Colt Model 1861 Special Musket . . . . **$***
Single shot muzzleloader. Caliber: 58. Barrel: 40 inches, round; three barrel bands. Iron mountings. Walnut stock. Made under U.S. Government contracts for use by Union Troops between 1861 and 1865.

Colt New Lightning Magazine Baby Carbines **$2000**
Same general specifications as standard New Lightning Carbines, except barrel was of slimmer construction. Weight: 5¼ to 8 pounds, depending on size of frame.

Colt New Lightning Small Frame Magazine Rifle **$525**
Caliber: 22 Long. 15- or 16-shot magazine. Slide action. Barrel: 24 inches; round or octagonal. Weight: 5¾ pounds w/round barrel; 6 pounds w/octagonal barrel. Walnut stock. Made from 1887 to 1904.

Colt Model 1861 Special Musket

**Colt 44 Cal. New Lightning
Medium Frame Rifle**

**Colt New Lightning Medium Frame Magazine
Carbine** **$995**
Same general specifications as medium frame New
Lightning Rifle, except barrel is 20 inches and maga-
zine holds 12 shots. Weight: 6¼ pounds.

**Colt New Lightning Medium Frame
Magazine Rifle** **$840**
Calibers: 32-20, 38-40, 44-40 centerfire. 15-shot mag-
azine. Slide action. Barrel: 26 inches. Walnut stock.
Made 1883 to 1902.

**Colt New Lightning Medium Frame Military
Carbine** **$1800**
Differs from the medium frame rifle in that it was made
in only 44-40 caliber, has shortened magazine tubes
and is equipped with sling swivels, bayonet lugs and
carbine-type butt plates. Made from about 1885 to
1902.

**Colt New Lightning Large Frame Magazine
Rifle** **$725**
Express Model. Calibers: 38-56, 40-60, 45-50, 45-85,
50-95 Express. Ten-shot magazine. Barrel: 28 inches,
round or octagonal. Weight: 9¾ to 10 pounds. Walnut
stock. Made from 1887 to 1894.

**Colt New Lightning Large Frame
Magazine Carbine** **$1800**
Same general specifications as the large frame rifle, except has a 22-inch round barrel, full magazine, military-style sights and carbine-type butt plates. Weight:
9 pounds. Walnut stock. Made about 1888 to 1894.

**Colt Paterson Model 1836 Percussion Rifle
(34 Cal.)** **$7500**
Caliber: 34. Eight-shot fluted cylinder. Earliest models
had no loading lever; it was added on later models. Barrel: 32 inches. Overall length: 50 inches. Weight: 12½
pounds. Walnut stock. Made from 1836 to 1843.

**Colt Paterson Model 1836 Percussion Rifle
(44 Cal.)** **$6995**
Caliber: 44. Eight-shot fluted cylinder. Earliest models
had no loading lever; it was added on later models. Barrel: 24 inches. Overall length: 42 inches. Weight: 12
pounds. Walnut stock. Made from 1836 to 1843.

Colt Paterson Model 1836 Rifle (69 Cal.) . . . **$8000**
Hammerless. Caliber: 69 percussion. Seven-shot
fluted cylinder. Earliest models had no loading lever; it
was added on later models. Walnut stock. Made from
1836 to 1838.

**Colt Paterson Model 1837 Percussion
Rifle** **$7225**
Caliber: 44. Eight-shot cylinder. Barrel: 24 inches.
Overall length: 40 inches. Weight: 10½ pounds. Only
about 20 made from 1837 to 1843.

Colt Paterson Model 1839 Carbine **$5500**
Caliber: 47. Six-shot cylinder. Barrel: 24½ inches.
Overall length: 42½ inches. Weight: 8½ pounds. Made
from 1839 to 1840.

Colt-Burgess 12-Shot Repeating Carbine . . . **$1425**
Lever action. Caliber: 44-40. 12-shot magazine. Barrel:
20 inches, round; blued finish. walnut stock. Based on
a design by Andrew Burgess, only about 2600 were
made from 1883 to 1885.

Colt-Burgess 15-Shot Repeating Rifle **$1800**
Lever action. Caliber: 44-40. 15-shot magazine. Barrel:
24 to 25½ inches; round and octagonal. Blued and
brown finishes with casehardened hammer and lever.
Walnut stock. Based on a design by Andrew Burgess,
only about 3800 were made from 1883 to 1885.

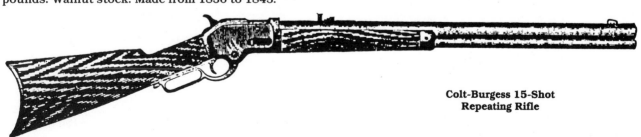

**Colt-Burgess 15-Shot
Repeating Rifle**

GEORGE W. CUNNINGHAM
Detroit, Michigan

Cunningham Percussion Rifle **$700**
Calibers: various. Barrel: various lengths, octagonal. Lock plate usually stamped "MOORE." Moore was a gunsmith and importer from Toronto, Ontario. The rifle pictured is undoubtedly one of the guns that Moore imported from the United States. Made from 1874 to 1878.

CZECHOSLOVAKIAN MILITARY
Various Manufacturers

Czech Model 1898 Mauser Military Rifle **$175**
Bolt action, straight handle. Caliber: 7.9mm (8x57mm) Mauser. Five-shot magazine. Barrel: 29 inches, stepped barrel. Weight: 9 pounds. Blade-front sight, adjustable rear sight. Military-type full-length stock. Adopted in 1898.

John Demuth Kentucky Sporting
Target Rifle

DANISH MILITARY
Various Manufacturers

Danish Model 1889 Krag-Jorgensen Military Rifle **$200**
Bolt action. Caliber: 8mmR. Five-shot magazine. Barrel: 33 inches. Weight: 9³/₄ pounds. Blade front sight, adjustable rear sight. Military-type stock, straight grip.

JOHN DEMUTH
Frederick Co., Maryland

Demuth Flintlock Target Rifle **$1800**
Caliber: 72. Barrel: Heavy octagonal with 16- groove rifling, 1¹/₄ inches across flats. Brass furniture. Made from 1794 to 1796.

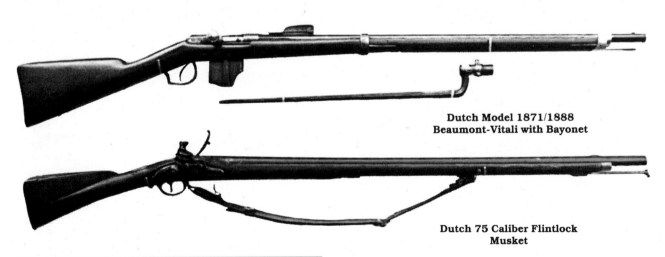

Dutch Model 1871/1888
Beaumont-Vitali with Bayonet

Dutch 75 Caliber Flintlock
Musket

DUTCH MILITARY
Various Manufacturers

Dutch Model 1871/88 Bolt Action Beaumont-Vitali Rifle **$200**
Caliber: 11mm. Marked 1873 and 91 "DELFT." Military model with bayonet.

Dutch Flintlock Musket **$600**
Caliber: 75. Typical of those used during the American Revolution.

ECUADOR MILITARY
Various Manufacturers

Ecuador Model 1891 Mauser Military Rifle . . **$115**
Bolt action. Caliber: 7.65 Belgian Mauser. Five-shot box magazine, clip loaded. Barrel: 29 inches. Weight: about 8³/₄ pounds. Open rear sight, inverted "V" front sight. Military-type full stock. Adopted in 1891 by Argentina and several other South American countries.

EVANS RIFLE MANUFACTURING CO.
Mechanic Falls, Maine

Warren E. Evans of Thomaston, Maine, was granted patents covering his unique rifle on December 8, 1868, and again on September 18, 1871.

The Evans rifles were manufactured in two distinct models known as the "old" and the "new." Both had a special four-column fluted magazine within the butt that held a maximum of 34 cartridges—making the Evans the greatest capacity repeating rifle ever to be placed on the market. The original Evans cartridge had a 215-grain lead bullet backed with 28 grains of black powder. The new model cartridge was slightly longer, using a 280-grain bullet in front of 42 grains of black powder.

Due to financial difficulties, the Evans Rifle Company was forced out of business about 1880.

Evans Old Model Military Rifle. **$1050**
Essentially the same as the Old Model Sporting Rifle, except for longer forearm, provisions for bayonet, and a 30-inch barrel. Also, some of the refinements of the sporting rifle were missing.

Evans Old Model Repeating Carbine. **$995**
Essentially the same as the Old Model Sporting Rifle, except for the butt plate and 22-inch barrel, which reduced the weight to 7¹/₂ pounds.

Evans Old Model Sporting Rifle. **$1100**
Lever-action repeater. Special four-column fluted magazine holding 34 shots. Caliber: 44 Evans. Barrel: 26, 28 and 30 inches; octagonal. Weight: 9 lbs. 10 oz. with 26-inch barrel. Overall length: 43 inches. Various sights, but globe front sight and vernier rear were common. Two-piece walnut butt stock; walnut forend. Made from 1875 to 1877.

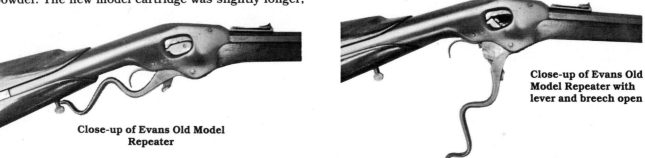

Close-up of Evans Old Model Repeater

Close-up of Evans Old Model Repeater with lever and breech open

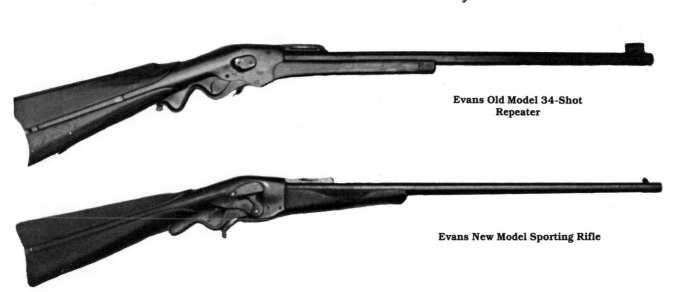

Evans Old Model 34-Shot Repeater

Evans New Model Sporting Rifle

Evans New Model Military Repeating Rifle . . $1195
Essentially the same as the New Model Sporting Rifle, except for longer forend and bayonet provisions.

Evans New Model Repeating Carbine $900
Essentially the same as the New Model Sporting Rifle, except for butt plate and shorter barrel. Made from 1877 to 1880.

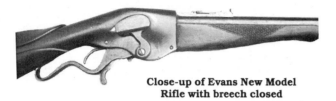

Close-up of Evans New Model
Rifle with breech closed

Evans New Model Sporting Rifle $795
Lever-action repeater. Four-column, 26-shot, fluted magazine. Caliber: a longer version of the Old Model 44 Evans. Barrel: various lengths from 26 to 31 inches; round or octagonal. Overall length: 47$\frac{1}{2}$ inches. Weight: 9$\frac{1}{2}$ pounds. Walnut stock and forearm. Made from 1877 to 1880.

FRENCH MILITARY
Various Manufacturers

French Model 1763 Musketoon $500
Caliber: 73. Lock stamped "HB ST ETIENNE". Regimentally marked on barrel. Many original muskets were altered to musketoon style, like the one pictured.

French Model 1777 Musket $500
Caliber: 75. Barrel marked "MRE IMP. LE DE VERSAILLES." Typical reconversion.

French Model 1866 Chassepot Rifle $300
Caliber: 11mm Needle Gun. Barrel: round with bayonet lug. Made circa 1867.

French Model 1886 Lebel Military Rifle $110
Bolt action. Caliber: 8mm Lebel (.315). Eight-shot tubular magazine. Barrel: 31$\frac{1}{2}$ inches. Overall length: 49 inches. Weight: 9$\frac{1}{4}$ pounds. Sights: blade front, adjustable rear. Two-piece military stock. Made with various modifications in Chatellerault, St. Étienne, France, from 1886 to about 1945.

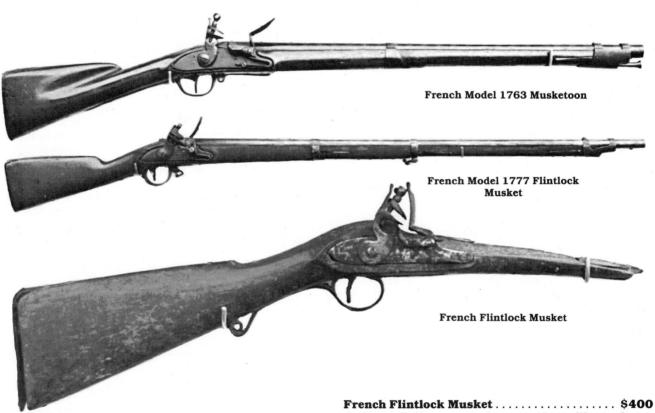

French Model 1763 Musketoon

French Model 1777 Flintlock
Musket

French Flintlock Musket

French Model 1892 Lebel Military Carbine . . $125
Same general specifications as the Lebel Rifle, except has 17$\frac{1}{2}$-inch barrel and weighs 6$\frac{3}{4}$ pounds.

French Flintlock Musket $400
Caliber: 73. Many made from surplus military pieces, so many variations exist. This musket stamped on butt "NIGER COAST PROTECTORATE FIREARMS PROTECTION."

MAHLON J. GALLAGHER
Philadelphia, Pennsylvania

Mahlon Gallagher patented certain percussion breechloading rifle designs as well as those designed for metallic cartridges. Most were manufactured between 1860 and 1865 at the Richardson and Overman plant in Philadelphia under Mr. Gallagher's supervision.

Gallagher Breech-Loading Metallic Cartridge Rifle **$395**
Same general specifications as the Gallagher Percussion Rifle, except used a metallic cartridge instead of a paper cartridge.

Gallagher Percussion Carbine **$525**
Same general specifications as the Gallagher Percussion Rifle, except had 22- or 24-inch barrel. Made from 1860 to 1865.

Gallagher Percussion Rifle **$495**
Caliber: 54. Barrel: various lengths to 32 inches; mostly round. Color casehardened back-lock action. Straight-grip buttstock; usually no wood forend. Combination trigger guard/lever released barrel latch for insertion of paper cartridge. Made from 1860 to 1865.

GERMAN MILITARY
Various Manufacturers

German Model 1871 Rifle **$500**
Caliber: 11mm. Brass hilt bayonet. This model manufactured circa 1879.

German Model 1888 Mauser-Mannlicher Carbine **$125**
Same general specifications as the Model 1888 Rifle, except has 18-inch barrel, flat turned-down bolt handle and weighs 6¾ pounds. Manufactured by Ludwig Loewe & Co., Berlin.

German Model 1888 Mauser-Mannlicher Military Rifle **$250**
Bolt action. Caliber: 7.9mm Mauser (8x57mm). Five-shot magazine. Barrel: 29 inches, round. Weight: 8½ pounds. Sights: adjustable rear; fixed front. Military stock. Made by Ludwig Loewe & Co., Berlin, from 1888 to 1898. The model shown is dated 1890.

German Model 1898 Mauser Military Rifle . . . **$175**
Bolt action. Caliber: 7.9mm (8x57mm). Five-shot magazine. Barrel: 29 inches, stepped. Weight: about 9 pounds. Sights: blade front; adjustable rear. Military-type full stock with rounded bottom pistol grip. Adopted 1898.

German Model 1898A Mauser Carbine **$200**
Same general specifications as the 1898 Mauser Rifle, except has turned-down bolt handle, smaller receiver sight, 23½-inch tapered barrel and weighs about 8 pounds.

C. G. HAENEL
Suhl, Germany

Haenel Mauser-Mannlicher Bolt Action Sporting Rifle **$495**
Bolt action. Calibers: 7x57, 8x57, 9x57. Five-shot Mannlicher clip-loading box magazine. Barrel: 22 or 24 inches; half or full octagonal with raised matte rib. Double-set triggers. Weight: 7½ pounds. Sights: ramp front; leaf-type open rear. Sporting walnut stock with checkered pistol grip, raised side-panels, schnabel tip and sling swivels.

Haenel Model '88 Mauser Sporter **$495**
Same general specifications as the Sporting Rifle, except has Mauser-type five-shot magazine instead of Mannlicher style.

**German Model 1871 Rifle
with Brass Hilt Bayonet**

ALEXANDER HENRY
Edinburgh, Scotland

This the "Henry" (1819–1894) who invented the system of rifling that was combined with the Martini action to produce the Martini-Henry Rifle, officially adopted by the British government in 1869. (*See* also British and Canadian listings.)

Alexander Henry Single Shot Rifle $2000
Caliber: 450 black powder. Checkered pistol grip and forend. Elaborately engraved. Made circa 1862 to 1894.

R. E. HODGES
London, England

Hodges Elastic Gun $2400
Caliber: 44. Barrel: octagonal with "R.E. HODGES PATENTEE LONDON" engraved on top flat. Walnut stock with checkered grip and iron butt plate. Copper nosecap and two brass busts of Britannia at the muzzle. Two elastics, one on each side of barrel. The projection below the forend is a grip for the palm of the hand. Hodges believed in the power of vulcanized caouthchouc (rubber) and described his elastic gun as follows: "constructed after the manner of an ordinary fowling piece which would be well adapted for deer shooting, as it will carry a long way and be attended with neither noise nor smell." This is an unusual piece, another example of 19th-century inventiveness. Only a few hundred were ever made circa 1849.

COBOURG C.W. HOLMES
Address Unknown

Holmes Percussion Rifle $1300
Caliber: 41. Lock by J.P. Moore of Union, N.Y. Walnut stock. Brass butt plate, trigger guard and ramrod thimbles, as well as side plate. Silver inlays.

HOWARD BROTHERS
Whitneyville, Connecticut

Charles Howard obtained patents for a breechloading hammerless sporting rifle from September 26, 1865, to May 15, 1866. Whitney Arms Co. at Whitneyville, Conn., made most of these rifles under contract, as is stated on the barrels of many early rifles; that is, "Mf'd for Howard Brothers by Whitney Arms Co., Whitneyville, Conn."

Howard Brothers Breech-Loading Hammerless Rifle $225
Caliber: 38 Long rimfire. Barrel: 24 inches. Overall length: 43 inches. Weight: 6 pounds. American walnut stock. Set triggers available as extra. Made from 1866 to 1869.

Howard Brothers Single-Shot Breech-Loading Sporting Rifle $245
Caliber: 44 RF. Barrel: 24½ inches. Overall length: 43¾ inches. Weight: 6 pounds. American walnut stock. Set triggers available for extra cost. Made from 1866 to 1869.

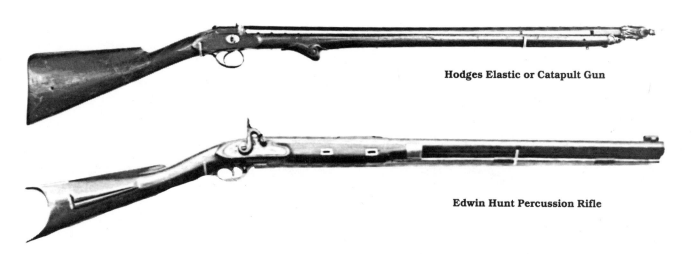

Hodges Elastic or Catapult Gun

Edwin Hunt Percussion Rifle

EDWIN HUNT
Canada

Hunt Percussion Rifle $750
Caliber: 36. Barrel: part octagonal. American walnut stock with cheekpiece. Silver escutcheons. Brass butt plate, trigger guard, rear thimble and nosecap.

WALTER HUNT
New York, New York

On August 21, 1849, Walter Hunt—a 53-year old machinist and inventor—was granted U.S. Patent No. 6663 for a lever-action, breechloading, repeating rifle known as the "Volition Repeater." This rifle was the forerunner of the Henry and Winchester actions, but mainly because of unsuitable cartridges, it was not successful.

Hunt "Volition" Repeating Rifle .... **$50,000+**
Caliber: 54 Tubular magazine under barrel. Small-frame style with exposed ring trigger. Used "Rocket-ball" conical lead bullet with self-contained powder charge and independent priming pill. Only one specimen is known at this time, which is in the Winchester Collection at the W. F. Cody Museum in Cody, Wyoming. Made in limited numbers between 1849 and 1853.

JAMES INNES
Edinburgh, Scotland

Innes Scottish Hunting Musket............ **$500**
Caliber: 80. Brass furniture. Adjustable single-set trigger. Walnut stock. Made 1793 to 1820; converted to percussion around 1835.

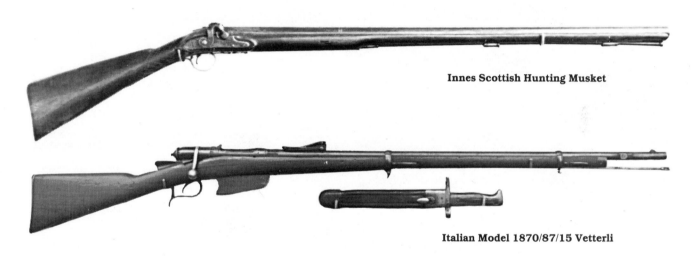

Innes Scottish Hunting Musket

Italian Model 1870/87/15 Vetterli

ITALIAN MILITARY
Various Manufacturers

Italian Model 1870/87/15 Vetterli **$200**
Caliber: 6.5x52mm. Walnut stock, full-length. Bayonet lug with bayonet and scabbard. Dated 1882 and stamped "BRESCIA."

Italian Model 1891 Mannlicher-Carcano Military Rifle..**$90**
Bolt action. Caliber: 6.5mm. Six-shot modified Mannlicher-style box magazine. Barrel: 30³/₄ inches. Weight: 9 pounds. Sights: blade front; adjustable rear. Military-style straight-grip stock. Adopted by the Italian Military Service in 1891.

Italian Model (18)91 TS Cavalry Carbine **$80**
Caliber: 6.5mm. Introduced in 1891.

JAPANESE MILITARY
Various Manufacturers

Japanese Matchlock...................... **$850**
Matchlock. Calibers: various. Barrel: 39¹/₂ inches. Inlaid in silver with trees and other designs.

LEWIS JENNINGS
Windsor, Vermont

Lewis Jennings simplified and improved an earlier repeating rifle design by Walter Hunt (*see* separate listing), and was granted a U.S. patent on December 25, 1849. The Jennings and the Walter Hunt rifles were the basic patents for the Henry and, later, the Winchester rifles. The Jennings rifles were manufactured by Robbins & Lawrence of Windsor, Vt., and are usually so marked.

Jennings Breechloading Rifle—First Model $2500
Caliber: 54, with automatic priming device. Single shot. Straight frame with ring trigger and oval trigger guard. Made from 1850 to 1853.

Jennings Breechloading Repeating Rifle. . . . $6000
Caliber: 54. Tubular magazine. Barrel: round with magazine tube below. Exposed hammer. Fixed rear and front sights. American walnut buttstock with crescent butt plate, straight grip. Made from 1851 to 1853.

Jennings Muzzle-Loading Rifle $1250
Caliber: 54 percussion. Single shot. Muzzleloading barrel with cleaning rod below. Curved trigger and indented trigger guard. American walnut stock with no forend. Assembled from remaining parts of the first and second Jennings models, this was made from 1852 to 1853.

BENJAMIN F. JOSLYN
Stonington, Connecticut

Benjamin Joslyn was patentee of the Joslyn breechloading carbine, patented August 23, 1855, and the Joslyn percussion revolver, patented May 4, 1858. Benjamin Joslyn established the Joslyn Arms Company in 1861 and was awarded U.S. Government contracts for both the carbines and revolvers. These arms were also manufactured by W.D. Freeman of Worcester, Mass., and the carbines by A.H. Waters & Co. of Millbury, Mass. The Joslyn Arms Co. operated until 1878.

For further specifications, *see* U.S. Military Single Shot Breechloading Carbines at the end of the Rifle Section.

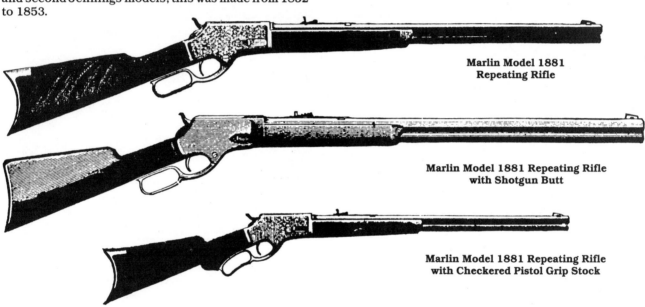

Marlin Model 1881
Repeating Rifle

Marlin Model 1881 Repeating Rifle
with Shotgun Butt

Marlin Model 1881 Repeating Rifle
with Checkered Pistol Grip Stock

MARLIN FIREARMS COMPANY
North Haven, Connecticut

The Marlin Firearms Company was founded in 1870 by John Mahlon Marlin who first started producing single-shot pistols, revolvers, and the famous Ballard single-shot rifles under the brand name, "J.M. Marlin."

In 1880 the Marlin firm was incorporated as the Marlin Firearms Company and operated successfully until John Marlin died in 1900. Ownership was then carried out by the Marlin family until the business was sold in 1915 to a firm known as the Marlin Arms Corporation.

Although the Marlin Company changed owners many times, the company is still in operation at 100 Kenna Drive, North Haven, Conn.

Marlin Model 1881 Repeating Rifle $750
Calibers: 45-70, 45-85-285, 40-60, 38-55 and 32-40. Barrel lengths: 28 and 30 inches. Weight: 9$^{1}/_{2}$ to 11$^{1}/_{4}$ pounds. Open rear sight, blade front sight. American walnut stock in either straight or pistol grip. Double-set triggers were introduced for this model in 1883, which was rather unique for a lever-action rifle. Several variations exist. Made from 1881 to 1892.

Marlin Model 1888 Repeating Rifle $895
Top-eject. Similar to the Model 1881, except it had a shorter action for use with 32-30, 38-40 and 44-40 cartridges. Barrel lengths: 24, 26, and 28 inches; octagonal. Weight: from 6$^{3}/_{4}$ pounds. Made from 1888 to 1889.

Marlin Model 1889 Slide Action Repeating Carbine. $600
Same general specifications as the Model 1889 Rifle, except had a 20-inch barrel and carbine-type stock.

Marlin Model 1889 Slide Action Repeating Rifle. **$525**
Solid frame. Calibers: 25-20, 32-30, 38-40 and 44-40. Barrels: 24 inches; round, octagonal, or half-octagonal most common. Plain or checkered American walnut stock and forend. Made from 1889 to 1893.

Marlin Model 1889 Slide Action Repeating Rifle (Fancy) **$895**
Same general specifications as Model 1889 Rifle, except had extra-fancy walnut stock and forend.

NOTE
Annie Oakley, famous female sharpshooter of the West, used a specially engraved Marlin Model 1889 Rifle, and often joined "Buffalo Bill" Cody in shooting exhibitions with Cody's Circus.

Marlin Model 1891 Repeating Rifle **$425**
Solid frame. Calibers: 22 RF, 32 RF long. 18-shot tubular magazine with long rifle cartridges. Barrels: 24, 25 and 26 inches average, but could be furnished in lengths of up to 32 inches; round or octagonal. Weight: 6 to 6½ pounds. American walnut stock and forend with either straight or pistol grip. Rifle-type butt plate. Made from 1891 to 1892.

Marlin Model 1891 Fancy Repeating Rifle . . . **$595**
Same general specifications as standard Model 1891 Rifle, except furnished with fancy grade walnut checkered stock and forend.

Marlin Model 1892 Lever Action Repeating Rifle. **$430**
Calibers: 22 Short, Long, Long Rifle; 32 Short, Long (rimfire or centerfire by changing firing pin). Tubular magazines holding: 25 Short, 20 Long, 18 Long Rifle (22); 17 Short, 14 long (32). 16-inch barrel model has shorter magazine holding 15 Short, 12 Long, 10 Long Rifle. Barrel lengths: 16 (22 cal. only), 24, 26, 28 inches; round or octagonal. Weight: 5½ pounds with 24-inch barrel. Open rear sight, blade front sight. Plain straight grip stock and forearm. Made from 1892 to 1916.

MODEL 1893 SERIES

Marlin Model 1893 Lever Action Repeating Rifle. **$425**
Solid frame or takedown. Calibers: 25-36 Marlin, 30-30, 32 Special, 32-40, 38-55. Tubular magazine holds 10 cartridges. Barrels: 26 inches, round or octagonal standard; also made in 28-, 30- and 32-inch lengths. Weight: 7¼ pounds. Open rear sight, bead front sight. Plain straight-grip stock and forearm. Made from 1893 to 1936.

Marlin Model 93 Carbine. **$1195**
Same as Standard Model 1893 Rifle, except made in calibers 30-30 and 32 Special only. Seven-shot magazine. Barrel: 20 inches, round. Weight: 6¾ pounds. Carbine sights.

Marlin Model 93 Musket **$895**
Same as standard Model 1893 Rifle, except has 30-inch barrel, angular bayonet, ramrod under barrel, musket stock, full-length military-style forearm. Weight: 8 pounds. Made from 1893 to 1915.

Marlin Model 93SC Sporting Carbine **$1250**
Same as Model 93 Carbine, except has two-thirds magazine that holds five shots. Weight: 6½ pounds.

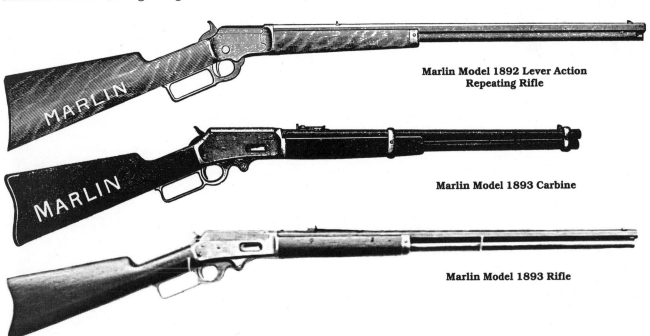

Marlin Model 1892 Lever Action Repeating Rifle

Marlin Model 1893 Carbine

Marlin Model 1893 Rifle

Marlin Model 1894 Lever Action Repeating Rifle. **$1200**
Solid frame or takedown. Calibers: 25-20, 32-30, 38-40, 44-40. Ten-shot tubular magazine. Barrel: 24 inches; round or octagonal. Weight: 7 pounds. Open rear sight, bead front sight. Plain straight-grip stock and forearm (also available with pistol-grip stock). Made from 1894 to 1934.

Marlin Model 1894
Takedown

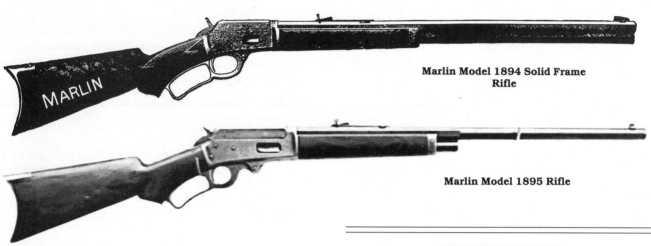

Marlin Model 1894 Solid Frame
Rifle

Marlin Model 1895 Rifle

Marlin Model 1895 Lever Action Repeating Rifle. **$1200**
Solid frame or takedown. Calibers: 33 WCF, 38-56, 40-65, 40-70, 40-82 and 45-70. Nine-shot tubular magazine. Barrel: 24 inches, round or octagonal standard (other lengths available). Weight: 8 pounds. Open rear sight, bead front sight. Plain stock and forearm (also available with pistol-grip stock). Made from 1895 to 1915.

Marlin Model 1897 Lever Action Repeating Rifle. **$445**
Takedown. Caliber: 22 Long Rifle, Long, Short. Tubular magazine; full length holds 25 Short, 20 Long, 18 Long Rifle; half length holds 16 Short, 12 Long and 10 Long Rifle. Barrel lengths: 16, 24, 26, 28 inches. Weight: 6 pounds. Open rear sight and bead front sight. Plain straight-grip stock and forearm (also available with pistol-grip stock). Made from 1897 to 1922.

MAUSER RIFLES
Various German Manufacturers

Mauser Model 1871 Rifle . . . .**$*****
Single shot. Bolt action. Caliber: 11mm. Barrel: round. Had claw-type extractor on left side of bolt and automatic cam cocking, which made it a self-cocking arm, with safety centerfire action locked securely at the rear. This model was an improvement over the earlier needle-type rifle, and became very popular. It was manufactured at various official German armories, as well as by Steyr in Austria; it was also sold to many foreign countries.

Mauser Model 1871 Carbine **$225**
Caliber: 11mm. Barrel: round, carbine length. Walnut stock. Made circa 1879.

───────── *NOTE* ─────────
*** after a dollar sign indicates that there was not enough trading at press time to establish a valid selling price.

Mauser Model 1871 Carbine

MERRIMACK ARMS MFG. COMPANY
Newburyport, Massachusetts

The Merrimack Arms Mfg. Company operated in the mid- to late 1860s, producing Ballard rifles (*see* separate listing) as well as its own arms. At the end of the decade, it became the Brown Mfg. Co.

Merrimack Double Barrel Rifle **$1210**
Calibers: various. Side by side. Barrel: octagonal.

MEXICAN MILITARY RIFLES
Various Manufacturers

The rifles that follow were purchased or produced for use by the Mexican Armed Forces during the 19th century. Prior to the introduction of these cartridge rifles, muzzleloaders of all types were used by Mexico. Some of the newer rifles were made by Mexican gunsmiths, but most were imported or confiscated from other countries.

Mexican/Mauser Model 1895 Carbine **$225**
Same general specifications as Mauser 1895 Rifle, except has 18¼-inch barrel, overall length of 37½ inches and weight of 7½ pounds.

Mexican/Mauser Model 1895 Rifle **$200**
Bolt action. Caliber: 7mm Mauser. Barrel: 29 inches, round. Overall length: 48½ inches. Weight: 8¾ pounds. Staggered box magazine holds 5 rounds. Inverted "V" front sight; adjustable leaf rear. Besides German markings, top of receiver stamped with eagle and "REPUBLICA MEXICANA."

Mexican/Mondragon Model 1893 Rifle **$400**
Straight-pull bolt action. Caliber: 6.5mm Mondragon. Barrel: 29 inches. Overall length: 48 inches. Weight: 7½ pounds. Box magazine holds 8 rounds. Front inverted "V" sight; adjustable leaf rear. Top tang marked, "FAB. D'ARMES. NEUHAUSEN."

Mexican/Mondragon Model 1894 Rifle **$400**
Straight-pull bolt action. Caliber: 5.2x68mm. Barrels: 21¾ to 34½ inches. Fixed box magazine holds 8 rounds. Inverted "V" front sight; various types of rear sights. Markings same as Model 1893 Mondragon Rifle.

Mexican/Pieper-Nagant Model 1893 Carbine. **$1700**
Revolving nine-shot cylinder. Single and double action. Caliber: 8mm Nagant. Barrel: 19¾ inches. Overall length: 36 inches. Weight: 6½ pounds. Plain straight-grip stock. Barleycorn front sight; adjustable leaf rear. Top of receiver marked "EJERCITO MEXICANO." Top tang marked "H. PIEPER Bte LIÈGE." Left-side plate marked "EJERCITO MEXICANO."

Mexican/Remington Model 1871 Carbine. . . . **$525**
Same general specifications as the Remington Model 1871 Rifle, except for 20½-inch barrel, overall length of 36 inches and weight of 6¾ pounds. Also carried saddle ring on left side of receiver.

Mexican/Remington Model 1871 Rifle. **$450**
Single-shot rolling block. Caliber: 11mm Spanish. Barrel: 35 inches. Overall length: 50½ inches. Weight: 8½ pounds. Barleycorn front sight; adjustable leaf rear sight. Plain walnut stock. Top of barrel marked at breech "R. DE MEXICO" or "RM" with issue number on breech top.

Mexican/Remington Model 1897 Carbine. . . . **$425**
Same general specifications as Remington 1897 Rifle, except has 20½-inch barrel and weighs 6¾ pounds.

Mexican/Remington Model 1897 Rifle. **$375**
Single-shot rolling block. Caliber: 7mm Mauser. Barrel: 30 inches, round. Overall length: 45½ inches. Weight: 8½ pounds. Inverted "V" front sight; adjustable leaf rear. Top of receiver stamped "REPUBLICA MEXICANA."

Mexican/Spencer Model 1865 Carbine . . . . **$*****
Manually operated lever action. Caliber: 50-50. Barrel: 20 inches. Overall length: 37 inches. Weight: 8¼ pounds. Tubular magazine in buttstock holds 7 rounds. Inverted "V" front sight; adjustable leaf rear. Color casehardened receiver; balance of metal parts blued. Purchased as U.S. surplus and given Mexican ownership marks, including the letters "R.M."

Mexican/Whitney Rolling Block Carbine **$625**
Same general specifications as the Whitney Rolling Block Rifle, except has 20½-inch barrel, overall length of 36 inches and weighs about 7 pounds. Saddle ring on left side of receiver.

Mexican/Remington Model 1897
7mm Rifle

Mexican/Whitney Rolling Block Rifle **$360**
Single-shot rolling block. Caliber: 11mm Spanish. Barrel: 35 inches. Overall length: 50½ inches. Weight: 9½ pounds. Barleycorn front sight; adjustable leaf rear. Serial number on lower tang; "RM" marked on top, right side of receiver.

Mexican/Winchester Model 1866 Rifle **$2300**
Manually operated lever action. Caliber: 44 RF. Barrel: 24 inches. Overall length: 43½ inches. Weight: 9½ pounds. Tubular magazine beneath barrel holds 17 rounds. Blade front sight, adjustable leaf rear sight. Very small eagle stamped on these rifles. Serial numbers, found on tang beneath lever, should be under 20,000. Top of notch barrel marked: "HENRY'S PATENT - OCT. 16, 1860, KING'S PATENT - MARCH 29, 1866." One thousand of these rifles ordered and purchased from Winchester in late 1866.

Mexican/Winchester Model 1894 Carbine **$495**
Manually operated lever action. Caliber: 30 WCF (30-30). Barrel: 20 inches, round. Overall length: 38 inches. Weight: 6½ pounds. Tubular magazine beneath barrel holds 6 rounds. Blade front sight; three-leaf rear sight.

Spanish Model Peabody Rifle . . . . **$*****
Single shot. Falling block action, lever actuated. Caliber: 11mm Spanish. Barrel: 33 inches. Overall length: 52 inches. Weight: 9¾ pounds. Front inverted "V" sight; adjustable leaf rear sight. The Mexican government purchased 8,500 of these rifles between 1870 and 1872 for testing, but they were not adopted by the Mexican authorities.

NOTE

*** after a dollar sign indicates that there was not enough trading at press time to establish a valid selling price.

JOSEPH NEEDHAM
London, England

Needham Model 1861 Percussion Rifle **$450**
Caliber: 58. Barrel: round. Lock stamped "BRIDESBURG 1864." This is commonly called the Finian's Rifle as it was the rifle used by them in their attacks on Canada in 1866 and 1870.

Needham Model 1861 Percussion
Rifle Rimfire Conversion

Portuguese Model 1886
Kropatschek Carbine

Prussian Model 1839 Military
Musket

PORTUGUESE MILITARY
Various Manufacturers

**Portuguese Model 1886 Kropatschek
Carbine** **$100**
Caliber: 8mm. Barrel: round; shorter carbine length. Iron furniture. Full stock, straight grip.

PRUSSIAN LONG ARMS
Various Manufacturers

Prussian Model 1839 Military Musket **$300**
Converted from the Model 1809 flintlock. Round barrel with full-length musket stock. Brass furniture.

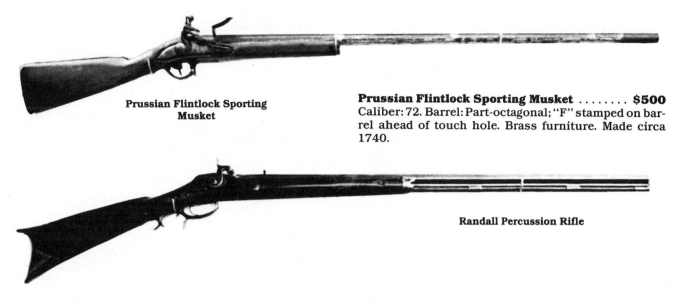

Prussian Flintlock Sporting
Musket

Prussian Flintlock Sporting Musket **$500**
Caliber: 72. Barrel: Part-octagonal; "F" stamped on barrel ahead of touch hole. Brass furniture. Made circa 1740.

Randall Percussion Rifle

JOSEPH C. RANDALL
Philadelphia, Pennsylvania

Randall Percussion Rifle **$450**
Caliber: 45. Barrel: octagonal. Pewter nose cap; silver propeller-style inlay on barrel. Double-set triggers. American walnut stock with brass and copper furniture. Made circa 1860.

REMINGTON ARMS CO.
Ilion, New York

Eliphalet Remington Jr. made his first rifle in 1816 as a young man. With his father, he produced custom rifles and gun parts at Ilion Gorge, N.Y. In 1828 they moved to a larger facility in Ilion, N.Y., to accommodate their growing business, only to be met with tragedy in the death of Eliphalet Sr. Undaunted, the son continued to expand the manufacturing operation and by 1844 he was able to take his son, Philo, into the business, changing the name to E. Remington & Son. Many U.S. Government contracts for rifles, carbines and eventually handguns were awarded to the Remingtons,

so that by 1856 the volume of business was great enough for Remington to take his other two sons into the business. The partnership formed, "E. Remington & Sons" continued from 1856 to 1865, when a corporation was formed. For more than twenty years the corporation successfully produced a variety of popular guns, until 1886 when it suffered severe loses, and failed. Two years later, Hartley and Graham, partners and founders of the Union Metallic Cartridge Co. of Bridgeport, Conn., purchased controlling interest in what became the Remington Arms Company. Other investors entered into the picture from time to time, but the firm is still in operation under the same name and is now a subsidiary of the du Pont Corporation.

See also Handguns and Shotguns for additional Remington arms.

Remington No. 1 Sporting Rifle **$395**
Rolling-block, casehardened action. Calibers: 22 RF, 32 RF, 38 RF, 44 RF, 46 RF; 32-20, 32-40, 38-40 Rem., 40-45, 40-50, 40-70, 40-70 straight, 44 S&W, 44-40, 44-77 Sharps, 45-70, 50-70, 58 Govt. and others. Barrel: 20 inches round; 26 inches in round, octagonal or half-octagonal; or 30 inches octagonal. Weight: from 6½ to 15 pounds. Open sights standard. American walnut stock and forend. Made from 1869 to 1889.

Remington No. 1 Sporting Rifle

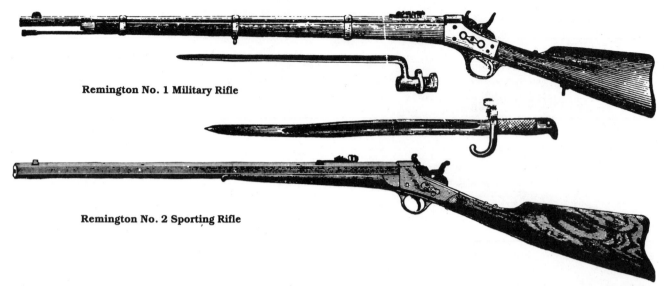

Remington No. 1 Military Rifle

Remington No. 2 Sporting Rifle

Remington No. 1 Military Rifle................**$*****
Large size rolling block action. Casehardened. Calibers: 43 (11mm), 50, 58 centerfire. With or without bayonets. Made for foreign countries from about the 1870s to 1900.

Remington No. 2 Sporting Rifle
Single-shot, rolling-block action. Calibers: 22, 25, 32, 38, 44 rimfire or centerfire. Barrel: 24, 26, 28 or 30 inches. Weight: 5½ to 8 pounds. Open rear sight, bead front sight. Straight-grip sporting stock and knob-tip forearm of walnut. Made from 1873 to 1910.
Calibers 22 through 32.....................**$245**
Calibers 38 through 44.......................**425**

Remington No. 3 Sporting Rifle............ **$675**
Single shot. Hepburn falling-block action with side lever. Calibers: 22 WCF, 22 Extra Long, 25-20 Stevens, 25-21 Stevens, 25-25 Stevens, 32 WCF, 32-40 Ballard & Marlin, 32-40 Remington, 38 WCF, 38-40 Remington, 38-50 Remington, 38-55 Ballard & Marlin, 40-60 Ballard & Marlin, 40-60 WCF, 40-65 Remington Straight, 40-82 WCF, 45-70 Govt., 45-90 WCF; also supplied on special order in bottle-necked 40-50, 40-70, 40-90, 44-77, 44-90, 44-105, 50-70 Govt., and 50-90 Sharps Straight. Barrel: 26 inches (22, 25, 32 cal. only); 28, 30 inches; half-octagonal or full octagonal. Weight: 8 to 10 pounds, depending upon barrel length and caliber. Open rear sight, blade front sight. Checkered pistol-grip stock and forearm. Made from 1880 to 1911.

Remington No. 3 Creedmoor and Schuetzen Rifles...................................**$5000+**
Produced in a variety of styles and calibers, these are collectors' items and bring far higher prices than the sporting types. The Schuetzen Special, which has an under-lever action, is especially rare—perhaps less than 100 having been made.

Remington No. 3 High Power Rifle
Single shot. Hepburn falling-block action with side lever. Calibers: 30-30, 30-40, 32 Special, 32-40, 38-55, 38-72 (high-power cartridges). Barrel: 26, 28 or 30 inches. Weight: 8 pounds. Open sporting sights. Checkered pistol-grip stock and forearm. Made from 1893 to 1907.
Calibers 30-30, 30-40, 32 Special, 32-40......**$1425**
Calibers 38-55, 38-72........................**1750**

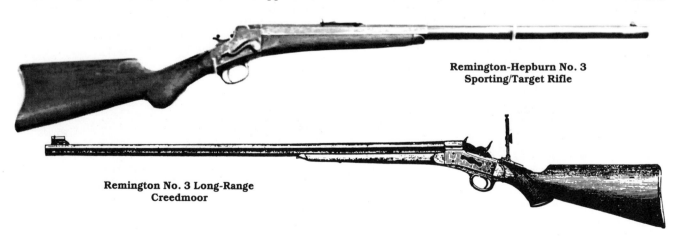

Remington-Hepburn No. 3
Sporting/Target Rifle

Remington No. 3 Long-Range
Creedmoor

Remington No. 4 Single Shot Rifle **$195**
Rolling-block action. Solid frame or takedown. Calibers: 22 Short and Long, 22 Long Rifle, 25 Stevens RF, 32 Short and Long RF. Barrel: 22½ inches; 24 inches (32 cal. only); octagonal. Weight: 4½ pounds. Open rear sight, blade front sight. Plain walnut stock and forearm. Made from 1890 to 1933.

Remington Light Baby Carbine **$325**
Single shot. Rolling-block action. Caliber: 44 Winchester. Barrel: 20 inches. Weight: 5¾ pounds. Open rear sight, blade front sight. Plain straight-grip carbine-stock and forearm, barrel band. Made from 1883 to 1910.

Remington "Split Breech" Carbine **$995**
Two-part breech system. Color casehardened receiver. Calibers: 46 Long RF, 56-50 RF, 56-52 RF. Barrel: 20 inches, blued. Weight: about 7½ pounds. Plain carbine stock. Made from 1865 to 1867.

Remington Springfield Model Rifle **$555**
Casehardened rolling-block action. Caliber: 58 centerfire. Barrel: 36 inches; round, blued. Weight: about 8½ pounds. Straight-grip military walnut stock and forend. Made from 1863 to 1883.

Remington U.S. Navy Carbine **$575**
Caliber: 50 carbine. Barrel: 23½ inches; octagonal, marked with anchor. Weight: about 7½ pounds. Plain carbine stock. Tang marked "Remington, Ilion, N.Y., U.S.A." and also patent dates. Open sights. Approximately 5,000 of these were made in 1867.

Remington-Lee Bolt Action Sporting Rifle
Calibers: 6mm U.S.N., 30-30, 30-40, 7mm Mauser, 7.65 Mauser, 32 Rem., 32-40, 35 Rem., 38-55, 38-72, 405 Win., 43 Spanish, 44-77 Sharps, 45-70, 45-90. Detachable box magazine held 5 cartridges. Barrel: 24 or 26 inches. Weight: 7 pounds. Open rear sight, bead or blade front sight. Walnut stock with checkered pistol grip. Made from 1880 to 1906.
Standard Model **$500**
Deluxe Model **750**

--- *NOTE* ---
A limited number of the Remington-Lee Bolt Action Sporting Rifle models were produced in "Special" Grade and command approximately twice the price of the Standard Grade.

RUSSIAN MILITARY
Various Manufacturers

Russian Model 1891 Mosin-Nagant Bolt Action Rifle **$130**
Nagant-system bolt action. Caliber: 7.62 x 54mm Russian. Five-shot box magazine. Barrel: 31½ inches, round. Weight: about 9 pounds. Open rear sight, blade front sight. Full stock with straight grip. Introduced 1891.

SAVAGE REPEATING ARMS COMPANY
Utica, New York

Arthur W. Savage had experimented with a new type of lever-action rifle for military use before he incorporated his enterprise on April 5, 1894. Although the incorporation was contracted under the laws of West Virginia, the principal offices were located in Utica, N.Y. In December of 1897, the business was re-incorporated under the name of the "Savage Arms Company," under which Savage introduced and made famous the various Savage rifles, some of which are described below.

Savage's success lasted until about 1915, when the Driggs-Seabury Ordnance Co. of Sharon, Penn., bought the business. For a short time, the name was changed to the Driggs-Seabury Corporation, but in 1917 the firm became the Savage Arms Corporation, which is still in operation today in Westfield, Mass.

Savage Model 1892 Repeating Military Rifle **$1595**
Lever-action mechanism with rotary. Nine-shot magazine. Caliber: 30-40 Krag. Barrel: 30 inches. Weight: 10 lbs. 4 oz. Made especially for military use, but was rejected by the U.S. Government in favor of the 30-40 Krag Rifle. Introduced in 1892.

Savage Model 1895 Carbine **$995**
Same general specifications as the 1895 Sporting Rifle, except had a 22-inch barrel, forearm band and saddle ring. Made from 1895 to 1899 at the time of the Savage Model 1899 with an improved action of the same general design as the Model 1895.

Savage Model 1895 Repeating Military Rifle **$995**
Same general specifications as the 1892 Repeating Military Rifle, except had a six-shot magazine and weighed 8¾ pounds. Made from 1895 to 1899.

Savage Model 1895 Sporting Rifle **$850**
Caliber: 303 Savage. Six-shot rotary magazine. Barrels: round, half-octagonal or full-octagonal. Weight: 7 to 7¾ pounds. American walnut stock and forearm. Approximately 5,000 of these rifles were made between 1895 to 1899.

Savage Model 1899 Repeating Military Carbine **$1695**
Same general specifications as the 1899 Military Rifle, except with shorter 22-inch barrel, lighter weight, and carbine barrel band. Made from 1899 to 1908.

Savage Model 1899 Repeating Military Rifle **$1425**
Same general specifications as Model 1899 Sporting Rifle, except had a military stock, 30-inch barrel and bayonet provisions. Made in calibers 303 Savage and later in 30-30. Made from 1899 to 1908.

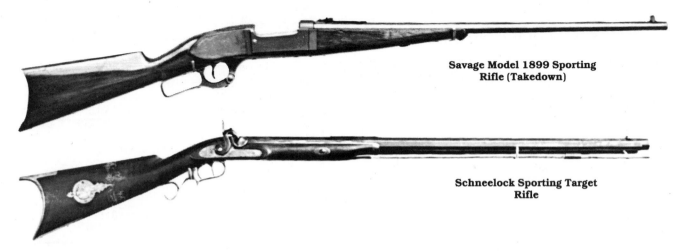

Savage Model 1899 Sporting
Rifle (Takedown)

Schneelock Sporting Target
Rifle

Savage Model 1899 Sporting Rifle.......... **$450**
Hammerless solid frame or takedown. Rotary magazine. Calibers: 303 Savage, 25-35, 30-30, 32-40 and 38-
55; later calibers included 22 Savage Hi-Power, 250-
3000 Savage, and 300 Savage. Barrels: 22 to 26 inches;
round, half-octagonal or full-octagonal. Weight: 7³/₄
pounds average. American stock and forearm with
either crescent or shotgun butt plate; also either
straight or pistol grip. Made from 1899 to date, with
several modifications.

OTTO SCHNEELOCK
Brooklyn, New York

Schneelock Sporting Target Rifle........... **$650**
Caliber: 44 percussion. Barrel: Medium-length, octag-
onal. American walnut stock with large cheekpiece.
German silver fittings. Made 1868 to 1878.

SHARPS RIFLE COMPANY
Hartford, Connecticut

Christian Sharps founded the Sharps Rifle Manufacturing Company in Hartford, where it began operation
in October 1851. After two years of problems with
"management," Sharps himself left the company and
formed another firm under his name in Philadelphia
(see C. Sharps & Co. under Handguns). There for a
short time during the Civil War, he collaborated with
Williams Hankins, producing handguns as well as rifles (see also Sharps & Hankins under Rifles).

The Sharps Rifle Mfg. Company in Hartford, however,
continued to manufacture rifles without any assis-
tance or apparent contact with Christian Sharps, and
in 1874 it changed its name to simply the Sharps Rifle
Company. In 1876 the operation was transferred to
Bridgeport, Conn., where it remained until 1881, when
it folded.

ESTABLISHED 1851.

ARMORY OF

Sharps Rifle Company,

BRIDGEPORT, CONN., U. S. A.

Breech Loading Fire Arms

AND

AMMUNITION.

(OLD RELIABLE.)
TRADE MARK.

EDW. G. WESTCOTT,   CHARLES H. POND,
President.   *Secretary.*

From the Sharps Catalog of 1877.

During the time of their manufacture, the Sharps
"Old Reliable" rifles were considered to be the strong-
est and most accurate of any available. They were used
extensively by buffalo hunters of the day for distance
shots and, as Civil War buffs know, they were instru-
mental in winning the war.

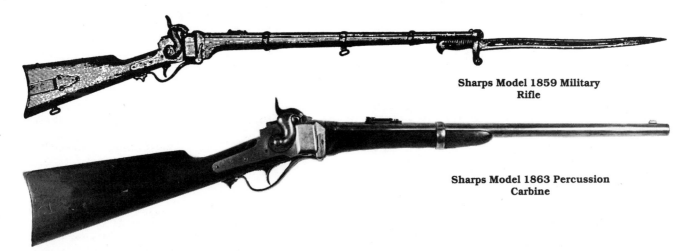

Sharps Model 1859 Military
Rifle

Sharps Model 1863 Percussion
Carbine

Sharps 1851 Boxlock Hunting Rifle. **$2000**
Boxlock action. Calibers: 44 and 36. Barrel: 27 inches. Overall length: 44½ inches. Weight: 9¾ pounds. Some barrels marked "Robbins & Lawrence, Winsdor, Vt." Before manufacturing was conducted in Hartford, Sharps had arranged for Robbins & Lawrence to produce his early rifles. American walnut stock. Introduced in 1851.

**Sharps 1851 "Original" Model Breech-Loading
Percussion Rifle**. **$2800**
Caliber: 52. Percussion, curved lock plate. Heavy barrel with ramrod beneath. American walnut stock. Introduced in 1851.

Sharps 1852 Slanting Breech Carbine **$995**
Caliber: 52 Linen. Barrel: 21½ inches. Overall length: 37¾ inches. Weight: 7¼ pounds. Barrel marked "Sharps Rifle Manufg. Co., Hartford, Conn." Tang and lock plate marked "C. Sharps, Pat. 1878." Introduced in 1852.

**Sharps Model 1855 Slanting Breech
Carbine**. **$1695**
Caliber: 52, with Maynard 1855 primer. Barrel: 21½ inches; six grooves. Overall length: 37¾ inches. Introduced in 1855.

**Sharps Model 1859 Breech-Loading Percussion
Carbine**. **$895**
Same general specifications as the 1859 Vertical Breech Percussion Carbine, except the patch box was omitted and the barrel was marked, "New Model 1859." Introduced in 1859.

**Sharps Model 1859 BL Percussion Military
Rifle**. **$1600**
Caliber: 52 Linen. Same general specifications as the Model 1859 Carbine, except this had a 30-inch barrel and an overall length of 47 inches. Weight: 9 pounds. This model was widely used by Berdan's Sharpshooters during the Civil War. Made from 1859 to 1862.

**Sharps 1859 Vertical Breech Percussion
Carbine**. **$1050**
Caliber: 52. Barrel: 22 inches, with flat brass barrel band. Overall length: 39 inches. Weight: 8 pounds. Rear sight marked "R.S. Lawrence, Patented February 15th, 1859." American walnut stock with brass butt plate and brass patch box. A few stocks supplied for this model were equipped with a coffee mill built into the stock, which was used by military personnel to grind coffee beans in the field. Introduced in 1859.

Sharps Model 1863 BL Percussion Carbine. . **$895**
Caliber: 52 Sharps Linen. Same general specifications as the Model 1859, except the barrel was marked, "New Model 1863." Serial numbers on the tang usually are preceded by the letter "C." Introduced in 1863.

**Sharps Model 1863 BL Percussion Military
Rifle**. **$1625**
Same general specifications as the Model 1863 Carbine, except made with full musket stock and rifle-length barrel.

**Sharps Model 1867 Breech-Loading
Carbine**. **$925**
Caliber: 52 Sharps RF. This carbine was assembled from old percussion gun parts or with surplus parts on hand. Introduced in 1867.

**Sharps Model 1868 Breech-Loading
Sporting Rifle**. **$2100**
Calibers: 40-50, 40-70, 44-77 Sharps and 50-70 Government. Made from 1868 to 1871.

**Sharps Model 1869 Breech-Loading
Carbine**. **$795**
Caliber: 50. Made from existing percussion carbines by replacing the breech block and relining the barrels. Introduced in 1869.

**Sharps Model 1869 Breech-Loading
Military Rifle**. **$1195**
Another alteration, chambered for the 50-70 Government centerfire cartridge. Introduced in 1869.

Sharps Model 1870 Breech-Loading Carbine. **$995**
Same general specifications as the Model 1870 BL Rifle, except made in short carbine style. Chambered for the 50-70 Government cartridge.

Sharps Model 1870 Breech-Loading Military Rifle. **$1125**
Caliber: 50-70 Government. Barrel: 32$\frac{1}{2}$ inches. Another alteration of a percussion rifle, introduced in 1870.

Sharps Model 1873 Creedmoor Rifle. **$3000**
Calibers: 44-90, 44-100 and 44-105 Sharps. Equipped with Vernier peep rear sight for 1000-yard shooting. Made from 1873 to 1874.

Sharps Model 1874
Business Rifle

Sharps Model 1874 Business Rifle. **$2400**
Caliber: 45-70 with 2$\frac{1}{10}$-inch case; 45-120 with 2$\frac{7}{8}$-inch case. Barrel: 28 inches; round; blued. Double-set trigger. Open sights. Plain wood straight stock and forend. Rifle butt. Made from 1877 to 1881.

Sharps 1874 Creedmoor Rifle #1. . . . . **$3000**
Calibers: 44-77 with 2$\frac{1}{4}$ or 2$\frac{7}{16}$-inch BN case; 44-90 with 2$\frac{5}{8}$-inch BN case. Barrel: 32 inches; octagonal or half-octagonal; blued. Weight: just under 10 pounds. Sights: Vernier tang rear; wind-gauge front. Checkered pistol grip stock and forend. Shotgun butt.

Sharps Model 1874 Creedmoor Rifle #2. . . . **$3000**
Calibers: 44-77 with 2$\frac{1}{4}$ or 2$\frac{7}{16}$-inch BN cases; 44-90 with 2$\frac{5}{8}$-inch case. Barrel: 32 inches; octagonal or half-octagonal; blued. Weight: just under 10 pounds. Sights: Vernier tang rear; wind-gauge front. Straight polished stock and forend. Shotgun butt.

Sharps 1874 Creedmoor Rifle #3. . . . . **$3000**
Calibers: 44-77 with 2$\frac{1}{4}$-inch BN case; 44-90 with 2$\frac{5}{8}$-inch BN case. Barrel: 30 inches; octagonal or half-octagonal; blued. Weight: just under 10 pounds. Sights: peep and open. Straight polished stock and forend. Shotgun butt.

Sharps 1874 Creedmoor Rifle #4. . . . . **$3500**
Same general specifications as the 1874 Creedmoor #3, except for a plainer wood rifle butt. Although the Model 1874 rifles were produced between about 1871 to 1881, this Creedmoor #4 was made only for a short time around 1875.

Sharps 1874 Military Rifle. **$1695**
Caliber: 45-70 with 2$\frac{1}{10}$-inch case. Barrel: 30 inches (rifle); 22 inches (carbine); round; blued. Plain straight stock and forend held by bands. Made from 1875 to 1877.

Sharps Model 1875 Rifle. **$20,000**
Only one is known to exist in an engraved version of Creedmoor pattern with extra fancy wood, and deluxe throughout. Hammer is operative like regular side hammer models.

Sharps Model 1876 BL Sporting Rifle. **$2300**
Calibers: 40-50, 40-70, 44-77, 44-90, 50-90 Sharps and 50-70 Government. Barrel: 28 or 30 inches; octagonal. Weight: 8 to 12 pounds. Oil-finished American walnut stock. Introduced in 1876.

Sharps 1876 Long Range Rifle #1. . . . . **$2995**
Calibers: 44-90 (2$\frac{5}{8}$-inch case); 45-90 (2$\frac{4}{10}$-inch case); 45-100 (2$\frac{6}{10}$-inch case). Barrel: 34 inches standard; 32 inches rare; octagonal or half-octagonal; blued. Weight: just under 10 pounds. Sights: Vernier tang rear; spirit level wind-gauge front. Checkered pistol-grip stock and forend of extra fancy wood with sterling silver inscription plate. Made from 1876 to 1881.

Sharps 1876 Long Range Rifle #2. . . . . **$2750**
Same general specifications as the Long Range #1 Rifle, except has plainer wood without inscription plate and wind-gauge front sight is without spirit level. Made from 1876 to 1881.

Sharps 1876 Long Range Rifle #3. . . . . **$2850**
Same general specifications as Long Range #2 Rifle, except has straight, checkered stock and forend. Made from 1876 to 1881.

Sharps Model 1874 Creedmoor
Rifle #1

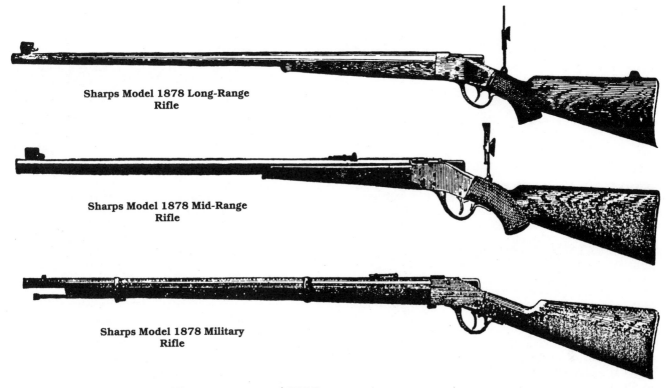

Sharps Model 1878 Long-Range
Rifle

Sharps Model 1878 Mid-Range
Rifle

Sharps Model 1878 Military
Rifle

Sharps 1876 Mid-Range Rifle #1 . . . . **$1995**
Caliber: 40-70 with 2¹/₂-inch case. Barrel: 30 inches;
octagonal or half-octagonal; blued. Weight: 9 pounds.
Sights: Vernier tang rear; wind-gauge spirit level front.
Nickel-plated rifle butt. Checkered pistol grip stock
and forend. Made from 1876 to 1879.

Sharps 1876 Mid-Range Rifle #2 . . . . **$1750**
Same general specifications as Mid-Range Rifle #1, except has plain wood straight stock and forend. Made
from 1876 to 1879.

Sharps 1876 Mid-Range Rifle #3 . . . . **$1900**
Same general specifications as Mid-Range Rifle #2, except in caliber 40-50 with 1⁷/₈-inch case; peep and
globe sights. Made from 1876 to 1879.

Sharps Model 1877 Rifle **$2750**
Side hammer, fourth lock form. With the exception of
the lock, these rifles were offered in three grades identical to the Long Range rifles introduced in 1876.

Sharps Model 1878 Business Rifle **$1295**
Caliber: 40-70 with 2¹/₂-inch case; 40-90 with 2⁵/₈-inch
BN case. Barrel: 28 inches; octagonal; blued. Open
sights. Plain polished American walnut stock and forend. Made from 1879 to 1881.

Sharps Model 1878 Hunter's Rifle **$1495**
Caliber: 40-50 with 1⁷/₈-inch case; 40-70 with 2¹/₂-inch
case. Barrel: 26 inches; round; blued. Open sights.
Plain polished American walnut stock and forend.
Made from 1879 to 1881.

Sharps Model 1878 Express Rifle **$2895**
Caliber: 45-120 with 2⁷/₈-inch case, 293 gr. bullet. Barrel: 26 inches; octagonal; flat-matte top. Borchardt action. Weight: about 9¹/₂ pounds. Sights: two-leaf rear
with platinum lines; long beaded front. Sling staples.
Fancy American walnut checkered pistol-grip stock
and forend. Hard rubber shotgun butt. Made from 1879
to 1881.

Sharps Model 1878 Long Range Rifle **$2650**
Caliber: 45-90 with 2⁴/₁₀-inch case. Barrel: 32 or 34
inches; round; blued finish. English walnut checkered
pistol-grip stock and forend. Hard rubber shotgun butt.
Sights: Vernier rear sight; wind-gauge spirit level front.
Hard rubber or wood paneled receiver. Made from 1878
to 1881.

Sharps Model 1878 Mid Range Rifle **$2300**
Caliber: 40-50 with 1⁷/₈ inch case; 40-70 with 2¹/₂-inch
case. Barrel: 30 inches; round; blued. Weight: about 9
pounds. Sights: Vernier tang rear; wind-gauge spirit
level front and open hunting sights. Checkered pistol-
grip stock and forend. Shotgun butt. Made from 1878
to 1881.

Sharps Model 1878 Military Rifle **$1495**
Caliber: 45-70 with 2¹/₁₀-inch case. Barrel: 32 inches
(rifle); 24 inches (carbine); round; blued. Sling swivel
on under side of action ahead of lever. Sling ring on left
side of action on carbine. Plain military straight stock
and forend. Made from 1878 to 1881.

**Sharps Model 1878 Sporting
Rifle with Double Triggers**

Sharps Model 1878 Officer's Rifle **$3100**
Same length, weight, and caliber as the 1878 Military
Rifle. Medium fancy American walnut stock, closely se-
lected barrels. Receiver inlaid with hard rubber.

Sharps Model 1878 Short Range Rifle. **$3000**
Caliber: 40-50 with $1^7/_8$-inch case; 40-70 with $2^1/_2$-inch
case. Borchardt action. Sights: short Vernier grip rear;
wind-gauge front. Plain American walnut checkered
pistol-grip stock and forend. Hard rubber shotgun butt.

Sharps Model 1878 Sporting Rifle. **$1325**
Caliber: 45-70 with $2^1/_{10}$-inch case; 45-120 with $2^7/_8$-
inch case. Barrel: 30 inches; round or octagonal; blued.
Double triggers. Open sights. Plain polished American
walnut stock and forend. Made from 1879 to 1881.

Sharps Breech-Loading Cartridge Carbine. . . . **$925**
Caliber: 52 Sharps centerfire. Same general specifications as the Model 1863 Percussion Carbine, as the
early cartridge carbines were merely an alteration using the old-style percussion frames. The same breech
block was use, the nipple plugged up with the priming
system milled off.

**Sharps Commercial Breech-Loading
Military Rifle.** **$1200**
Calibers: 52-70 and 50-67-487 Sharps. Barrel: 30
inches. Overall length: 47 inches. Weight: 11 pounds.
This rifle was assembled about 1867 from recovered
percussion actions.

**Sharps & Hankins Model 1861
Navy Rifle**

SHARPS & HANKINS
Philadelphia, Pennsylvania

Christian Sharps and William Hankins collaborated
during the Civil War to produce handguns and long
arms primarily for military use. Sharps had before this
time organized the Sharps Rifle Manufacturing Company (*see* separate listing), which had nothing to do
with the Sharps & Hankins operation in Philadelphia.
In about 1853, Sharps had left Hartford and started
his own business called C. Sharps & Co. in Philadel-

phia. After the war, Sharps again went alone in his pursuit of producing firearms under his former name and
stayed in business in the "City of Brotherly Love" until
he died in 1874.

Sharps & Hankins Model 1861 Navy Rifle . . **$1200**
Civil War breechloader based on Sharps patent of 1859.
Caliber: 52 RF. Barrel: $32^1/_2$ inches. Overall length: $47^1/_2$
inches. Weight: $8^1/_2$ pounds. Lug under barrel for saber
bayonet. Walnut stock. Made in limited quantity for a
short period from 1861 to 1862.

Sharps & Hankins Model 1862
Cavalry Carbine

**Sharps & Hankins Model 1862 Cavalry
Carbine**. **$925**
Civil War breechloader. Caliber: 52 RF. Barrel: 19
inches. Overall length: 33⅝ inches. Weight: 7½
pounds. Walnut stock. Introduced in 1862.

SMITH ARMS
Chicopee Falls, Massachusetts

Smith carbines were manufactured by the Massachusetts Arms Co. This firm was founded by Daniel B. Wesson to manufacture percussion revolvers based on Edwin Wesson patents. The company had several U.S. Government contracts during the Civil War, making Green, Maynard and Smith percussion carbines. For further information, *see* specifications under U.S. Military Single Shot Breechloading Carbines.

SMITH & WESSON
Springfield, Massachusetts

S&W Model .320 Caliber Revolving Rifle. . . . **$1500**
Double-action revolver frame, blued or nickel-plated. Caliber: 320 S&W Rifle. Barrels: 16, 18 or 20 inches. Open sights with optional tang peep sight. Weight: about 6 pounds. Circassian detachable walnut buttstock. Mottled hard rubber forend. Approximately 1,000 of these were made between 1880 and 1887.

J. STEVENS ARMS & TOOL CO.
Chicopee Falls, Massachusetts

Joshua Stevens started out as a toolmaker in Chester, Mass., his home town, then went to work for Cyrus Allen, a gunmaker in Springfield, Mass. For a short time he was employed by a small arms manufacturer in Hartford, Conn. before moving to Chicopee Falls, where he began working for the Massachusetts Arms Company.

At age 50, after receiving a patent on a simple breechloading single shot pistol, Stevens decided to start his own arms making business, J. Stevens & Company. The first plant was located in a converted grist mill along the Chicopee River and produced a small single shot pistol in pocket and vest pocket models, based on Stevens' patent of September 6, 1864. It also turned out precision machinists' tools, which probably kept the company afloat in its early days.

In 1886, the company was incorporated as the J. Stevens Arms & Tool Company. By this time, Stevens was building target rifles and introduced many new cartridges to the shooting fraternity of a century or more ago. Of the Stevens rifle series, the Old Model Pocket rifles were among the first. These rifles were very light in weight (and strength), and eventually were followed by the heavier target rifles. The firm manufactured the Stevens Tip-Up or "Favorite" 22 single shot rifle, a popular arm of the day. All of the Stevens rifles are choice among today's collectors.

Joshua Stevens remained with the firm until 1896 when he sold his interests in the business. The J. Stevens Arms & Tool Company became a subsidiary of Savage Arms in 1936.

Stevens No. 2 Single Shot
Rifle

(Illustration courtesy Savage Arms)

Although today a subsidiary of Savage Arms, the J. Stevens & Co. enterprise was launched in 1864 in an old grist mill along the Chicopee River. For many years, it produced popular pocket rifles and was one of the leading arms manufacturers of its time.

Stevens No. 1 Single Shot Rifle **$225**
Tip up, exposed hammer. Calibers: 32, 38, and 44 rimfire or centerfire. Barrel: 24 to 30 inches, octagonal. Weight: about 8$\frac{1}{2}$ pounds. Open rear sight; blade front sight. Nickel-plated frame and buttplate. Plain straight grip, oiled walnut stock; no forend. Made from 1888 to 1902.

Stevens No. 2 Single Shot Rifle **$195**
Tip up, exposed hammer. Same general specifications as Single Shot No. 1 Rifle, except chambered for 22 Long Rifle RF and weight is 6$\frac{1}{2}$ to 7$\frac{1}{2}$ pounds. Made from 1888 to 1902. (*See* photo, preceding page.)

Stevens No. 3 Single Shot Rifle **$200**
Tip-up action. Calibers: 32, 38 and 44 RF. Barrel: 24 to 30 inches; full or half-octagonal. Weight: 6$\frac{1}{4}$ to 8$\frac{1}{4}$ pounds. Folding-type combination front sight with pin-head bead inside a globe and a blade for hunting; tang rear peep sight. Plain straight-grip walnut stock; no forend. Made from 1888 to 1895.

Stevens No. 4 Tip-Up Single Shot Rifle **$200**
Same general specifications as the No. 3 Single Shot Rifle, except chambered for 22 Short RF only. Half or full octagonal barrel.

Stevens No. 5 Tip-Up Expert Single Shot Rifle **$245**
Tip up, exposed hammer. Calibers: 22, 25 and 32 RF; also 32-20, 38-40 and 44-40. Barrel: 24, 26, 28 or 30 inches; half-octagonal. Weight: 5$\frac{1}{2}$ to 6$\frac{1}{2}$ pounds, depending on barrel length. Vernier peep rear sight; leaf middle sight; Beach combination front sight. Plain straight-grip stock. Finger ring rest on lower tang. Crescent butt plate; no forearm. Made from 1888 to 1902. (*See* photo, next page.)

Stevens No. 6 Tip-Up Expert Single Shot Rifle **$265**
Tip up, exposed hammer. Same general specifications as No. 5 Tip-Up Expert Single Shot Rilfe, except for fancy finish.

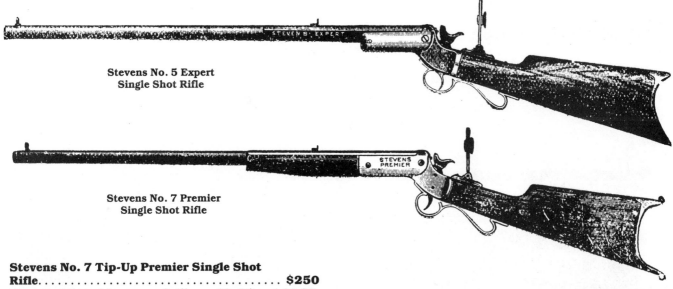

Stevens No. 5 Expert
Single Shot Rifle

Stevens No. 7 Premier
Single Shot Rifle

**Stevens No. 7 Tip-Up Premier Single Shot
Rifle**. **$250**
Tip up, exposed hammer. Calibers: 22, 25 and 32 RF;
32-20, 38-40, and 44-40. Barrel: 24, 26, 28 or 30 inches;
half-octagonal. Weight: 5$\frac{1}{2}$ to 6$\frac{3}{4}$ pounds, depending
on barrel length. Vernier and open rear sights and also
globe sight. Plain straight-grip stock and forend. Finger ring rest on lower tang. Swiss-type butt plate. Made
from 1888 to 1902.

**Stevens No. 8 Tip-Up Premier Single Shot
Rifle**. **$225**
Tip up, exposed hammer model. Basically the same
specifications as the No. 7 Premier, except in fancier
grade finish.

**Stevens No. 9 Single Shot Tip-Up Range
Model** **$195**
Tip up, exposed hammer. Calibers: 32, 38 and 44 RF or
Centerfire; 32, 38 and 44 Everlasting CF, 22-10-45, 32-
35 Stevens. Barrel: 24 to 30 inches; half-octagonal or
octagonal; other lengths available up to 36 inches.
Weight: 7 to 9$\frac{1}{4}$ pounds. Straight-grip stock.
Schuetzen-type butt plate. Made from 1886 to 1902.

**Stevens No. 10 Single Shot Tip-Up Range
Rifle**. **$225**
Same general specifications as the No. 9 Range Model,
except for fancy stock and checkering.

Stevens No. 11 Single Shot Ladies Rifle **$200**
Same general specifications as the No. 8 and No. 9
Range Rifles, except for smaller stock, smaller forearm
and lighter barrel. Caliber: 22 RF and 25 Stevens. Made
from 1888 to 1900.

Stevens No. 12 Single Shot Ladies Rifle **$295**
Same general specifications as the No. 11 Ladies Rifle,
except for extra fancy oil-finished stock. Both the stock
and forend were checkered. Made from 1888 to about
1900.

Stevens No. 13 Single Shot Ladies Rifle **$250**
Same general specifications as No. 11 Ladies Rifle, except for Beach combination front sight and Vernier
peep rear sight mounted on upper tang. Made from
1888 to 1902.

Stevens No. 14 Single Shot Ladies Rifle **$325**
Same general specifications as No. 13 Ladies Rifle, except for fancy checkered stock and forend. Made from
about 1888 to 1895.

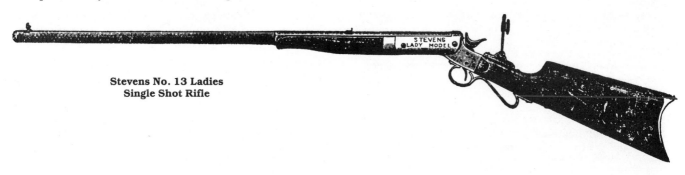

Stevens No. 13 Ladies
Single Shot Rifle

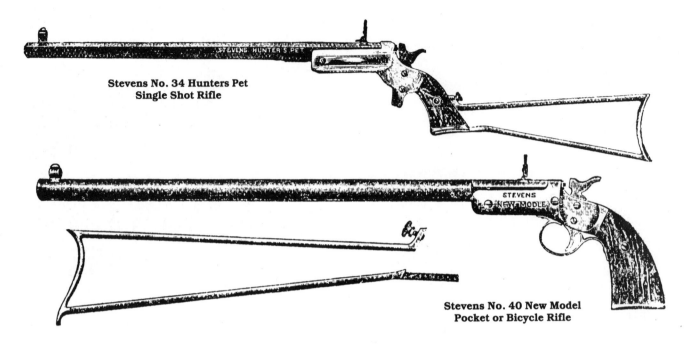

Stevens No. 34 Hunters Pet
Single Shot Rifle

Stevens No. 40 New Model
Pocket or Bicycle Rifle

Stevens No. 15 Crack Shot Single Shot Rifle. **$175**
Single shot. Calibers: 22, 25, 32, 38 and 44 RF; also 25, 32, 38 and 44 centerfire. Barrel: 24, 26, 28 and 30 inches; octagonal. Weight: 6½ to 8¾ pounds. Sights: Lyman ivory bead front sight and Lyman combination rear sight on tang. Plain straight stock and forend. Made from 1900 to 1938.

Stevens No. 16 Crack Shot Single Shot Rifle. **$165**
Rolling-block action. Takedown. Calibers: 22 and 32 RF. Barrel: 20 inches, round. Weight: 3¾ pounds. Blade front sight and dovetail non-adjustable rear sight on barrel. Made from 1900 to 1913.

Stevens No. 17 Favorite Single Shot Rifle . . . **$125**
Swinging block, lever operated. Takedown. Calibers: 22, 25 and 32 RF. Barrel: 22 inches, half-octagonal; 24 inches, round or octagonal; other lengths were available. Weight: about 4½ pounds. Casehardened receiver; blued receiver optional. Early models were non-automatic ejecting. Open rear sight, Rocky Mountain front sight. Plain straight-grip stock, small tapered forearm. Made from 1889 to 1935.

Stevens No. 18 Favorite Single Shot Rifle . . . **$180**
Same general specifications as No. 17 Favorite, except has Vernier peep rear sight, left middle sight, Beach combination front sight. Made from 1895 to 1917.

Stevens No. 19 Favorite Single Shot Rifle . . . **$195**
Same general specifications as the No. 17 Favorite, except has Lyman combination rear sight, leaf sight, Lyman front sight. Made from 1895 to 1917.

Stevens No. 23 Sure Shot Rifle **$350**
Single-shot takedown model. Caliber: 22 RF. Barrel: 20 inches, round. Weight: 3½ pounds. Conventional trigger. Detachable butt stock. Made in the 1890s.

Stevens No. 34 Hunters Pet Pocket Single Shot Rifle. **$175**
Tip-up action. Calibers: all pistol cartridges ranging from 22 short to 44 WCF. Barrel: 18, 20, 22 or 24 inches; half or full octagonal; other lengths available up to 36 inches. Weight: about 5¾ pounds with 18-inch barrel. Spur trigger. Sights: combination globe and blade rear; combination peep and V-notch adjustable for elevation only. Walnut grips. Detachable shoulder rest. Brass or iron nickel-plated frame. Made from 1872 to 1900.

Stevens No. 40 New Model Pocket or Bicycle Rifle. **$225**
Single shot. Tip-up action. Calibers: 22 Long Rifle, 22 WRF, 22 Stevens-Pope, 25 Stevens, 32 Long RF or CF. Barrel: 10, 12, 15 or 18 inches; half or full octagonal. Iron frame nickel-plated. Sights: combination globe front and blade rear; folding combination peep and V-notch, adjustable for elevation. Conventional trigger. Walnut grips. Detachable nickel-plated shoulder stock. Made 1896 to 1916.

Stevens No. 44 Ideal Single Shot Rifle. **$390**
Rolling block, lever operated. Takedown. Calibers: 22 Long Rifle, 25 RF, 32 RF, 25-20, 32-20, 32-40, 38-40, 38-55, 44-40. Barrel: 24 and 26 inches in round, half-octagonal or full-octagonal. Weight: about 7 pounds with 26-inch round barrel. Open rear sight, Rocky Mountain front sight. Plain straight-grip stock and forearm. Made from 1894 to 1932.

Stevens Sporting Single
Shot Rifle

Stevens No. 44¹/₂ Ideal Single Shot Rifle **$495**
Falling-block, lever operated. Practically the same
specifications as the Model No. 44 Ideal.

Stevens No. 45 Ideal Range Model **$225**
Same general specifications as the No. 44 Ideal, available
in many calibers with Beach combination front
and open rear sights, Vernier tang and Swiss butt plate.
Made 1896 to 1916.

**Stevens Central Fire Sporting Single Shot
Rifle**. **$180**
Similar specifications to the rimfire Sporting Single
Shot Rifle, except adapted to centerfire cartridges: 38-
33 Stevens, 38-45 Stevens, 44-50 Stevens, 44-65 Stevens,
38 long and extra long special cartridges made by
the Union Metallic Cartridge Co., and the UMC 44 long
or extra long centerfire. Made from 1875 to about 1888.

**Stevens Hunters Pet Pocket Centerfire Single Shot
Rifle**. **$175**
Same general specifications as the No. 34 standard
Hunters Pet, except adapted to centerfire cartridges.
Made from 1877 to 1897.

Stevens Old Model Pocket Single Shot Rifle. . **$210**
Tip-up action. Caliber: 22 Short or 22 Long RF. Barrel:
8 or 10 inches; half-octagonal. Lightweight brass
frame. Weight: about 11 ounces with 10-inch barrel.
Spur trigger. Rosewood or walnut pistol-grip stock,
with detachable skeleton stock either nickel-plated or
Japanned finish. No forend. This was the first of the
Stevens pocket rifles and is basically a long-barreled
version of the Old Model Pocket Pistol. Made from 1869
to 1886.

Stevens Sporting Single Shot Rifle. **$175**
Tip-up action. Calibers: 22, 32, 38 and 44 RF. Barrel: 24
to 36 inches, octagonal. Weight: 6¹/₂ pounds with 24-
inch barrel. Nickel-plated frame. Standard non-adjustable
sights; adjustable sights were fitted on special order.
Made from 1872 to about 1888.

Swiss Model 1871 Vetterli
Bolt Action Rifle

SWISS MILITARY
Various Manufacturers

Swiss Model 1871 Vetterli Bolt Action Rifle . **$250**
Caliber: 10.5mm. Full-length military stock. Iron furniture.
Stamped "WAFFENFABRIK BERN."

Swiss Model 1891 Military Rifle. **$130**
Same specifications as the Russian Mosin-Nagant. Caliber:
7.62 x 54mm Russian. Five-shot box magazine.
Barrel: 31¹/₂ inches, round. Weight: about 9 pounds.
Open rear sight, blade front sight. Full stock with
straight grip. Introduced 1891.

TURKISH MILITARY
Various Manufacturers

Turkish Mauser Model 1903 Military Rifle . . **$125**
Caliber: 8x57mm. Five-shot magazine. Straight bolt.
Barrel: 23¹/₂ inches, round. Weight: 8¹/₂ pounds. Blade
front sight, adjustable rear sight. Walnut, military-type
stock. Mauser trademark on receiver ring.

WHITNEY ARMS COMPANY
New Haven, Connecticut

The original Whitney firearms business was founded by Eli Whitney, born in 1763 and today well-known as the inventor of the cotton gin. Many of Whitney's patents were used by other manufacturers, but Whitney also manufactured several models under his own name.

Eli Whitney established his firearms factory in 1798 in Hampton, Conn., when he received a Government contract for 10,000 muskets to be delivered within two years. He received another contract for 15,000 muskets and a few years later, an additional contract for 3,000 more. His fourth contract called for still another 15,000 muskets.

On January 8, 1825, Whitney died in New Haven, and his two nephews, Philos and Eli Whitney Blake carried on the business. Eli Whitney Jr. came into control of the business in 1841, and the following year he was offered a Government contract for the Whitney Navy Percussion Musket, which was the first percussion arm made by the Whitney Company.

The Whitney Arms Co. continued to make muskets, rifles, carbines and revolvers for the government, as well as some sporting arms. The last rifles made were Kennedy magazine rifles, patented January 7, 1873. The Whitney plant ceased operation in 1888.

Whitney Creedmoor No. 1 Long Range Rifle . . **$945**
Calibers: 44-90, 44-100 and 44-105 Sharps necked. Barrel: 32 or 34 inches; octagonal or half-octagonal. Deluxe stock with checkered pistol grip and forearm. Vernier and wind-gauge sights.

Whitney Creedmoor No. 2 Mid-Range Rifle . . . **$745**
Calibers: 40-50 to 40-90 Sharps straight. Barrel: 30 or 32 inches; octagonal, half-octagonal or round. Checkered pistol-grip stock and forearm. Vernier peep rear and wind-gauge front sights.

Whitney Gallery Rifle **$625**
Caliber: 22 short or long RF. Barrel: 24 or 26 inches. Same general type of action as the Whitney Sporting and Target Rifle. Equipped either with inexpensive or deluxe sights. Weight: 7½ to 8½ pounds.

Whitney Light Carbine **$675**
Calibers: 44 Henry RF, 44 Short RF, 44 S&W, 46 Long RF. Barrel: 19½ inches. Weight: 5 pounds. This was widely used as a saddle weapon.

Whitney Military Carbine **$695**
Calibers: 43 Spanish Mauser centerfire, 45-70 Government and 50-70 Government. Barrel: 20½ inches, round. Overall length: 36 inches. Weight: 7 lbs. 2 oz. This model was built the same as the rifle.

Whitney Military Rifle **$640**
Caliber: 43 Spanish Mauser centerfire, 45-70 and 50-70 Government. Barrel: 35 inches; 32½ inches in 50/70 Govt. Overall length: 50½ inches with 35-inch barrel. Weight: 9 pounds.

Whitney Phoenix Gallery Rifle **$745**
Caliber: 22 short or long. Barrel: 24 inches; octagonal or half-octagonal. Weight: 7 to 8½ pounds.

Whitney Phoenix Military Carbine **$845**
Calibers: same as for the Phoenix Military Rifle. Barrel: 20½ inches. Weight: 7 pounds. Half-stock with carbine-type butt plate and ring on the side of the receiver.

Whitney Phoenix Military Rifle **$800**
Calibers: 43 Spanish Mauser centerfire, 45-70 Government and 50-70 Government. Barrel: 35 inches. Weight: 9 pounds. Full rifle stock.

Whitney Phoenix Sporting & Target Rifle **$895**
Calibers: 38 long or extra long RF, 44 long or extra long RF, 40-50 Sharps necked, 40-70 Sharps necked centerfire, 44-60 Sharps necked, 44-70 Sharps necked, 44-90, 44-100, 44-105 Sharps necked, 45-70 Government and 50-70 Government. Barrel: 26 to 30 inches; round or octagonal. Weight: 7 to 10 pounds.

Whitney Phoenix-Schuetzen Target Rifle **$910**
Caliber: 38 extra long centerfire and Sharps straight. Barrel: 30 or 32 inches; octagonal or half-octagonal. Weight: 10 to 12 pounds. Sights: Vernier peep rear; wind-gauge front. Walnut stock with checkered grip and forearm. Nickel-plated butt plate.

Whitney Sporting & Target Rifle **$425**
Calibers: 38 Long Centerfire, 38-40 WCF, 44-60 Sharps, 44-77 Sharps necked, 40-50 and 40-70 Sharps straight, 40-90 Sharps straight, 44-40 WCF, 45-70 Government, 50-70 Government; 32 short or long RF, 32-20 WCF, 38 long RF, and 44 long RF. Barrel: 26 to 32 inches; round and octagonal. Weight: 7½ pounds.

Whitney-Burgess Repeating Military Carbine **$2195**
Caliber: 45-70 Government. Seven-shot tubular magazine. Barrel: 22 inches. Weight: 7½ pounds. Full stock.

Whitney-Burgess Repeating Military Rifle . . **$2100**
Caliber: 45-70 Government. Barrel: 33 inches, round. Full stock with an 11-round tubular magazine enclosed in the forearm beneath the barrel. Weight: 9 lbs. 1 oz.

Whitney-Burgess Repeating Sporting Rifle **$1895**
Caliber: 45-70 Government. Barrel: 28 inches, round or octagonal. Nine-shot tubular magazine. Weight: 9 to 10 pounds. Introduced in 1879.

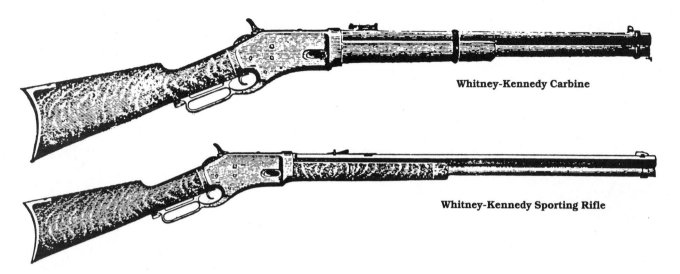

Whitney-Kennedy Carbine

Whitney-Kennedy Sporting Rifle

Whitney-Kennedy Repeating Military Rifle... **$700**
Calibers: 44-40 WCF and 45-60 WCF. Seventeen- and 13-shot magazine. Barrel: 30 inches, round. Weight: 9 pounds.

**Whitney-Kennedy Repeating Sporting
Carbine**.................................. **$725**
Calibers: same calibers as the Whitney-Kennedy Repeating Sporting Rifle. Barrel: 20 inches, round. Weight: 7 lbs. 4 oz.

Whitney-Kennedy Repeating Sporting Rifle.. **$695**
Calibers: 32-20, 38-40, 40-60 WCF, 44 centerfire, 44-40, 45-60 WCF, 45-75 WCF, 50-95 Express. Barrel: 24, 26 or 28 inches, depending on caliber; octagonal or round. Weight: 9 to $9^{1}/_{2}$ pounds, depending on shape and length of barrel.

**Winchester Model 1866
Saddle Ring Carbine**

WINCHESTER REPEATING ARMS CO.
New Haven, Connecticut

Although Oliver F. Winchester had offered financial backing to firearms makers earlier, he did not meet with financial success until he hired an engineering genius named B. Tyler Henry. A resident of Windsor, Vt., Henry completely revolutionized the firearms industry with the .44 Henry cartridge and a complementary lever-action repeater known as the .44 Henry Rifle. This popular arm was based on U.S. Patent No. 30,446, granted to Henry on October 16, 1860, and later assigned to Oliver Winchester. In 1860, Winchester's firm, the New Haven Arms Company, concentrated on this one rifle, producing numerous grades in quality—from the plainest to the most elaborately decorated and engraved.

In 1866, with his firearms business flourishing, Winchester decided to terminate the affairs of the New Haven Arms Co. and expand the business under his own name. The Winchester Repeating Arms Company was based in Bridgeport, Conn., where it operated until 1870. At that time a new plant was built in New Haven and the firm moved back to Winchester's home town. From then on, and well into the 20th century, the Winchester Company thrived, developing many successful rifles and shotguns. At one time, it was the largest manufacturer of firearms in the world.

**Winchester Model 1866 Lever-Action
Carbine**................................... **$1895**
Same general specifications as the Model 1866 Rifle, except manufactured with a 20-inch barrel and 13-shot magazine, barrel bands, and saddle ring on left side. Weight: 7 lbs. 12 oz.

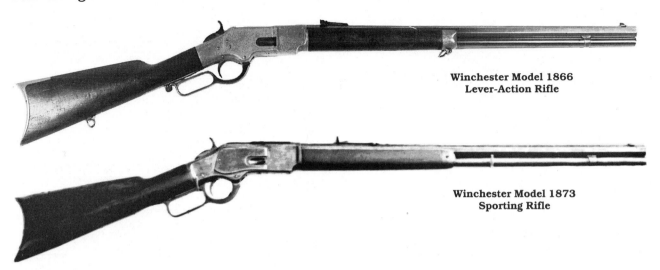

Winchester Model 1866
Lever-Action Rifle

Winchester Model 1873
Sporting Rifle

Winchester Model 1866 Lever-Action Military Musket **$2000**
Same general specifications as the Model 1866 Rifle, except it was fitted with a 27-inch barrel, had a 17-shot magazine, and weighed 8 lbs. 4 oz. A full-length military-type stock was attached by two barrel bands and was equipped with either triangular or saber-type bayonets. These muskets were manufactured mostly for the Turkish Government.

Winchester Model 1866 Lever-Action Rifle **$2400**
The original brass-frame model was made only in 44 Henry rimfire. Barrel: 24 inches; octagonal, half-octagonal, and round. Overall length: 43 inches. Barrel marked "Winchester's Repeating Arms, Bridgeport, Conn." and later "New Haven, Conn., King's Improvement, Pat. March 29, 1866, Oct. 16, 1860." Weight: 8 lbs. 6 oz. Open, adjustable rear sights, fixed blade front sight. American walnut stock and forend with crescent butt plate. Approximately 170,100 of these rifles were made between 1866 and 1898.

Winchester Model 1873 Carbine **$2800**
Same as standard Model 1873 Rifle, except has a 20-inch barrel, 12-shot magazine and weighs 7¼ pounds.

Winchester Model 1873 Fancy Sporting Rifle **$2100**
Same general specifications as standard Model 73 Rifle, except made with casehardened receiver and trimmings, pistol-grip stock of selected walnut, octagonal barrel or half-octagonal in most cases.

Winchester Model 1873 Lever-Action Sporting Rifle **$1500**
Solid frame. Calibers: 22 RF; 32-20, 38-40 and 44-40. 15-shot full magazine; 6-shot half-magazine. Barrel: 24 inches; round, half-octagonal, and octagonal. Weight: about 8½ pounds. Open rear sight, bead or blade front sight. Plain straight-grip stock and forearm. 720,610 rifles of this model manufactured from 1873 to 1924.

During the last half of the 19th century, the Apache Indians of the American Southwest were fond of Winchester rifles. Not only did the long arms aid them in their buffalo hunts, the guns also provided them with the lethal weapons to destroy unwanted intruders in their territories. Here Apache Warrior, Nabakala, readies a Winchester 1873 Sporting Rifle.

Winchester Model 1885
Hi-Wall Single Shot Rifle

Winchester Model 1873 Rifle—One of One Thousand............................ $25,000+

During the late 1870s Winchester offered Model 73 rifles of superior accuracy and extra finish, designated "One of One Thousand" grade at a price of $100 each. These rifles are marked "1 of 1000" or "One of One Thousand." Only 136 are known to have been manufactured. This is one of the rarest of shoulder arms, and because so few have been sold in recent years, it is extremely difficult to assign a value. One such rifle—in perfect condition—was sold at a New York auction in 1981 for about $35,000. Beware of fakes!

Winchester Model 1885 Single Shot Engraved Rifle .... $2500 to $5000

Same general specifications as standard grade 1885 Rifle, except fancy-grade American walnut stock, and various grades of metal engraving. Some furnished with set triggers and other luxuries.

Winchester Model 1885 Single Shot Fancy Grade Rifle.................................... $1895

Same general specifications as standard grade 1885 Rifle, except fancy grade checkered walnut stock and forearm.

Winchester Model 1885 Single Shot Hi-Wall Rifle.................................... $795

Solid frame or takedown. Caliber: practically all calibers used at the time. Plain trigger, standard lever. Barrel: No. 3, No. 4, and No. 5; round, half-octagonal, or full-octagonal. Weight: 9½ pounds average. Open rear sight, blade front sight. Plain American walnut stock and forearm.

Winchester Model 1885 Single Shot Low-Wall Rifle............................ $595

Solid frame. The low-wall model was used mainly for low-powered small calibers such as 22 RF, 22 Win. Centerfire, etc. Barrel: No. 1 lightweight, 28 inches round, or octagonal. Weight: 7 pounds. Open rear sight, blade front sight. Plain American walnut stock and forearm.

Winchester Model 1885 Single Shot Musket................................... $495

Same general specifications as the 1885 Winder Musket, except solid-frame low-wall receiver and Lyman rear peep sight. The U.S. Government purchased a large quantity of these muskets during World War I for training purposes.

Winchester Model 1885 Single Shot Schuetzen Rifle.................................... $2400

Solid frame or takedown. High-wall receiver. Calibers: various, but most common is 38-55. Double-set triggers, spur finger lever. Barrel: No. 3 weight; 30 inches, octagonal. Weight: 12 pounds. Vernier rear peep sight, wind-gauge front sight. Fancy walnut Schuetzen stock with checkered pistol grip and forearm. Schuetzen butt plate. Adjustable palm rest.

Winchester Model 1885 Single Shot Winder Musket................................... $595

Solid frame or takedown. High-wall receiver. Calibers: 22 Short, 22 Long Rifle. Barrel: 28 inches, round. Weight: 8½ pounds. Musket rear sight, blade front sight. Plain trigger. Standard finger lever. Military-type stock and forearm.

Winchester Model 1886 Carbine........... $4000

Same general specifications as standard Model 1886, except furnished with 22-inch barrel, carbine stock and forearm, and saddle ring on left-hand side of receiver. Very few of these carbines were made in the Model 1886, and it is estimated that less than 500 of these are now in circulation.

Winchester Model 1886 Fancy Sporting Rifle.................................... $2800

Same general specification as the standard 1886 Sporting Rifle, except had fancy walnut checkered pistol-grip stock and forend.

Winchester Model 1886 Lightweight Rifle .. $1295

Same general specifications as the standard 1886 Sporting Rifle, except furnished with lightweight, rapid-taper barrel; 22 inches in 45-70 and 24 inches in 33 Winchester, in both solid frame and takedown. Made from about 1898 to 1935.

Winchester Model 1886
Saddle Ring Carbine

Winchester Model 1886
Sporting Rifle

Winchester Model 1892
Lever Action Sporting Rifle

Winchester Model 1886 Sporting Rifle $1250
Solid frame or takedown. Caliber: (in order of introduction) 45-70, 45-90, 40-82, 40-65, 38-56, 50-110 Express, 40-70, 38-70, 50-100 and 33 WCF. Eight-shot tubular magazine; 4-shot half-magazine. Barrel: 26 inches; round, half-octagonal, and octagonal was standard. Other lengths were available on special order; odd-length barrels bring a premium price. Weight: from 7½ pounds and up. Plain walnut stock and forearm, straight grip. Crescent and shotgun butt plate. Early models had casehardened receivers, hammer, lever, butt plate and forend cap; balance of gun blued. Made from 1886 to 1935.

**Winchester Model (18)90 Slide Action
Repeater $895**
Visible hammer, solid frame or takedown. Calibers: 22 Short, Long, Long Rifle, 22 WCF. Tubular magazine. Barrel: 24 inches, octagonal. Weight: 5¾ pounds. Open rear sight, bead front sight. Plain straight-grip stock, grooved slide handle. Made from 1890 to 1932.

**Winchester Model (18)90 Slide Action Repeater
Fancy Grade $1095**
Same general specifications as standard Model 90, except furnished with fancy grade walnut pistol-grip stock. Made from 1890 to 1932.

Winchester Model 1892 Carbine $795
Same general specifications as the standard 1892 Sporting Rifle, except had 20-inch barrel, carbine stock and forearm, barrel bands and saddle ring. Weight: about 5¾ pounds. Made from 1892 to 1941.

**Winchester Model 1892 Fancy Engraved
Models . . . . $2500 to $5000**
Same general specifications as standard 1892 models, except had fancy-grade walnut stock and forend with higher grades of checkering and engraved receiver parts, sometimes extending a short distance onto the barrel.

**Winchester Model 1892 Fancy Sporting
Rifle. $1295**
Same general specifications as standard Model 1892 Sporting Rifle, except fancy walnut stock with checkered pistol grip and forend.

**Winchester Model 1892 Lever Action Repeating
Sporting Rifle $495**
Solid frame or takedown. 13-shot magazine. Calibers: 25-20, 32-20, 38-40 and 44-40. Barrel: 24 inches; half-octagonal or octagonal. Weight: 6¾ pounds. Open rear sight, bead or blade front sight. American walnut, straight-grip stock and forend. 1,004,067 of these were made between 1892 and 1932.

**Winchester Model 1892 Long Barrel
Models $1500**
Longer barrel lengths up to 36 inches were available at extra cost. However, this option was discontinued by the Winchester factory in 1908.

Winchester Model 1892 Musket $825
Same general specifications as standard sporting rifle except 30 inch round barrel, 17-shot magazine, and weighed 8 pounds. Musket stock and barrel bands.

**Winchester Model 1892 Short Barrel
Model $1500**
Shorter barrel lengths were available in the Model 1892; that is, 14, 15, 16 and 18 inches. These short-barreled models were sometimes called Trapper Carbines, but were used mainly by the rubber industry in South America.

Winchester Model 1894 Carbine $295
Same general specifications as standard Model 94 Rifle, except furnished with 20-inch barrel, carbine-style forend (long and short), and straight-grip buttstock with shotgun butt plate. Made in 30-30, 32 Special, and 25-35 from 1894 to 1950; the 25-35 was dropped from the line in 1936, reinstated in 1940 and again dropped in 1950. Both the 30-30 and 32 Special remained until 1964 when the model went through some modifications, and only the 30-30 remained thereafter. The Winchester Model 94 was the first sporting rifle to exceed 1,000,000 in sales. Pre-War Model (before 1941) bring a premium price of perhaps 25 percent more than those manufactured between 1945 and 1964.

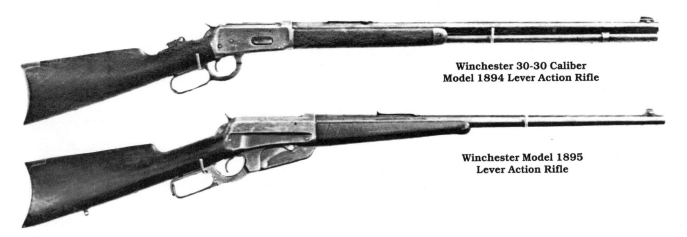

Winchester 30-30 Caliber
Model 1894 Lever Action Rifle

Winchester Model 1895
Lever Action Rifle

Winchester Model 1894 Fancy Sporting
Rifle $995
Same general specifications as standard 1894 Rifle, except furnished with fancy grade walnut checkered stock and forend.

Winchester Model 1894 Repeating Rifle $450
Solid frame or takedown. Lever action. Calibers: 25-35, 30-30, 32 Win. Special, 32-40 and 38-55. Eight-shot magazine. Barrel: 26 inches; round, half-octagonal or octagonal. Extra length barrels up to 36 inches were also furnished at extra cost. Weight: 7 1/2 pounds average. Plain, straight-grip stock and forend. Crescent or shotgun-type butt plates. Made from 1894 to 1936.

Winchester Model 1894 Saddle Ring
Carbine $595
Same general specifications as standard Model 94, except furnished with 20-inch barrel, carbine stock and forend, barrel bands, and saddle ring on left-hand side of receiver. Made from 1894 to 1925.

Winchester Model 1895 Carbine $995
Same general specifications as standard 1895 Rifle, except had 28-inch barrel and carbine stock and forend.

Winchester Model 1895 Fancy Sporting
Rifle $995
Same general specifications as standard 1895 Rifle, except with fancy-grade walnut checkered pistol-grip stock.

Winchester Model 1895 Musket $895
Same general specifications as standard 1895 Rifle, except had 28-inch round barrel and total weight of 9 3/4 pounds.

Winchester Model 1895 Repeating Rifle $695
Solid frame or takedown. Non-detachable six-shot box magazine. Lever action. Calibers: 30 US Army (30-40 Krag), 38-72, 40-72, 303 British, 35 Winchester, 405 Winchester, 30-03 Government, and 30-06. A number of these were also made for the Russian Government chambered for 7.63mm Russian. Barrel: 26 inches; round, half-octagonal or octagonal. Weight: 7 1/2 pounds. Walnut stock and forend. Crescent or shotgun butt plate. 425,881 were made between 1895 and 1931, with the line continuing from already-manufactured parts until 1938.

Winchester-Hotchkiss 1879 Bolt-Action Repeating
Rifle—First Model $695
Solid frame. Caliber: 45-70 Govt. Six-shot tubular magazine in buttstock. Barrel: 26 inches; round, half-octagonal and octagonal. Weight: 8 1/2 pounds average. Plain walnut stock with crescent or shotgun butt plates. Designed by Benjamin Hotchkiss, who sold the rights to Winchester, this first model had a magazine cutoff and safety control in one unit in the form of a turn button on the right-hand side above the trigger guard. 6,419 were made between 1879 and 1880.

Winchester-Hotchkiss 1879 Repeating Rifle
Second Model $750
Same general specifications as the 1879 First Model, except had the magazine cutoff on the right side, top of receiver, rear of bolt handle. Safety was on the left side of the receiver opposite the magazine cuttoff. About 16,102 of these rifles were made between 1880 and 1883.

Winchester-Hotchkiss 1883 Repeating Rifle
Third Model $950
Same general specifications as Winchester-Hotchkiss 1879 Second Model Repeater, except this had a two-piece stock. 62,034 of this model were made between 1883 and 1899.

Winchester-Hotchkiss Repeating Carbine
Same general specifications as the 1879 Repeating Rifle, except early models had a 24-inch round barrel, which was changed to 22 1/2 inches around 1884. Carbine stock with barrel band. Weight: about 8 1/4 pounds.
First Model $695
Second Model 795
Third Model 895

Winchester-Hotchkiss Repeating Musket . . . . . . $***
Same general specifications as the 1879 Repeating Rifle, except had a 32-inch round barrel, later changed to 28 inches (Second Model). Musket stock with barrel bands. Weight: 9 pounds.

Winchester-Lee Straight-Pull Bolt-Action Musket **$695**
Same general specifications as Winchester-Lee Rifle, except had a 28-inch round barrel and weight of 8¹/₂ pounds.

Winchester-Lee Straight Pull Bolt-Action Rifle **$795**
Solid frame. Non-detachable five-shot magazine. Caliber: 236 or 6mm Lee Navy. Barrel: 24 inches, round. Weight: 7¹/₂ pounds. Walnut stock and forend. Designed by James Paris Lee, about 20,000 of these rifles

were made from 1895 to 1900 primarily for use by the U.S. Navy. Some remained on the market until about 1916.

> ———— *NOTE* ————
> *** after a dollar sign indicates that there was not enough trading at press time to establish a valid selling price.

H. T. WOOD & CO.
Bradford, Ontario

H.T. Wood Percussion Rifle **$600**
Caliber: 44. Barrel: heavy, part octagonal. Walnut stock with mounted brass. Rectangular silver escutcheon on grip. Pewter nose cap. Made circa 1830s to 1840s.

H.T. Wood Percussion Rifle

SUCCESSFUL RIFLE MAGAZINES

Six basic types of magazines were successfully employed in military rifles and carbines during the last half of the 19th century and into the 20th.

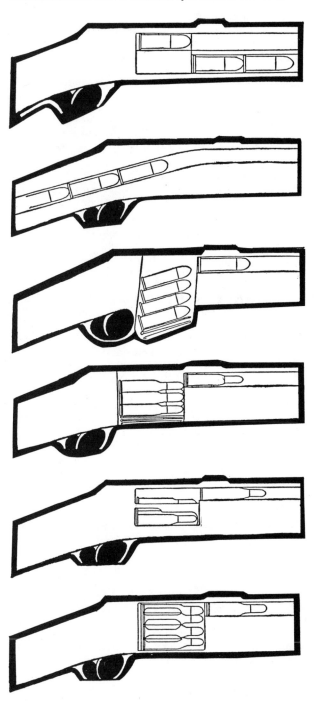

1. The first type of magazine was the invention of B. Tyler Henry, introduced in the United States with the famous lever-action Henry Rifle in 1860. In this rifle magazine, the cartridges are inserted in a tube underneath the barrel and fed into the chamber by a coiled spring. In addition to the Henry Rifle, it has been used in the Ball, U.S., 1863; the Swiss Vetterli, 1874; the French Kropatschek, 1878; the Lebel, 1886; and others.

2. The next magazine to be brought out was the Spencer type, with the feed tube in the buttstock. Christopher Spencer was the inventor in 1860. Other rifles that used this were the U.S. models Triplett and Scott, 1865; the Hotchkiss 1878 and 1883 models; the Chaffee-Reece, 1884; the Evans, 1885; the Austrian Mannlicher, 1880; and the Chinese Schulhof, 1884.

3. The third type was the invention of James P. Lee, dated 1879. This is the first of the centrally located magazines. Initially the cartridges were loaded one at a time, but later a clip was designed. Some famous guns have used this system, notably the Remington-Lee, U.S.N., 1880; the Italian Vetterli-Vitali, 1887; the Dutch Beaumont-Vitali, 1888; the Mannlicher, 1888; the Belgian Mauser, 1889; the Canadian Ross Mark III; the English Lee-Enfield, 1892–1921; the Winchester Model 1895; and the Lee Straight Pull, U.S.N., 1895; and others.

4. The fourth type is the famous Mauser design—the most successful of all rifle magazine systems. First introduced in the Spanish Model of 1893, this magazine is berthed entirely within the stock. It was also used in the U.S. Springfield 1903, and the Mausers dated 1895, 1896, 1898, 1899, 1902, 1903, 1904 and 1917.

5. The fifth system is the Krag-Jorgensen, invented by two Danish military officers. In this system, the cartridges are loaded singly and fed by a spring from the right side to the left, and then upwards into the chamber. It was introduced in the Danish Model of 1889, and used in Norway in 1894 and in the U.S. in 1892.

6. The last magazine type is the Schulhof, a product of Austria in 1888. This system revolves the cartridges on a ratchet wheel, and with a bolt, the top shell is forced into the chamber. Shells were loaded either by clip or singly in the Greek Mannlicher-Schoenauer; the U.S. Savage Mannlicher, 1887, 1888, and 1900; and the Blake Rifle, 1895.

AMERICAN KENTUCKY FLINTLOCK RIFLES

The Kentucky rifle was America's first great contribution to firearms technology. This type of rifle was born on the frontier around 1750 and was developed by gunsmiths who were artists as well as mechanics. These accurate rifles were made well into the 1800s until the development of the percussion cap around 1830. In general, the age of the Kentucky Rifle is usually considered to be between 1750 and 1850, when it made its most important contributions to American history.

Although called "Kentucky" Rifle, the main center of its production was Pennsylvania. But regardless of its origin, it was the supreme American hunting rifle for the period—at least for the eastern half of the country. The typical rifle averaged .50 caliber, had barrels of 42 to 46 inches, with both full and half-length stocks of curly maple. The butt plate was crescent-shaped to fit the shoulder snugly, and the patch box was usually an integral part of the buttstock. A cheekpiece was standard on most models.

The Kentucky Rifle started to decline in popularity soon after the introduction of the successful percussion lock rifles. Some rifles, however, continued to be made long after cartridge rifles came into use. Currently, many reproduction models are being manufactured for blackpowder enthusiasts. The following are some of the more well-known original Kentucky Rifle makers.

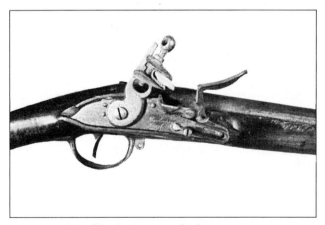

Close-up of the flint lock on a typical Pennsylvania-produced American "Kentucky" Flintlock Rifle.

ANDREW ALBRECHT
Warwick Township, Pennsylvania

Albrecht Kentucky Flintlock Rifle **$1500**
Lock: casehardened flintlock. Calibers: various. Barrel length: 36 inches average. Weight: 7 to 7½ pounds average. Curly maple one-piece stock, although walnut was sometimes used. Single- and double-set trigger. Brass fittings, including patch box, ramrod ferrules, butt plate, etc. Made from 1779 to 1782.

Albrecht Fancy Grade Kentucky Flintlock . . **$4500**
Same general specifications as standard Albrecht Flintlock, above, except gun has some modest stock carvings, silver inlays, etc.

Albrecht Extra Fancy Grade Kentucky Flintlock Rifle. **$7000**
Same general specifications as standard Albrecht Flintlock Rifle, except extra fancy wood, much carving, engraving on metal with gold or silver inlays.

M. ALDENDERFER
Lancaster, Pennsylvania

Aldenderfer Kentucky Flintlock Rifle. **$1500**
Lock: casehardened flintlock. Calibers: various. Barrel length: 36 inches average. Weight: 7 to 7½ pounds average. Curly maple one-piece stock, although walnut was sometimes used. Single- and double-set trigger. Brass fittings, including patch box, ramrod ferrules, butt plate, etc. Made from 1763 to 1817.

Aldenderfer Fancy Grade Kentucky Flintlock. **$4500**
Same general specification as standard Aldenerfer Flintlock, above, except gun has some modest stock carvings, silver inlays, etc.

Aldenderfer Extra Fancy Grade Kentucky Flintlock Rifle. **$7000**
Same general specifications as standard Aldenerfer Flintlock Rifle, except extra fancy wood, much carving, engraving on metal with gold or silver inlays.

SILAS ALLEN
Shrewsbury, Massachusetts

Allen Flintlock Kentucky Rifle **$1500**
Lock: casehardened flintlock. Calibers: various. Barrel length: 36 inches average. Weight: 7 to 7½ pounds average. Curly maple one-piece stock, although walnut was sometimes used. Single- and double-set trigger. Brass fittings, including patch box, ramrod ferrules, butt plate, etc. Made from 1796 to 1843.

Allen Smoothbore Musket................. **$995**
Lock: casehardened flintlock. Calibers: various. Barrel
length: 41 inches average, smoothbore. American walnut or maple one-piece stock. Brass or iron fittings.
Made from 1796 to 1843.

THOMAS ALLEN
New York, New York

T. Allen Flintlock Kentucky Rifle **$1500**
Lock: casehardened flintlock. Calibers: various. Barrel:
36 inches average. Weight: 7 to 7½ pounds average.
Curly maple one-piece stock, although walnut was
sometimes used. Single- and double-set trigger. Brass
fittings, including patch box, ramrod ferrules, butt
plate, etc. Made from 1768 to 1785.

WILLIAM ALLEN
New York, New York

W. Allen Kentucky Flintlock Rifle **$1500**
Lock: casehardened flintlock. Calibers: various. Barrel
length: 36 inches average. Weight: 7 to 7½ pounds average. Curly maple one-piece stock, although walnut
was sometimes used. Single- and double-set trigger.
Brass fittings, including patch box, ramrod ferrules,
butt plate, etc. Made from 1801 to 1812.

W. Allen Fancy Grade Kentucky Flintlock... **$4500**
Same general specifications as standard Allen Flintlock, above, except gun has some modest stock carvings, silver inlays, etc.

**W. Allen Extra Fancy Grade Kentucky Flintlock
Rifle**...................................**$7000**
Same general specifications as standard Allen Flintlock Rifle, except extra fancy wood, much carving, engraving on metal with gold or silver inlays.

PETER ANGSTADT
Lancaster, Pennsylvania

Angstadt Kentucky Flintlock Rifle **$1500**
Lock: casehardened flintlock. Calibers: various. Barrel
length: 36 inches average. Weight: 7 to 7½ pounds average. Curly maple one-piece stock, although walnut
was sometimes used. Single- and double-set trigger.
Brass fittings, including patch box, ramrod ferrules,
butt plate, etc. Made from 1779 to 1782.

Angstadt Fancy Grade Kentucky Flintlock.. **$4500**
Same general specifications as standard Angstadt
Flintlock, above, except gun has some modest stock
carvings, silver inlays, etc.

**Angstadt Extra Fancy Grade Kentucky Flintlock
Rifle**...................................... **$7000**
Same general specifications as standard Angstadt
Flintlock Rifle, except extra fancy wood, much carving,
engraving on metal with gold or silver inlays.

JAMES ANGUSH
Lancaster, Pennsylvania

Angush Kentucky Flintlock Rifle.......... **$1500**
Lock: casehardened flintlock. Calibers: various. Barrel
length: 36 inches average. Weight: 7 to 7½ pounds average. Curly maple one-piece stock, although walnut
was sometimes used. Single- and double-set trigger.
Brass fittings, including patch box, ramrod ferrules,
butt plate, etc. Made from 1775 to 1776.

Angush Fancy Grade Kentucky Flintlock ... **$4500**
Same general specifications as standard Angush Flintlock, above, except gun has some modest stock carvings, silver inlays, etc.

JACOB ANSTADT
Kutztown, Pennsylvania

Anstadt Kentucky Flintlock Rifle **$1500**
Lock: casehardened flintlock. Calibers: various. Barrel
length: 36 inches average. Weight: 7 to 7½ pounds average. Curly maple one-piece stock, although walnut
was sometimes used. Single- and double-set trigger.
Brass fittings, including patch box, ramrod ferrules,
butt plate, etc. Made from 1815 to 1816.

WILLIAM ANTIS
Fredericktown, Pennsylvania

Antis Kentucky Flintlock Rifle............ **$1500**
Lock: casehardened flintlock. Calibers: various. Barrel
length: 36 inches average. Weight: 7 to 7½ pounds average. Curly maple one-piece stock, although walnut
was sometimes used. Single- and double-set trigger.
Brass fittings, including patch box, ramrod ferrules,
butt plate, etc. Made from 1775 to 1782.

Antis Fancy Grade Kentucky Flintlock **$4500**
Same general specifications as standard Antis Flintlock, above, except gun has some modest stock carvings, silver inlays, etc.

**Antis Extra Fancy Grade Kentucky
Flintlock Rifle**.......................... **$7000**
Same general specifications as standard Antis Flintlock Rifle, except extra fancy wood, much carving, engraving on metal with gold or silver inlays.

G. AVERY
Hamburg, Pennsylvania

Avery Kentucky Flintlock Rifle **$1500**
Lock: casehardened flintlock. Calibers: various. Barrel length: 36 inches average. Weight: 7 to 7½ pounds average. Curly maple one-piece stock, although walnut was sometimes used. Single- and double-set trigger. Brass fittings, including patch box, ramrod ferrules, butt plate, etc. Made from 1779 to 1782.

Avery Fancy Grade Kentucky Flintlock **$4500**
Same general specifications as standard very Flintlock, above, except gun has some modest stock carvings, silver inlays, etc.

RICHARD BACKHOUSE
Easton, Pennsylvania

Backhouse Kentucky Flintlock Rifle **$1450**
Lock: casehardened flintlock. Calibers: various. Barrel length: 36 inches average. Weight: 7 to 7½ pounds average. Curly maple one-piece stock, although walnut was sometimes used. Single- and double-set trigger. Brass fittings, including patch box, ramrod ferrules, butt plate, etc. Made from 1774 to 1781.

Backhouse Fancy Grade Kentucky Flintlock **$4400**
Same general specifications as standard Backhouse Flintlock, above, except gun has some modest stock carvings, silver inlays, etc.

Backhouse Extra Fancy Grade Kentucky Flintlock Rifle **$6500**
Same general specifications as standard Backhouse Flintlock Rifle, except extra fancy wood, much carving, engraving on metal with gold or silver inlays.

ROBERT BAILEY
York, Pennsylvania

Bailey Kentucky Flintlock Rifle **$1250**
Lock: casehardened flintlock. Calibers: various. Barrel length: 36 inches average. Weight: 7 to 7½ pounds average. Curly maple one-piece stock, although walnut was sometimes used. Single- and double-set trigger. Brass fittings, including patch box, ramrod ferrules, butt plate, etc. Made from 1776 to 1777.

JACOB BAKER
Philadelphia, Pennsylvania

Baker Kentucky Flintlock Rifle **$1500**
Lock: casehardened flintlock. Calibers: various, usually 36 to 50. Barrel length: 36 to 41 inches. Weight: 7 to 7½ pounds average. Curly maple one-piece stock, although walnut was sometimes used. Single- and double-set trigger. Brass fittings, including patch box, ramrod ferrules, butt plate, etc. Made from 1820 to 1833.

Baker Fancy Grade Kentucky Flintlock **$4500**
Same general specifications as standard Baker Flintlock, above, except gun has some modest stock carvings, silver inlays, etc.

Baker Extra Fancy Grade Kentucky Flintlock Rifle **$7000**
Same general specifications as standard Baker Flintlock Rifle, except extra fancy wood, much carving, engraving on metal with gold or silver inlays.

JOHN BAKER
Newburgh, New York

Baker Kentucky Flintlock Rifle **$1500**
Lock: casehardened flintlock. Calibers: various, usually 36 to 50. Barrel length: 36 to 41 inches. Weight: 7 to 7½ pounds average. Curly maple one-piece stock, although walnut was sometimes used. Single- and double-set trigger. Brass fittings, including patch box, ramrod ferrules, butt plate, etc. Made from 1837 to 1850.

MELCHIOR BAKER
Fayette County, Pennsylvania

M. Baker Kentucky Flintlock Rifle **$1500**
Lock: casehardened flintlock. Calibers: various usually 36 to 50. Barrel length: 36 to 41 inches. Weight: 7 to 7½ pounds average. Curly maple one-piece stock, although walnut was sometimes used. Single- and double-set trigger. Brass fittings, including patch box, ramrod ferrules, butt plate, etc. Made from 1779 to 1805.

M. Baker Fancy Grade Kentucky Flintlock . . **$4500**
Same general specifications as standard Baker Flintlock, above, except gun has some modest stock carvings, silver inlays, etc.

M. Baker Extra Fancy Grade Kentucky Flintlock Rifle **$7000**
Same general specifications as standard Baker Flintlock Rifle, except extra fancy wood, much carving, engraving on metal with gold or silver inlays.

CHRISTIAN BALSLEY
Dickinson Township, Pennsylvania

Balsley Kentucky Flintlock Rifle **$1500**
Lock: casehardened flintlock. Calibers: various usually 36 to 50. Barrel length: 36 to 41 inches. Weight: 7 to 7½ pounds average. Curly maple one-piece stock, although walnut was sometimes used. Single- and double-set trigger. Brass fittings, including patch box, ramrod ferrules, butt plate, etc. Made from 1795 to 1796.

Balsley Fancy Grade Kentucky Flintlock. . . . **$4500**
Same general specifications as standard Balsley Flintlock, above, except gun has some modest stock carvings, silver inlays, etc.

Balsley Extra Fancy Grade Kentucky Flintlock Rifle. **$7000**
Same general specifications as standard Balsley Flintlock Rifle, except extra fancy wood, much carving, engraving on metal with gold or silver inlays.

GEORGE BARNHART
Jackson, Ohio

Barnhart Kentucky Flintlock Rifle **$1500**
Lock: casehardened flintlock. Calibers: various usually 36 to 50. Barrel length: 36 to 41 inches. Weight: 7 to 7½ pounds average. Curly maple one-piece stock, although walnut was sometimes used. Single- and double-set trigger. Brass fittings, including patch box, ramrod ferrules, butt plate, etc. Made from 1818 to 1844.

Barnhart Fancy Grade Kentucky Flintlock. . **$4500**
Same general specifications as standard Barnhart Flintlock, above, except gun has some modest stock carvings, silver inlays, etc.

Barnhart Extra Fancy Grade Kentucky Flintlock Rifle. **$7000**
Same general specifications as standard Barnhart Flintlock Rifle, except extra fancy wood, much carving, engraving on metal with gold or silver inlays.

SAMUEL BAUM
Mahoning Township, Pennsylvania

Baum Kentucky Flintlock Rifle **$1450**
Casehardened flintlock. Calibers: various, usually 36 to 50. Barrels: 36 to 41 inches. Weight: 7½ pounds average. Curly maple one-piece stock; sometimes walnut. Single- and double-set triggers. Brass fittings, including patch box, ramrod ferrules, butt plate, etc. Made from 1819 to 1821.

Baum Fancy Grade Kentucky Flintlock Rifle. **$4000**
Same general specifications as above rifle, except some modest stock carvings, silver inlays, minute metal engraving, etc.

Baum Extra Fancy Grade Kentucky Flintlock Rifle. **$6500**
Same general specifications as above rifle, except has extra fancy grade wood, much wood carving, engraving on metal with gold or silver inlays.

GIDEON BECK
Lancaster, Pennsylvania

G. Beck Kentucky Flintlock Rifle. **$1500**
Lock: casehardened flintlock. Calibers: various, usually 36 to 50. Barrel length: 36 to 41 inches. Weight: 7½ pounds average. Curly maple one-piece stock, although walnut was sometimes used. Single- and double-set trigger. Brass fittings, including patch box, ramrod ferrules, butt plate, etc. Made from 1780 to 1788.

G. Beck Fancy Grade Kentucky Flintlock Rifle. **$4500**
Same general specifications as standard Beck Flintlock, above, except gun has some modest stock carvings, silver inlays, minute metal engraving, etc.

G. Beck Extra Fancy Grade Kentucky Flintlock Rifle. **$7000**
Same general specifications as standard Beck Flintlock Rifle, except extra fancy grade wood, much carving, engraving on metal with gold or silver inlays.

JOHN BECK
Lancaster, Pennsylvania

J. Beck Kentucky Flintlock Rifle. **$1500**
Lock: casehardened flintlock. Calibers: various, usually 36 to 50. Barrel length: 36 to 41 inches average. Weight: 7½ pounds average. Curly maple one-piece stock, although walnut was sometimes used. Single- and double-set trigger. Brass fittings, including patch box, ramrod ferrules, butt plate, etc. Made from 1772 to 1777.

J. Beck Fancy Grade Kentucky Flintlock Rifle. **$4500**
Same general specifications as above rifle, except gun has some modest stock carvings, silver inlays, and minute metal engraving, etc.

J. Beck Extra Fancy Grade Kentucky Flintlock Rifle. **$7000**
Same general specifications as above rifle, except extra fancy wood, much carving, engraving on metal with gold or silver inlays.

JOHN PHILLIP BECK
Dauphin County, Pennsylvania

J.P. Beck Kentucky Flintlock Rifle. **$2500**
Lock: casehardened flintlock. Calibers: various, usually 36 to 50. Barrel length: 36 to 41 inches. Weight: 7½ pounds average. Curly maple one-piece stock, although walnut was sometimes used. Single- and double-set trigger. Brass fittings, including patch box, ramrod ferrules, butt plate, etc. Made from 1785 to 1811.

J.P. Beck Fancy Grade Kentucky Flintlock Rifle. **$6500**
Same general specifications as above rifle, except has some modest stock carvings, silver inlays, minute metal engraving, etc.

J.P. Beck Extra Fancy Grade Kentucky Flintlock Rifle. **$1000**
Same general specifications as above rifle, except extra fancy wood, much carving, engraving on metal with gold or silver inlays. One such rifle has the inscription "To the President George Washington AD 1791."

J. BECKER
Lebanon, Pennsylvania

Becker Kentucky Flintlock Rifle. **$1500**
Lock: casehardened flintlock. Calibers: various, usually 36 to 50. Barrel length: 36 to 41 inches average. Weight: 7½ pounds average. Curly maple one-piece stock, although walnut was sometimes used. Single- and double-set trigger. Brass fittings, including patch box, ramrod ferrules, butt plate, etc. Made from 1808 to 1810.

Becker Fancy Grade Kentucky Flintlock Rifle. **$4500**
Same general specifications as above rifle, except gun has some modest stock carvings, silver inlays, and minute metal engraving, etc.

Becker Extra Fancy Grade Kentucky Flintlock Rifle. **$7000**
Same general specifications as above rifle, except extra fancy wood, much carving, engraving on metal with gold or silver inlays.

S. BEIG
Lancaster County, Pennsylvania

Beig Kentucky Flintlock Rifle. **$1500**
Lock: casehardened flintlock. Calibers: various, usually 36 to 50. Barrel length: 36 to 41 inches average. Weight: 7½ pounds average. Curly maple one-piece stock, although walnut was sometimes used. Single- and double-set trigger. Brass fittings, including patch box, ramrod ferrules, butt plate, etc. Made from 1789 to 1790.

Beig Fancy Grade Kentucky Flintlock Rifle. **$4500**
Same general specifications as above rifle, except gun has some modest stock carvings, silver inlays, and minute metal engraving, etc.

Beig Extra Fancy Grade Kentucky Flintlock Rifle. **$7000**
Same general specifications as above rifle, except extra fancy wood, much carving, engraving on metal with gold or silver inlays.

JOHN BELL
Carlisle, Pennsylvania

Bell Kentucky Flintlock Rifle. **$1550**
Lock: casehardened flintlock. Calibers: various, usually 36 to 50. Barrel length: 36 to 41 inches average. Weight: 7½ pounds average. Curly maple one-piece stock, although walnut was sometimes used. Single- and double-set trigger. Brass fittings, including patch box, ramrod ferrules, butt plate, etc. Made from 1799 to 1800.

Bell Fancy Grade Kentucky Flintlock Rifle. . **$4550**
Same general specifications as above rifle, except gun has some modest stock carvings, silver inlays, and minute metal engraving, etc.

Bell Extra Fancy Grade Kentucky Flintlock Rifle. **$7050**
Same general specifications as above rifle, except extra fancy wood, much carving, engraving on metal with gold or silver inlays.

AMOS BENFER
Beaverstown, Pennsylvania

Benfer Kentucky Flintlock Rifle. **$1500**
Lock: casehardened flintlock. Calibers: various, usually 36 to 50. Barrel length: 36 to 41 inches average. Weight: 7½ pounds average. Curly maple one-piece stock, although walnut was sometimes used. Single- and double-set trigger. Brass fittings, including patch box, ramrod ferrules, butt plate, etc. Made 1814 to 1815.

**Benfer Fancy Grade Kentucky Flintlock
Rifle**................................... **$4500**
Same general specifications as above rifle, except gun
has some modest stock carvings, silver inlays, and
minute metal engraving, etc.

**Benfer Extra Fancy Grade Kentucky
Flintlock Rifle**........................ **$7000**
Same general specifications as above rifle, except extra
fancy wood, much carving, engraving on metal with
gold or silver inlays.

ABRAHAM BERLIN
Easton, Pennsylvania

Berlin Kentucky Flintlock Rifle........... **$1500**
Lock: casehardened flintlock. Calibers: various, usually 36 to 50. Barrel length: 36 to 41 inches average.
Weight: 7¹/₂ pounds average. Curly maple one-piece
stock, although walnut was sometimes used. Single-
and double-set trigger. Brass fittings, including patch
box, ramrod ferrules, butt plate, etc. Made from 1773 to
1786.

**Berlin Fancy Grade Kentucky Flintlock
Rifle**................................... **$4500**
Same general specifications as above rifle, except gun
has some modest stock carvings, silver inlays, and
minute metal engraving, etc.

**Berlin Extra Fancy Grade Kentucky
Flintlock Rifle**......................... **$7000**
Same general specifications as above rifle, except extra
fancy wood, much carving, engraving on metal with
gold or silver inlays.

ISAAC BERLIN
Easton, Pennsylvania

I. Berlin Kentucky Flintlock Rifle......... **$1525**
Lock: casehardened flintlock. Calibers: various, usually 36 to 50. Barrel length: 36 to 41 inches average.
Weight: 7¹/₂ pounds average. Curly maple one-piece
stock, although walnut was sometimes used. Single-
and double-set trigger. Brass fittings, including patch
box, ramrod ferrules, butt plate, etc. Made from 1781 to
1817.

**I. Berlin Fancy Grade Kentucky Flintlock
Rifle**................................... **$4525**
Same general specifications as above rifle, except gun
has some modest stock carvings, silver inlays, and
minute metal engraving, etc.

**I. Berlin Extra Fancy Grade Kentucky Flintlock
Rifle**................................... **$7025**
Same general specifications as above rifle, except extra
fancy wood, much carving, engraving on metal with
gold or silver inlays.

BEST
Lancaster, Pennsylvania

Best Kentucky Flintlock Rifle............. **$1500**
Lock: casehardened flintlock. Calibers: various, usually 36 to 50. Barrel length: 36 to 41 inches average.
Weight: 7¹/₂ pounds average. Curly maple one-piece
stock, although walnut was sometimes used. Single-
and double-set trigger. Brass fittings, including patch
box, ramrod ferrules, butt plate, etc. Made from 1760 to
1775.

**Best Fancy Grade Kentucky Flintlock
Rifle**................................... **$4500**
Same general specifications as above rifle, except gun
has some modest stock carvings, silver inlays, and
minute metal engraving, etc.

**Best Extra Fancy Grade Kentucky Flintlock
Rifle**................................... **$7000**
Same general specifications as above rifle, except extra
fancy wood, much carving, engraving on metal with
gold or silver inlays.

N. BEYER
Lebanon, Pennsylvania

Beyer Kentucky Flintlock Rifle........... **$1500**
Lock: casehardened flintlock. Calibers: various, usually 36 to 50. Barrel length: 36 to 41 inches average.
Weight: 7¹/₂ pounds average. Curly maple one-piece
stock, although walnut was sometimes used. Single-
and double-set trigger. Brass fittings, including patch
box, ramrod ferrules, butt plate, etc. Made from 1769 to
1770.

**Beyer Fancy Grade Kentucky Flintlock
Rifle**................................... **$4500**
Same general specifications as above rifle, except gun
has some modest stock carvings, silver inlays, and
minute metal engraving, etc.

**Beyer Extra Fancy Grade Kentucky
Flintlock Rifle**......................... **$7000**
Same general specifications as above rifle, except extra
fancy wood, much carving, engraving on metal with
gold or silver inlays.

HENRY BICKEL
York, Pennsylvania

Bickel Kentucky Flintlock Rifle............ **$1500**
Lock: casehardened flintlock. Calibers: various, usually 36 to 50. Barrel length: 36 to 41 inches average. Weight: 7½ pounds average. Curly maple one-piece stock, although walnut was sometimes used. Single- and double-set trigger. Brass fittings, including patch box, ramrod ferrules, butt plate, etc. Made from 1799 to 1800.

Bickel Fancy Grade Kentucky Flintlock Rifle..................................... **$4500**
Same general specifications as above rifle, except gun has some modest stock carvings, silver inlays, and minute metal engraving, etc.

Bickel Extra Fancy Grade Kentucky Flintlock Rifle.......................... **$7000**
Same general specifications as above rifle, except extra fancy wood, much carving, engraving on metal with gold or silver inlays.

R. & W. C. BIDDLE
Philadelphia, Pennsylvania

Biddle Kentucky Flintlock Rifle........... **$1550**
Lock: casehardened flintlock. Calibers: various, usually 36 to 50. Barrel length: 36 to 41 inches average. Weight: 7½ pounds average. Curly maple one-piece stock, although walnut was sometimes used. Single- and double-set trigger. Brass fittings, including patch box, ramrod ferrules, butt plate, etc. Made from 1800 to 1835.

Biddle Fancy Grade Kentucky Flintlock Rifle..................................... **$4550**
Same general specifications as above rifle, except gun has some modest stock carvings, silver inlays, and minute metal engraving, etc.

Biddle Extra Fancy Grade Kentucky Flintlock Rifle.......................... **$7050**
Same general specifications as above rifle, except extra fancy wood, much carving, engraving on metal with gold or silver inlays.

ANTHONY BOBB
Reading, Pennsylvania

Bobb Kentucky Flintlock Rifle............ **$1500**
Lock: casehardened flintlock. Calibers: various, usually 36 to 50. Barrel length: 36 to 41 inches average. Weight: 7½ pounds average. Curly maple one-piece stock, although walnut was sometimes used. Single- and double-set trigger. Brass fittings, including patch box, ramrod ferrules, butt plate, etc. Made from 1778 to 1881.

Bobb Fancy Grade Kentucky Flintlock Rifle..................................... **$4500**
Same general specifications as above rifle, except gun has some modest stock carvings, silver inlays, and minute metal engraving, etc.

Bobb Extra Fancy Grade Kentucky Flintlock Rifle.......................... **$7000**
Same general specifications as above rifle, except extra fancy wood, much carving, engraving on metal with gold or silver inlays.

SAMUEL BOONE
Berks County, Pennsylvania

Boone Kentucky Flintlock Rifle........... **$1550**
Lock: casehardened flintlock. Calibers: various, usually 36 to 50. Barrel length: 36 to 41 inches average. Weight: 7½ pounds average. Curly maple one-piece stock, although walnut was sometimes used. Single- and double-set trigger. Brass fittings, including patch box, ramrod ferrules, butt plate, etc. Made from 1769 to 1770.

Boone Fancy Grade Kentucky Flintlock Rifle..................................... **$4550**
Same general specifications as above rifle, except gun has some modest stock carvings, silver inlays, and minute metal engraving, etc.

Boone Extra Fancy Grade Kentucky Flintlock Rifle.......................... **$7050**
Same general specifications as above rifle, except extra fancy wood, much carving, engraving on metal with gold or silver inlays.

SAMUEL BORDER
Somerset County, Pennsylvania

Border Kentucky Flintlock Rifle **$1500**
Lock: casehardened flintlock. Calibers: various, usually 36 to 50. Barrel length: 36 to 41 inches average. Weight: 7½ pounds average. Curly maple one-piece stock, although walnut was sometimes used. Single- and double-set trigger. Brass fittings, including patch box, ramrod ferrules, butt plate, etc. Made from 1825 to 1861.

Border Fancy Grade Kentucky Flintlock Rifle..................................... **$4500**
Same general specifications as above rifle, except gun has some modest stock carvings, silver inlays, and minute metal engraving, etc.

**Border Extra Fancy Grade Kentucky
Flintlock Rifle**.......................... **$7000**
Same general specifications as above rifle, except extra
fancy wood, much carving, engraving on metal with
gold or silver inlays.

BOSWORTH
Lancaster, Pennsylvania

Bosworth Kentucky Flintlock Rifle......... **$1500**
Lock: casehardened flintlock. Calibers: various, usually 36 to 50. Barrel length: 36 to 41 inches average.
Weight: 7¹/₂ pounds average. Curly maple one-piece
stock, although walnut was sometimes used. Single-
and double-set trigger. Brass fittings, including patch
box, ramrod ferrules, butt plate, etc. Made from 1760 to
1775.

**Bosworth Fancy Grade Kentucky Flintlock
Rifle**...................................... **$4500**
Same general specifications as above rifle, except gun
has some modest stock carvings, silver inlays, and
minute metal engraving, etc.

**Bosworth Extra Fancy Grade Kentucky Flintlock
Rifle**...................................... **$7000**
Same general specifications as above rifle, except extra
fancy wood, much carving, engraving on metal with
gold or silver inlays.

DANIEL & HENRY BOYER
Orwigsburg, Pennsylvania

Boyer Kentucky Flintlock Rifle **$1525**
Lock: casehardened flintlock. Calibers: various, usually 36 to 50. Barrel length: 36 to 41 inches average.
Weight: 7¹/₂ pounds average. Curly maple one-piece
stock, although walnut was sometimes used. Single-
and double-set trigger. Brass fittings, including patch
box, ramrod ferrules, butt plate, etc. Made from 1790 to
1810.

**Boyer Fancy Grade Kentucky Flintlock
Rifle**...................................... **$4525**
Same general specifications as above rifle, except gun
has some modest stock carvings, silver inlays, and
minute metal engraving, etc.

**Boyer Extra Fancy Grade Kentucky
Flintlock Rifle**........................... **$7025**
Same general specifications as above rifle, except extra
fancy wood, much carving, engraving on metal with
gold or silver inlays.

GEORGE BRAMMER
Chesapeake County, Ohio

Brammer Kentucky Flintlock Rifle......... **$1500**
Lock: casehardened flintlock. Calibers: various, usually 36 to 50. Barrel length: 36 to 41 inches average.
Weight: 7¹/₂ pounds average. Curly maple one-piece
stock, although walnut was sometimes used. Single-
and double-set trigger. Brass fittings, including patch
box, ramrod ferrules, butt plate, etc. Made from 1795 to
1820.

**Brammer Fancy Grade Kentucky Flintlock
Rifle**...................................... **$4500**
Same general specifications as above rifle, except gun
has some modest stock carvings, silver inlays, and
minute metal engraving, etc.

**Brammer Extra Fancy Grade Kentucky Flintlock
Rifle**...................................... **$7000**
Same general specifications as above rifle, except extra
fancy wood, much carving, engraving on metal with
gold or silver inlays.

JOSEPH BRONG
Lancaster, Pennsylvania

J. Brong Kentucky Flintlock Rifle.......... **$1500**
Lock: casehardened flintlock. Calibers: various, usually 36 to 50. Barrel length: 36 to 41 inches average.
Weight: 7¹/₂ pounds average. Curly maple one-piece
stock, although walnut was sometimes used. Single-
and double-set trigger. Brass fittings, including patch
box, ramrod ferrules, butt plate, etc. Made from 1760 to
1800.

**J. Brong Fancy Grade Kentucky Flintlock
Rifle**...................................... **$4500**
Same general specifications as above rifle, except gun
has some modest stock carvings, silver inlays, and
minute metal engraving, etc.

**J. Brong Extra Fancy Grade Kentucky
Flintlock Rifle**........................... **$7000**
Same general specifications as above rifle, except extra
fancy wood, much carving, engraving on metal with
gold or silver inlays.

PETER BRONG
Lancaster, Pennsylvania

P. Brong Kentucky Flintlock Rifle.......... **$1550**
Lock: casehardened flintlock. Calibers: various, usually 36 to 50. Barrel length: 36 to 41 inches average.
Weight: 7¹/₂ pounds average. Curly maple one-piece
stock, although walnut was sometimes used. Single-
and double-set trigger. Brass fittings, including patch
box, ramrod ferrules, butt plate, etc. Made from 1795 to
1816.

P. Brong Fancy Grade Kentucky Flintlock Rifle. **$4550**
Same general specifications as above rifle, except gun has some modest stock carvings, silver inlays, and minute metal engraving, etc.

P. Brong Extra Fancy Grade Kentucky Flintlock Rifle. **$7050**
Same general specifications as above rifle, except extra fancy wood, much carving, engraving on metal with gold or silver inlays.

JOHN BROOKS
Lancaster, Pennsylvania

Brooks Kentucky Flintlock Rifle **$1500**
Lock: casehardened flintlock. Calibers: various, usually 36 to 50. Barrel length: 36 to 41 inches average. Weight: 7½ pounds average. Curly maple one-piece stock, although walnut was sometimes used. Single- and double-set trigger. Brass fittings, including patch box, ramrod ferrules, butt plate, etc. Made from 1804 to 1805.

Brooks Fancy Grade Kentucky Flintlock Rifle. **$4500**
Same general specifications as above rifle, except gun has some modest stock carvings, silver inlays, and minute metal engraving, etc.

Brooks Extra Fancy Grade Kentucky Flintlock Rifle. **$7000**
Same general specifications as above rifle, except extra fancy wood, much carving, engraving on metal with gold or silver inlays.

JAMES BROWN
Pittsburg, Pennsylvania

Brown Kentucky Flintlock Rifle. **$1500**
Lock: casehardened flintlock. Calibers: various, usually 36 to 50. Barrel length: 36 to 41 inches average. Weight: 7½ pounds average. Curly maple one-piece stock, although walnut was sometimes used. Single- and double-set trigger. Brass fittings, including patch box, ramrod ferrules, butt plate, etc. Made from 1810 to 1848.

Brown Fancy Grade Kentucky Flintlock Rifle. **$4500**
Same general specifications as above rifle, except gun has some modest stock carvings, silver inlays, and minute metal engraving, etc.

Brown Extra Fancy Grade Kentucky Flintlock Rifle. **$7000**
Same general specifications as above rifle, except extra fancy wood, much carving, engraving on metal with gold or silver inlays.

JAMES BRYANT
Lancaster County, Pennsylvania

Bryant Kentucky Flintlock Rifle **$1525**
Lock: casehardened flintlock. Calibers: various, usually 36 to 50. Barrel length: 36 to 41 inches average. Weight: 7½ pounds average. Curly maple one-piece stock, although walnut was sometimes used. Single- and double-set trigger. Brass fittings, including patch box, ramrod ferrules, butt plate, etc. Made from 1799 to 1800.

Bryant Fancy Grade Kentucky Flintlock Rifle. **$4525**
Same general specifications as above rifle, except gun has some modest stock carvings, silver inlays, and minute metal engraving, etc.

Bryant Extra Fancy Grade Kentucky Flintlock Rifle. **$7025**
Same general specifications as above rifle, except extra fancy wood, much carving, engraving on metal with gold or silver inlays.

ABRAHAM, HENRY & JOHN BUCKWALTER
Lancaster County, Pennsylvania

Buckwalter Kentucky Flintlock Rifle **$1500**
Lock: casehardened flintlock. Calibers: various, usually 36 to 50. Barrel length: 36 to 41 inches average. Weight: 7½ pounds average. Curly maple one-piece stock, although walnut was sometimes used. Single- and double-set trigger. Brass fittings, including patch box, ramrod ferrules, butt plate, etc. Made from 1771 to 1780.

Buckwalter Fancy Grade Kentucky Flintlock Rifle. **$4500**
Same general specifications as above rifle, except gun has some modest stock carvings, silver inlays, and minute metal engraving, etc.

Buckwalter Extra Fancy Grade Kentucky Flintlock Rifle. **$7000**
Same general specifications as above rifle, except extra fancy wood, much carving, engraving on metal with gold or silver inlays.

CHARLES BULOW
Lancaster, Pennsylvania

Bulow Kentucky Flintlock Rifle **$1500**
Lock: casehardened flintlock. Calibers: various, usually 36 to 50. Barrel length: 36 to 41 inches average. Weight: 7½ pounds average. Curly maple one-piece stock, although walnut was sometimes used. Single- and double-set trigger. Brass fittings, including patch box, ramrod ferrules, butt plate, etc. Made from 1794 to 1795.

Bulow Fancy Grade Kentucky Flintlock Rifle. **$4500**
Same general specifications as above rifle, except gun has some modest stock carvings, silver inlays, and minute metal engraving, etc.

Bulow Extra Fancy Grade Kentucky Flintlock Rifle. **$7000**
Same general specifications as above rifle, except extra fancy wood, much carving, engraving on metal with gold or silver inlays.

JOHN BURT
Donegal Township, Pennsylvania

Burt Kentucky Flintlock Rifle **$1550**
Lock: casehardened flintlock. Calibers: various, usually 36 to 50. Barrel length: 36 to 41 inches average. Weight: 7½ pounds average. Curly maple one-piece stock, although walnut was sometimes used. Single- and double-set trigger. Brass fittings, including patch box, ramrod ferrules, butt plate, etc. Made from 1769 to 1770.

Burt Fancy Grade Kentucky Flintlock Rifle. **$4550**
Same general specifications as above rifle, except gun has some modest stock carvings, silver inlays, and minute metal engraving, etc.

Burt Extra Fancy Grade Kentucky Flintlock Rifle. **$7050**
Same general specifications as above rifle, except extra fancy wood, much carving, engraving on metal with gold or silver inlays.

BUSCH
Lancaster, Pennsylvania

Busch Kentucky Flintlock Rifle **$1525**
Lock: casehardened flintlock. Calibers: various, usually 36 to 50. Barrel length: 36 to 41 inches average.

Weight: 7½ pounds average. Curly maple one-piece stock, although walnut was sometimes used. Single- and double-set trigger. Brass fittings, including patch box, ramrod ferrules, butt plate, etc. Made from 1774 to 1775.

Busch Fancy Grade Kentucky Flintlock Rifle. **$4525**
Same general specifications as above rifle, except gun has some modest stock carvings, silver inlays, and minute metal engraving, etc.

Busch Extra Fancy Grade Kentucky Flintlock Rifle. **$7025**
Same general specifications as above rifle, except extra fancy wood, much carving, engraving on metal with gold or silver inlays.

WILLIAM CALDERWOOD
Philadelphia, Pennsylvania

Calderwood Kentucky Flintlock Rifle **$1500**
Lock: casehardened flintlock. Calibers: various, usually 36 to 50. Barrel length: 36 to 41 inches average. Weight: 7½ pounds average. Curly maple one-piece stock, although walnut was sometimes used. Single- and double-set trigger. Brass fittings, including patch box, ramrod ferrules, butt plate, etc. Made from 1807 to 1819.

GEORGE CALL
Lancaster, Pennsylvania

Call Kentucky Flintlock Rifle **$1250**
Lock: casehardened flintlock. Calibers: various, usually 36 to 50. Barrel length: 36 to 41 inches average. Weight: 7½ pounds average. Curly maple one-piece stock, although walnut was sometimes used. Single- and double-set trigger. Brass fittings, including patch box, ramrod ferrules, butt plate, etc. Made from 1775 to 1780.

Call Fancy Grade Kentucky Flintlock Rifle. . **$4100**
Same general specifications as above rifle, except gun has some modest stock carvings, silver inlays, and minute metal engraving, etc.

Call Extra Fancy Grade Kentucky Flintlock Rifle. **$6300**
Same general specifications as above rifle, except extra fancy wood, much carving, engraving on metal with gold or silver inlays.

H. CARLILE
Lancaster, Pennsylvania

Carlile Kentucky Flintlock Rifle. **$1500**
Lock: casehardened flintlock. Calibers: various, usually 36 to 50. Barrel length: 36 to 41 inches average. Weight: 7½ pounds average. Curly maple one-piece stock, although walnut was sometimes used. Single- and double-set trigger. Brass fittings, including patch box, ramrod ferrules, butt plate, etc. Made from 1779 to 1780.

THOMAS P. CHERRINGTON
Cattawissa, Pennsylvania

Cherrington Kentucky Flintlock Rifle **$1650**
Lock: casehardened flintlock. Calibers: various, usually 36 to 50. Barrel length: 36 to 41 inches average. Weight: 7½ pounds average. Curly maple one-piece stock, although walnut was sometimes used. Single- and double-set trigger. Brass fittings, including patch box, ramrod ferrules, butt plate, etc. Made from 1765 to 1805.

**Cherrington Fancy Grade Kentucky
Flintlock Rifle**. **$4650**
Same general specifications as above rifle, except gun has some modest stock carvings, silver inlays, and minute metal engraving, etc.

JOHN CLARK
Reading, Pennsylvania

Clark Kentucky Flintlock Rifle. **$1500**
Lock: casehardened flintlock. Calibers: various, usually 36 to 50. Barrel length: 36 to 41 inches average. Weight: 7½ pounds average. Curly maple one-piece stock, although walnut was sometimes used. Single- and double-set trigger. Brass fittings, including patch box, ramrod ferrules, butt plate, etc. Made from 1804 to 1805.

CONESTOGA RIFLE WORKS
Lancaster, Pennsylvania

Conestoga Kentucky Flintlock Rifle **$1225**
Lock: casehardened flintlock. Calibers: various, usually 36 to 50. Barrel length: 36 to 41 inches average. Weight: 7½ pounds average. Curly maple one-piece stock, although walnut was sometimes used. Single- and double-set trigger. Brass fittings, including patch box, ramrod ferrules, butt plate, etc. Made from 1779 to 1780.

ABRAHAM COSTER
Philadelphia, Pennsylvania

Coster Kentucky Flintlock Rifle. **$1500**
Lock: casehardened flintlock. Calibers: various, usually 36 to 50. Barrel length: 36 to 41 inches average. Weight: 7½ pounds average. Curly maple one-piece stock, although walnut was sometimes used. Single- and double-set trigger. Brass fittings, including patch box, ramrod ferrules, butt plate, etc. Made from 1810 to 1814.

**Coster Fancy Grade Kentucky Flintlock
Rifle**. **$4500**
Same general specifications as above rifle, except gun has some modest stock carvings, silver inlays, and minute metal engraving, etc.

**Coster Extra Fancy Grade Kentucky
Flintlock Rifle**. **$7000**
Same general specifications as above rifle, except extra fancy wood, much carving, engraving on metal with gold or silver inlays.

GEORGE CUNKLE
Harrisburg, Pennsylvania

Cunkle Kentucky Flintlock Rifle **$1500**
Lock: casehardened flintlock. Calibers: various, usually 36 to 50. Barrel length: 36 to 41 inches average. Weight: 7½ pounds average. Curly maple one-piece stock, although walnut was sometimes used. Single- and double-set trigger. Brass fittings, including patch box, ramrod ferrules, butt plate, etc. Made from 1839 to 1840.

JACOB DANNER
Canton, Ohio

Danner Kentucky Flintlock Rifle. **$1500**
Lock: casehardened flintlock. Calibers: various, usually 36 to 50. Barrel length: 36 to 41 inches average. Weight: 7½ pounds average. Curly maple one-piece stock, although walnut was sometimes used. Single- and double-set trigger. Brass fittings, including patch box, ramrod ferrules, butt plate, etc. Made from 1821 to 1844.

Danner Fancy Grade Kentucky Flintlock Rifle................................... **$4500**
Same general specifications as above rifle, except gun has some modest stock carvings, silver inlays, and minute metal engraving, etc.

Danner Extra Fancy Grade Kentucky Flintlock Rifle.................................. **$7000**
Same general specifications as above rifle, except extra fancy wood, much carving, engraving on metal with gold or silver inlays.

H. W. DEEDS
Reading, Pennsylvania

Deeds Kentucky Flintlock Rifle........... **$1500**
Lock: casehardened flintlock. Calibers: various, usually 36 to 50. Barrel length: 36 to 41 inches average. Weight: 7½ pounds average. Curly maple one-piece stock, although walnut was sometimes used. Single- and double-set trigger. Brass fittings, including patch box, ramrod ferrules, butt plate, etc. Made from 1774 to 1775.

JOHN DERR(E)
Lancaster, Pennsylvania

Derr(e) Kentucky Flintlock Rifle........... **$6300**
Flintlock ignition system. Caliber: 42. Barrel: 42½ inches; half-octagonal. Overall length: 57½ inches. Weight: 7½ pounds. Full maple stock. Brass patch box. Made from 1810 to 1844.

ADAM DETERER
Lancaster, Pennsylvania

Deterer Kentucky Flintlock Rifle.......... **$1500**
Lock: casehardened flintlock. Calibers: various, usually 36 to 50. Barrel length: 36 to 41 inches average. Weight: 7½ pounds average. Curly maple one-piece stock, although walnut was sometimes used. Single- and double-set trigger. Brass fittings, including patch box, ramrod ferrules, butt plate, etc. Made from 1740 to 1778.

Deterer Fancy Grade Kentucky Flintlock Rifle................................... **$4500**
Same general specifications as above rifle, except gun has some modest stock carvings, silver inlays, and minute metal engraving, etc.

JACOB DOLL
York, Pennsylvania

Doll Kentucky Flintlock Rifle............. **$1500**
Lock: casehardened flintlock. Calibers: various, usually 36 to 50. Barrel length: 36 to 41 inches average. Weight: 7½ pounds average. Curly maple one-piece stock, although walnut was sometimes used. Single- and double-set trigger. Brass fittings, including patch box, ramrod ferrules, butt plate, etc. Made from 1780 to 1805.

Doll Fancy Grade Kentucky Flintlock Rifle.. **$4500**
Same general specifications as above rifle, except gun has some modest stock carvings, silver inlays, and minute metal engraving, etc.

Doll Extra Fancy Grade Kentucky Flintlock Rifle................................... **$7000**
Same general specifications as above rifle, except extra fancy wood, much carving, engraving on metal with gold or silver inlays.

JACOB DULL
Lancaster, Pennsylvania

Dull Kentucky Flintlock Rifle............. **$1200**
Lock: casehardened flintlock. Calibers: various, usually 36 to 50. Barrel length: 36 to 41 inches average. Weight: 7½ pounds average. Curly maple one-piece stock, although walnut was sometimes used. Single- and double-set trigger. Brass fittings, including patch box, ramrod ferrules, butt plate, etc. Made from 1799 to 1800.

HENRY EBERMAN
Lancaster, Pennsylvania

Eberman Kentucky Flintlock Rifle......... **$1500**
Lock: casehardened flintlock. Calibers: various, usually 36 to 50. Barrel length: 36 to 41 inches average. Weight: 7½ pounds average. Curly maple one-piece stock, although walnut was sometimes used. Single- and double-set trigger. Brass fittings, including patch box, ramrod ferrules, butt plate, etc. Made from 1819 to 1820.

Eberman Fancy Grade Kentucky Flintlock Rifle................................... **$4500**
Same general specifications as above rifle, except gun has some modest stock carvings, silver inlays, and minute metal engraving, etc.

Eberman Extra Fancy Grade Kentucky Flintlock Rifle **$7000**
Same general specifications as above rifle, except extra fancy wood, much carving, engraving on metal with gold or silver inlays.

H. EHRMS
Address Unknown

Ehrms Kentucky Flintlock Rifle **$1500**
Caliber: 52. Barrel: 41½ inches, full octagonal. Overall length: 56½ inches. Weight: 9 pounds. Full maple stock; all silver mountings.

H. ELWELL
Liverpool, Pennsylvania

Elwell Kentucky Flintlock Rifle **$1500**
Lock: casehardened flintlock. Calibers: various, usually 36 to 50. Barrel length: 36 to 41 inches average. Weight: 7½ pounds average. Curly maple one-piece stock, although walnut was sometimes used. Single- and double-set trigger. Brass fittings, including patch box, ramrod ferrules, butt plate, etc. Made from 1769 to 1770.

FREDERICK, FRANK & JACOB FARNOT
Lancaster, Pennsylvania

Farnot Kentucky Flintlock Rifle **$1500**
Lock: casehardened flintlock. Calibers: various, usually 36 to 50. Barrel length: 36 to 41 inches average. Weight: 7½ pounds average. Curly maple one-piece stock, although walnut was sometimes used. Single- and double-set trigger. Brass fittings, including patch box, ramrod ferrules, butt plate, etc. Made from 1775 to 1783.

Farnot Fancy Grade Kentucky Flintlock Rifle **$4500**
Same general specifications as above rifle, except gun has some modest stock carvings, silver inlays, and minute metal engraving, etc.

Farnot Extra Fancy Grade Kentucky Flintlock Rifle **$7000**
Same general specifications as above rifle, except extra fancy wood, much carving, engraving on metal with gold or silver inlays.

PHILIP FISHBURN
Dauphin County, Pennsylvania

Fishburn Kentucky Flintlock Rifle **$1500**
Lock: casehardened flintlock. Calibers: various, usually 36 to 50. Barrel length: 36 to 41 inches average. Weight: 7½ pounds average. Curly maple one-piece stock, although walnut was sometimes used. Single- and double-set trigger. Brass fittings, including patch box, ramrod ferrules, butt plate, etc. Made from 1776 to 1795.

Fishburn Fancy Grade Kentucky Flintlock Rifle **$4500**
Same general specifications as above rifle, except gun has some modest stock carvings, silver inlays, and minute metal engraving, etc.

Fishburn Extra Fancy Grade Kentucky Flintlock Rifle **$7000**
Same general specifications as above rifle, except extra fancy wood, much carving, engraving on metal with gold or silver inlays.

GEORGE FONDERSMITH
Stasburg Township, Pennsylvania

Fondersmith Kentucky Flintlock Rifle **$1500**
Lock: casehardened flintlock. Calibers: various, usually 36 to 50. Barrel length: 36 to 41 inches average. Weight: 7½ pounds average. Curly maple one-piece stock, although walnut was sometimes used. Single- and double-set trigger. Brass fittings, including patch box, ramrod ferrules, butt plate, etc. Made from 1779 to 1780.

C. FORDNEY
Cumberland, Pennsylvania

Fordney Kentucky Flintlock Rifle **$1500**
Lock: casehardened flintlock. Calibers: various, usually 36 to 50. Barrel length: 36 to 41 inches average. Weight: 7½ pounds average. Curly maple one-piece stock, although walnut was sometimes used. Single- and double-set trigger. Brass fittings, including patch box, ramrod ferrules, butt plate, etc. Made from 1800 to 1830.

Fordney Fancy Grade Kentucky Flintlock Rifle **$4500**
Same general specifications as above rifle, except gun has some modest stock carvings, silver inlays, and minute metal engraving, etc.

**Fordney Extra Fancy Grade Kentucky Flintlock
Rifle.** **$7000**
Same general specifications as above rifle, except extra
fancy wood, much carving, engraving on metal with
gold or silver inlays.

MARTIN FREY
York, Pennsylvania

Frey Kentucky Flintlock Rifle. **$1500**
Lock: casehardened flintlock. Calibers: various, usually 36 to 50. Barrels: 36 to 41 inches. Weight: 7½
pounds average. Curly maple one-piece stock, although walnut was sometimes used. Single- and double-set trigger. Brass fittings, including patch box,
ramrod ferrules, butt plate, etc. Made from 1799 to
1800.

PETER GANDER
Lancaster, Pennsylvania

Gander Kentucky Flintlock Rifle. **$1500**
Lock: casehardened flintlock. Calibers: various, usually 36 to 50. Barrel length: 36 to 41 inches average.
Weight: 7½ pounds average. Curly maple one-piece
stock, although walnut was sometimes used. Single-
and double-set trigger. Brass fittings, including patch
box, ramrod ferrules, butt plate, etc. Made from 1779 to
1780.

JOHN GETZ
Lancaster, Pennsylvania

Getz Kentucky Flintlock Rifle **$1500**
Lock: casehardened flintlock. Calibers: various, usually 36 to 50. Barrel length: 36 to 41 inches average.
Weight: 7½ pounds average. Curly maple one-piece
stock, although walnut was sometimes used. Single-
and double-set trigger. Brass fittings, including patch
box, ramrod ferrules, butt plate, etc. Made from 1773 to
1782.

**Getz Fancy Grade Kentucky Flintlock
Rifle.** **$4500**
Same general specifications as standard rifle, except
gun has some modest stock carvings, silver inlays, and
minute metal engraving, etc.

**Getz Extra Fancy Grade Kentucky Flintlock
Rifle.** **$7000**
Same general specifications as Fancy Grade rifle, ex-
cept extra fancy wood, much carving, engraving on
metal with gold or silver inlays.

FREDERICK GOETZ
Philadelphia, Pennsylvania

Goetz Kentucky Flintlock Rifle **$1500**
Lock: casehardened flintlock. Calibers: various, usually 36 to 50. Barrel length: 36 to 41 inches average.
Weight: 7½ pounds average. Curly maple one-piece
stock, although walnut was sometimes used. Single-
and double-set trigger. Brass fittings, including patch
box, ramrod ferrules, butt plate, etc. Made from 1806 to
1812.

**Goetz Fancy Grade Kentucky Flintlock
Rifle.** **$4500**
Same general specifications as standard rifle, except
gun has some modest stock carvings, silver inlays, and
minute metal engraving, etc.

**Goetz Extra Fancy Grade Kentucky
Flintlock Rifle.** **$7000**
Same general specifications as Fancy Grade rifle, ex-
cept extra fancy wood, much carving, engraving on
metal with gold or silver inlays.

J. GRESHEIM
Lancaster, Pennsylvania

Gresheim Kentucky Flintlock Rifle. **$1500**
Lock: casehardened flintlock. Calibers: various, usually 36 to 50. Barrel length: 36 to 41 inches average.
Weight: 7½ pounds average. Curly maple one-piece
stock, although walnut was sometimes used. Single-
and double-set trigger. Brass fittings, including patch
box, ramrod ferrules, butt plate, etc. Made from 1775 to
1783.

SAMUEL GROVE
York County, Pennsylvania

Grove Kentucky Flintlock Rifle **$1500**
Lock: casehardened flintlock. Calibers: various, usually 36 to 50. Barrel length: 36 to 41 inches average.
Weight: 7½ pounds average. Curly maple one-piece
stock, although walnut was sometimes used. Single-
and double-set trigger. Brass fittings, including patch
box, ramrod ferrules, butt plate, etc. Made from 1779 to
1783.

**Grove Fancy Grade Kentucky Flintlock
Rifle.** **$4500**
Same general specifications as standard rifle, except
gun has some modest stock carvings, silver inlays, and
minute metal engraving, etc.

**Grove Extra Fancy Grade Kentucky
Flintlock Rifle**. **$7000**
Same general specifications as Fancy Grade rifle, except extra fancy wood, much carving, engraving on metal with gold or silver inlays.

CHRISTIAN GUMP
Lancaster, Pennsylvania

Gump Kentucky Flintlock Rifle **$1500**
Lock: casehardened flintlock. Calibers: various, usually 36 to 50. Barrel length: 36 to 41 inches average. Weight: 7½ pounds average. Curly maple one-piece stock, although walnut was sometimes used. Single- and double-set trigger. Brass fittings, including patch box, ramrod ferrules, butt plate, etc. Made from 1799 to 1800.

ISAAC HAINES
Lampeter Township, Pennsylvania

Haines Kentucky Flintlock Rifle **$1500**
Lock: casehardened flintlock. Calibers: various, usually 36 to 50. Barrel length: 36 to 41 inches average. Weight: 7½ pounds average. Curly maple one-piece stock, although walnut was sometimes used. Single- and double-set trigger. Brass fittings, including patch box, ramrod ferrules, butt plate, etc. Made from 1730 to 1775.

**Haines Fancy Grade Kentucky Flintlock
Rifle**. **$4500**
Same general specifications as standard rifle, except gun has some modest stock carvings, silver inlays, and minute metal engraving, etc.

**Haines Extra Fancy Grade Kentucky
Flintlock Rifle**. **$7000**
Same general specifications as Fancy Grade rifle, except extra fancy wood, much carving, engraving on metal with gold or silver inlays.

JOHN N. HAMPTON
Hanover Township, Pennsylvania

Hampton Kentucky Flintlock Rifle **$1500**
Lock: casehardened flintlock. Calibers: various, usually 36 to 50. Barrel length: 36 to 41 inches average. Weight: 7½ pounds average. Curly maple one-piece stock, although walnut was sometimes used. Single- and double-set trigger. Brass fittings, including patch box, ramrod ferrules, butt plate, etc. Made from 1834 to 1835.

HENRY HARRIS
Lancaster, Pennsylvania

Harris Kentucky Flintlock Rifle. **$1500**
Lock: casehardened flintlock. Calibers: various, usually 36 to 50. Barrel length: 36 to 41 inches average. Weight: 7½ pounds average. Curly maple one-piece stock, although walnut was sometimes used. Single- and double-set trigger. Brass fittings, including patch box, ramrod ferrules, butt plate, etc. Made from 1834 to 1841.

**Harris Fancy Grade Kentucky Flintlock
Rifle**. **$4500**
Same general specifications as standard rifle, except gun has some modest stock carvings, silver inlays, and minute metal engraving, etc.

**Harris Extra Fancy Grade Kentucky
Flintlock Rifle**. **$7000**
Same general specifications as Fancy Grade rifle, except extra fancy wood, much carving, engraving on metal with gold or silver inlays.

PETER HENCH
Lancaster, Pennsylvania

Hench Kentucky Flintlock Rifle. **$1500**
Lock: casehardened flintlock. Calibers: various, usually 36 to 50. Barrel length: 36 to 41 inches average. Weight: 7½ pounds average. Curly maple one-piece stock, although walnut was sometimes used. Single- and double-set trigger. Brass fittings, including patch box, ramrod ferrules, butt plate, etc. Made from 1740 to 1775.

J. HILLEGAS
Pottsville, Pennsylvania

Hillegas Kentucky Flintlock Rifle **$1500**
Lock: casehardened flintlock. Calibers: various, usually 36 to 50. Barrel length: 36 to 41 inches average. Weight: 7½ pounds average. Curly maple one-piece stock, although walnut was sometimes used. Single- and double-set trigger. Brass fittings, including patch box, ramrod ferrules, butt plate, etc. Made from 1810 to 1830.

**Hillegas Fancy Grade Kentucky Flintlock
Rifle**. **$4500**
Same general specifications as standard rifle, except gun has some modest stock carvings, silver inlays, and minute metal engraving, etc.

Hillegas Extra Fancy Grade Kentucky Flintlock Rifle. **$7000**
Same general specifications as Fancy Grade rifle, except extra fancy wood, much carving, engraving on metal with gold or silver inlays.

MATHIAS HOAK
Lancaster, Pennsylvania

Hoak Kentucky Flintlock Rifle. **$1500**
Lock: casehardened flintlock. Calibers: various, usually 36 to 50. Barrel length: 36 to 41 inches average. Weight: 7½ pounds average. Curly maple one-piece stock, although walnut was sometimes used. Single- and double-set trigger. Brass fittings, including patch box, ramrod ferrules, butt plate, etc. Made from 1799 to 1800.

MICHAEL HUMBLE
Louisville, Kentucky

Humble Kentucky Flintlock Rifle. **$1995**
Lock: casehardened flintlock. Calibers: various, usually 36 to 50. Barrel length: 36 to 41 inches average. Weight: 7½ pounds average. Curly maple one-piece stock, although walnut was sometimes used. Single- and double-set trigger. Brass fittings, including patch box, ramrod ferrules, butt plate, etc. Made from 1775 to 1795.

Humble Fancy Grade Kentucky Flintlock Rifle. **$4900**
Same general specifications as standard rifle, except gun has some modest stock carvings, silver inlays, and minute metal engraving, etc.

Humble Extra Fancy Grade Kentucky Flintlock Rifle. **$9000**
Same general specifications as Fancy Grade rifle, except extra fancy wood, much carving, engraving on metal with gold or silver inlays.

V. HUNTINGTON
Allentown, Pennsylvania

Huntington Kentucky Flintlock Rifle. **$1500**
Lock: casehardened flintlock. Calibers: various, usually 36 to 50. Barrel length: 36 to 41 inches average. Weight: 7½ pounds average. Curly maple one-piece stock, although walnut was sometimes used. Single- and double-set trigger. Brass fittings, including patch box, ramrod ferrules, butt plate, etc. Made from 1798 to 1800.

BENEDICT IMHOFF
Heidelberg Township, Pennsylvania

Imhoff Kentucky Flintlock Rifle. **$1500**
Lock: casehardened flintlock. Calibers: various, usually 36 to 50. Weight: 7½ pounds average. Curly maple one-piece stock; sometimes of walnut. Single- and double-set triggers. Brass fittings, including patch box, ramrod ferrules, butt plate, etc. Made from 1784 to 1785.

Imhoff Fancy Grade Kentucky Flintlock Rifle. **$4500**
Same general specifications as standard rifle, except with some modest stock carvings, silver inlays, minute metal engraving, etc.

Imhoff Extra Fancy Grade Kentucky Flintlock Rifle. **$7000**
Same general specifications as Fancy Grade Rifle, except has extra fancy grade wood, elaborate wood carving, engraving on metal with gold or silver inlays.

JACOB JORG
Berks County, Pennsylvania

Jorg Kentucky Flintlock Rifle **$1500**
Lock: casehardened flintlock. Calibers: various, usually 36 to 50. Barrel length: 36 to 41 inches average. Weight: 7½ pounds average. Curly maple one-piece stock, although walnut was sometimes used. Single- and double-set trigger. Brass fittings, including patch box, ramrod ferrules, butt plate, etc. Made from 1814 to 1815.

JOHN KELLER
Carlisle, Pennsylvania

Keller Kentucky Flintlock Rifle **$1500**
Lock: casehardened flintlock. Calibers: various, usually 36 to 50. Barrel length: 36 to 41 inches average. Weight: 7½ pounds average. Curly maple one-piece stock, although walnut was sometimes used. Single- and double-set trigger. Brass fittings, including patch box, ramrod ferrules, butt plate, etc. Made from 1823 to 1842.

Keller Fancy Grade Kentucky Flintlock Rifle. **$4500**
Same general specifications as standard rifle, except gun has some modest stock carvings, silver inlays, and minute metal engraving, etc.

**Keller Extra Fancy Grade Kentucky
Flintlock Rifle** **$7000**
Same general specifications as Fancy Grade rifle, except extra fancy wood, much carving, engraving on metal with gold or silver inlays.

JOHN S. KINTER
Harriston County, Indiana

Kinter Kentucky Flintlock Rifle **$1500**
Lock: casehardened flintlock. Calibers: various, usually 36 to 50. Barrel length: 36 to 41 inches average. Weight: 7½ pounds average. Curly maple one-piece stock, although walnut was sometimes used. Single- and double-set trigger. Brass fittings, including patch box, ramrod ferrules, butt plate, etc. Made from 1820 to 1851.

JOHN MAURER
Lancaster, Pennsylvania

Maurer (Mauger) Kentucky Flintlock Rifle . . **$6800**
Flintlock ignition system. Caliber: 42. Overall length: 61 inches. Weight: 9¾ pounds. Full maple stock, hand carved. Brass patch box. Made circa 1800.

PETER NEIHARD
Whitehall Township, Pennsylvania

Neihard Kentucky Flintlock Rifle **$950**
Flintlock. Caliber: 45 most common. Barrel length: 40 inches; round and octagonal. Weight: 9 pounds. Curly maple full-length stock. Brass fittings. Made from 1785 to 1793.

CHRISTIAN OBERHOLZER
Lancaster, Pennsylvania

Oberholzer Kentucky Flintlock Musket **$795**
Calibers: 45, 54 and others. Barrel: 40 inches; round and octagonal. Weight: 9 pounds. Curly maple full-length stock. Brass fittings. Made from 1775 to 1778.

JOHN PAGE
Lancaster, Pennsylvania

Page Kentucky Flintlock Rifle **$975**
Flintlock. Calibers: 36 and 45. Barrel: 40 inches; round and octagonal. Weight: 9 pounds. Curly maple full-length stock; brass fittings. Made from 1770 to 1777.

RAPPAHANNOCK FORGE
Falmouth, Virginia

Rappahannock Forge was established by Act of the Assembly of Virginia, June 1775. The forge was previously owned by the Hunter Iron Works. Rappahannock Forge was considered to have produced some of the earliest "true" American military arms.

Rappahannock Forge Flintlock Musket **$1400**
Calibers: 45, 54 and others. Barrel: 40 inches, round. Weight: 9½ pounds. American walnut stock with iron and brass fittings. Made from 1775 to 1781.

WILLIAM SCHEANER
Reading, Pennsylvania

Scheaner Kentucky Flintlock Rifle **$1725**
Calibers: 36 and 45. Barrel: 40 inches; round and octagonal. Weight: 8½ to 9¼ pounds. American walnut and curly maple stock. Mostly brass fittings. Made from 1779 to 1790.

Scheaner Kentucky Flintlock Rifle, Deluxe . . **$1725**
Calibers: 36 and 45. Barrel: 40 inches; round and octagonal. Weight: 8½ to 9¼ pounds. American walnut and curly maple stock. Mostly brass fittings. Silver inlays and wood carvings. Made from 1779 to 1790.

WELSHANTZ BROTHERS
York, Pennsylvania

**Welshantz Kentucky Flintlock Rifle,
Deluxe** **$1425**
Caliber: 45 most common. Barrel: 40 inches; round and octagonal. Weight: 9½ pounds. Curly maple stock. Mostly brass fittings. Made from 1777 to 1811.

CONFEDERATE MILITARY RIFLES

Firearms used by the Confederacy are usually grouped into five general categories: U.S. arms already in possession of the Southern troops: U.S. arms captured by the Confederacy; arms imported from abroad; firearms manufactured by the southern states, and private firearms owned by individuals.

Rifles manufactured by the Union may be found in the section on U.S. Military Breechloading Carbines, while privately owned firearms may be found under individual listings. The firearms that follow were those most often found in use by the Confederacy and were for the most part either manufactured in the South or "adapted" by Southern armories.

C.S. & P. Rising-Breech Carbine **$4690**
Caliber: 54 percussion. Barrel: 21 inches; marked "C.S.&P."

Confederate Asheville Rifle **$5000**
Caplock side plate. Caliber: 58. Barrel: 32⅝ inches with bayonet lug. Overall length: 48⅝ inches. Weight: 8 lbs. 6 oz. Fixed sights. Brass butt plate, stock tip and trigger guard. Iron barrel bands. Lock plate marked "ASHEVILLE, N.C."

Confederate Austrian Rifle **$2250**
Caplock. Caliber: 54. Barrel: 37¼ inches. Overall length: 53 inches. Weight: approximately 9 pounds. Iron mountings. Two bands. Sling swivels attached to top band and trigger guard. "Austrian Rifle, Tyler, Tex. Cal. 54" marked on rear of hammer; some were also marked with "C.S." and the year of manufacture.

Confederate Baker Rifle **$2500**
Percussion, converted from flintlock. Caliber: 52. Barrel: 36 inches, with lug for sword bayonet. Overall length: 51 inches. Weight: approximately 9 pounds. Barrel marked "N. Carolina" with date on tang. "M.A. Baker, Fayetteville, N.C." marked on lock plate. "U.S" marked on butt plate tang.

Confederate Billups Rifle **$2300**

Confederate Cook & Brother Artillery Rifle **$3700**
Percussion lock. Caliber: 58. Barrel: 24 inches. Overall length: 40 inches. Weight: approximately 7 pounds. All brass mountings. Markings include "Cook & Brother, Athens, Ga." year plus serial number on lock plate; Confederate flag rear of hammer; serial number on butt plate; "Athens, year, proved." on barrel. Black walnut stock.

Confederate Cook & Brother Infantry Rifle. . **$2900**
Percussion lock. Caliber: 58. Barrel: 33 inches. Overall length: 49 inches. Weight: approximately 8 pounds. Iron ramrod with brass cup-shaped end. Cherry stock. Other markings same as Artillery Rifle.

Confederate Cook & Brother Musketoon **$2800**
Percussion. Caliber: 58. Barrel: 21 inches. Overall length: 36½ inches. Weight: approximately 6½ pounds. Swivel ramrod with large button head end; clamping bands. Brass mountings. Other markings same as the Artillery Rifle.

Confederate Davis & Bozeman Rifle **$4375**
Percussion. Caliber: 58. Barrel: 33 inches. Overall length: 48 inches. Weight: 8 pounds. Barrel marked "Ala. 1864." and lock plate marked "D & B Ala., 1864." Brass mountings.

Confederate Dickson, Nelson & Co. Carbine. **$4750**
Percussion. Caliber: 58. Barrel: 24 inches. Overall length: 40 inches. Weight: approximately 6½ pounds. "Dickson, Nelson & Company, Ala., 1864" marked on lock plate. Brass furniture. Fixed rear sight. Swivel ramrod.

Confederate Dickson, Nelson & Co. Rifle. . . . **$2995**
Percussion. Caliber: 58. Barrel: 33 inches. Overall length: 49 inches. Weight: 8 pounds. Two-leaf rear sight. Brass furniture. Lock plate marked "Dickson, Nelson & Co., C.S." in front of hammer and "Ala." plus the date behind the hammer. Barrel may also be marked "Ala." and the date. Cherry or walnut stock.

Confederate Fayetteville Rifle **$3125**
Percussion. Caliber: 58. Barrel: 33 inches. Overall length: 49 inches. Weight: 8¾ pounds. Markings include "V.P." with eagle head and year on barrel breech, "C.S." on butt plate tang, "Fayetteville" with spread eagle over "C.S.A." on lock plate. Made from parts and tools taken from Harper's Ferry, W.V.

Confederate Georgia Armory Rifle **$2900**
Percussion. Caliber: 58. Barrel: 33 inches, some equipped with saber-bayonet lug. Overall length: 49 inches. Weight: 8¾ pounds. "Ga. Armory" and the year marked on lock plate in rear of hammer. Brass furniture.

Confederate Lamb Rifle **$4500**
Caplock, plain lock plate. Caliber: 58. Barrel: 33 inches; part octagonal, part round. Weight: approximately 9 pounds. Yellow oak stock stamped "H.C. Lamb & Co., N.C." Serial number on breech, inside of hammer and sometimes on stock.

Confederate Richmond
Model 1863 Carbine

Confederate LeMat Carbine **$5000**
Percussion, two-barrel revolving carbine; nine-shot cylinder. Caliber: 42. Barrel: 20 inches; part-round, part-octagonal. Overall length: 38¼ inches. Weight: 7½ pounds. Of French manufacture, but designed and patented by Dr. LeMat of New Orleans.

Confederate "M" Rifle.................... **$5000**
Percussion, caplock. Caliber: 58. Barrel: 39 inches; with British proof marks. Marked "L.S.M." on lower tang, "1862" on lock plate in front of hammer, and "M" and a spread eagle at rear of hammer.

Confederate Mendenhall, Jones & Gardner Rifle.. **$2250**
Percussion. Caliber: 58. Barrel: 33 inches with sword-type bayonet lug. Weight: approximately 9 pounds. Iron butt plate and ramrod. Brass mountings. Lock plate marked "M.J. & G., N.C." forward of hammer; rear of hammer marked "C.S. 1863."

Confederate Morse Breech-Loading Altered Musket **$5000**
Action used metallic, self-primed cartridges. Caliber: 69. Barrel: 40½ inches with bayonet provisions. Weight: approximately 9 pounds. Lock plate marked "U.S. spread eagle, Springfield 1839."

Confederate Morse Breech-Loading Carbine................................... **$3750**
Hinged breech action. Caliber: 50. Barrel: 20 inches, round. Weight: approximately 7 pounds. Butternut stock; brass frame and mountings. Serial numbers on bottom of frame. No other markings.

Confederate Murray Cavalry Carbine **$2550**
Same general description as Murray Carbine Musketoon, except had 23-inch barrel and weighed approximately 6¾ pounds.

Confederate Murray Carbine Musketoon.... **$2550**
Percussion. Caliber: 58. Barrel: 24 inches, round. Weight: approximately 7 pounds. Brass mountings; iron sling swivels and ramrod. Walnut stock. Lock plate marked "J.P. Murray, Columbus, GA." Breech marked "Ala 1864" and "F.C.H."

Confederate Murray Rifle................. **$2550**
Same general description as Murray Carbine, except had 32¾-inch barrel.

Confederate Murray Sharpshooter's Rifle... **$3750**
Same general description as Murray Carbine, except had 29-inch heavy octagonal barrel. Caliber: 50.

Confederate "P" Breech-Loading Carbine... **$4500**
Bronze-lined breech block with spiral groove to seat cartridge firmly. Caliber: 52. Barrel: 22½ inches, round. Marked "P" on breech block.

Confederate "P" Rifled Carbine (Hodgkins Carbine)................................. **$3750**
Percussion lock. Caliber: 58. Barrel: 22 inches, round. Iron mountings except brass forearm tip. Barrel marked "P.C.S.A"; inside of lock marked "C 44." Walnut stock. Sling ring mounted on rear of trigger guard bow.

Confederate Pulaski Rifle **$900**
Percussion lock. Caliber: 58. Barrel: 32¼ inches. Brass mountings. Marked "Pulaski, T.C.S.A. 61." Walnut stock.

Confederate Richmond Carbine........... **$2000**
Percussion lock. Caliber: 58. Barrel: 25 inches, with two barrel bands. Weight: approximately 7½ pounds. Full walnut stock; three sling swivels. Bronze butt plate marked "C.S." Barrel marked with year and "C.S." Lock plate marked "C.S. Richmond" plus the year.

Confederate Richmond Navy Musketoon.... **$2400**
Percussion lock. Caliber: 62. Barrel: 30 inches, round. Lock plate marked "C.S. Richmond, VA." plus year.

Confederate Richmond Rifled Musket **$1800**
Percussion lock. Caliber: 58. Barrel: 40 inches, round. Weight: approximately 9½ pounds. Walnut stock with three barrel bands. Close copy of U.S. Model 1855. Brass butt plate. Lock plate marked "C.S. Richmond, Va." and also the year near rear of lock plate. Barrel marked with year.

Confederate Robinson-Sharps Carbine..... **$2400**
Percussion breechloader. Caliber: 52. Barrel: 22 inches. Weight: approximately 7½ pounds. Lock plate marked "S.C. Robinson Arms Mfg. Co., Richmond, Va." Year plus serial number. Similar markings on barrel.

Confederate Sturdivant Rifle **$2100**
Percussion. Caliber: 54. Barrel: 32 inches. All brass
mountings. No markings except serial number.

**Confederate Tallassee Enfield Pattern
Carbine.** **$5000**
Percussion muzzleloader. Caliber: 58. Barrel: 25
inches, round; brass clamping barrel bands. Weight:
approximately 7³/₄ pounds. Brass trigger guard and
butt plate. Lock plate marked "S.C. Tallassee, Ala."
Date marked at rear of hammer.

Confederate Tanner Rifle. **$1750**
Percussion. Caliber: 54. Barrel: 33 inches, round. Se-
rial number is the only marking. This is similar to the
Mississippi Rifle.

Confederate Tarpley Carbine **$8500**
Percussion breechloader. Caliber: 52. Barrel: 23
inches, round. Weight: approximately 7 pounds. Iron
butt plate; brass breech.

Confederate Texas-Enfield Rifle **$7500**
Percussion. Caliber: 57. Barrel: 33 inches; round, with
bayonet lug. Brass mountings. Two-leafed rear sight.
Lock plate marked "Texas Rifle, Tyler, Cal. 57." Barrel
and butt plate marked "C.S."

Confederate Todd Rifled Musket **$750**
Percussion. Caliber: 58. Barrel: 40 inches, round.
Weight: approximately 9 pounds. Walnut stock. Lock
plate marked "Geo. H. Todd, Montgomery, Ala."

Confederate Wallis Rifle. **$900**
Similar to the Mississippi Rifle, except without the bayonet lug and patch box.

**Confederate Whitney-Enfield Mississippi
Rifle.** **$850**
Percussion lock. Caliber: 61. Barrel: 33 inches; round,
with bayonet lug. Weight: approximately 8¹/₂ pounds.
Brass trigger guard; iron butt plate. Close copy of En-
field Model 1858. Lock plate marked "E. Whitney."

Confederate Whitney Rifled Musket **$750**
Similar to U.S. Model 1855, except has brass butt plate
and no markings except "E. Whitney, New Haven" on
lock plate.

Confederate Wytheville-Hall Rifle **$2400**
Many variations of this model exist, as all were hand-
made from parts captured at Harpers Ferry. One-piece
brass casting was used to convert breechloader to
muzzleloader.

U.S. MILITARY FLINTLOCK RIFLES

The first U.S. Military muskets were known as the "Committee of Safety" arms. In the spring of 1775 the 13 colonies, through the various "Committees," provided muskets to arm the patriots for the ensuing "Revolution." The arms were produced by about 200 different gunsmiths, so wide variations are common. Some were stamped with the maker's name; some with simply an initial, and some without any markings at all. From about 1774 to 1775, the letters "C.P."—to designate "Continental Property"—were used. After Sep-

tember 9, 1776, the marking "U.S." was added to most arms. The later models were of course used during other wars and some were even converted to percussion and employed during the Civil War.

Harpers Ferry Flintlock Musket **$2700**
Same general specifications as Harpers Ferry Rifle, except smooth bore with longer barrel.

Harpers Ferry Flintlock Rifle **$2600**
Flintlock ignition system. Caliber: 53. Barrel: 33 inches; seven-grooved rifling. Weight: 9¾ pounds. American walnut stock without barrel bands. Buttstock is provided with patch box. Made from 1814 to 1819.

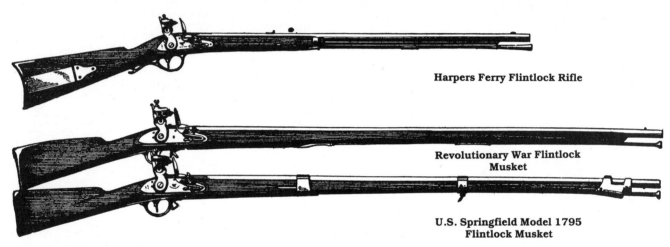

Harpers Ferry Flintlock Rifle

Revolutionary War Flintlock Musket

U.S. Springfield Model 1795 Flintlock Musket

Revolutionary Flintlock Musket **$3700**
Flintlock ignition system. Calibers: 72 to 80. Barrel: approximately 44½ inches long; round, smooth bore, but variations exist. Weight: over 10 pounds. Stock generally without barrel bands. Made principally in Massachusetts, Rhode Island, Maryland and Pennsylvania between 1775 and 1795.

U.S. Springfield Model 1795 Flintlock Musket **$2450**
Flintlock ignition system. Caliber: 70. Barrel: 45 inches; round, smoothbore. Weight: 9½ pounds. American walnut stock with barrel bands. Made from 1795 to 1808.

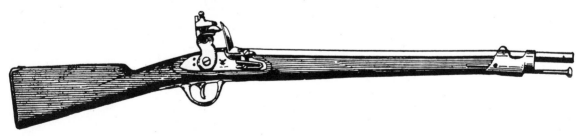

U.S. Springfield Model 1809 Flintlock Carbine

U.S. Springfield Model 1809 Flintlock Carbine **$12000**
Flintlock ignition system. Caliber: 56. Barrel: 19½ inches; round, smoothbore. Weight: 4¾ pounds. American walnut stock; sling swivels. No center barrel band.

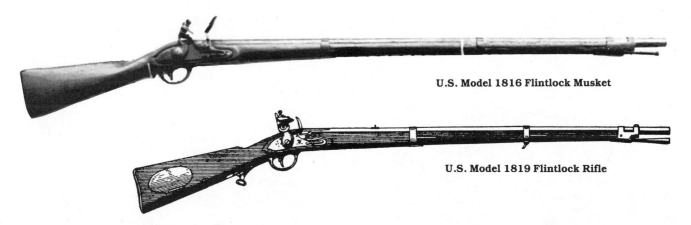

U.S. Model 1816 Flintlock Musket

U.S. Model 1819 Flintlock Rifle

U.S. Model 1816 Flintlock Musket **$2350**
Caliber: 69. Barrel: 42 inches, smoothbore. Weight: 10 pounds with bayonet. American walnut stock with barrel bands and 16-inch bayonet. Made from about 1816 to 1840, although sources disagree.

U.S. Model of 1819 Flintlock Rifle **$2550**
Officially known as the "Common Rifle." Caliber: 54. Barrel: 36 inches, round. Weight: 10¼ pounds. Stock with barrel bands. No bayonets provided. Made principally in Middletown, Conn., and Philadelphia.

U.S. Springfield Model 1840
Musketoon

U.S. Springfield Model 1840 Musketoon Smooth Bore. **$2400**
Flintlock ignition. Caliber: 69. Barrel: 26 inches; round, smoothbore. Copied from the French arm of 1836. The lock and its parts are slightly smaller than the musket of the same date.

Union soldier of the 22nd New York Infantry at Harpers Ferry, W. Va., during the Civil War.

U.S. MILITARY SINGLE SHOT BREECHLOADING CARBINES

All of the carbines described below were designed just prior to and during the Civil War. They could be loaded from the breech, which made them faster to load than muzzleloaders, and most were used by the Union troops. They were, however, single-shot arms, and slower than the repeaters, like the Spencer, for example, that were very successful during the war. Other Civil War-era breechloaders can be found under individual manufacturers listings.

Burnside Breech-Loading Carbine **$2550**
Caliber: 54. During the Civil War over 56,000 of these carbines, invented by A.E. Burnside, were purchased. George P. Foster, the primary manufacturer, brought out several improvements. This carbine used the first metallic shell cartridge designed for a military arm. The tapered end was open for the purpose of igniting the powder charge by the percussion cap. Patented in 1856.

Cosmopolitan Breech-Loading Carbine **$1125**
Caliber: 50. Made in Hamilton, Ohio, these guns, also called "Union," consisted of three models. During the Civil War 342 were purchased. This carbine, which weighs slightly under seven pounds, has an extremely lengthy hammer caused by the fact that it spans the entire breech block.

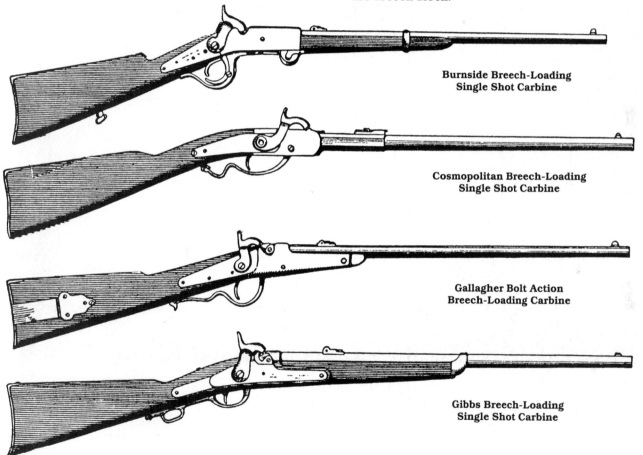

Burnside Breech-Loading
Single Shot Carbine

Cosmopolitan Breech-Loading
Single Shot Carbine

Gallagher Bolt Action
Breech-Loading Carbine

Gibbs Breech-Loading
Single Shot Carbine

Gallagher Breech-Loading Bolt Action Carbine **$750**
Caliber: 54. Made in Philadelphia by Richardson & Overman, who in 1865 altered a specimen to rimfire, calling it the Richardson, and submitted it to the Hancock Board on breechloading arms. For this particular carbine, over $212,000 were expended for cartridges. The barrel tilted up to load like a shotgun and the cartridge was linen covered. Patented in 1860.

Gibbs Breech-Loading Carbine **$1275**
Caliber: 52. W.F. Brooks of New York was given a contract in 1861 for 10,000 of these carbines, of which he completed and delivered only 1052. The barrel slides forward and tilts up at breech to load. The gun uses a paper cartridge. Although patented in 1856, none were made until 1863.

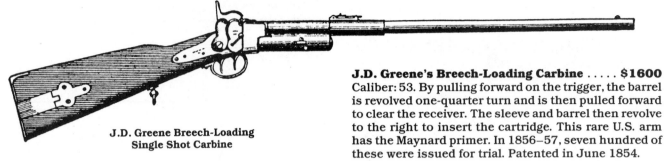

J.D. Greene Breech-Loading
Single Shot Carbine

J.D. Greene's Breech-Loading Carbine **$1600**
Caliber: 53. By pulling forward on the trigger, the barrel is revolved one-quarter turn and is then pulled forward to clear the receiver. The sleeve and barrel then revolve to the right to insert the cartridge. This rare U.S. arm has the Maynard primer. In 1856–57, seven hundred of these were issued for trial. Patented in June 1854.

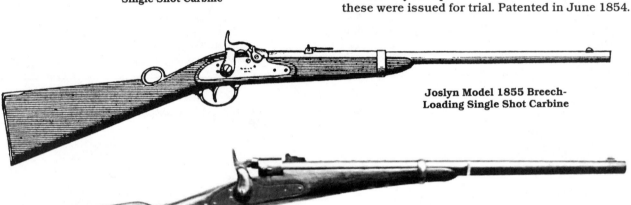

Joslyn Model 1855 Breech-
Loading Single Shot Carbine

Joslyn Model 1864 Civil War
Carbine

Joslyn Model 1855 Breech-Loading Carbine. **$1275**
Caliber: 54. Made by A.H. Waters of Millbury, Conn., for B.F. Joslyn, these were the first of the Joslyn systems, the rest being cartridge arms. The strap on the small of the stock lifts up and uncovers the breech when the ring on top of the butt is released. Patented in 1855. (*See* also Benjamin F. Joslyn under Rifles.)

Joslyn Model 1864 Carbine **$650**
Caliber: 52 RF. Single-shot breechloader. Barrel: 22 inches average; round. Casehardened lock plate. Iron mountings. Walnut stock. Patented in 1864. Made under government contract and used at the end of the Civil War.

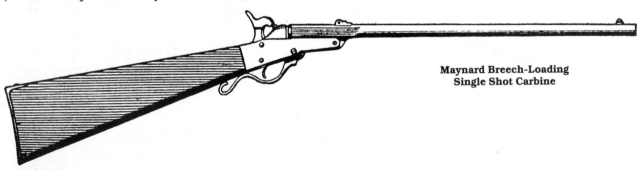

Maynard Breech-Loading
Single Shot Carbine

Maynard Breech-Loading Percussion Carbine. **$715**
Caliber: 50. Twenty thousand of these were purchased during the Civil War. The first few models of these carbines were equipped with the Maynard primer. The bar-

rel tilts up to load like a shotgun and it uses a metallic cartridge, the base of which filled the space between the barrel and breech. Patented by Dr. Edward Maynard in 1859.

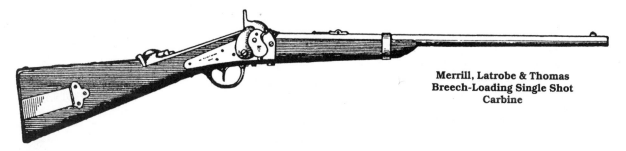

**Merrill, Latrobe & Thomas
Breech-Loading Single Shot
Carbine**

**Merrill, Latrobe and Thomas Breech-Loading
Carbine.** **$4500**
Caliber: 54. Made by Remington at Ilion, N.Y., but no
records have been found as to the quantity produced,
so they may be called rare. The carbine has the familiar
Maynard primer, but it had an unusual method of loading, which consisted of pushing the cartridge in place
with a piston worked by hand against the action of a
spring. The strap along the top of the stock is brought
up and forward to open the breech, which is merely a
circular piece of metal with a hole extending through
it. Patented in 1856.

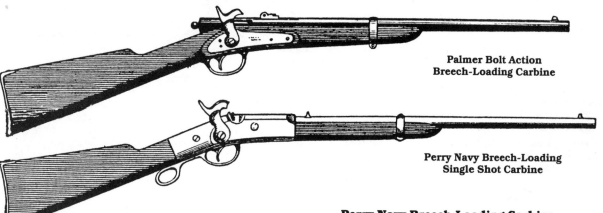

**Palmer Bolt Action
Breech-Loading Carbine**

**Perry Navy Breech-Loading
Single Shot Carbine**

**Palmer Breech-Loading Bolt Action
Carbine.** **$825**
Caliber: 50. This was the first metallic cartridge (rim-
fire) bolt gun used in the U.S. One of the lightest of the
Civil War guns, it weighed only 5³/₄ pounds. Another
feature was that the sectional locking screw of the bolt
was similar to the breech blocks of our modern cannon. Patented in December 1863, one thousand of
these were delivered before the end of the war.

Perry Navy Breech-Loading Carbine. **$1275**
Caliber: 54. Made in Newark, N.J., 200 were purchased
for trial in February, 1855, and in 1856 they were fa-
vorably commented upon by Admiral Dahlgren. This
arm has a magazine primer, consisting of a tube that is
inserted through the butt plate. The caps are fed by the
action of a spring exactly like the cartridge in the Spencer carbines and rifles. The arm is the second model of
Perry's breech action; the first is the so-called "Rebel"
Perry. This name was applied because some of the rifles made their way to the South in the early days of the
Civil War. Patented in 1855.

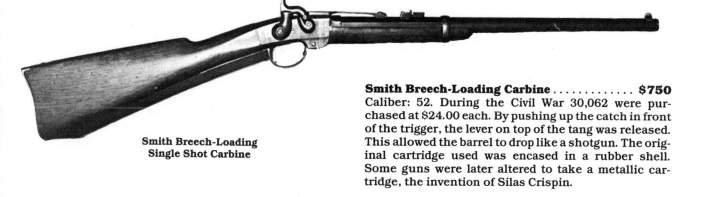

**Smith Breech-Loading
Single Shot Carbine**

Smith Breech-Loading Carbine **$750**
Caliber: 52. During the Civil War 30,062 were purchased at $24.00 each. By pushing up the catch in front
of the trigger, the lever on top of the tang was released.
This allowed the barrel to drop like a shotgun. The original cartridge used was encased in a rubber shell.
Some guns were later altered to take a metallic cartridge, the invention of Silas Crispin.

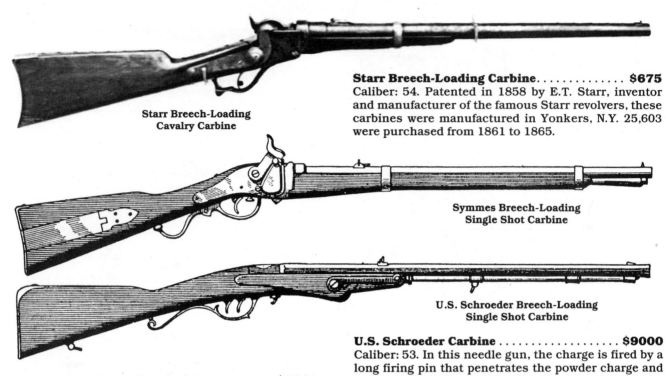

**Starr Breech-Loading
Cavalry Carbine**

Starr Breech-Loading Carbine............. **$675**
Caliber: 54. Patented in 1858 by E.T. Starr, inventor
and manufacturer of the famous Starr revolvers, these
carbines were manufactured in Yonkers, N.Y. 25,603
were purchased from 1861 to 1865.

**Symmes Breech-Loading
Single Shot Carbine**

**U.S. Schroeder Breech-Loading
Single Shot Carbine**

Symmes Breech-Loading Carbine.......... **$9000**
Caliber: 54. One of the early experimental pieces, only
200 being purchased by the U.S. Government. The
breech block rotates upward and has the Maynard magazine primer. Patented in 1858.

U.S. Schroeder Carbine.................. **$9000**
Caliber: 53. In this needle gun, the charge is fired by a
long firing pin that penetrates the powder charge and
ignites the fulminate, which is at the base of the bullet
in front of the cartridge. Used in 1858, these very rare
guns have a sliding forward barrel with an eagle and
U.S. on the tang. Several are in government collections.
Patented in 1856.

**Warner Breech-Loading
Single Shot Carbine**

**Weston Breech-Loading
Single Shot Carbine**

Warner Breech-Loading Carbine.......... **$1125**
Caliber: 50. This rimfiring carbine has a breech block
that swings to the right like the Joslyn; the extractor,
however, was worked by hand. Although 4,001 of these
guns were purchased during the Civil War, not many
were used because of the extra movement needed to
eject the shell. These guns, weighing less than seven
pounds, have an extractor handle that shows at the
bottom of the stock in front of the trigger guard. Patented in 1864.

Wesson Carbine.......................... **$625**
Caliber: 44. The barrel of this carbine tilts up like the
Gallager and Maynard and the front trigger releases the
catch holding it. The cartridge was all metal and rimfire. This gun was a great favorite with the Indians because it weighed less than six pounds. Some can be
found with Indian ornamentation of brass-headed
tacks on the buttstock. Invented by Frank Wesson who
later became one of the founders of the firm of Smith
and Wesson, this was patented in 1859. More than 150
of these breechloading arms were purchased by the
U.S. during the Civil War.

CHAPTER THREE
SHOTGUNS

Shotguns trace their descent from the ancient bell-mouth blunderbuss. The fowling piece that developed after that was simply a shorter, lighter version of the smoothbore musket.

The slow ignition of flintlock arms limited the success of hitting birds on the wing, and fowling pieces were seldom used until the introduction of the percussion cap. With its more rapid ignition, wing shooting became more practical.

The average shooter of the 1800s found that the .69 caliber smoothbore musket, loaded with a charge of shot pellets, served well enough for sitting ducks. But rifles barrels were unsuited for shot loads. As rifled barrels started to replace the smoothbore musket and bores gradually became smaller in size, a special fowling gun was developed. This fowling piece started to be called "shotgun" and was made with both single and double barrels. It rapidly acquired the characteristics that are found in the single-shot and side-by-side double-barreled shotguns of today.

Although breechloading shotguns appeared earlier, they did not come into common usage until about 1880, when the modern shotshell evolved. Shortly after, choke boring was discovered. By constricting the bore at the muzzle, it was found that a gun would throw a narrower, denser pattern of shot, tremendously extending its effective range. Except for minor refinements in design, metallurgy and the new operating concepts, the early breechloading shotguns were very similar to the designs in use today.

Like its muzzleloading predecessor, the fowling piece, the breechloading shotgun utilized a smooth bore of relatively large size to accommodate the load of shot pellets. The size of the bore, as the British call it, or gauge, as the Americans call it, is derived from the number of round lead balls required to make a pound. For example, a 12-gauge gun has a bore, which, if it had no choke, would accept one round ball—12 of which would weigh a pound. This antiquated means of measurement is longer used by manufacturers, but it has stuck in the marketplace because it serves its descriptive purpose well. The smaller the number, the larger the gauge. Twelve-gauge shotguns have larger diameter barrels than 16 gauge guns; 16 gauge are larger than 20 gauge, and so on. The .410 bore is the exception; it is the actual barrel diameter of .410", which is equivalent to about a 67 gauge. Since this size bore was a relative late-comer, it has escaped the older nomenclature.

Shotgun ammunition in England is termed "cartridge", but "shotshells" is the common term in the United States. For information on the composition of shotshells, please turn to Shotshells in the Obsolete Cartridges Section.

Although the production and variety of 19th-century shotguns does not approximate that of either handguns or rifles, the following pages contain an assortment of shotgun makers and models, many of which are of foreign origin.

J. F. ABBEY & CO.
Chicago, Illinois

**J.F. Abbey Single Barrel Muzzle-Loading
Shotgun** **$250**
Percussion side lock. Gauges: 12 to 30 bore. Barrel: 30
to 40 inches, iron. Weight: 5 to 8¾ pounds. Oil or varnished stock with checkered pistol grip. Made from
1871 to 1875.

**J.F. Abbey Double Barrel Muzzle-Loading
Shotgun** **$525**
Percussion back locks. Gauges: 12 to 30 bore. Barrel:
30 to 36 inches, iron. Weight: 6 to 8½ pounds. Double
triggers. Oil or varnished American walnut stock with
checkered pistol grip. Made from 1871 to 1875.

ACME ARMS
Chicopee Falls, Massachusetts

Acme Arms Double Barrel Shotgun. **$200**
Side-by-side. Manufactured by J. P. Stevens Arms
Company of Chicopee Falls, Mass.

E. B. ALDEN
Claremont, New Hampshire

**Alden Double Barrel Muzzle-Loading
Shotgun** **$495**
Swivel back-action locks. Gauges: 12 and 16 standard.
Barrels: 30 to 35 inches, iron. Weight: 7 to 8½ pounds.
Double triggers. Oiled or varnished American walnut
stock and forearm. Blued and engraved steel mount-
ing. German silver escutcheons and name plate. Made
from 1863 to 1868.

ARABIAN SHOTGUNS
Various Manufacturers

Arabian DAG Blunderbuss **$415**
flintlock. Barrel heavily engraved with Arabic inscrip-
tions, usually prayers or religious sayings, much of it
in silver inlay. Iron trigger guard. Brass wire inlay in
stock. Butt plate and saddle bar on left side.

A. J. AUBREY
Meriden, Connecticut

In the 1890s, Sears, Roebuck & Co. of Chicago, Ill.,
established a manufacturing facility in Meriden, Conn.,
called the Meriden Fire Arms Company. It was designed to produce firearms for the successful Sears
mail-order business. A. J. Aubrey was the manager of
the Meriden plant, and many of the guns turned out
there bear the name "A.J. Aubrey" as a brand name.

Firearms manufactured under the Aubrey name included hammer and hammerless single- and double-
barreled shotguns, as well as hammer and hammerless
revolvers of different styles.

A.J. Aubrey Standard Grade Double Barrel Shotgun
Sidelock action. Gauge: 12. Barrels: 30 or 32 inches; ar-
mory steel, laminated steel or two-blade Damascus.
Weight: 7½ to 8 pounds. Walnut stock with modest
checkering.
Armory Steel Barrels **$150**
Laminated Steel Barrels. **100**
Two-blade Damascus Barrels **100**

**A.J. Aubrey Hand-Engraved Double Barrel
Shotgun** **$125**
Sidelock action, modestly engraved. Gauge: 12. Bar-
rels: 30 or 32 inches; laminated steel or two-blade Damascus. Weight: 7½ to 8 pounds. Walnut stock with
modest checkering.

**A.J. Aubrey Highest Grade Double Barrel
Shotgun** **$175**
Sidelock action, modestly engraved. Gauge: 12. Bar-
rels: 30 or 32 inches; laminated steel or two-blade Damascus. Weight: 7¼ to 7¾ pounds. Good grade walnut
stock with nice checkering.

A.J. Aubrey Custom Grade Double Barrel Shotgun
Sidelock action, custom engraved. Gauges: any de-
sired. Barrels: any specified length, but usually made
in 30- or 32-inch length; laminated steel or two-blade
Damascus. Weight: 7 to 8¾ pounds. Any grade walnut
stock with various checkering, carving, embellish-
ments, etc. available.
Lower Grade Custom **$150**
Medium Grade Custom. **225**
Highest Grade Custom. **395**

Arabian DAG Blunderbuss

A.J. Aubrey Hammerless Single Shot
Shotgun **$75**
Top lever. Break-open. Single shot. Gauge: 12. Barrel:
30 or 32 inches. Weight: 6¹/₂ pounds. Walnut stock and
forend with checkering on buttstock grips.

BAKER GUN & FORGING CO.
Batavia, New York

The Baker Gun & Forging Company manufactured
firearms in the late 1800s and into the first third of the
1900s. They produced an extensive array of single- and
double-barreled arms that differed by grade and the
amount of customizing done.

Baker Batavia Leader Double Barrel Shotgun
Standard Model **$445**
Special Shotgun 575
Grade C Shotgun 250

Baker Black Beauty Double Shotgun
Standard Double Barrel **$675**
Special Double Barrel Model 750

Baker Deluxe Double Barrel Shotgun
Grade H . . . . $ 3,800
$300 Grade 5,000
$1000 Grade 15,000

Baker Double Barrel Shotgun
Grade A **$375**
Grade B 325
Grade R 700
Grade S 600
Model 1896 275
Model 1897 300
New Model Double 275

Baker Paragon Double Barrel Shotgun
With Non-automatic Ejector **$1200**
With Automatic Ejector 1500
Special Model 1895

Baker Pigeon Double Barrel Shotgun
Grade L Pigeon Grade **$2400**

Baker Single Shot Shotguns
Elite Model **$1295**
Sterling Model 800

Baker Trap Guns
N Krupp Double Barrel Trap **$1500**
Superba Single Shot Trap 3000

BAYARD SHOTGUNS
Herstal (Liège), Belgium

"Bayard" was the trade name of firearms produced
by the well-known firm of Anciens Establissements
Pieper, founded by Belgian gun manufacturer, Henri
Pieper (1840–1905). Pieper contributed to the evolu-
tion of cartridge revolvers and automatic pistols in addition to making quality shotguns.

Bayard Hammer Double Barrel Shotguns
Standard w/Damascus Barrels **$165**
Standard w/Steel Barrels 195
Fancy Grade 325

Bayard Hammerless Shotgun
Standard Double Barrel **$250**

BELGIAN SHOTGUNS
Various Manufacturers

Toward the end of the 19th century, Belgium was virtually the production center of Damascus barrels that
had become so popular at that time. These barrels were
imported by numerous U.S. arms manufacturers because they were in such demand. Nearly a third of all
the Belgian shotguns as well sported Damascus barrels.

Belgian Bolt Action Shotgun

Belgian Bolt Action Shotgun **$100**
Gauges: 12 and others. Barrel: 28, 30 and 32 inches,
round. Half-stock with checkered grip. Made circa
1890.

Belgian Double Barrel
Percussion Shotgun

Belgian Sidelock Double
Barrel Percussion Shotgun

Belgian Double Barrel Shotgun **$185**
Gauges: 16 and others. Barrels: 28, 30 and 32 inches;
side-by-side Damascus. Gold triggers and shield escutcheon in butt. High-grade walnut with checkered
grip and forend.

Belgian Double Barrel Percussion Shotgun . . **$200**
Gauges: 12 and others. Barrels: 28, 30 and 32 inches;
Damascus. Fern engraving. Fine wood with checkered
grip. Made circa 1850.

**Belgian Sidelock Double Barrel Percussion
Shotgun** **$200**
Gauges: 12 and others. Barrels: 28, 30 and 32 inches;
Damascus. Plain metal and wood, except for simple
checkered pattern on grip.

BOND & JAMES
London, England

**Bond & James Double Barrel Percussion
Shotgun** **$375**
Gauges: various (17 gauge shown.) Barrels: various
lengths, marked "LONDON FINE TWIST." Checkered
grip and forend. Iron furniture. Engraved, silver escutcheon in buttstock. Made from 1868 to 1875.

BRITISH SHOTGUNS
Various Manufacturers

See also individual listings.

British Double Barrel Percussion Shotgun . . . **$250**
Gauges: various. Barrels: various lengths. Stocks usually checkered at grip; no checkering on forend. Several silver escutcheons.

British Double Barrel Percussion Shotgun . . . **$300**
Gauges: 12 and others. Barrel: Damascus in various
lengths. Iron furniture, usually modestly engraved.
Checkered grips with silver escutcheon. Made in England circa 1840.

British Flintlock Fowler **$1000**
Gauge: 16. Barrel: 47 inches, round. Brass furniture.
Relief carving at barrel tang, front of comb and around
lock. Large brass escutcheon on wrist. Made in England circa 1735.

British Fowler Conversion **$175**
Percussion lock. Gauge: 20. Barrel: 43 inches. During
the early 1800s many British fowlers were converted
from flintlock to percussion. Many were unnamed, and
this is one typical example of their current value. Converted circa 1840.

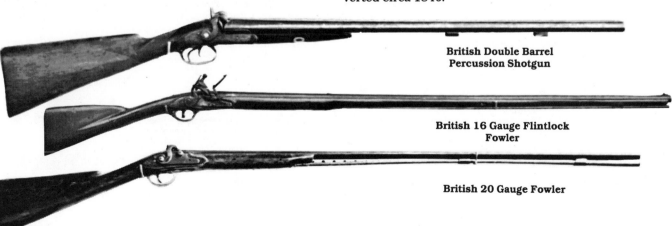

British Double Barrel
Percussion Shotgun

British 16 Gauge Flintlock
Fowler

British 20 Gauge Fowler

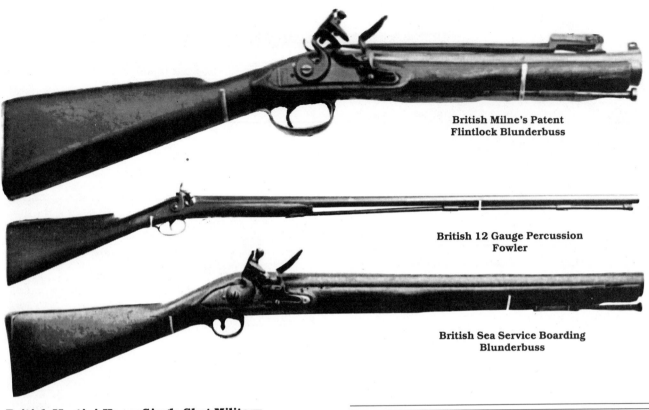

British Milne's Patent
Flintlock Blunderbuss

British 12 Gauge Percussion
Fowler

British Sea Service Boarding
Blunderbuss

**British Martini-Henry Single Shot Military
Shotgun** **$175**

**British Milne's Patent Flintlock
Blunderbuss** **$1400**
Engraved lockplate. Spring bayonet. Made circa 1795.

British Percussion Fowler. **$150**
Gauge: 12. Barrel: 39¹/₂ inches, round. Iron furniture,
lightly engraved. Silver escutcheon on grip.

**British Sea Service Boarding
Blunderbuss** **$2000**
Flintlock engraved, "TRULOCK 1757." Bore: 1 inch.
Brass furniture. Full-length plain stock. Made circa
1750s.

British Southall Blunderbuss. **$900**
Percussion lock. Brass barrel. Checkered grip. Iron
furniture, nicely engraved. Made circa 1835.

ANDREW BURGESS
Oswego, New York

Burgess Slide Action Shotgun
Takedown **$425**
Folding Gun **750**

WILLIAM CHANCE & SON
London, England

Wm. Chance & Son Percussion Fowler **$300**
Gauge: 12. Barrel: various lengths. Walnut stock with
iron furniture and German silver nose cap. German silver escutcheons and cap box in bottom of buttstock.
Modest metal engraving. One of the better quality fowlers. Made circa 1840.

Wm. Chance Percussion Fowler

Wm. Chance Double Barrel
Percussion Shotgun

**Wm. Chance & Son Double Barrel Percussion
Shotgun** **$300**
Gauge: 12. Barrel: various lengths. Three silver bars at
breech; silver patch box with iron door. Checkered
grip. Platinum blow plugs. Made from 1835 to 1845.

CHARLES CLEMENT
Liège, Belgium

Clement Double Barrel Hammer Shotgun
Standard Model **$195**

Clement Double Barrel Hammerless Shotgun
Damascus Barrels **$195**
Steel Barrels 225

J. B. CLEMENT
Belgium

J. B. Clement Double Barrel Shotguns
Hammer Model **$210**
Hammerless Model 225

COLT'S PATENT FIRE ARMS MFG. CO.
Hartford, Connecticut

Although Colt manufactured only two basic model
shotguns, they became renown throughout the world
for their craftsmanship and quality, as Colt's other firearms. In fact, shortly after the Model 1878 Shotgun de-
buted, it won a Gold Medal and Diploma of Merit at the
Melbourne Exposition of 1881 and the "Highest Re-
ward" by the Massachusetts Charitable Mechanic Association in 1881.

Colt Model 1878 Hammer Shotgun **$850**
Side-by-side double barrel. Gauges: 10 and 12. Barrels:
28, 30 or 32 inches; blued or brown. Weight: about 7¹/₂
pounds with 28-inch barrel. Rebounding lock. Color
casehardened breech. Double triggers. Colt markings
rolled on the lock plates and sometimes on the barrel
rib. Semi-pistol grip standard, but English straight grip
often found. Checkered English or Circassian walnut
stock and forend. Available in a variety of styles with
twist, fine twist, laminated or Damascus barrels, custom engravings, inlaids, etc. 22,683 guns made between 1878 and 1889.

Colt Model 1883 Hammerless Shotgun **$900**
Side-by-side double barrel. Gauges: 10 and 12. Barrel:
28, 30 or 32 inches; blued or brown. Double triggers.
This was virtually a custom shotgun, similar to the
Model 1878, and made in much smaller quantity, with
great variation of engravings, inlaids, etc. Made from
1883 to 1895.

CRESCENT FIREARMS COMPANY
Norwich, Connecticut

The Crescent Firearms Company was founded about
1888 and operated in Norwich, Conn. It has been said
that this company was the most prolific of all manufacturers of private label guns, producing not less than
100 different brand names.

In 1893, Crescent was purchased by H & D Folsom
Arms Company of New York City (*see* separate listing).
This firm sold guns manufactured by Crescent under a
variety of names. In fact, if a certain number of the
same model of gun was ordered, the buyer could have
almost any label he wished stamped on the arm. For
this reason, many hardware stores of the time, who always sold dozens of single- and double-barreled shotguns each year, had their own firm name stamped on
the guns—providing even more confusion among gun
collectors. The following shotguns were known to have
been produced by the Crescent Firearms Co. and carried any of the brand names or private labels in the listing that follows them. In effect, all of the double-
barreled side-by-side shotguns, for example, were
identical, except for the names stamped on them.

Double Barrel Side-by-Side Shotgun
Outside hammers. Sidelock action. Gauges: various.
Barrels: 28 to 32 inches; steel or Damascus. Weight:
7¹/₂ to 9¹/₂ pounds. Checkered standard grade American walnut pistol-grip stock.
With Damascus Barrels **$155**
With Steel Barrels **200**

Double Barrel Side-by-Side Hammerless Shotgun
Sidelock action. Gauges: various. Barrels: 28 to 32
inches; steel or Damascus. Weight: 7¹/₂ to 8¹/₂ pounds.
Checkered standard grade American walnut pistol-grip
stock.
With Steel Barrels **$210**
With Damascus Barrels **165**

Single Barrel Shotgun **$85**
Single-shot, break-open, breechloading action.
Gauges: 12, 16 and others. Barrels: 28 to 32 inches,
steel. Weight: 5³/₄ to 6¹/₂ pounds. Plain walnut stock
and forearm with light checkering on some models.

The following "Brand Names" are those known to
have been carried on Crescent Firearms Co. shotguns:

Barker Gun Company
Bellmore Gun Company
Carolina Arms Company
Central Arms Company
Cherokee Arms Company
Chesapeake Gun Company
Columbian New York Arms Company
Compeer
Cruso
Cumberland Arms Company
Elgin Arms Company
Elmira Arms Company
Empire
Empire Arms Company
Enders Oak Leaf
Enders Royal Service
Essex
Faultless
Faultless Goose Gun
F. F. Forbes
Hartford Arms Company
Harvard
Hermitage Arms Company
Hermitage Gun Company
Howard Arms Company
Interstate Arms Company
Jackson Arms Company
Kingsland Special
Kingsland 10 Star
Knickerbocker
Knox-All
Lakeside
J. H. Lau & Company
Leader Gun Company
Lee Special

Lee's Munner Special
Marshwood
Massachusetts Arms Company
Metropolitan
Minnesota Arms Company
Mississippi Valley Arms Co.
Mohawk
Monitor
National Arms Company
New Rival
New York Arms Company
Nitro Bird
Nitro Hunter
Norwich Arms Company
Not-Nac Manufacturing Co.
Occidental Arms
Oxford Arms Company
Peerless
Perfection
Piedmont
Pioneer Arms Company
Quail
Queen City
Rev-O-Noc
Charles Richter
Rickard Arms Company
Royal Service
Rummel
Shue's Special
Southern Arms Company
Special Service
Spencer Gun Company
Sportsman
Springfield Arms Company
Square Deal
State Arms Company
Sterling
Sullivan Arms Company
U. S. Arms Company
Victor
Victor Special
Virginia Arms Company
Volunteer
Vulcan Arms Company
Wilshire Arms Company
Winfield Arms Company
Winoca Arms Company
Wolverine Arms Company
Worthington Arms Company

W. H. DAVENPORT
Providence, Rhode Island

Davenport Shotguns
Double Barrel Shotgun. **$575**
Single Shot Shotgun. **85**

DAMASCUS BARRELS

The Damascus barrels that were an integral part of many 19th-century shotguns are distinctive for their often intricate patterning. The term "Damascus" is derived from the ancient Middle Eastern city of the same name, the capital of now modern Syria. In this city, swords were forged with wavy patterns, and it is from these patterns that the barrels borrow their distinction.

Damascus barrels consisted of a combination of forged iron and steel strips that were braided in different forms into a band. The band was then wound around a mandrel and welded. The manufacture proceeded gradually as the form was worked with light hammering until all the small rods or wires were joined into a solid piece. The mandrel used as the form was then removed by boring it out. Depending upon how the wires were braided and twisted, a more or less fine Damascus-like or damascened pattern would appear upon the finished barrel after browning or bluing. The finer and more regular the patterning, the greater the worth of the barrel.

Because of the construction, these barrels were lighter and usually stronger than their predecessors. Not only did these features make pro-duction cheaper, but demand for them increased considerably, because, especially with double-barreled shotguns, for example, carrying them into the field was all the more easy.

Confidence in the quality of Damascus barrels was so great before the turn of the century that even ordinary steel barrels were either painted or covered with decalcomania to imitate the real damascened patterns.

The cheapest Damascus barrels were the so-called "band" Damascus barrels. Better grades, based on the quality of the workmanship, are the "Horseshoe," "Rose," "Bernard," "Crolle," "Moire," and "Laminette.' Other fine types of Damascus were the "Laminated Steel," type and "Genuine Damascus" made in England. The primary source of Damascus barrels, however, was Belgium, specifically the Liège area, and about one-third of all the Belgian shotguns produced before 1900 had Damascus barrels.

New technology in metallurgy, however, has all but made Damascus barrels obsolete in terms of use. They will *take only blackpowder loads and not the modern smokeless loads* of today.

Braiding strips of forged iron and steel was the first step in constructing a Damascus barrel.

Step two was wrapping the braided strips around a mandrel, then lightly hammering all the small rods or wires until the "braids" were a solid piece.

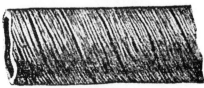

Band

Bernard

Horseshoe

Laminette

Rose

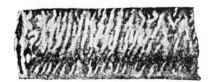

Laminated Steel

N. R. DAVIS & CO.
Freetown, Massachusetts

N.R. Davis Percussion Shotguns
Standard Model $510
Percussion Shotgun No. 3 .400

N.R. Davis Double Barrel Hammer Shotgun
Damascus Barrels $170
Steel Barrels 195

N.R. Davis Double Barrel Hammerless Shotgun
Damascus Barrels $165
Steel Barrels 190

WILLIAM EVANS
London, England

Evans Double Barrel Shotgun
Pistol Grip, Single Weapon $2000
Pistol Grip, Cased Pair 6000
Straight Grip, Single Weapon 3000
Straight Grip, Cased Pair 8000

CARL AUGUST FISCHER
Lubek, Germany

Fischer Double Barrel Percussion Shotgun . . $725
Percussion locks. Gauge: 14 and possibly others. Barrel: 28³/₄ inches, Damascus; lettered "C.A. Fischer in Lubek." Finely engraved locks. Checkered stock and forearm with carved borders. Fischer shotguns were manufactured between 1845 and 1853.

H & D FOLSOM ARMS COMPANY
New York, New York

In about 1893, H & D Folsom purchased the Bacon Arms Company as well as Crescent Firearms Company (*see* separate listings). These two companies produced, and Folsom sold, a vast number of firearms under a host of brand names, probably around 100 different ones.

During this same period, Folsom Arms imported thousands of firearms from Europe (primarily Belgium) and sold them under a variety of private labels. Firearms manufactured in Europe are readily identifiable by the European proof marks on the underside of the barrels. The H & D Folsom Arms Co. was purchased by Savage Arms Corporation in 1931.

The following shotguns are representative of the shotguns imported by H & D Folsom Arms and may have carried any one of the brand names that are listed afterward.

Double Barrel Side-by-Side Hammer Shotgun
Outside hammers. Sidelock action. Gauges: 12 and 16. Barrels: 28 to 32 inches; steel or Damascus. Weight: 6¹/₂ to 8¹/₂ pounds. Checkered European walnut stock with half-pistol grip and forearm. Made circa 1895.
With Damascus Barrels $155
With Steel Barrels 195

Double Barrel Side-by-Side Hammerless Shotgun
Hammerless. Boxlock action. Gauges: 12 and 16. Barrels: 28 to 32 inches; steel or Damascus. Weight: 6¹/₂ to 8¹/₂ pounds. European walnut stock and forearm. Made circa 1895.
With Steel Barrels $200
With Damascus Barrels 160

Single Shot Hammer Shotgun $75
Single-shot. Break-open, breechloading action. Gauge: 12 most common. Barrels: 30 to 32 inches, steel. Weight: 5³/₄ to 6¹/₄ pounds. Plain European walnut stock and forearm with light checkering on some models. Made circa 1895.

The following "Brand Names" are those most often found on H & D Folsom Arms Co. imported shotguns:

T. Barker
C. G. Bonehill
C. W. Franklin
Harrison Arms Company
Henry Gun Company
Hummer
Liège Arms Company
J. Manton & Company
William Moore & Company
Mt. Vernon Arms Company
C. Parker & Company
W. Richards
St. Louis Arms Company
Sickels Arms Company
Stanley
Ten Star
Ten Star Heavy Duty
Tiger
Warren Arms Company
Wilkinson Arms Company
Wilmont Arms Company
Wiltshire Arms Company

FOREHAND & WADSWORTH
Worcester, Massachusetts

Sullivan Forehand and Henry Wadsworth were the sons-in-law of Ethan Allen and the successors to his firearms interests. As the arms-producing firm of Forehand & Wadsworth, which operated from 1871 to about 1890, they manufactured handguns and rifles as well as shotguns (*see* separate listings). Although they were well-built, the shotguns detailed below have never gained much popularity as collectors' items.

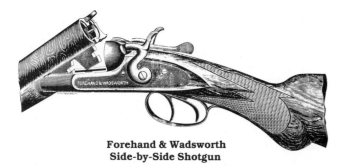

Forehand & Wadsworth
Side-by-Side Shotgun

Forehand Arms Co. Hammer
Side-by-Side Shotgun

Forehand & Wadsworth Double Barrel Side-by-Side Shotgun **$200**
Gauges: 10 and 12. Barrels: various lengths and chokes to order; Belgian-twist steel. Weight: 6½ to 8½ pounds (12 Ga.); 8 to 10 pounds (10 Ga.). Color casehardened frame. Outside hammers. Side locks. Italian or Circassian walnut pistol-grip stock and forend, checkered. Snap forend and extension rib. Made from 1880 to 1890.

Forehand Hammer Side-by-Side Shotgun. . . . **$150**
Outside hammers. Plain receiver. Gauges: 12 and 16. Barrels: various lengths and chokes; twist or Damascus steel; extension rib, straight and matted. Weight: 7 to 8½ pounds. French or Italian half-pistol grip stock, finely checkered. Made from about 1895 to 1902.

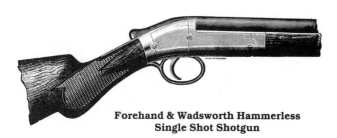

Forehand & Wadsworth Hammerless
Single Shot Shotgun

Forehand & Wadsworth Hammerless Shotgun **$150**
Single shot. Top-snap action. Gauge: 12. Barrel: 30 to 36 inches; twist or Damascus steel. Weight: about 7 pounds. Automatic safety. Checkered walnut semipistol-grip stock and forend. Made from 1880 to 1890.

Forehand & Wadsworth Single Shot Shotgun . .**$90**
Breechloading, top-snap action. Barrel: various lengths, slightly choked. Weight: 7 to 9¾ pounds. Plain walnut pistol-grip stock and forend. Made from the 1870s to 1890s.

Forehand Arms Co. Hammerless
Side-by-Side Shotgun

Forehand Hammerless Double Barrel Side-by-Side Shotgun
Boxlock action. Gauges: 12 and 16. Barrels: various lengths and chokes made to order. Made from 1896 to 1902 in the following grades:

Grade No. 0: Finest Belgian twist barrels, fine walnut stock, full or half-pistol grip, well checkered; no engraving. **$150**
Grade No. 1: Two-blade Damascus steel barrels, full or half-pistol grip stock of French walnut, lightly checkered and engraved **$200**
Grade No. 2: Fine three-blade or chain Damascus steel barrels, selected French walnut stock with full or half-pistol grip, finely checkered and engraved **$250**
Grade No. 3: Very fine Damascus barrels, extra fine French walnut stock with full or half-pistol grip, finely checkered and extra quality engraving **$350**

FOREHAND ARMS COMPANY
Worcester, Massachusetts

After Henry Wadsworth retired in 1890, Sullivan Forehand continued the business they had partnered in (*see* Forehand & Wadsworth) and changed the firm name to simply Forehand Arms Co. The legacy of producing fine firearms, begun by Ethan Allen in 1837, extended into the 20th century until 1902.

**Forehand Arms Co. Hammer
Single Shot Shotgun**

**Forehand Arms Co. Hammerless
Single Shot Shotgun**

Forehand Hammer Single Shot Shotgun.......**$90**
Same general specifications as the Forehand & Wadsworth Single Shot Shotgun. Breechloading. Top-snap action. Barrel: various lengths, slightly choked. Weight: 7 to 9¾ pounds. Plain walnut pistol-grip stock and forend. Made from about 1890 to 1895.

Forehand Hammerless Shotgun.............. **$150**
Single shot. Same general specifications as the Forehand & Wadsworth Hammerless. Top-snap action. Gauge: 12. Barrel: 30 to 36 inches; twist or Damascus steel. Weight: about 7 pounds. Automatic safety. Checkered semipistol-grip walnut stock and forend. Made from 1890 to 1902.

French Trade Gun

FRENCH SHOTGUNS
Various Manufacturers

French Trade Shotgun.................... **$2500**
Flintlock. Gauge: 10. Barrel: 47 inches. Iron furniture. French proof mark on lock. Made circa 1745.

**Golcher American Percussion
Fowler**

JOSEPH GOLCHER
Address Unknown

Golcher locks were used on many American and British shotguns made by different gunsmiths. The following are two examples, but prices may vary tremendously depending upon quality of gun and embellishments.

American Percussion Fowler **$100**
Back-action lock. Iron furniture, silver escutcheons on grips.

British Percussion Fowler................. **$100**
Lock marked "Joseph Golcher." Partridges also engraved on lock. Iron furniture with low-quality wood in stock. Made circa 1850.

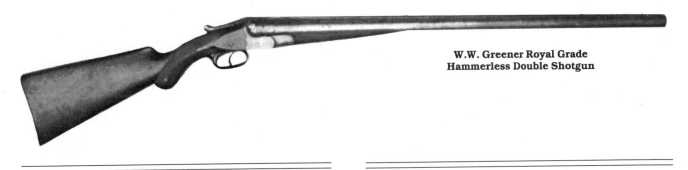

W.W. Greener Royal Grade
Hammerless Double Shotgun

W. W. GREENER & SONS
Birmingham, England

Greener Hammerless Ejector Double Barrel Shotgun
Crown Model Grade DH55 . . . . **$3900**
Jubilee Model Grade DH35 . . . . **2200**
Royal Model Grade DH75 . . . . **3900**
Sovereign Model Grade DH40 . . . . **2550**

Greener Far-Killer Model Grade FH35 Double Barrel Shotgun
12 Gauge, Non-ejector **$2395**
12 Gauge, Ejector **3000**
10 or 8 Gauge, Non-ejector **2500**
10 or 8 Gauge, Ejector **3300**

Greener Empire Model Double Barrel Shotgun
Non-ejector Model. **$1650**
Ejector Model. **1750**
Deluxe, Non-ejector Model. **1900**
Deluxe Ejector Model **2000**

Greener Single Barrel Shotgun
General Purpose Model **$345**

HARRINGTON & RICHARDSON ARMS
Worcester, Massachusetts

H&R Double Barrel Shotgun. **$150**
Hammerless. Gauges: 10 and 12. Barrels: 28, 30 or 32 inches; Damascus. Casehardened frame. Checkered semipistol-grip stock. Made in the 1880s.

HOLLIS & SHEATH
London, England

Hollis & Sheath 12 Gauge Percussion Shotgun **$595**
Percussion locks. Gauge: 12. Double barrels: 30 inches; Damascus; marked "LONDON FINE STUB TWIST." Locks, hammers, short tang and trigger guard finely engraved. Checkered walnut stock with metal butt plate.

Hollis & Sheath 10 Gauge Percussion Shotgun **$250**
Gauge: 10. Massive stock and double barrels. Two wedges in forewood to hold barrels. Iron furniture.

HOWARD BROTHERS
Whitneyville, Connecticut

   Charles Howard obtained patents for a breechloading hammerless action, which were applied to handguns, rifles and shotguns from September 26, 1865 to May 15, 1866. The Whitney Arms Co. of Whitneyville, Conn., made most of these arms under contract, as is stamped on the barrels of many of the early models, "Mf'd for Howard Brothers by Whitney Arms Co., Whitneyville, Conn."

Howard Brothers Single Shot Shotgun **$150**
Breechloading shotgun. Gauge: 20. Barrel: $30\frac{1}{2}$ inches. Overall length: $49\frac{3}{4}$ inches. Weight: 6 pounds. American walnut stock. Made from 1866 to 1869.

Hollis & Sheath 10 Gauge
Percussion Shotgun

JAPANESE MILITARY
Various Manufacturers

Japanese Matchlock "Blunderbuss"........ **$925**
Matchlock. Calibers: various. Barrel: 38 inches; heavy, octagonal. Overall length: 50 inches. Two brass bands, brass outside hammer spring. Brass escutcheons, brass flower ornament at tang. Imperial seal inlaid in silver on barrel.

IVER JOHNSON'S ARMS & CYCLE WORKS
Fitchburg, Massachusetts

Iver Johnson, from Norway, and Martin Bye, from Sweden, joined efforts in 1871 to manufacture muzzle-loading pistols under the firm name of Johnson, Bye and Co. The original firm, quite small, consisted of the two gunsmiths and a staff of three assistants. They occupied two rooms in a building in Worcester, Mass. However, in 1873 they purchased a five-story building and rapid expansion followed.

In 1883 after Bye retired, Johnson changed the name twice until in 1884 the company became known as Iver Johnson's Arms & Cycle Works, relocated in Fitchburg. This company produced bicycles, and it was as a bicycle manufacturer that the firm name became a household word. In addition to bicycles, however, the plant made a great assortment of revolvers and pistols (*see* Handgun Section), as well as single- and double-barreled shotguns. They also sold a line of police equipment, handcuffs and accessories.

Iver John Single Barrel Shotguns
Side Snap Model $75
Top Snap Model............................. 85

NICANOR KENDALL
Windsor, Vermont

Kendall Percussion Underhammer Single Barrel Shotgun **$400**
Underhammer percussion lock. Gauges: various. Barrel: 37 inches; part round, part octagonal; marked "N. KENDALL/WINDSOR, VT./PATENT." Engraved tang and breech marked, "SMITH'S/IMPROVED/PATENT/STUD/LOCK." One-piece walnut stock.

CASIMIR LEFAUCHEUX
Paris, France

Casimir Lefaucheux (1802–1852) was a French gun-maker who invented the pinfire cartridge in the 1830s, which was covered in the 1835 addition to his initial 1832 patent. His son, Eugène, carried on the gunmaking tradition and helped introduce pinfire cartridge revolvers to the world during the mid-19th century (*see* separate listing under Handguns). The shotgun detailed below was one of the first to use pinfire cartridges.

Lefaucheux Double Barrel Shotgun **$175**
Highly engraved frame and lock. Outside hammers. Side locks. Gauges: various pinfire cartridges. Barrels: 30 inches standard, but other lengths made. Weight: about 6 pounds. Straight-grip, finely figured walnut stock and forend, usually checkered. Introduced in 1836.

LEFEVER ARMS CO.
Syracuse, New York

Daniel "Uncle Dan" Lefever learned his trade as a gunsmith in Rochester, New York. When the Civil War broke out in 1861, Lefever had a little gun shop in Canandaigua, N.Y., where he made superior rifles for some of the sharpshooters in the Northern Army. A few years later he moved to Auburn, where he did high-class gunsmithing and produced a few shotguns on special order. The Lefever was the first double-barrel breech-loading hammerless gun made in America.

The original breechloading Lefever hammerless was cocked by a side lever, which the shooter pushed down directly after firing the gun. This motion cocked the gun so it could be loaded and fired again. A short time later, however, this design was modified to cock the hammers automatically upon opening the breech. Patents on the first Lefever hammerless were issued in 1872. (For a brief time in the 1870s, Lefever partnered with John Nichols to make Nichols & Lefever fine grade shotguns with Damascus barrels.)

From Auburn, Uncle Dan moved to Syracuse, where the Lefever Arms Company was incorporated in 1884. Lefever went into the extensive manufacture of shotguns bearing his name, and for many years he superintended the building of his famous line of hand-finished guns.

In 1901, a few years before his death, Lefever sold his interests in Lefever Arms Co. and moved to Bowling Green, Ohio. There he started another factory under the name of D.M. Lefever & Son, which produced shotguns until Lefever died in 1906.

The Syracuse company, however, operated independently a little longer, and was eventually sold to the Ithaca Gun Company of Ithaca, N.Y., in about 1915.

Lewis & Tomes Percussion
Double Barrel Shotgun

Lefever shotguns are still coveted by collectors of fine shotguns, and continue to rise in price each year.

Lefever Hammerless Double Barrel Shotguns
Hammerless, boxlock breechloader. Full "compensated" action with square-shouldered top fastener. Gauges: 10, 12, 14, 16, 20; 8 gauge was available at additional cost. Barrel: Damascus or laminated steel, tapered, with matted rib; length varies. Weight: 10 gauge, 8 to 10 lbs.; 12 gauge, 7 to 9 lbs. Auto or non-auto safety. Checkered pistol-grip stock and forend. Double triggers. In 1889, according to the Lefever catalog of that year, prices ranged from **$80** for F Grade to **$400** for Optimus Grade. Today, those prices range from **$250** to about **$1200.**

Optimus. Whitworth fluid steel or Kilby barrels; finest French walnut stock; full pistol grip with horn cap; horn or skeleton butt plate; special gold designs; highest grade of engraving, checkering and finish.

AA Grade. Finest Damascus or laminated steel barrels; finest French walnut stock; full pistol grip with horn cap; horn or skeleton butt plate; elegantly engraved, checkered and finished.

A Grade. Same as above, but differs in finish and engraving.

B Grade. Fine Damascus or laminated steel barrels; fine English walnut stock; full pistol grip with horn cap; horn heel plate; handsomely engraved and checkered.

C Grade. Fine Damascus or laminated steel barrels; choice English walnut stock; full pistol grip with horn or steel cap; rubber heel plate; richly engraved and checkered.

D Grade. Damascus or laminated steel barrels; fine English walnut stock; full pistol grip with horn cap; rubber heel plate; finely engraved and checkered.

E Grade. Damascus or laminated steel barrels; English walnut stock; full pistol grip with horn cap; horn or rubber plate; nicely engraved and checkered.

F Grade. Damascus or laminated steel barrels; English walnut stock; horn or rubber butt plate; full pistol grip; checkered and engraved.

LEWIS & TOMES
London, England

Lewis & Tomes Percussion Double Barrel Shotgun **$275**
Gauges: various. Barrel: London Fine Twist Damascus. Iron butt plate and trigger guard. German silver nose cap, wedge escutcheons and cap box in butt stock. Checkered grip.

THE MARLIN FIRE ARMS CO.
New Haven, Connecticut

The Marlin Firearms Co. entered the shotgun business with their Model 1898 Slide Action Shotgun, and its later variations: the Models 16, 17, 19, 21, 24, 26, 28 and 30. However, only the Model 1898 was manufactured prior to 1900; the remaining models were not produced until at least 1904, with the Model 16; 1906, with the Model 17, etc.

Marlin Model 1898 Slide Action Repeating Shotgun
Takedown. Five-shot tubular magazine. Gauge: 12. Barrel: 26, 28, 30 or 32 inches; various chokes. Weight: 7½ pounds. Pistol-grip stock, grooved slide handle; checkering on higher grades.
Grade A (Field) .... **$ 535**
Grade B: plain gun with checkered, fancy walnut and matte barrel rib 695
Grade C: same as B, except simple engraving on receiver 995
Grade D: European walnut, fancy checkering, engraving on receiver, gold-plated screws and trigger 2000

MASSACHUSETTS ARMS CO.
Chicopee Falls, Massachusetts

Founded by Daniel B. Wesson of Smith & Wesson fame, the Massachusetts Arms Company had several U.S. Government contracts for the manufacture of firearms during the Civil War. The original operation was supposedly discontinued around 1866, but the name has since been used on many inexpensive shotguns.

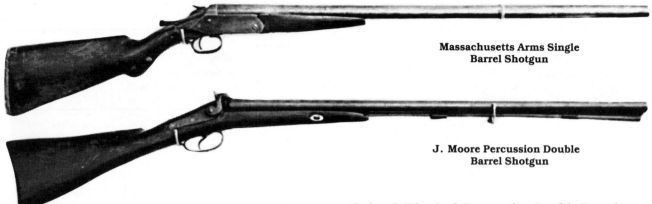

Massachusetts Arms Single
Barrel Shotgun

J. Moore Percussion Double
Barrel Shotgun

Mass. Arms Co. Single Barrel Shotgun **$75**
Gauge: 12. Barrel: various lengths from 28 to 32 inches.
Typical break-open, single-shot shotgun with barrel
latch on upper tang. Made circa 1890s.

JOHN P. MOORE & CO.
Toronto, Canada

John P. Moore was an importer and wholesaler of
guns; most of the shotguns that bear his name were
produced in Belgium.

**John P. Moore Double Barrel Percussion
Shotgun** **$175**
Gauge: 12 and others. Barrel: browned Damascus. Iron
furniture. Imported between 1884 and 1886.

WILLIAM MOORE & CO.
London, England

**William Moore & Co. Double Barrel Percussion
Shotgun** **$500**
Percussion front-action locks. Gauges: 10 and 12. Bar-
rel: 30 inches; browned Damascus steel. Lock plates
marked, "W. Moore & Co." Fine English-style checkering on walnut stock and forend.

ONION & WHEELOCK
London, England

Onion & Wheelock was one of the British manufacturers who produced percussion shotguns for export
to America. This firm made a medium-quality shotgun
for the sportsman who wanted a reliable weapon, but
who was unwilling (or unable) to pay a great amount of
money for the extras—the elaborate ornamentation,
for example, that was found on such shotguns as those
produced by W & C Scott and others.

**Onion & Wheelock Percussion Double Barrel
Shotgun** **$385**
Color casehardened frame. Outside hammers. Side
locks. Gauge: 12. Barrels: various lengths, but most
measured approximately 30 inches; marked "Fine Damascus London Double Proof"; Damascus steel. English walnut straight-grip stock. Plain ornamentation.
Wood ramrod. Made circa 1850.

F. ORGAN
London, England

**F. Organ Percussion Double Barrel
Shotgun** **$575**
Percussion locks. Gauge: 12. Barrels: 30 inches; Lon-
don twist steel; marked "LONDON FINE TWIST." Locks
lightly engraved in coarse pattern. Walnut stocks,
checkered at grip; metal butt plate.

PARKER BROTHERS
Meriden, Connecticut

Under the leadership of Charles Parker, the first
models of the commercial Parker Double Barrel Shotgun were completed and marketed in 1868. It was a
breechloading, 14-gauge shotgun with 29-inch barrels
using outside primed ammunition, similar to the ignition system used on the Sharps carbine.

The locking mechanism on the first Parker was operated by means of a lever under the breech mechanism, which was both crude and inconvenient when
compared to the later shotgun development of the
1870s. Therefore, with the help of designer Charles A.
King, the Parker Shotgun was given a new streamlined
locking system, using what has become known as the
"doll's head" extension to the top rib of the barrel; also
a hardened, tapered wedge was set into the vertical lug
below the barrels. This design was so satisfactory that
it remained an integral part of the Parker Shotgun until
it was discontinued in the early 1940s.

Although The Parker Gun is often referred to as an
"American Classic," the laminated-twist barrels were
manufactured in Belgium, as were the barrels for the
majority of shotguns made in the United States at the
time.

Unlike some other types of antique firearms, the later Parker shotguns are worth more than the earlier models. One Parker A-1 Special in 28 gauge, for example, sold for the sum of $95,000 a few years ago at a New York auction. None of the antique varieties of the same shotgun will even approach this figure. You will find a broad range of prices in dealing with Parker shotguns, starting at **$175** for the lowest grades, to about **$9000** for the highest quality with intricate engraving.

Parker Hammerless Side-by-Side Shotgun
Color casehardened boxlock action. Non-automatic ejectors. Gauges: 10, 12, and 16. Barrels: various lengths with various chokes. Weight: 6¼ to 8 pounds. Double triggers. Checkered pistol-grip stock and forend. Made from 1899 to 1912 in the following grades: AAH Pigeon, AH, BH, CH, DH, EH, GH, NH, PH and VH.

Parker Outside Hammer Double Barrel Shotgun
Color casehardened receiver. Engraved side locks. Gauges: 8 to 12. Barrel: 30 to 36 inches. Weight: 7 to 13 pounds. Top lever, double bolt, rebounding locks, patent forend bolt, solid head plungers, improved check hook, and choke bore. Various grades as follows:

Quality A "Premier": Gauge: 10. Barrels: 32 inches; finest Damascus steel. Weight: 9 to 10½ pounds. Finest imported pistol-grip walnut stock, gold shield, finest checkering and engraving combined with the best finish available.

Quality D: Gauge: 10. Barrels: 32 inches; fine Damascus steel. Weight: 9 to 10½ pounds. Fine imported pistol-grip walnut stock, silver shield, fine checkering and engraving, skeleton butt plate.

Quality 3: Same as Grade D, except made in 12 gauge with 32-inch barrels. Weight: 7 to 9 pounds.

Quality E: Gauge: 10. Barrels: 32 inches; Damascus steel. Fine figured American or imported walnut pistol-grip stock, checkered and engraved.

Quality G: Similar to Quality E, except chambered for 12 gauge and weighs 9 pounds.

Quality I: Gauge: 10. Barrels: 32 inches; fine laminated steel. Weight: 10¼ to 10½ pounds. Fine figured American walnut pistol-grip stock, checkered and engraved with rubber butt plate.

Quality 8: Gauge: 8. Barrels: 34 inches; fine laminated steel. Weight: 13 pounds. Fine figured American walnut pistol-grip stock, checkered and engraved. Rubber butt plate.

Quality R: Gauge: 10. Barrels: 32 inches; twist. Weight: 10 pounds. Pistol-grip American walnut stock and forend, lightly checkered and engraved.

Quality S: Basically the same as Quality R, except for straight grip and slightly lighter weight.

Quality T: Gauge: 12. Barrels: 32 inches; twist. Weight: 9 pounds. American walnut pistol-grip stock and forend, very lightly engraved with modest checkering.

Quality U: Basically the same as Quality T, except for straight grip and slightly lighter weight.

Parker Under Lever Side-by Side Shotgun . . $1100
Outside hammers. Under-lever locked action. Gauges: various. Barrels: various lengths; laminated-twist steel. Weight: about 8½ pounds average.

REMINGTON ARMS COMPANY
Ilion, New York

The Remington Arms Co., America's oldest firearms manufacturer, was one of the first successful producers of shotguns in this country.

Remington Breechloading Single Barrel Shotgun
Single-shot, rolling-block action. Gauge: 16. Barrel: 30 or 32 inches; laminated. Overall length: 48 inches. Weight: 6½ pounds. Straight-grip walnut stock and forend; plain on standard model. Made from about 1873 to 1909.
Engraved Model **$450**
Extra-fancy Engraved Model **500**

Remington Muzzleloading Single Barrel
Shotgun . . . . **$***
Hammer model. Straight-grip walnut stock. Offered in 1877.

Remington Breechloading
Single Barrel Shotgun

Remington Muzzleloading
Single Barrel Shotgun

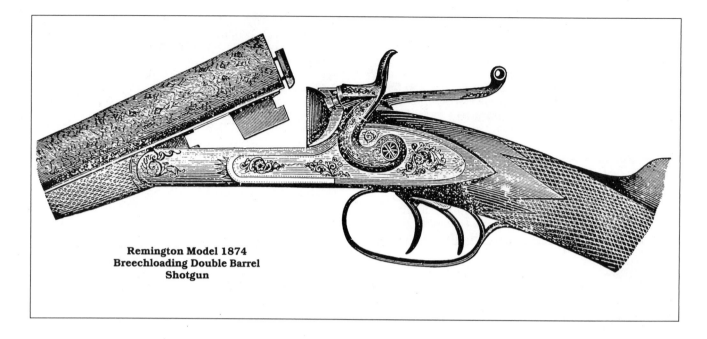

**Remington Model 1874
Breechloading Double Barrel
Shotgun**

**Remington Model 1874 Side-by-Side Breech-
Loading Shotgun** . . . . $300 – $675
Outside hammers. Sidelock action. Gauges: 10 and 12.
Barrels: 28 or 30 inches; decarbonized steel, twist or
Damascus. Weight: 8 to 8½ pounds. Double triggers.
Stock varied from plain walnut to select and English
walnut, with various grades of checkering and ornamentation. Double gun with one barrel rifle and one decarbonized steel barrel available; also double rifle with
decarbonized steel barrels available, with price rising
accordingly. Made in the 1870s.

NOTE

Lt. Col. H. A. Gildersleeve of the American Rifle Team wrote
in November 1876 that "I have just returned from the Big
South Bay, where I have been gunning for ducks. I tried for
the first time the Remington 10 gauge (shot)gun. My success
with it was excellent. In my judgment its shooting capacity
cannot be surpassed. I want no better gun, and if I did, I don't
believe I could find it, even among the expensive grades of
English ones." (Originally published in the 1877 Remington Catalog about the Model 1874.)

**Remington New Model 1882 Double Barrel
Shotgun** **$450**
Outside hammers. Side lock. Gauges: 10, 12 and 16.
Barrels: 28 to 32 inches; plain or Damascus. Weight:
6¾ to 10¼ pounds. Double triggers. Checkered pistol-
grip stock and forend. Made from 1882 to 1910.

**Remington Model 1889 Double Barrel
Shotgun** **$795**
Gauges: 10, 12 and 16. Barrels: 28 to 32 inches; steel or
Damascus. Weight: 7 to 10 pounds. Checkered pistol-
grip stock and forend. Made from 1889 to 1908.

Remington Model 1894 Double Barrel Shotgun
Box lock. Automatic ejector. Gauges: 10, 12 and 16.
Barrels: 28 to 32 inches; ordnance steel or Damascus.
Weight: 7 to 10 pounds. Double triggers. Checkered
stock and forend. Different grades consisted of fancier
wood, elaborate checkering and engraving, and other
ornamentation. Made from 1894 to 1910.

Grade	Price
A.E. Grade	$ 360
A.E.O. Grade	595
AO Grade	540
B Grade	260
BE Grade	435
BEO Grade	825
BO Grade	555
C Grade	455
CE Grade	545
CEO Grade	1100
CO Grade	795
D Grade	695
DE Grade	795
DEO Grade	1600
DO Grade	1450
E Grade	1010
EE Grade	1295
EEO Grade	2995
EO Grade	2750
Special Grade	7500

**Remington Model 1900 Double Barrel
Shotgun** **$440**
Improved version of Remington Model 1894 Shotgun.
Same general specifications as above. Made from 1900
to 1910.

WESTLEY RICHARDS & CO. LTD.
Birmingham, England

Westley Richards Double Barrel Shotgun . . . $7800
Box lock. Hammerless. Gauges: 12, 16 and 20. Barrels: lengths and boring to order; side-by-side. Weight: 5½ to 6¼ pounds, depending on gauge and barrel length. Hand-detachable locks and hinged cover plate. Selective ejectors. Double triggers or selective single trigger. Straight or half-pistol grip checkered stock and forend. Although there are various grades, the price does not vary significantly. Made from 1899 to the mid-1900s.

Westley Richards Single Barrel Shotgun $300
Gauge: 16. Barrel engraved "W. Richards London Fine Damascus." Lock engraved with flying geese and "W. Richards." Checkered grip and forend. Fanny gutta percha butt plate. A family of deer among trees in cartouche.

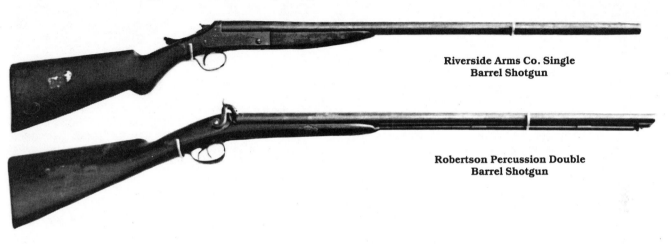

Riverside Arms Co. Single
Barrel Shotgun

Robertson Percussion Double
Barrel Shotgun

RIVERSIDE ARMS CO.
Address Unknown

Riverside Single Shot Shotgun $75
Gauges: 12 and others. Barrel stamped "Electro Steel Choke Bored." Typical of inexpensive break-open, single-shot shotguns.

ROBERTSON
Scotland

**Robertson Double Barrel Percussion
Shotgun $250**
Gauges: 12 and others. Iron furniture. Half stock. Made circa 1840.

W. & C. SCOTT & SON
London, England

**W & C Scott Double Barrel Percussion
Shotgun $900**
Bar and wood percussion locks, engraved with high-quality line drawings and maker's name. Gauges: 11 and others. Barrels: 32 inches; Damascus steel; top rib marked "W & C Scott & Sons, Makers, 10 Gt Castle St., Regent Circus London." Serial number usually marked on trigger guard. Checkered straight-grip stock with plain steel butt plate.

L. C. SMITH
Syracuse, New York

Lyman Cornelius Smith began the manufacture and sale of shotguns as early as 1877 with the Baker double and three-barreled shotguns. The official L.C. Smith Shotgun did not debut until 1884, however, and was the exposed-hammer double-barrel, side-by-side model, manufactured in Syracuse, N.Y. In 1886, a hammerless model was introduced that established the reputation of performance and quality that the L.C. Smith shotgun still enjoys.

In 1888, John Hunter Sr. of Fulton, N.Y., purchased the Smith gun business and moved the entire operation to Fulton. The firm name was changed to Hunter Arms Co., but the name of the gun remained "The L.C. Smith Shotgun." Hunter Arms continued to manufacture L.C. Smith shotguns well into the 20th century until the Hunter holdings were sold prior to the outbreak of WWI. The L.C. Smith name maintained its appearance on newly manufactured firearms until 1971, when Marlin purchased the rights.

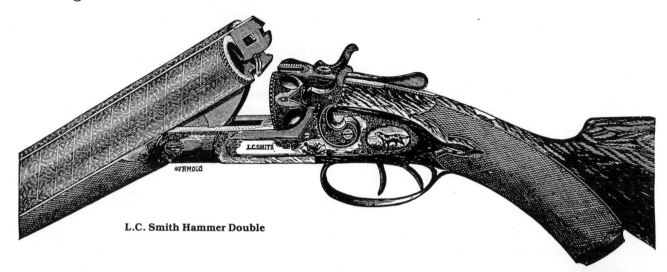

L.C. Smith Hammer Double

L.C. Smith Hammer Double Barrel Shotguns
Back-action, double cross-bolted. Breechloading. Gauges: 10 and 12. Barrels: 26 to 32 inches; Damascus; any standard boring. Weight: $8^1/_2$ to 12 pounds (10 Ga.); $7^1/_2$ to 10 pounds (12 Ga.). Plain extractors. Double triggers.

A Grade: very fine Damascus steel barrels, extra fine English walnut stock with pistol grip, extra fine checkering and engraving **$480**

B Grade: extra fine Damascus steel barrels, fine English walnut stock with pistol grip, fine checkering and engraving **$360**

C Grade: fine Damascus steel barrels, fine English walnut stock with pistol grip, fine checkering and engraving **$300**

D Grade: fine Damascus steel barrels, good English walnut stock with pistol grip, checkering, engraved metal **$228**

E Grade: Damascus steel barrels, good imported English walnut stock with pistol grip, checkering, engraved metal **$168**

F Grade: English stub twist barrels, checkered American walnut stock with pistol grip, engraved metal **$132**

L.C. Smith Hammerless Side-by-Side Shotguns (I)
Side lock. Gauges: 10 and 12. Barrels: 30 or 32 inches; Damascus. Weight: $7^1/_2$ to 12 pounds. Plain extractors. Compensating forend. Interchangeable main spring. Grades differ only in quality of workmanship, wood, style and amount of checkering and engraving, and quality of steel barrels. Manufactured by Smith in Syracuse from 1886 to 1888.

No. 2 Grade: good Damascus steel barrels, good English walnut stock and forend, half-pistol grip **$210**

No. 3 Grade: fine Damascus steel barrels, fine English walnut stock and forend with pistol grip or half-pistol grip, nicely checkered and engraved . . . **$240**

No. 4 Grade: very fine Damascus steel barrels, very fine walnut stock and forend, full pistol grip or half-pistol grip, fine checkering and engraving . . . **$360**

No. 5 Grade: very fine Damascus steel barrels, extra fine walnut stock and forend, full or half-pistol grip, extra fine checkering and engraving **$480**

No. 6 Grade: finest Damascus steel barrels, finest imported English walnut stock, full or half-pistol grip, finest checkering and engraving, very finest finish **$720**

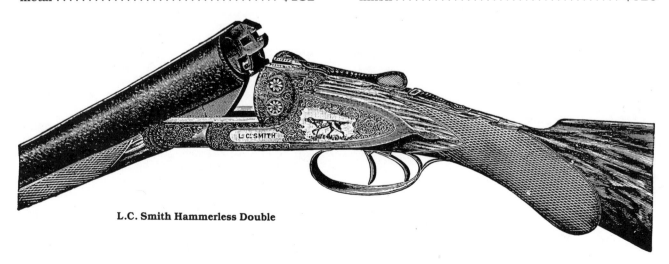

L.C. Smith Hammerless Double

L.C. Smith Hammerless Side-by-Side Shotguns (II)
Side lock. Gauges: 8, 10, 12, 16. Barrels: 26 to 32
inches. Weight: 6½ to 8 pounds. Automatic ejectors
standard on higher grades, extra on lower grades.
Checkered stock and forend; choice of straight, half- or
full pistol grip. Beavertail or splinter forend. Grades
differ only in quality of workmanship, wood, checkering, engraving, etc. Made by Hunter Arms from 1888 to
1900.

00 Grade	$ 1,095
0 Grade	1,295
1 Grade	1,475
2 Grade	1,595
3 Grade	1,695
Pigeon Grade	3,450
4 Grade	4,595
5 Grade	5,000
Monogram Grade	8,500
A1 Grade	6,000
A2 Grade	8,700
A3 Grade	15,000+

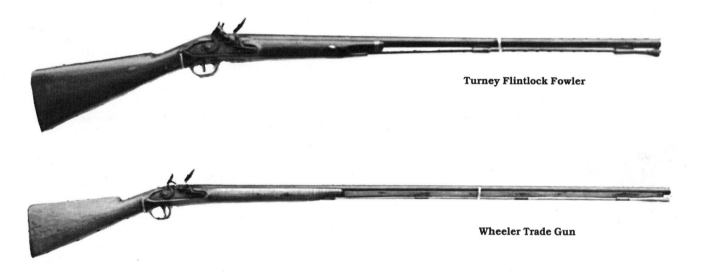

Turney Flintlock Fowler

Wheeler Trade Gun

J. TURNEY
London, England

Turney Flintlock Fowler.................. **$600**
Gauges: 12 and other. Brass furniture. High-quality
fowling piece. Made from 1820 to 1832.

ROBERT WHEELER
England/Canada

Robert Wheeler had a contract to produce arms for
the Hudson's Bay Co. in Canada.

Wheeler Trade Shotgun **$900**
Gauge: 12. Barrel: 48 inches. Plain iron furniture of
typical trade gun style. Proof marks stamped on barrel.
Made circa 1800.

WINCHESTER REPEATING ARMS CO.
New Haven, Connecticut

The Winchester Repeating Arms Co., prior to 1879,
manufactured only repeating rifles (*see* Winchester
under Rifles). In 1876 the company experimented with
a few handguns, but none were ever produced for public use. Owning to the popularity of double-barreled
breechloading shotguns of the time, and because there
was a shortage of such weapons in the U.S., an agent
from Winchester was sent to Birmingham, England, to
purchase a quantity of the cheaper grade English "dou-
bles." The first shipment of shotguns, purchased in
1878 from W. C. McEntree & Company, Richard Rodman, C. G. Bonehill, and some better grades from W. C.
Scott & Sons, sold out so quickly that Winchester decided to purchase another quantity. This time it was
the better grades marked with the Winchester name.

These imported shotguns bearing the Winchester
name were available in five grades and were offered between 1879 and 1884, when serious consideration was

given to a Winchester-manufactured line of shotguns. The first was the Model 1887 Lever Action, followed by the Model 1893 Pump or Slide Action Repeating Shotgun and finally an improved version of the 1893, called the Model 1897 Repeating Shotgun. These three models, offered in several grades, were the only true Winchester-produced shotguns before 1900.

Winchester Imported Side-by-Side Shotgun
Side lock. Outside exposed hammers. Gauges: 10 and 12. Barrels: 30 and 32 inches; top rib marked "Winchester Repeating Arms Co./New Haven, Connecticut U.S.A., Class A" (or whatever class it was). Weight: 7½ to 10 pounds. Double triggers. Distributed by Winchester from 1879 to 1884.

Winchester Match Gun **$3300**
Winchester Class A **2700**

Winchester Class B **2325**
Winchester Class C **1940**
Winchester Class D **1550**

Winchester Model 1887 Lever Action Repeating Shotgun
Casehardened solid frame. Gauges: 10 and 12. Four-shot tubular magazine under barrel. Barrels: 30 or 32 inches; full choke. Weight: 8 pounds (12 Ga.; 9 pounds (10 Ga.). Pistol-grip stock and forend. Made from 1887 to 1901.

Standard Model **$525**
Fancy Wood, Plain Stock **600**
Fancy Wood, Checkering, Damascus Barrel **800**

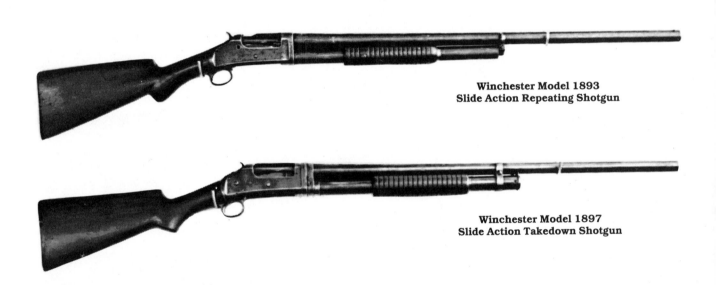

Winchester Model 1893
Slide Action Repeating Shotgun

Winchester Model 1897
Slide Action Takedown Shotgun

Winchester Model 1893 Slide Action Repeating Shotgun
Solid frame. Five-shot tubular magazine. Gauge: 12. Barrel: 30 or 32 inches; full choke. Weight: 7¾ pounds with 30-inch barrel. Pistol-grip stock. Rounded slide handle with semicircular notches on standard model. About 34,000 made from 1893 to 1897.

Standard Model **$325**
Fancy Wood, Plain Stock **375**
Fancy Wood, Checkering **450**

Winchester Model 1897 Slide Action Repeating Shotgun
Visible hammer. Takedown or solid frame. Gauges: 12 and 16. Five-shot tubular magazine. Barrels: 26 to 32 inches; choked full to cylinder. Weight: about 7¾ pounds. Made from 1897 to 1957.

Standard Model . . . . **$ 325**
Trap Grade **595**
Tournament Grade **775**
Pigeon Grade **1250**

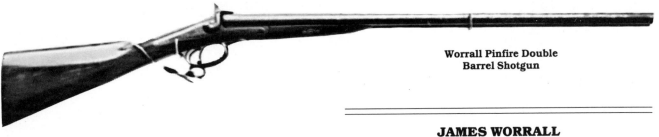

Worrall Pinfire Double
Barrel Shotgun

JAMES WORRALL
Chester, England

Worrall Pinfire Double Barrel Shotgun **$400**
Gauge: 15. Barrels: browned Damascus. High-grade
walnut stock with checkered forend. Nicely engraved
locks and trigger guard. Made from 1859 to 1864.

NOTE

In the late 1800s, it was recommended by many gun manufacturers that the best oil—sperm oil—be used to clean the
barrels thoroughly, inside and out.

CHAPTER FOUR
BLACKPOWDER REPLICAS

During the mid-1950s, a number of blackpowder buffs began importing replica arms from Europe. Although many take the credit for being the first, Turner Kirkland of Dixie Gun Works probably offered the first production replica in 1955. This was a typical Kentucky rifle manufactured to Kirkland's specifications in Belgium. Val Forgett of Navy Arms followed shortly thereafter with a basic Remington percussion revolver design manufactured in Italy.

The sale of these replica arms surpassed all expectations, and sales quickly exceeded the supply. Eventually, other models were introduced by the major importers, and soon several additional firms entered into the replica business. Custom shops also sprang up in the United States where higher quality blackpowder arms were produced on a limited basis, similar to the custom cartridge rifles made to individual specifications. It did not take long for replica arms to become big business nationwide, and even the major firearms manufacturers scrambled for a piece of the pie. Colt brought back into production several of the original Colt percussion designs; H&R came out with a replica model of the 1873 Springfield rifle chambered for the .45-70 cartridge; and Ruger introduced a replica stainless steel percussion revolver. The trend continues today.

Although replica arms are not antiques in the true sense, they are of great interest to antique collectors and shooters. Many blackpowder shooters who once utilized an original collector's item now keep their highly prized collector pieces in the gun cabinet, and use one of the replicas for their shooting requirements. Also, there is a need for trading information on replica arms since many exchange hands each year, and detailed pricing information for used models is sometimes difficult to obtain . . . especially with identifying specifications. Thus, the reason for including this section in **Antique Guns — The Collector's Guide**.

ARMSPORT, INC.
Miami, Florida

HANDGUNS

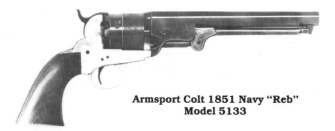

Armsport Colt 1851 Navy "Reb"
Model 5133

Armsport Colt 1851 Navy "Reb" Percussion Revolver Model 5133 .... **$55**
Caliber: 36. Six-shot cylinder. Barrel: 7 inches. Polished walnut grips. Finish: blued barrel and cylinder; brass frame and trigger guard.

Armsport Colt 1851 Navy "Reb" Percussion Revolver Model 5134 .... **$55**
Same general specifications as Model 5133, except manufactured in 44 caliber.

Armsport Colt 1851 Navy Percussion Revolver Model 5135 .... **$95**
Same general specifications as Model 5133, except with steel frame.

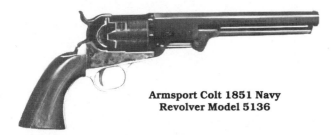

Armsport Colt 1851 Navy
Revolver Model 5136

Armsport Colt Navy 1851 Percussion Revolver Model 5136 .... **$75**
Caliber: 36. Six-shot engraved cylinder. Barrel: 7 inches, round. Walnut grips. Finish: blued steel frame and cylinder; polished brass trigger guard.

Armsport Remington Army
Revolver

Armsport Colt 1860 Army Percussion Revolver Model 5139 .... **$80**
Caliber: 44. Six-shot unfluted cylinder. Barrel: 8 inches, round. Weight: about 42 ounces. Walnut grips. Finish: blued barrel and frame; polished brass trigger guard.

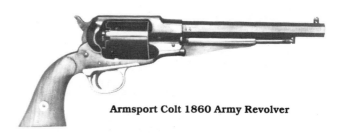

Armsport Colt 1860 Army Revolver

Armsport Remington Army Percussion Revolver Model 5120 .... **$85**
Caliber: 44. Six-shot cylinder. Barrel: 8 inches, octagonal. Walnut grips. Finish: blued steel frame and cylinder; polished brass trigger guard.

Armsport Remington Army
Stainless

Armsport Remington Army Revolver Model 5138 Stainless Steel **$140**
Same general specifications as Model 5120, except made with stainless steel frame.

LONG ARMS

Armsport Hawken Rifle Model 5101 .... **$145**
Lock: color casehardened, percussion. Caliber: 45. Barrel: 28 inches, octagon. Weight: about 7 pounds. High-luster walnut stock. Double-set triggers. Brass fittings, including patch box, ferrules, butt plate, etc.

Armsport Hawken Rifle Model 5102 .... **$145**
Same general specifications as Model 5101, except available in 50 caliber.

Armsport Hawken Smoothbore Rifle Model 5102S **$145**
Same general specifications as Model 5101, except made in 50 caliber smoothbore.

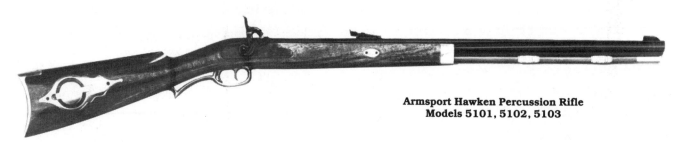

**Armsport Hawken Percussion Rifle
Models 5101, 5102, 5103**

Armsport Hawken Rifle Model 5102V **$145**
Lock: color casehardened, percussion. Caliber: 36.
Barrel: 28 inches, octagonal. Weight: about 6³/₄
pounds. High-luster walnut stock. Double-set triggers.
Brass fittings, including patch box, ferrules, butt plate,
etc.

Armsport Hawken Rifle Model 5103 . . . . **$145**
Same general specifications as Model 5102, except
manufactured in 54 caliber.

Armsport Hawken Rifle Model 5103C **$145**
Same general specifications as Model 5103, except
manufactured in 58 caliber.

Armsport Hawken Rifle Model 5103CS **$145**
Same general specifications as Model 5103, except
made with 58 caliber smoothbore barrel.

Armsport Hawken Rifle Model 5103S **$145**
Same general specifications as Model 5103, except
with smoothbore barrel.

**Armsport Hawken Flintlock Rifle
Model 5104**

Armsport Hawken Rifle Model 5104 . . . . **$155**
Lock: color casehardened, flintlock. Caliber: 50. Barrel:
28 inches, octagonal. Weight: about 7¹/₂ pounds. Walnut stock. Double-set triggers. Brass fittings, including patch box, ferrules, butt plate, etc.

Armsport Hawken Rifle Model 5104B **$155**
Same general specifications as Model 5104, except
manufactured in 54 caliber.

Armsport Hawkentucky Rifle **$150**
Lock: color casehardened, percussion. Calibers: 36 or
50. Barrel: 28 inches, octagonal. Weight: 6 pounds.
Walnut stock. Double-set triggers. Brass fittings, including patch box, ferrules, butt plate, etc.

Armsport Kentucky Rifle Deluxe **$175**
Lock: color casehardened, percussion. Caliber: 45.
Barrel: 28 inches, octagonal. Weight: about 7¹/₄
pounds. Selected walnut stock. Single trigger. Brass
fittings, including patch box, ferrules, butt plate, etc.

Armsport Kentucky Rifle Model 5108 . . . . **$145**
Lock: color casehardened, percussion. Caliber: 45.
Barrel: 28 inches; octagonal, chrome-lined. Weight:
about 7 pounds. Walnut stock. Single trigger. Brass fittings, including patch box, ferrules, butt plate, etc.

Armsport Kentucky Rifle Model 5108V **$145**
Same general specifications as Model 5108, except
manufactured in 36 caliber without chrome-lined barrels.

Armsport Kentucky Rifle Model 5109 . . . . **$145**
Lock: color casehardened, percussion. Caliber: 50.
Barrel: 28 inches; octagonal, chrome-lined. Weight:
about 7 pounds. Walnut stock. Single trigger. Brass fittings, including patch box, ferrules, butt plate, etc.

Armsport Kentucky Flintlock Rifle
Model 5110

Armsport Kentucky Rifle Model 5110....... **$150**
Lock: color casehardened, flintlock. Caliber: 45. Barrel: 28 inches; octagonal, chrome-lined. Weight: about 7½ pounds. Walnut stock. Single trigger. Brass fittings, including patch box, ferrules, butt plate, etc.

Armsport Kentucky Rifle Model 5110A..... **$150**
Same general specifications as Model 5110, except manufactured in 50 caliber.

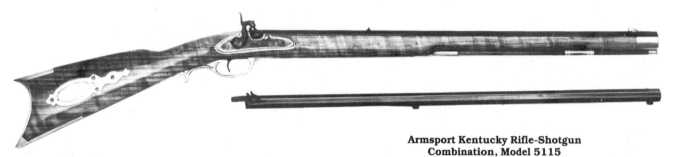

Armsport Kentucky Rifle-Shotgun
Combination, Model 5115

Armsport Kentucky Rifle-Shotgun Combination, Model 5115............................. **$185**
Lock: color casehardened, percussion. Caliber/gauge: 50 with 20 gauge. Barrel: 28 inches, octagonal. Weight: about 7 pounds. Select-grain walnut stock. Single trigger. Brass fittings, including patch box, ferrules, butt plate, etc.

Armsport Kentucky Rifle-Shotgun Combination, Model 5115C............................. **$185**
Same general specifications as Model 5115, except made in 45 caliber.

Armsport Tryon Trailblazer

Armsport Tryon Trailblazer Rifle.......... **$225**
Lock: color casehardened, percussion. Calibers: 50 or 54. Barrels: 28 or 32 inches; octagonal, chrome-lined. Weight: about 7 pounds. European walnut stock. Double-set triggers. Brass fittings, including patch box, ferrules, butt plate, etc. Engraved Model 5131 commands a higher price.

Armsport Double Barrel Shotgun

Armsport Double Barrel Muzzleloading Shotgun **$280**
Lock: color casehardened, percussion. Gauges: 10 or 12. Barrel: 28 inches, octagonal. Weight: 6½ pounds. Straight grip, checkered stock. Double triggers.

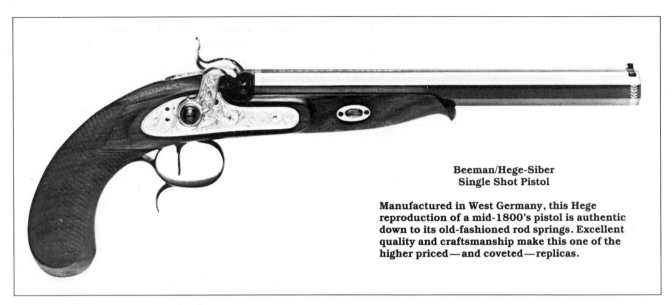

**Beeman/Hege-Siber
Single Shot Pistol**

Manufactured in West Germany, this Hege
reproduction of a mid-1800's pistol is authentic
down to its old-fashioned rod springs. Excellent
quality and craftsmanship make this one of the
higher priced—and coveted—replicas.

BEEMAN PRECISION ARMS, INC.
Santa Rosa, California

Beeman Precision Arms, Inc., began operations primarily distributing high-quality air guns. During the
1980s, they created a new division that now imports a
variety of modern quality firearms and accessories for
distribution in the U.S. For their entry into the blackpowder replica market, they have made available the
following reproductions, produced by the West German firm of Hege.

Hege Waffenschmiede im Zeughaus, located in Über-
lingen, was established by the Hebsacker family in
1959. The owner, Frederick, is a master gunmaker who
studied at the government arms engineering school in
Austria. One of the foremost weapons dealers in Germany today, the company caters to serious shooters
and collectors and prides itself on its outstanding
craftsmanship. The family also owns one of the largest
collections of antique and modern arms and accessories.

Beeman/Hege-Siber Single Shot Pistol
An exact replica of the 33-caliber pistol made by Jean
Frederick Siber in the mid-1800s. A master gunmaker,
engraver and medalist, Siber (1812–1898) came from a
Swiss watch-making family and lived in the French-
speaking section of Lausanne in Switzerland. In con-
stant touch with exacting European marksmen (Lord
Byron was one of his clients), he designed this pistol
to satisfy the demands of small caliber, high-precision
barrel, low recoil, fast ignition and "natural" 70-degree
grip angle.

Specifications. The Siber formula: 33-3-333, or 33
caliber, .3mm groove depth, 333mm rifling twist (one
turn in 13.1 inch). Engraved, percussion, precision-
made lock. Barrel: 10 inches, octagonal. Overall length:
15½ inches. Weight: 2.4 pounds. French-style single-

set trigger. Barleycorn dovetailed front sight; micro-ad-
justable rear sight. Oil-finished hand-checkered stock
of European walnut rounded at 70-degree angle. Tulip
forend.

French Deluxe Model has rust blued barrel and trigger guard, elaborate, original engraving, 24-carat gold
inlay on top of barrel inscribed "Siber A Lausanne."

English Standard Model is similar to the French version, except has less elaborate engraving on lockplate
and hammer; barrel and trigger guard are plum brown.

Paired, cased sets available.

French Deluxe Model **$1200**
English Standard Model. **695**

Beeman/Hege-Manton Flintlock Pistol **$1100**
An excellent reproduction of the high-performance,
highly desired flintlock pistol designed by the Manton
brothers, John and Joseph, in the early 1800s. John
held the patent for the lock and gun design, while Joseph designed the breeching.

Caliber: 44. Barrel: octagonal, rifled or smoothbore.
Flintlock ignition that worked very fast because of the
profile of the hammer and V-shaped pan emitting only
a thin layer of powder. Rounded European walnut
stock with hand-checkering. Engraved hammer and
lockplate inscribed "John Manton."

COLT FIREARMS
Hartford, Connecticut

In January 1979, Colt Firearms, a division of Colt Industries, announced the introduction of an expanded
range of famous Colt blackpowder revolvers to be offered to the public as part of a new program—"The Authentic Colt Blackpowder Series." In addition to the
Third Model Dragoon and 1851 Navy revolvers—reintroduced in 1974—Colt offered the 1861 Navy, 1860
Army, 1862 Pocket Navy and 1862 Pocket Police, 1847

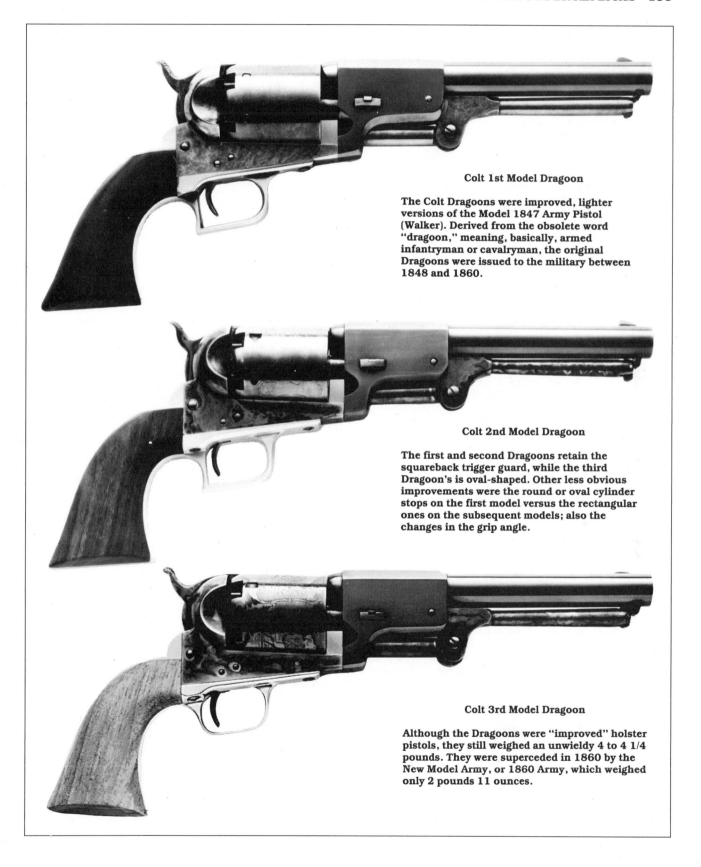

Colt 1st Model Dragoon

The Colt Dragoons were improved, lighter versions of the Model 1847 Army Pistol (Walker). Derived from the obsolete word "dragoon," meaning, basically, armed infantryman or cavalryman, the original Dragoons were issued to the military between 1848 and 1860.

Colt 2nd Model Dragoon

The first and second Dragoons retain the squareback trigger guard, while the third Dragoon's is oval-shaped. Other less obvious improvements were the round or oval cylinder stops on the first model versus the rectangular ones on the subsequent models; also the changes in the grip angle.

Colt 3rd Model Dragoon

Although the Dragoons were "improved" holster pistols, they still weighed an unwieldy 4 to 4 1/4 pounds. They were superceded in 1860 by the New Model Army, or 1860 Army, which weighed only 2 pounds 11 ounces.

Colt Walker, Baby Dragoon, and the First and Second Dragoons.

These Colt blackpowder handguns are authentic in every detail and continue to bear serial numbers following those stamped on earlier issues. Therefore, rather than be considered reproductions or replicas, they are a continuation of the legacy laid down by Colonel Samuel Colt and his predecessors more than 150 years ago. *See* also Colt listings in Handguns, Section One.

Colt Baby Dragoon Percussion Revolver **$250**
Caliber: 31. Unfluted, straight cylinder engraved with Ranger-Indian scene. Barrel: 4 inches. Finish: color casehardened frame and hammer; blued barrel, trigger, wedge, cylinder and screws. Silver backstrap and trigger guard. Varnished grips. Made from 1979 to 1984.

**Colt 1st Model Dragoon Percussion
Revolver** **$280**
Caliber: 44. Six-shot cylinder engraved with Ranger-Indian scene. Barrel: 7¹/₂ inches, part round, part octagonal. Weight: 66 ounces. Finish: color casehardened frame, loading lever, plunger and hammer; blued barrel, cylinder, trigger and wedge. Polished brass backstrap and squareback trigger guard. One-piece, oil-finished walnut stocks. German silver front sight. Made from 1979 to 1984.

**Colt 2nd Model Dragoon Percussion
Revolver** **$280**
Caliber: 44. Six-shot cylinder engraved with Ranger-Indian scene. Barrel: 7¹/₂ inches, part round, part octagon. Weight: 66 ounces. Finish: color casehardened frame, loading lever, plunger and hammer; blued barrel, cylinder, trigger and wedge. Polished brass backstrap and squareback trigger guard. One-piece, oil-finished walnut stocks. Made from 1979 to 1984.

**Colt 3rd Model Dragoon Percussion
Revolver** **$260**
Caliber: 44. Six-shot cylinder engraved with Ranger-Indian scene. Barrel: 7¹/₂ inches, part round, part octagon. Weight: 66 ounces. Finish: color casehardened frame, loading lever, plunger and hammer; blued barrel, cylinder, trigger and wedge. Polished brass backstrap and oval trigger guard. One-piece, oil-finished walnut stocks. Made from 1974 to 1984.

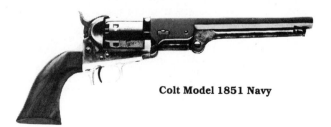

Colt Model 1851 Navy

Colt Model 1851 Navy Percussion Revolver . . **$265**
Caliber: 36. Six-shot cylinder with engraved Naval scene. Barrel: 7¹/₂ inches, octagonal. Weight: 42 ounces. Finish: color casehardened frame, loading lever, plunger, hammer and latch; blued cylinder, trigger, barrel, screws and wedge. Silver-plated trigger guard and backstrap. Brass front sight. One-piece varnished walnut grips. Made from 1974 to 1984.

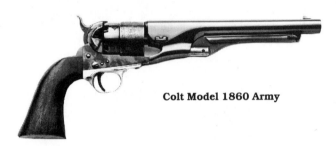

Colt Model 1860 Army

Colt Model 1860 Army Percussion Revolver . . **$270**
Caliber: 44. Six-shot unfluted cylinder with engraving of navy scene and markings "Patented Sept. 10th, 1850." Barrel: 8 inches, round. Weight: 42 ounces. Finish: color casehardened frame, loading lever, plunger, hammer and latch; brush blued cylinder, trigger, barrel, backstrap, screws and wedge. Polished brass trigger guard. German silver front sight. Oiled walnut grips. Made from 1979 to 1984.

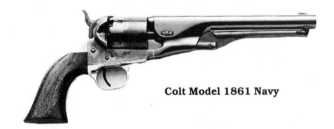

Colt Model 1861 Navy

Colt Model 1861 Navy Percussion Revolver . . **$260**
Caliber: 36. Six-shot round cylinder engraved with naval scene. Barrel: 7¹/₂ inches, round. Weight: 42 ounces. Finish: color casehardened frame, loading lever, plunger, hammer and latch; blued cylinder, trigger, barrel screws and wedge. Silver-plated trigger guard and backstrap. German silver front sight. Varnished one-piece walnut grips. Made from 1979 to 1984.

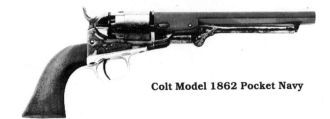

Colt Model 1862 Pocket Navy

Colt Model 1862 Pocket Navy Percussion Revolver **$245**
Caliber: 36. Five-shot, round-rebated cylinder engraved with stage coach scene. Barrel: 5¹/₂ inches, octagonal. Weight: 27 ounces. Finish: color casehardened frame, hammer, loading lever, plunger and latch; blued barrel, wedge, cylinder, trigger guard and backstrap. Brass pin front sight. Varnished one-piece walnut grips. Made from 1979 to 1984.

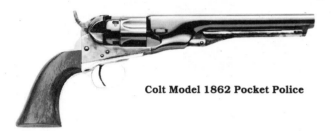

Colt Model 1862 Pocket Police

Colt Model 1862 Pocket Police Percussion Revolver **$245**
Caliber: 36. Five-shot, rebated, fluted cylinder. Barrel: 5¹/₂ inches, round. Weight: 25 ounces. Finish: color casehardened frame, hammer, loading lever, plunger and latch; blued barrel, wedge, cylinder, trigger and screws. Silver-plated trigger guard and backstrap. Brass front sight. Varnished one-piece walnut grips. Made from 1979 to 1984.

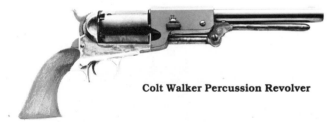

Colt Walker Percussion Revolver

Colt Walker Percussion Revolver **$260**
Caliber: 44. Six-shot cylinder with engraving of soldiers fighting Indians. Barrel: 9 inches, round. Weight: 73 ounces. Finish: color casehardened frame, hammer, loading lever and plunger; blued barrel, cylinder, backstrap, trigger and wedge. Polished brass trigger guard. German silver sight. Oil-finished walnut grips. Made from 1979 to 1984.

CVA
Norcross, Georgia

Connecticut Valley Arms, Inc. (CVA) was founded in 1971 by David Silk and was located in Haddam, Connecticut. Its chief aim was to provide the American market with an extensive line of replica arms, knives and blackpowder accessories manufactured at various European plants. Most CVA items are moderate in cost,

although a few higher priced, presentation-grade models are now available. The current line-up includes flint and percussion firearms such as cap-and-ball revolvers, mountain guns, Hawken rifles, Kentucky pistols and rifles, and the like.

PISTOLS

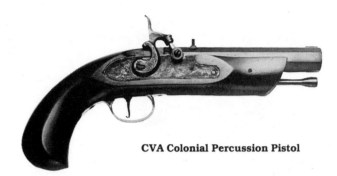

CVA Colonial Percussion Pistol

CVA Colonial Pistol **$55**
Lock: color casehardened, engraved flintlock or percussion. Caliber: 45 (.451). Barrel: 6³/₄ inches, octagonal. Overall length: 12³/₄ inches. Weight: 31 ounces. Blade front sight; fixed rear. Finish: blued barrel; brass hardware. Dark walnut-tone stock.

CVA Hawken Flintlock Pistol **$90**
Same general specifications as Hawken Percussion model, except for flintlock ignition.

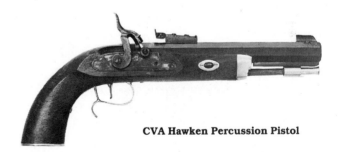

CVA Hawken Percussion Pistol

CVA Hawken Percussion Pistol **$85**
Lock: color casehardened, engraved percussion. Caliber: 50. Barrel: 9³/₄ inches; octagonal, 1 inch across the flats. Overall length: 16¹/₂ inches. Weight: 50 ounces. Beaded blade front sight; adjustable rear. Finish: blued barrel; brass wedge plate, nose cap, ramrod thimbles, trigger guard and grip cap. Select walnut stock.

CVA Kentucky Flintlock Pistol **$80**
Same general specifications as Kentucky Percussion model, except has flintlock ignition.

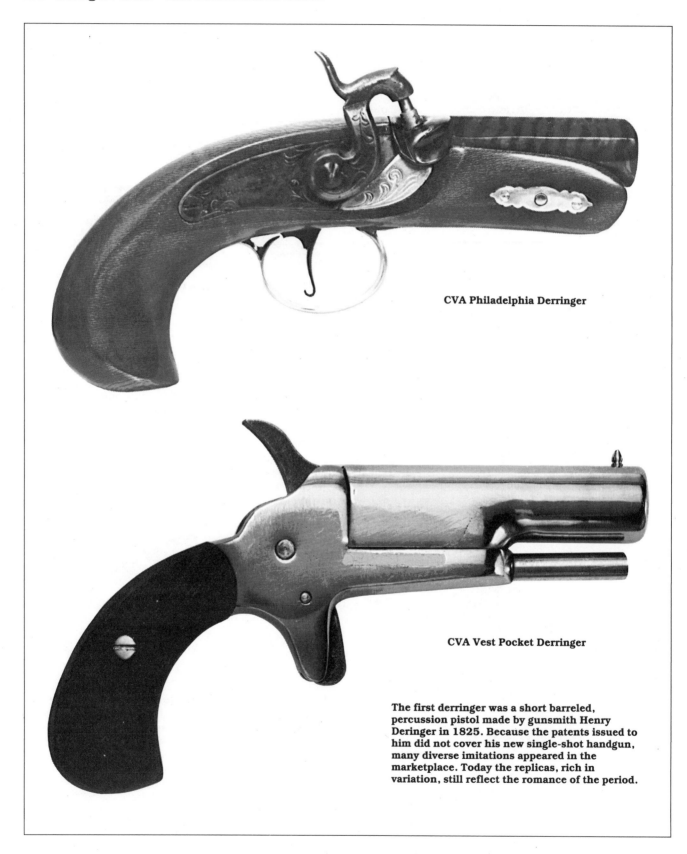

CVA Philadelphia Derringer

CVA Vest Pocket Derringer

The first derringer was a short barreled, percussion pistol made by gunsmith Henry Deringer in 1825. Because the patents issued to him did not cover his new single-shot handgun, many diverse imitations appeared in the marketplace. Today the replicas, rich in variation, still reflect the romance of the period.

CVA Kentucky Percussion Pistol

CVA Kentucky Percussion Pistol............$75
Lock: color casehardened, engraved percussion. Caliber: 45. Barrel: 10¼ inches, octagonal. Overall length: 15¼ inches. Weight: 40 ounces. Finish: blued barrel; brass hardware. Dovetailed Kentucky front and rear sights.

CVA Mountain Flintlock Pistol............ $100
Same general specifications as Mountain Percussion model, except for flintlock ignition.

CVA Mountain Percussion Pistol

CVA Mountain Percussion Pistol........... $100
Lock: color casehardened, engraved percussion. Caliber: 50. Barrel: 9 inches; octagonal, 15⁄16 inch across flats. Overall length: 14 inches. Weight: 40 ounces. Finish: brown steel, German silver wedge plates. German silver blade front sight; fixed primitive rear. American maple stock.

CVA Philadelphia Derringer.................$45
Lock: color casehardened, engraved, coil-spring back-action percussion lock. Caliber: 45. Barrel: 3¼ inches, octagon. Overall length: 7⅛ inches. Weight: 16 ounces. Finish: blued barrel, brass hardware. No sights. Walnut-toned stock. (*See* photo, opposite.)

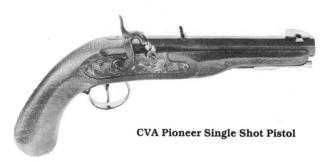

CVA Pioneer Single Shot Pistol

CVA Pioneer Single Shot Percussion Pistol $55
Lock: color casehardened, engraved percussion. Caliber: 32. Barrel: 7½ inches; octagonal, 7⁄8 inch across flats. Overall length: 13 inches. Weight: 14 ounces. Brass blade front sight; open rear sight.

CVA Prospector Single Shot Pistol

CVA Prospector Single Shot Pistol...........$50
Caliber: 44. Barrel: 8½ inches, tapering octagonal. Overall length: 12¾ inches. Weight: 42 ounces. Blade front sight; notch in hammer rear sight. Grips are of one-piece walnut.

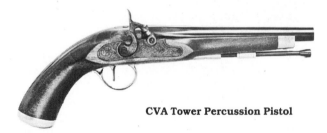

CVA Tower Percussion Pistol

CVA Tower Percussion Pistol.................$80
Lock: color casehardened, engraved percussion. Caliber: 45. Barrel: 9 inches; octagonal at breech tapering to round at muzzle. Overall length: 15¾ inches overall. Weight: 36 ounces. Finish: blued barrel, brass hardware. Cark-grained walnut stocks.

CVA Vest Pocket Derringer...................$45
Caliber: 31. Single shot. Barrel: 2½ inches. Overall length: 5 inches. Weight: 16 ounces. Finish: brass frame and barrel. Two-piece walnut grips. (*See* photo, opposite.)

REVOLVERS

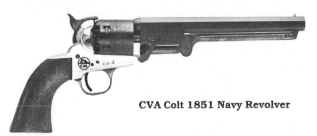

CVA Colt 1851 Navy Revolver

CVA Colt 1851 Navy Percussion Revolver......$75
Caliber: 36. Six-shot engraved cylinder. Barrel: 7½ inches, octagonal. Overall length: 13 inches. Weight:

CVA Colt 1851 Navy Percussion Revolver (cont.)
44 ounces. Post front sight; hammer notch rear. One-piece walnut grips. Hinged-style loading lever. Finish: blued barrel and cylinder; brass frame, trigger guard and backstrap; color casehardened loading lever and hammer.

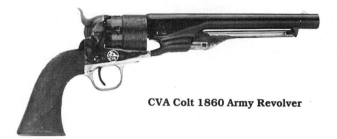

CVA Colt 1860 Army Revolver

CVA Colt 1860 Army Percussion Revolver ... $125
Caliber: 44. Six-shot engraved cylinder. Barrel: 7¹/₂ inches, rounded; creeping style. Weight: 44 ounces. Blade front sight; hammer notch rear. One-piece walnut grips. Hinged-style loading lever. Finish: blued barrel and cylinder with color casehardened loading lever, hammer and frame; brass trigger guard.

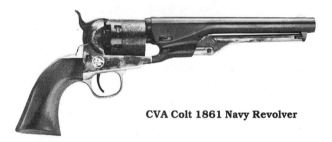

CVA Colt 1861 Navy Revolver

CVA Colt 1861 Navy Percussion Revolver.... $120
Caliber: 36. Six-shot engraved cylinder. Barrel: 7¹/₂ inches, rounded. Overall length: 13 inches. Weight: 44 ounces. Creeping-style loading lever. Blade front sight; hammer notch rear. Walnut grips. Finish: blued barrel and cylinder; color casehardened loading lever, hammer and frame. Brass trigger guard and backstrap.

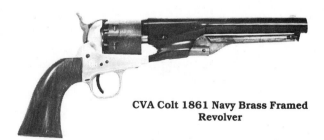

CVA Colt 1861 Navy Brass Framed Revolver

CVA Colt 1861 Navy Percussion Revolver (Brass Frame) $130
Same general specifications as blued model, except has brass frame.

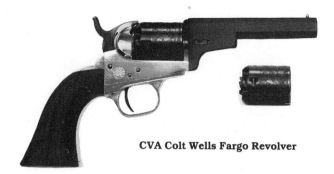

CVA Colt Wells Fargo Revolver

CVA Colt Wells Fargo Percussion Revolver $98
Caliber: 31. Five-shot engraved cylinder with extra 5-shot cylinder. Barrel: 4 inches, octagonal. Overall length: 9 inches. Weight: 28¹/₂ ounces w/extra cylinder. Post front sight; hammer notch rear sight. Finish: solid brass frame, trigger guard and backstrap. Blued steel barrel and cylinder; color casehardened hammer. One-piece walnut grip.

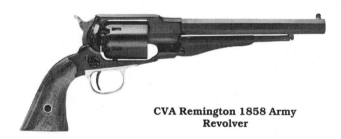

CVA Remington 1858 Army Revolver

CVA Remington 1858 Army Percussion Revolver $75
Caliber: 44. Barrel: 8 inches, octagonal. Weight: about 2¹/₂ pounds. Overall length: 13 to 14 inches. Adjustable front sight. Finish: blued frame, cylinder and barrel; brass trigger guard. Walnut stocks.

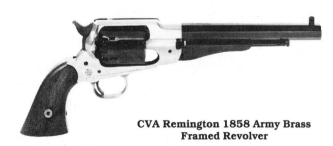

CVA Remington 1858 Army Brass Framed Revolver

CVA Remington 1858 Army Percussion Revolver (Brass Frame)................................$75
Same general specifications as steel frame model, except for brass frame, trigger guard and backstrap.

CVA Remington New Pocket Revolver

CVA Remington New Model Pocket Percussion Revolver **$55**
Caliber: 31. Five-shot cylinder. Barrel: 4 inches, octagonal. 7 1/2 inches overall. Weight: 15 1/2 ounces. Post front sight; groove in frame at rear. Finish: blued barrel, cylinder and loading lever; solid brass frame.

LONG ARMS

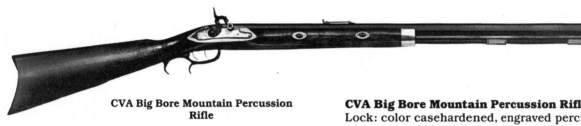

CVA Big Bore Mountain Percussion Rifle

CVA Big Bore Mountain Flintlock Rifle **$225**
Same general specifications as Big Bore Percussion version, except has flintlock ignition system.

CVA Big Bore Mountain Percussion Rifle **$235**
Lock: color casehardened, engraved percussion. Calibers: 54 and 58. Barrel: 32 inches; octagonal, 1 inch across flats. Overall length: 48 inches. Weight: 8 lbs. 2 oz. Double-set triggers. German silver front sight; adjustable dovetail rear. Selected hardwood stock with fully formed cheekpiece. Finish: browned steel and wedge plates; authentic pewter-type nose cap.

CVA Blazer Rifle

CVA Blazer Rifle. **$80**
Lightweight percussion rifle with straight-through ignition. Caliber: 50. Barrel: 28 inches; octagonal, 15/16 inch across flats. Overall length: 43 1/2 inches. Weight: 6 lbs. 12 oz. Select hardwood stock with pistol grip. Front brass blade sight; fixed semibuckhorn rear.

CVA Blazer II **$72**
Scaled-down version of the CVA Blazer Rifle. Caliber: 45 percussion. Barrel: 24 1/2 inches; octagonal, 11/16 inch across flats. Overall length: 38 1/2 inches. Weight: 5 lbs. 12 oz.

CVA Double Barreled Express Rifle

CVA Express Rifle **$250**
Locks: color casehardened, engraved percussion style. Caliber: 50. Barrels: two 28-inch tapered, round. Overall length: 44 1/4 inches. Weight: 9 lbs. 3 oz. Select

hardwood stock. Sights: dovetail, beaded blade front; adjustable, hunting-style rear. Finish: polished steel wedge plates; color casehardened hammers, double triggers and trigger guard; blued barrels.

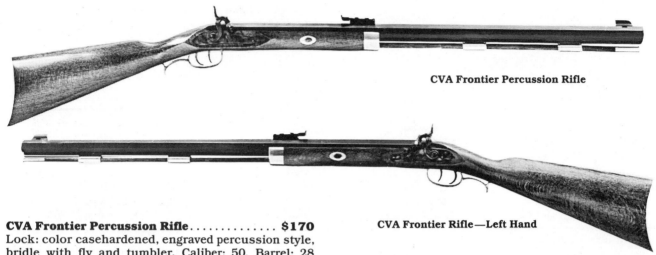

CVA Frontier Percussion Rifle

CVA Frontier Rifle—Left Hand

CVA Frontier Percussion Rifle **$170**
Lock: color casehardened, engraved percussion style,
bridle with fly and tumbler. Caliber: 50. Barrel: 28
inches; octagonal, $^{15}/_{16}$ inch across flats. Overall
length: 44 inches. Weight: 6 lbs. 14 oz. Selected hardwood stock. Double-set triggers. Brass blade front
sight; adjustable open rear sight. Finish: blued steel;
brass wedge plates; brass nose cap, trigger guard and
butt plate.

CVA Frontier Percussion Rifle, Left Hand . . . **$175**
Same general specifications as above rifle, except lock
and nipple are located on left-hand side for left-hand
shooter.

CVA Hawken Percussion Rifle

CVA Hawken Percussion Rifle **$200**
Lock: color casehardened, engraved percussion style.
Calibers: 50 and 54. Barrel: 28 inches; octagonal, 1
inch across flats. Overall length: 44 inches. Weight: 7
lbs. 15 oz. Selected walnut stock with fully formed

beavertail cheekpiece. Double-set triggers. Dovetail,
beaded blade front sight; adjustable, dovetail open rear
sight. Finish: blued steel; brass patch box, wedge
plates, nose cap, ramrod thimbles, trigger guard and
butt plate.

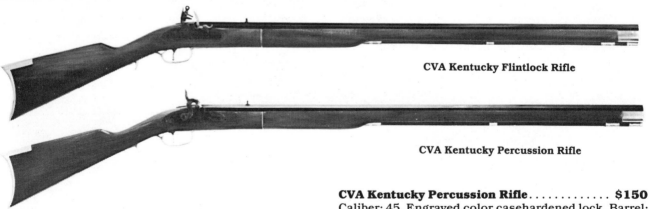

CVA Kentucky Flintlock Rifle

CVA Kentucky Percussion Rifle

CVA Kentucky Percussion Rifle **$150**
Caliber: 45. Engraved color casehardened lock. Barrel:
$33^1/_2$ inches; octagonal. Overall length: 48 inches.
Weight: $7^1/_4$ pounds. Kentucky-style front and rear
sights. Brass furniture. Blued barrel. Dark walnut-
toned stock.

CVA Kentucky Flintlock Rifle **$160**
Same general specifications as Kentucky Percussion
model, except with flintlock ignition.

CVA Mountain Flintlock Rifle

CVA Mountain Percussion Rifle

CVA Mountain Percussion Rifle **$225**
Lock: color casehardened, engraved percussion. Calibers: 45 and 50. Barrel: 32 inches; octagonal, $^{15}/_{16}$ inch across flats. Overall length: 48 inches. Weight: 7 lbs. 14 oz. Select hardwood stock with fully formed cheekpiece. Double-set triggers. German silver blade front; adjustable rear. Finish: brown steel, German silver patch box and wedge plates; pewter-type nose cap.

CVA Mountain Flintlock Rifle **$225**
Same general specifications as Mountain Percussion Rifle, except has flintlock ignition system.

CVA Pennsylvania Flintlock
Long Rifle

CVA Pennsylvania Flintlock Long Rifle **$225**
Lock: color casehardened, engraved flintlock. Caliber: 50. Barrel: 40 inches; octagonal, $^{7}/_{8}$ inch across flats. Overall length: 55$^{3}/_{4}$ inches. Weight: 8 lbs. 3 oz. Double-set triggers. Fixed semibuckhorn rear sight. Selected walnut stock. Finish: brass butt plate, patch box, trigger guard, thimbles and nose cap.

CVA Pennsylvania Percussion Long Rifle **$225**
Same general specifications as Pennsylvania Flintlock above, except made with percussion lock. Discontinued in 1984.

CVA Squirrel Flintlock Rifle

CVA Squirrel Percussion Rifle

CVA Squirrel Rifle **$150**
Lock: color casehardened, engraved percussion or flintlock ignition. Caliber: 32. Barrel: 25 inches; octagonal, $^{11}/_{16}$ inch across flats. Overall length: 40$^{3}/_{4}$ inches.

Weight: 5 lbs. 12 oz. Double-set triggers. Dovetailed, beaded blade front sight; adjustable, open hunting-style rear sight. Selected hardwood stock. Finish: blued steel; brass butt plate, trigger guard, wedge plates and thimbles.

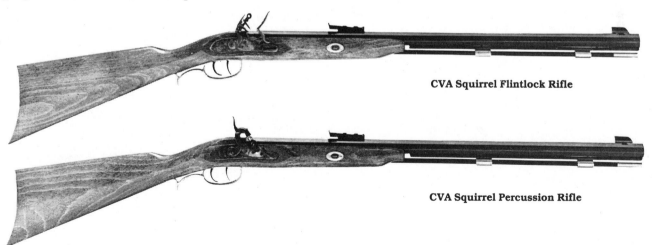

CVA Squirrel Percussion Rifle, Left Hand. . . . **$150**
Same general specifications as standard Squirrel Percussion model, except lock and nipple are on left side for left-hand shooter.

CVA Squirrel Rifle—Left Hand

CVA St. Louis Hawken Rifle **$120**
Caliber: 50. Percussion lock. Barrel: 28 inches; octagonal, $^{15}/_{16}$ inch across the flats, rifled one turn in 66 inches. Overall length: 44 inches. Weight: 7 lbs. 13 oz. Hooked breech. Double-set triggers. Adjustable trigger pull. Dovetailed blade front sight; adjustable open hunting-style rear. Solid brass wedge plates, nose cap, ramrod thimbles, finger spur trigger guard and patch box. Select hardwood stock with beavertail cheekpiece.

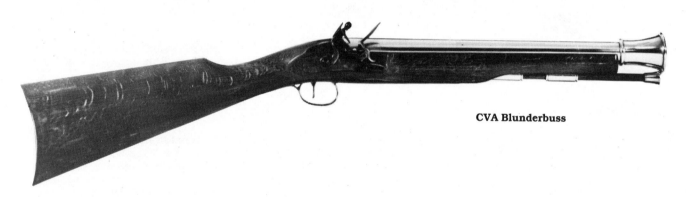

CVA Blunderbuss

CVA Blunderbuss. **$185**
Lock: engraved flintlock. Bore: .690. Barrel: 16 inches; tapered to flared muzzle. Weight: 5 lbs. 5 oz. Select hardwood stock. Finish: solid brass butt plate, ramrod thimbles, trigger, trigger guard, barrel, and engraved side plate.

CVA Double Barreled Shotgun

CVA Double Barrel Percussion Shotgun **$195**
Locks: polished steel, engraved percussion. Gauge: 12. Barrels: 28 inches; round, smoothbore. Overall length: 44½ inches. Weight: 6 lbs. 10 oz. Double triggers. Brass bead front sight. Finish: blued steel; polished steel wedge plates, trigger guard, triggers, tang. Engraved lock, hammers, tang and trigger guard. Select hardwood checkered stock.

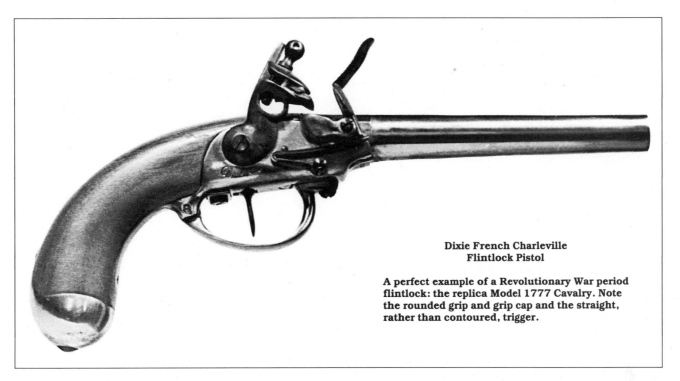

**Dixie French Charleville
Flintlock Pistol**

A perfect example of a Revolutionary War period flintlock: the replica Model 1777 Cavalry. Note the rounded grip and grip cap and the straight, rather than contoured, trigger.

DIXIE GUN WORKS, INC.
Union City, Tennessee

Dixie Gun Works is the largest and oldest dealer of antique and replica blackpowder arms in the U.S. Under the direction of Turner Kirkland, the firm has bought, sold and traded muzzleloaders since 1954. It publishes a 500-plus-page catalog, "Blackpowder Shooting and Antique Gun Supplies" that details an inventory of more than 7,000 blackpowder-related items. Among their offering of replicas are the following.

HANDGUNS

Dixie 1848 Baby Dragoon Percussion Revolver **$85**
Caliber: 31. Five-shot cylinder. Barrel: 6 inches, octagonal. Overall length: 10¹/₂ inches. Weight: 1¹/₂ pounds. Color casehardened frame and loading lever. One-piece walnut grip. Polished brass backstrap and square bowed trigger guard.

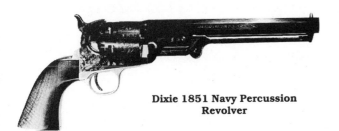

**Dixie 1851 Navy Percussion
Revolver**

Dixie 1851 Navy Percussion Revolver (Steel). . .**$90**
Caliber: 36. Six-shot engraved cylinder. Barrel: 7¹/₂ inches, octagonal. Overall length: 13³/₄ inches. Weight: 3 pounds. Color casehardened steel frame and loading lever brass backstrap and trigger guard. Blued barrel and cylinder. Italian reproduction of Civil War favorite.

**Dixie 1860 Army Percussion
Revolver**

Dixie 1860 Army Percussion Revolver **$95**
Caliber: 44. Six-shot half-fluted cylinder. Barrel: 8 inches. Overall length: 14 inches. Weight: 2³/₄ pounds. Cut for shoulder stock.

Dixie French Charleville Flintlock Pistol **$100**
Reproduction of the Model 1777 Cavalry pistol of the Revolutionary War period. Color casehardened hammer, frizzen and trigger. Round barrel and rounded European walnut stock. Shoots .680 ball with 40 gr. FFg powder. (*See* photo, above.)

Dixie Navy Percussion Revolver (Brass).......$70
Caliber: 36. Six-shot cylinder. Barrel: 7½ inches. Overall length: 12⅞ inches. Weight: 3 pounds. Brass frame with blued steel barrel and cylinder.

Dixie Remington Army Revolver

Dixie Remington Army Revolver $95
Caliber: 44, percussion. Six-shot cylinder. Barrel: 8 inches, octagonal. Overall length: 13½ inches. Weight: 2½ pounds. Brass trigger guard. Blued steel. Color casehardened hammer.

Dixie Spiller & Burr Brass Frame Revolver $50
Caliber: 36. Six-shot cylinder. Barrel: 7 inches, octagonal. Overall length: 12¾ inches. Weight: 2½ pounds. Brass frame, trigger guard and backstrap. Color casehardened loading lever, hammer and trigger.

Dixie Third Model Dragoon Percussion Revolver $95
Caliber: 44. Six-shot engraved cylinder. Barrel: 7⅜ inches. Overall length: 14 inches. Weight: 4½ pounds. Brass backstrap and trigger guard. Color casehardened steel frame. Blued barrel and cylinder.

Dixie Walker Revolver

Dixie Walker Percussion Revolver............$90
Modeled after the largest Colt pistol ever made. Caliber: 44. Six-shot engraved cylinder. Barrel: 9 inches, round. Overall length: 15½ inches. Weight: 4½ pounds. Steel back strap and brass squareback trigger guard. Walnut grips. Metal parts blued. Col. Walker of Mexican War fame suggested this style pistol instead of the Paterson, and only about 1,000 of the original were produced.

Dixie Wyatt Earp Percussion Revolver........$70
Caliber: 45. Five-shot cylinder. Barrel: 12 inches, octagonal. Overall length: 18¼ inches. Weight: 3 pounds. Brass frame, backstrap and trigger guard. Blued barrel and cylinder. Color casehardened hammer, trigger and loading lever.

LONG ARMS

Dixie Brown Bess Musket, Second Model $230
Lock: color casehardened, flintlock. Caliber: 75. Barrel: 41¾ inches, octagonal. Weight: 9½ pounds. Walnut stock. Single trigger. Brass fittings, including patch box, ferrules, butt plate, etc.

Dixie Buffalo Hunter...................... $185
Lock: color casehardened, percussion. Caliber: 58. Barrel: 26 inches, octagonal. Weight: 8¼ pounds. Walnut stock. Single trigger. Brass fittings, including patch box, ferrules, butt plate, etc.

Dixie Deluxe Cub Rifle $190
Lock: color casehardened, percussion or flintlock. Caliber: 40. Barrel: 28 inches, octagonal. Weight: 6¾ pounds. Walnut stock. Double-set triggers. Brass fittings, including patch box, ferrules, butt plate, etc.

Dixie Brown Bess Musket
Second Model

Dixie Enfield Model 1858 Two-Band Rifle . . . **$250**
Lock: color casehardened, percussion. Caliber: 58.
Barrel: 33 inches, octagonal. Weight: 9¼ pounds. European walnut stock. Single trigger. Brass fittings, including patch box, ferrules, butt plate, etc.

Dixie Enfield Three-Band Rifled Musket **$285**
Lock: color casehardened, percussion. Caliber: 58.
Barrel: 39 inches, octagonal. Weight: 10½ pounds. European walnut stock. Single trigger. Brass fittings, including patch box, ferrules, butt plate, etc.

Dixie Hawken Percussion Rifle **$165**
Lock: color casehardened, percussion. Calibers: 45
and 50. Barrel: 28 inches, octagonal. Weight: 9 pounds.
Walnut stock. Double-set triggers. Brass fittings, including patch box, ferrules, butt plate, etc.

Dixie Indian Gun **$300**
Lock: color casehardened, flintlock. Caliber: 75. Barrel:
31 inches, octagonal. Weight: 8 pounds. Walnut-stained stock. Single trigger. Brass fittings, including patch box, ferrules, butt plate, etc.

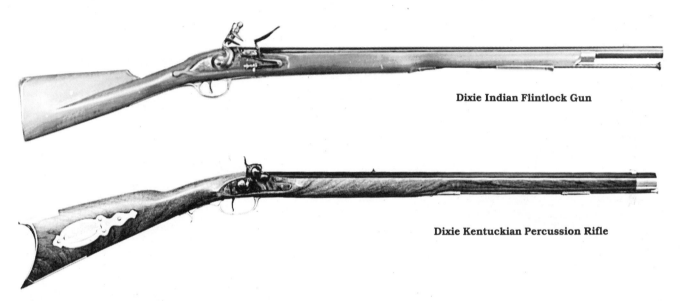

Dixie Indian Flintlock Gun

Dixie Kentuckian Percussion Rifle

Dixie Kentuckian Carbine
Lock: color casehardened, flintlock or percussion. Caliber: 45. Barrel: 27½ inches, octagonal. Weight: 5½
pounds. European walnut stock. Single trigger. Brass
fittings, including patch box, ferrules, butt plate, etc.
Flintlock **$150**
Percussion **140**

Dixie Kentuckian Rifle
Lock: color casehardened, flintlock or percussion. Caliber: 45. Barrel: 33½ inches; octagonal, 13/16 inch
across the flats. Overall length: 48 inches. Weight: 6¼
pounds. European walnut stock. Single trigger. Brass
fittings, including patch box, ferrules, butt plate, etc.
Flintlock **$150**
Percussion **140**

Dixie Mississippi Rifle

Dixie Mississippi Rifle **$180**
Lock: color casehardened, percussion. Caliber: 58.
Barrel: 33½ inches, octagonal. Weight: 10 pounds.
Walnut-stained stock. Single trigger. Brass fittings, including patch box, ferrules, butt plate, etc.

Dixie Pennsylvania Rifle **$230**
Lock: color casehardened, percussion or flintlock. Caliber: 45. Barrels: 41½ inches, octagonal. Weight: 8
pounds. Walnut stock. Double-set, double-phase triggers. Brass fittings, including patch box, ferrules, butt
plate, etc.

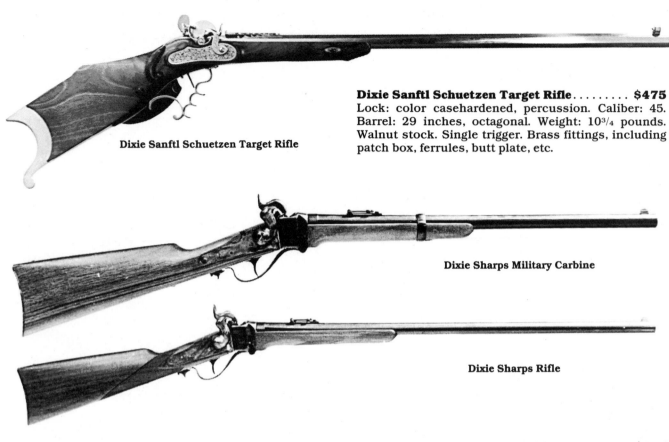

Dixie Sanftl Schuetzen Target Rifle

Dixie Sharps Military Carbine

Dixie Sharps Rifle

Dixie Sanftl Schuetzen Target Rifle **$475**
Lock: color casehardened, percussion. Caliber: 45.
Barrel: 29 inches, octagonal. Weight: 10³/₄ pounds.
Walnut stock. Single trigger. Brass fittings, including
patch box, ferrules, butt plate, etc.

Dixie Sharps Military Carbine **$265**
Lock: color casehardened, percussion. Caliber: 54.
Barrel: 22 inches, round. Weight: 7¹/₂ pounds. Walnut
stock. Single trigger. Brass fittings, including patch
box, ferrules, butt plate, etc.

Dixie Sharps Rifle **$280**
Lock: color casehardened, percussion. Caliber: 54.
Barrel: 28¹/₂ inches, round. Weight: 8¹/₂ pounds. Walnut stock. Single trigger. Brass fittings, including
patch box, ferrules, butt plate, etc.

**Dixie Springfield Model 1863 Civil War
Musket** **$230**
Lock: color casehardened, percussion. Caliber: 58.
Barrel: 40 inches, octagonal. Weight: 9¹/₂ pounds. Wal-
nut-stained stock. Single trigger. Brass fittings, in-
cluding patch box, ferrules, butt plate, etc.

Dixie Swiss Federal Target Rifle **$635**
Lock: color casehardened, percussion. Caliber: 45.
Barrel: 32 inches, octagonal. Weight: 13¹/₄ pounds.
Walnut stock. Double-set triggers. Brass fittings, in-
cluding patch box, ferrules, butt plate, etc.

Dixie Tennessee Mountain Rifle **$200**
Flintlock or percussion. Caliber: 50. Barrel: octagonal,
15/16 inch across the flats. Overall length: 41¹/₂ inches.

Dixie Tryon Rifle **$240**
Lock: color casehardened, percussion. Caliber: 50.
Barrels: 32 inches, octagonal. Walnut stock. Adjustable double-set triggers. Brass fittings, including patch
box, ferrules, butt plate, etc.

Dixie Tennessee Mountain
Flintlock Rifle

Dixie Wesson Percussion Rifle

Dixie Wesson Rifle. **$260**
Lock: color casehardened, percussion. Caliber: 1¹/₈″ ×
50. Barrels: 28 inches, octagonal. Weight: 10¹/₄ pounds.

European walnut stock. Double-set triggers. Brass fittings, including patch box, ferrules, butt plate, etc.

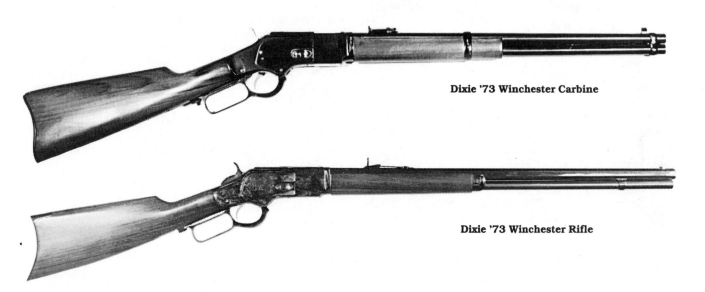

Dixie '73 Winchester Carbine

Dixie '73 Winchester Rifle

Dixie Winchester 1873 Carbine **$345**
Caliber: 44/40. Barrel: 20 inches, round. Overall length:
39 inches. Weight: 7 pounds. Full tubular magazine
holds 11 shots. Blade front sight; leaf rear sight. High-
luster blued steel. Walnut forearm and buttstock.

Dixie Winchester 1873 Rifle **$485**
Caliber: 44/40. Barrel: 23¹/₂ inches, octagonal. Weight:
8 pounds. Color casehardened frame with engraving.
Walnut forearm and buttstock.

Dixie York County Pennsylvania Rifle
Lock: color casehardened, percussion or flintlock. Caliber: 450. Barrels: 36 inches, octagonal. Overall length:
51¹/₂ inches. Weight: 7¹/₂ pounds. Walnut one-piece
stock. Double-set triggers. Brass fittings, including
patch box, ferrules, butt plate, etc.
Flintlock **$185**
Percussion **180**

Dixie Zouave Carbine **$170**
Lock: color casehardened, percussion. Caliber: 58.
Barrel: 26 inches, octagonal. Weight: 8¹/₂ pounds. Walnut-stained stock. Single trigger. Brass fittings, including patch box, ferrules, butt plate, etc.

Dixie Zouave Model 1863 Rifle **$200**
Lock: color casehardened, percussion. Caliber: 58.
Barrel: 33¹/₂ inches, octagonal. Weight: 9³/₄ pounds.
Walnut-stained stock. Single trigger. Brass fittings, in-
cluding patch box, ferrules, butt plate, etc.

EUROARMS OF AMERICA
Winchester, Virginia

HANDGUNS

Euroarms 1851 Navy Revolver..............**$95**
Model 1120. Caliber: 36 percussion; #11 cap. Barrel: 7½ inches, octagonal. Overall length: 13 inches. Weight: 42 ounces. Blued finish. Walnut grips. Brass backstrap and trigger guard.

Euroarms 1851 Navy Sheriff

Euroarms 1851 Navy Sheriff Model 1080 ..... **$95**
Caliber: 36 percussion; #11 cap; .375 round or conical lead ball. Barrel: 5 inches, octagonal. Overall length: 11½ inches. Weight: 38 ounces. Brass cone front sight; V-notch rear sight. Blued finish. Walnut grips. Brass backstrap and trigger guard.

Euroarms 1851 Navy Sheriff Model 1090 ..... **$95**
Same general specifications as Model 1080, except available in 44 caliber percussion with .451 round or conical ball.

Euroarms New Model Army Revolver Model 1010...**$85**
Caliber: 36 percussion. Barrel: 6½ inches. Weight: 34 ounces. Blued finish. Polished walnut stock. Brass trigger guard.

Euroarms New Model Army Revolver Model 1020.. **$100**
Same general specifications as Model 1010, except caliber 44 percussion, 8-inch barrel, overall length of 14¾ inches and weight of 40 ounces. (*See* photo, opposite.)

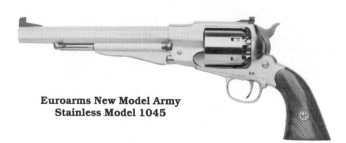

Euroarms New Model Army
Stainless Model 1045

Euroarms New Model Army Target Revolver
Caliber: 44 percussion. Barrel: 8 inches. Overall length: 14¾ inches. Weight: 41 ounces. Adjustable rear sight; ramp front sight. Polished walnut grips. Brass trigger guard.
Blued Model 1030 ....**$130**
Stainless Steel Model 1045 ....**200**

Euroarms Remington 1858 New Model Army Engraved **$195**
Caliber: 44 percussion. Barrel: 8 inches. Overall length: 14¾ inches. Weight: 41 ounces. Adjustable rear sight, ramp front sight. Classical 19th-century scroll engraving. Blued finish. Polished walnut grips. Brass trigger guard.

Euroarms Remington 1858 New Model Army Stainless Revolver
Caliber: 44 percussion. Overall length with 8-inch barrel: 13¼ inches. Weight: 40 ounces. Stainless steel finish with polished walnut stock and brass trigger guard.
Model 1047 with 6½-inch barrel **$145**
Model 1048 with 8-inch barrel **165**

Euroarms Rogers & Spencer
Revolver

Euroarms Rogers & Spencer Revolver **$130**
Model 1005. Caliber: 44 percussion; #11 cap. Barrel: 7½ inches. Overall length: 13¾ inches. Weight: 47 ounces. Blued finish with flared walnut grip.

Euroarms Rogers & Spencer
Army Revolver

Euroarms Rogers & Spencer Army Target Revolver **$175**
Model 1006. Caliber: 44 percussion; #11 cap. Barrel: 7½ inches. Overall length: 13¾ inches. Weight: 47 ounces. Adjustable rear sight; ramp front sight. Blued finish with flared walnut grip.

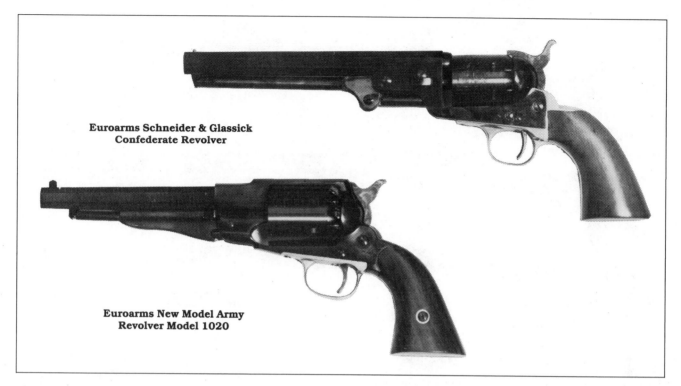

Euroarms Schneider & Glassick Confederate Revolver

Euroarms New Model Army Revolver Model 1020

Euroarms Rogers & Spencer London Gray Revolver
Same general specifications as Model 1005, except made with London gray finish.
Model 1007................................ **$150**
Engraved Model 1008.......................**200**

Euroarms Schneider & Glassick Confederate Revolver **$95**
Calibers: 36 and 44 percussion. Barrel: 7¹/₂ inches. Overall length: 13 inches. Weight: 40 ounces. Blued barrel. Color casehardened hammer and loading lever. Brass frame, backstrap and trigger guard. Engraved cylinder with naval battle scene. Model 1050, 36 caliber; Model 1060, 44 caliber. (*See* photo, above.)

LONG ARMS

Euroarms Cook & Brother Confederate Carbine.................................... **$245**
Model 2300. Caliber: 58 percussion. Barrel: 24 inches, round. Overall length: 40¹/₂ inches. Weight: 7¹/₂ pounds. Antique brown finish. Brass trigger guard, butt plate, barrel bands, sling swivels, nose cap.

Euroarms Hawken Rifle Model 2210A....... **$175**
Caliber: 50 percussion. Barrel: 28 inches, octagonal. Weight: about 9¹/₂ pounds. Solid one-piece walnut stock. Adjustable target rear sight; blade front sight. Double-set triggers. Polished brass mountings.

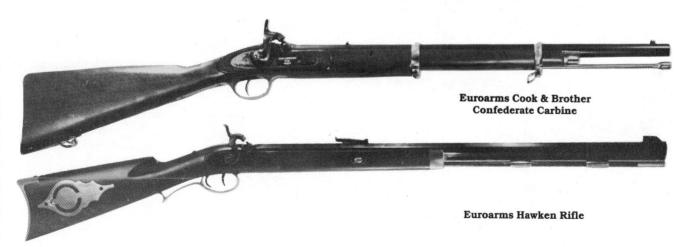

Euroarms Cook & Brother Confederate Carbine

Euroarms Hawken Rifle

Euroarms London Armory Co.
Enfield Musketoon

Euroarms London Armory Co.
Two-Band Enfield Musket

Euroarms London Armory Co.
Three-Band Enfield Musket

**Euroarms London Armory Company Enfield
Musketoon** **$200**
Model 2280. Caliber: 58 percussion; Minie ball. Barrel:
24 inches. Overall length: 40½ inches. Weight: 7 to 7½
pounds. Walnut stock with sling swivels. Blued finish
with brass trigger guard, nose cap and butt plate.

**Euroarms London Armory Company Two-Band
Enfield Musket** **$260**
Model 2270. Caliber: 58 percussion. Barrel: 33 inches,
round and rifled. Overall length: 49 inches. Weight:

about 8⅝ pounds. One-piece walnut stock. Brass butt
plate, trigger guard and nose cap. Blued barrel and barrel bands.

**Euroarms London Armory Company Three-Band
Enfield Musket** **$305**
Model 2260. Caliber: 58 percussion. Barrel: 39 inches,
round and rifled. Overall length: 54 inches. Weight:
about 9⅝ pounds. Enfield folding ladder-type rear
sight; inverted "V" front sight. One-piece walnut stock.
Blued barrel and barrel bands. Brass butt plate, trigger
guard, nose cap.

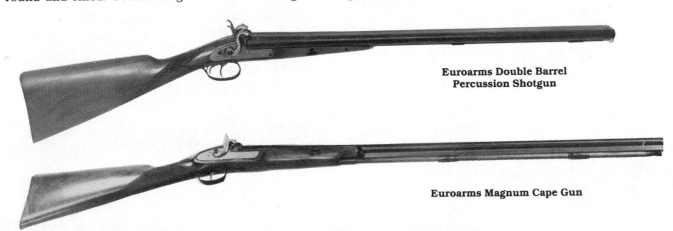

Euroarms Double Barrel
Percussion Shotgun

Euroarms Magnum Cape Gun

**Euroarms Percussion Double Barrel
Shotgun** **$305**
Model 2290. Gauge: 12. Chokes: modified/full. Weight:
about 6 pounds. Checkered, English-style walnut
stock. Blued barrels. Engraved side locks.

Euroarms Magnum Cape Gun **$245**
Model 2295. Single barrel. Gauge: 12. Barrel: 32 inches;
open choke. Overall length: 47½ inches. Weight: 7½
pounds. Classic English-styled stock of oil-finished
European walnut. Blued barrel, trigger guard and butt
plate. Scroll-engraved lock.

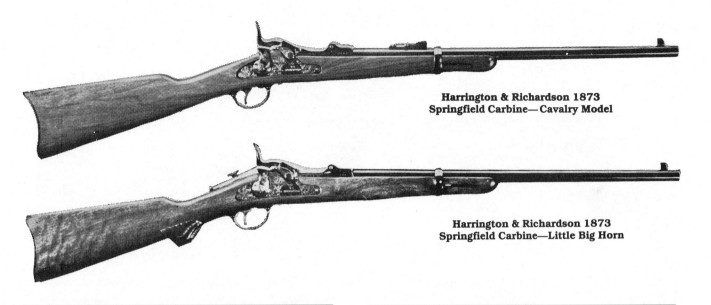

**Harrington & Richardson 1873
Springfield Carbine—Cavalry Model**

**Harrington & Richardson 1873
Springfield Carbine—Little Big Horn**

HARRINGTON & RICHARDSON, INC.
Gardner, Massachusetts

The firm of Harrington & Richardson was established by Gilbert Harrington and William Richardson in Worcester, Mass., in 1874. Originally producing shotguns and metallic cartridge revolvers, their enterprise soon expanded to many types of firearms. It was in 1986, after more than a century in business, that the company closed its doors.

**H & R 1873 Springfield Carbine—Cavalry
Model** **$275**
Model 171. Trapdoor, single-shot action. Caliber: 45-70 Govt. Barrel: 22 inches. Overall length: 41 inches. Weight: 7 pounds. Blade front sight; original military-style rear. Engraved action. Blue-black finish.

**H & R 1873 Springfield Carbine—Little Big Horn
Commemorative** **$275**
Model 174. Trapdoor, single-shot action. Caliber: 45-70 Govt. Barrel: 22 inches. Overall length: 41 inches. Weight: 7 lbs. 8 oz. Blade front sight; tang-mounted aperture rear. American walnut stock with metal grip adapter. Blue-black finish.

H & R 1873 Springfield Officer's Rifle **$275**
Model 173. Trapdoor, single-shot action. Caliber: 45-70 Govt. Barrel: 26 inches. Overall length: 45 inches. Weight: 8 pounds. Blade front sight; tang-mounted aperture rear. Hand-checkered American walnut stock. Blue-black finish. Color casehardened receiver.

HOPKINS & ALLEN
Hawthorne, New Jersey

The firm of Hopkins & Allen has been in the blackpowder replica business for many years. Its underhammer designs are exclusively American; they are manufactured in the U.S. and stem from 1830 New England. Some of the other replicas, particularly the handguns, are produced in Italy with German-made parts.

Hopkins & Allen 1851 Navy Revolver **$110**
Caliber: 36 percussion. Casehardened hammer, frame and loading lever. Blued barrel. Brass square-back trigger guard and back strap. Steel frame. Engraved cylinder.

Hopkins & Allen 1860 Army Revolver **$115**
Caliber: 44 percussion. Color casehardened hammer, frame and loading lever. Roll engraved cylinder. Walnut grips.

PISTOLS

**Hopkins & Allen Underhammer
Boot Pistol**

Hopkins & Allen Boot Pistol **$60**
Underhammer percussion lock. Calibers: 36 or 45. Barrel: 6 inches, octagonal. Weight: 40 ounces. Overall length: 13 inches. Open post-type front sight; open rear sight with step elevator. Sculptured walnut pistol grip. Match trigger. Blue-black finish.

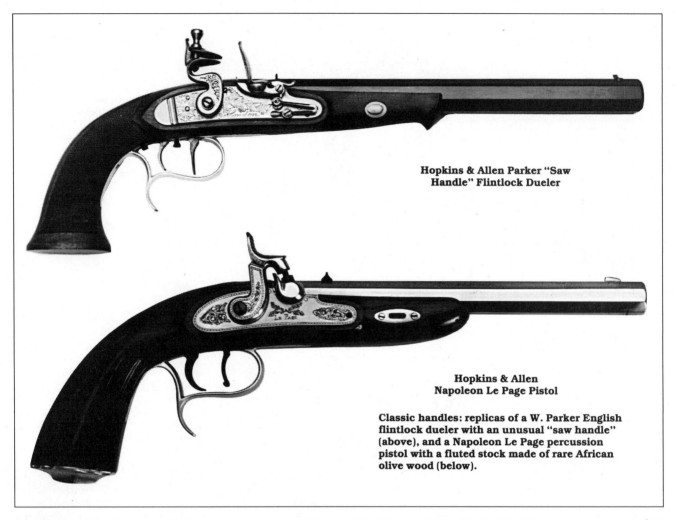

Hopkins & Allen Parker "Saw Handle" Flintlock Dueler

Hopkins & Allen Napoleon Le Page Pistol

Classic handles: replicas of a W. Parker English flintlock dueler with an unusual "saw handle" (above), and a Napoleon Le Page percussion pistol with a fluted stock made of rare African olive wood (below).

Hopkins & Allen Bounty Hunter Pistol **$90**
Caliber: 45 percussion. Barrel: 17 inches; octagonal, 13/16 inch across the flats. Overall length: 22 inches. Weight: 52 ounces. Solid brass nose cap and rib.

Hopkins & Allen J. S. Hawken Pistol **$165**
Calibers: 50 or 54 percussion. Barrel: octagonal, 15/16 inch across the flats; German-made. Overall length: 14 inches. Weight: 36 ounces. Full hooked breech. Finger spur trigger guard. Engraved lock plate and hammer. Checkered European walnut stock. Blue-black barrel. Early models have Italian-made barrels, brass trim, no engraving.

Hopkins & Allen Kentucky Pistol **$75**
Model 10. Flintlock or percussion; convertible ignition system. Caliber: 44. Barrel: 10 inches; octagonal, rifled. Overall length: 15 1/2 inches. Weight: 48 ounces.

Hopkins & Allen John Manton Pistol **$165**
Caliber: 45 percussion. Barrel: 10 inches; octagonal, 7/8 inch across the flats; German-made, precision-rifled. Overall length: 15 1/2 inches. Weight: 40 ounces. Two barrel wedges. Polished steel finish. Hand-checkered European walnut stock. Engraved lock plate and hammer. Early models have Italian-made barrels, no engraving and brass trim.

Hopkins & Allen Kentucky Percussion Pistol

Hopkins & Allen W. Moore Flintlock Pistol

**Hopkins & Allen W. Moore Flintlock
Target Pistol**............................ **$160**
Model 1800. Flintlock or percussion. Caliber: 45. Barrel: 10 inches; octagonal, 7/8 inch across the flats; German-made precision match, brown. Single trigger. Engraved lock in white. German silver-plated furniture. Rounded European walnut stock with checkered grip.

Hopkins & Allen Mountain Pistol **$90**
Caliber: 50. Color casehardened lock. Bronzed barrel. Single trigger. Checkered, engraved stock. Brass furniture, solid brass forend.

Hopkins & Allen Napoleon Le Page Pistol.... **$165**
Percussion dueling pistol. Caliber: 45. Barrel: 10 inches; octagonal, 7/8 inch across the flats; German-made, precision-rifled. Overall length: 16 inches. Weight: 40 ounces. Double-set triggers. Fixed sights. Stock of African olive wood (rare and higher priced) has unusual fluted grip and silver-plated grip cap; some newer stocks of fluted European walnut. Engraved silver-plated lock plate and hammer. Finger spur trigger guard. (*See* photo, opposite.)

**Hopkins & Allen W. Parker English Flintlock
Dueling Pistol**........................... **$170**
Same general specifications as Parker English Percussion model, except with flintlock ignition and engraved lock plate and hammer. (*See* photo, opposite.)

**Hopkins & Allen Parker "Saw
Handle" Percussion Dueler**

**Hopkins & Allen W. Parker English Percussion
Dueling Pistol**........................... **$160**
Caliber: 45. Barrel: 10 inches; octagonal, 7/8 inch across the flats; German-made precision match in brown finish. Double-set triggers. Fixed sights. Checkered "saw handle" European walnut stock with German silver inlay. Silver-plated furniture.

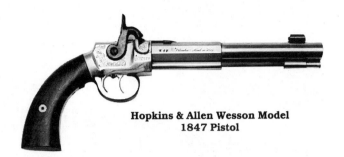

**Hopkins & Allen Wesson Model
1847 Pistol**

**Hopkins & Allen Wesson Model 1847
Pistol**.................................... **$120**
Reproduction of Daniel Wesson's 1847 percussion pistol. Caliber: 45 percussion. Barrel: 10 inches; half-octagonal, half-round. Overall length: 15 inches. Weight: 48 ounces. Double-set triggers. Polished steel barrel threaded to brass receiver.

LONG ARMS

**Hopkins & Allen All-American Percussion
Rifle**......................................**$90**
Underhammer percussion rifle. Calibers: 36 and 45. Barrel: 18 1/2 inches; half-round, half-octagonal, 8-grooved rifling. Overall length: 39 inches. Weight: 4 1/2 pounds. Walnut-stained, one-piece stock.

Hopkins & Allen Brush Rifle............... **$150**
Flintlock or percussion; convertible ignition system. Calibers: 36 and 45. Barrel: 25 inches; octagonal, 15/16 inch across the flats. Weight: 6 1/2 to 7 pounds. Overall length: 40 inches. Silver blade front sight; notched rear sight. Select hardwood stock.

**Hopkins & Allen Buggy Deluxe Percussion
Rifle**.................................... **$130**
Underhammer percussion lock. Calibers: 36 and 45. Barrel: 20 inches; octagonal, 8 grooved. Weight: 6 pounds. American walnut stock and forend.

Hopkins & Allen Brush Rifle

**Hopkins & Allen Deerstalker
Underhammer Percussion Rifle**

**Hopkins & Allen Heritage
Percussion Rifle**

Hopkins & Allen Deerstalker Rifle **$150**
Underhammer percussion lock. Caliber: 58. Barrel: 28
inches; octagonal, 1¹/₈ inches across flats, one turn in
72 inches. Weight: 9¹/₂ pounds. American walnut stock
and forearm.

Hopkins & Allen Heritage Percussion Rifle . . **$140**
Underhammer percussion lock. Calibers: 36, 45, 50.
Barrel: 32 inches; octagonal with either uniform or
grain twist rifling. Three aperture adjustable long-
range rear target sights. Weight: 7¹/₂ to 8 pounds. Brass
crescent-shaped butt plate, cap box and trigger guard
extension. American black walnut stock and forend.

**Hopkins & Allen
Minuteman Rifle**

Hopkins & Allen Minuteman Brush Rifle **$240**
Flintlock or percussion. Calibers: 45 and 50. Barrel: 24
inches; octagonal, rifled or smoothbore. Weight: 8
pounds. Silver blade front sight; notched Kentucky
rear sight. Blued finish. Maple stock. Brass patch box,
butt plate and trigger guard.

Hopkins & Allen Minuteman Rifle **$225**
Flintlock or percussion. Calibers: 31, 36 and 45. Barrel:
39 inches; octagonal, ¹⁵/₁₆ inch across flats, 8-groove rifling. Overall length: 55 inches. Weight: 10¹/₂ pounds.
High polished brass trimmings. Maple stock.

**Hopkins & Allen Offhand Deluxe Percussion
Rifle.** **$130**
Underhammer percussion lock. Calibers: 36 and 45.
Barrel: 32 inches; octagonal, 8-grooved, uniform twist.
Weight: 8¹/₂ pounds. American walnut stock and for-
end.

Hopkins & Allen Over/Under Rifle **$200**
Caliber: 45 percussion. Barrels: 28 inches; octagonal,
each with own set of sights. Custom blued finish. Overall length: 43 inches. Weight: 8¹/₂ pounds. Crescent
butt plate. American walnut stock. Introduced in 1969.

**Hopkins & Allen Pennsylvania Half-Stock
Rifle.** **$250**
Flintlock or percussion. Caliber: 45 or 50. Barrel: 32
inches, smoothbore or rifled. Weight: 10 pounds. Brass
furniture. Maple stock.

**Hopkins & Allen Pennsylvania Hawken
Rifle.** **$155**
Model 29. Flintlock or percussion; convertible ignition
system. Caliber: 50. Barrel: 29 inches; octagonal, ¹⁵/₁₆
inch across flats; rifled with round ball twist. Overall
length: 44 inches. Weight: 7¹/₄ pounds. Walnut stock
with cheekpiece. Brass furniture.

**Hopkins & Allen Pennsylvania
Hawken Percussion Rifle**

Hopkins & Allen Target
Percussion Rifle

Hopkins & Allen Lightweight
Percussion Shotgun

Hopkins & Allen Target Percussion Rifle **$130**
Underhammer percussion rifle. Caliber: 45. Barrel: 32
inches; octagonal, $1^{1}/_{8}$ inches across flats, 8-grooved
rifling. Weight: 11 pounds. American walnut stock.
Blued barrel and receiver.

Hopkins & Allen Double Barrel Shotgun **$200**
Percussion. Gauge: 12. Barrels: 28 inches; choked cylinder. Weight: 6 pounds. Blued barrels. Walnut stock
with checkered wrist and forearm. Engraved lock
plates.

Hopkins & Allen Lightweight Shotgun **$240**
Percussion. Gauge: 12. Barrel: 28 inches, smoothbore.
Weight: just under 6 pounds. Front bead sight. Blued
finish. Brass furniture. Maple stock.

INTERCONTINENTAL ARMS (E.M.F.)
Santa Ana, California

Intercontinental Arms was one of the many importers that sprang up during the late 1960s and early '70s,
importing replica Colt Army Single Action revolvers
and blackpowder firearms. The E.M.F. Company eventually took over the line and added a few of its own "Dakota" replicas. Although available in used gun circles,
most of these are not currently being produced.

Dakota Single Action Revolver. **$75**
Calibers: 22LR, 22WRM, 357 Mag. and 45 Colt. Six-shot
cylinder. Barrel: $4^{5}/_{8}$ and $5^{1}/_{2}$ inches. Overall length:
$10^{1}/_{4}$ and 11 inches, respectively. Weights: 35 and 40
ounces, respectively. Fixed sights. Knurled hammer
spur. Casehardened frame; blued barrel and cylinder;
brass trigger guard and backstrap. One-piece, smooth
walnut stocks.

Dakota Single Action Revolver—Engraved ... **$175**
Same general specifications as standard model, except
comes with finely engraved frame, barrel, cylinder,
hammer, trigger guard and back strap.

**Dakota Single Action Revolver—Long
Barrel** **$100**
Same general specifications as regular model, except
for $7^{1}/_{2}$-inch barrel and weight of 42 ounces.

Intercontinental Duck's Foot Pistol **$75**
Four-barreled percussion volley-pistol. Four, or any
lesser number of loaded barrels may be fired at one
time. Caliber: 36. Barrel: 3-inch tubes with 1-inch
chamber. Overall length: 7 inches. Weight: 24 ounces.
Walnut stock.

Intercontinental Kentucky Pistol **$75**
Casehardened flintlock or percussion. Caliber: 44. Barrel: $9^{1}/_{2}$ inches, octagonal. Overall length: 15 inches.
Weight: 40 ounces. Blued steel rifled barrel, engraved
lock plate. Solid brass trigger guard, barrel cap. Dovetailed front and rear sights. Single-piece, selected walnut stock.

Intercontinental Kiwi Pocket Pistol **$50**
Percussion lock. Caliber: 36. Barrel: $3^{3}/_{4}$ inches, round.
Weight: $9^{3}/_{4}$ ounces.

**Intercontinental Kiwi Pocket Pistol—Cased
Set** **$150**
Two Kiwi Pocket Pistols in lined case with all acces-
sories.

Intercontinental Kiwi Vest Pocket Pistol **$50**
Same general specifications as standard Kiwi Pocket
Pistol, except for 1-inch barrel and weight of $6^{1}/_{4}$
ounces.

Intercontinental Renegade Double Barrel Pistol. **$75**
Percussion locks with engraved side plates and hammers. Calibers: 36 and 44. Barrels: 8¼ inches, round. Overall length: 13¼ inches. Weight: 31 ounces. Single-piece walnut stock.

LONG ARMS

Intercontinental Kentuckian Carbine **$140**
Same general specifications as Kentuckian Rifle, except for 27½-inch barrel and slightly lesser weight.

Intercontinental Kentuckian Rifle **$135**
Flint or percussion lock. Caliber: 44. Barrel: 35 inches, octagonal. Overall length: 48 inches. Weight: 6¼ pounds. European walnut stock.

LYMAN PRODUCTS CORPORATION
Middlefield, Connecticut

Known primarily for its precision handloading tools and firearms accessories, Lyman also produces its own blackpowder replica arms. Based on tests done by in-house technicians, the company publishes a handbook as well that contains comprehensive load information for the modern blackpowder shooter.

Lyman Plains Pistol

Lyman Plains Pistol **$105**
Caliber: 50 or 54, percussion. Replica of mid-1800s pistol. Octagonal barrel. Authentic rib and thimble styling. Pistol-sized, coil-spring Hawken lock. Blackened iron furniture; brass trigger guard and ramrod tip. Hawken-style walnut "half" stock. Detachable belt hook.

Lyman Great Plains Rifle
Caliber: 50 or 54. Flintlock or percussion. Barrel: 32 inches; octagonal, one turn in 66 inches. Double-set triggers with Hawken-style trigger guard. Steel front sight; buckhorn adjustable or fixed primitive rear sight. Blackened steel furniture. Walnut stock.
Flintlock **$228**
Percussion. **220**

Lyman Trade Rifle
Caliber: 50 or 54. Flintlock or percussion. Barrel: 28 inches; octagonal, rifled one turn in 48 inches. Overall length: 45 inches. Spring-loaded single trigger. Hooked breech. Fixed steel sights. Steel barrel rib and ramrod ferrules. Polished brass furniture with blued steel parts. European walnut stock.
Flintlock **$165**
Percussion. **155**

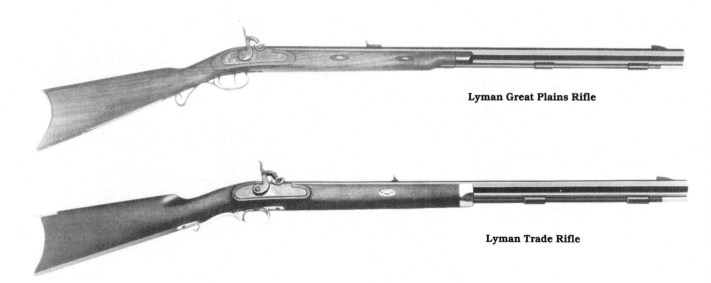

Lyman Great Plains Rifle

Lyman Trade Rifle

W. L. MOWREY GUN WORKS
Olney, Texas

Mowrey Allen & Thurber Replica Rifle **$200**
Percussion. Calibers: 45, 50, 54 or 58. Barrel: 32 inches; octagonal, 8-grooved rifling. Weight: 10¼ pounds. Adjustable open sights. Walnut stock. Polished brass furniture.

Mowrey Allen & Thurber Special Rifle **$220**
Percussion. Calibers: 45, 50, 54 or 58. Barrel: 32 inches, octagonal. Overall length: 48 inches. Weight: 10 pounds. Walnut stock and forend. Brass furniture.

Mowrey Hawk Short Stock Rifle. **$250**
Percussion lock. Calibers: 45, 50, 54 or 58. Barrel: 32 inches, octagonal. Overall length: 49 inches. Weight: 9½ pounds. Walnut sporter-type stock with cheekpiece. Fully adjustable open sights. Hawkins-type butt plate and action housing of brass. Adjustable trigger.

Mowrey Hawkins Full Stock Rifle **$300**
Percussion. Calibers: 45, 50, 54 or 58. Barrel: 27½ inches, octagonal. Overall length: 45 inches. Weight: 8¼ pounds. Blade front sight, adjustable rear. Double-set triggers. Maple stock.

Mowrey Hawkins Half-Stock Rifle. **$275**
Same general specifications as full stock rifle, except for maple half stock.

Mowrey Texas Carbine. **$400**
Percussion. Caliber: 58. Barrel: 24 inches, octagonal; 4-grooved. Overall length: 39 inches. Weight: 8 pounds. Adjustable front and rear sights. Maple or walnut stock. "1 of 100" inscribed on first 100 and "1 of 1000" inscribed on remaining 1000. Made from 1973 to 1974.

Mowrey 12 gauge Percussion Shotgun. **$200**
Percussion. Gauge: 12. Barrel: 32 inches; half-octagon, half-round. Overall length: 48 inches. Weight: 7½ pounds. Bead front sight. Oil-finished maple stock. Brass furniture.

NAVY ARMS COMPANY, INC.
Ridgefield, New Jersey

Since its establishment in 1958, Navy Arms has been a forerunner in the birth and development of the muzzleloading reproduction market. The "Yank" and the "Reb" were the first replica revolvers produced to meet the needs of blackpowder shooters who wanted to preserve their original antique arms. In fact, the "Yank," based on the Colt 1851 Navy revolver, inspired the name of the firm. Under the direction of owner Val Forgett, Navy Arms has accumulated a list of "firsts" in the industry, among them using stainless steel and progressive rifling in its reproduction handguns. The company also deals in cartridge arms, military surplus and of course antique guns.

PISTOLS

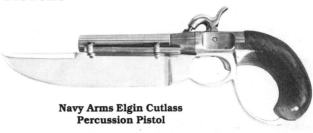

**Navy Arms Elgin Cutlass
Percussion Pistol**

Navy Arms Elgin Cutlass Percussion Pistol **$80**
Caliber: 44. Combination knife and gun pistol. Overall length: 9 inches. 12-inch knife blade. Weight: 2 pounds. This was the only combination gun ever issued by the U.S. military service and one of the first percussion arms officially used by the U.S.

Navy Arms Harper's Ferry Pistol

Navy Arms Harper's Ferry Pistol. **$135**
Caliber: 58 smoothbore. Flintlock. Barrel: 10 inches. Overall length: 16 inches. Weight: 2 lbs. 9 oz. Color casehardened lock. Brass-mounted browned barrel. Walnut stock. One of America's famous pistols, authentically reproduced.

**Navy Arms Kentucky Flintlock
Pistol**

Navy Arms Kentucky Flintlock Pistol
This is a representative replica of the pistol that forged American history, dating back to the Revolution. Caliber: 45. Barrel: 10⅛ inches, octagonal. Overall length: 15½ inches. Weight: 2 pounds. Color casehardened lock. Brass furniture. One-piece walnut stock.
Flintlock Model **$110**
Single Cased Set **175**
Double Cased Set **295**

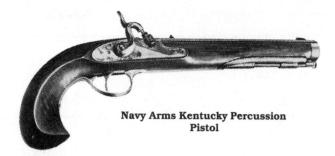

Navy Arms Kentucky Percussion
Pistol

Navy Arms Kentucky Percussion Pistol

Same general specifications as Kentucky Flintlock
Pistol, except with percussion lock.

Percussion Model . . . . $ 80
Single Cased Set 170
Double Cased Set 280

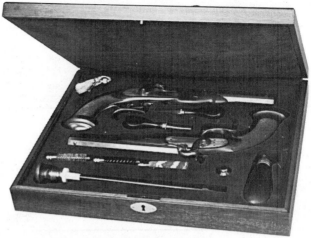

Navy Arms Le Page Percussion,
Double Cased Set

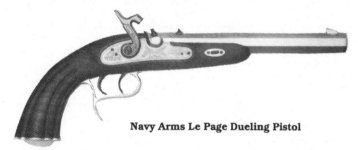

Navy Arms Le Page Dueling Pistol

Navy Arms Le Page Dueling Pistol $190

Reproduction of French percussion pistol. Caliber: 44.
Barrel: 9 inches, octagonal. Overall length: 15 inches.
Weight: 2 lbs. 2 oz. Engraved lock plate and hammer.
Double-set triggers. Finger spur trigger guard. Fluted
stock of European walnut. Discontinued 1986.

Navy Arms Le Page Percussion
Pistol

Navy Arms Le Page Percussion Pistol

Caliber: 45. Barrel: 9 inches; rifled, octagonal. Overall
length: 15 inches. Weight: 2 lbs. 2 oz. Adjustable single-set trigger. Boutet-style European walnut stock.
Finger spur trigger guard. Adjustable rear sight and
dovetailed front sight.

Standard Pistol $220
Single Cased Set 350
Double Cased Set 590

Navy Arms Le Page Flintlock Pistol

Navy Arms Le Page Flintlock Pistol

Caliber: 45. Barrel: 10¹/₂ inches, rifled or smoothbore.
Overall length: 17 inches. Weight 2 lbs. 2 oz. Hand-
checkered walnut stock with hinged buttcap and
carved motif of a shell at the forward portion of the
stock. Single-set trigger. Finger spur trigger guard.
Brown finish.

Standard Flintlock Model. $290
Single Cased Set 420
Double Cased Set 730

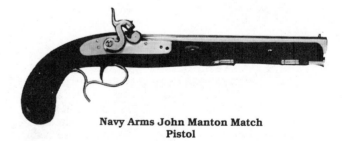

Navy Arms John Manton Match
Pistol

Navy Arms John Manton Match Pistol $170

Caliber: 45 percussion. Barrel: 10 inches, rifled. Overall length: 15¹/₂ inches. Weight: 2 lbs. 4 oz. High-pol-
ished steel barrel. Rounded, checkered European
walnut stock. Brass furniture. Finger spur trigger
guard. Discontinued 1986.

Navy Arms Moore & Patrick
English Percussion Pistol

Navy Arms Moore & Patrick English Pistol
Caliber: 45. Flintlock or percussion. Barrel: 10 inches.
Overall length: 14½ inches. Weight: 2 pounds.
Flintlock Model **$220**
Percussion Model **215**

Navy Arms F. Rochatte Percussion
Target Pistol

Navy Arms F. Rochatte Percussion Pistol. . . . **$190**
Caliber: 45 percussion. Barrel: 10 inches, round. Overall length: 16½ inches. Weight: 2 pounds. Single-set
trigger. All steel furniture. Checkered European walnut half-stock. Finger spur trigger guard. Discontinued
1986.

REVOLVERS

Navy Arms 1851 Navy "Yank"
Revolver

Navy Arms 1851 Navy "Yank" Revolver
Calibers: 36 or 44. Six-shot. Barrel: 7½ inches, octag-
onal. Overall length: 14 inches. Weight: 2 lbs. 9 oz.
Steel frame. Cylinder roll-engraved with naval battle
scene. Brass backstrap and trigger guard. Popular with
Union troops during the Civil War, this revolver was
originally manufactured by Colt in the mid-1800s.
Made from 1958 to date.
Standard Revolver. . . . . **$ 95**
Single Cased Set **165**
Double Cased Set **270**

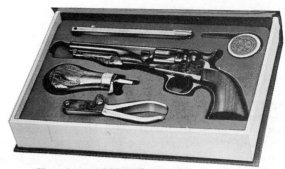

Navy Arms 1862 Police Model
Law & Order Set

Navy Arms 1862 Police Model Revolver
Percussion. Caliber: 36. Five shot. Barrel: 5½ inches.
Half-fluted and rebated cylinder. Brass trigger guard
and backstrap. Color casehardened frame, loading le-
ver and hammer.
Standard Revolver. **$125**
Law and Order Set. **170**

Navy Arms Army 60 Sheriff's Model Revolver . .**$70**
Calibers: 36 or 44. Six-shot. Full fluted cylinder. Barrel:
5½ inches. Shortened version of the Colt Army Model
1860 Revolver. Original snub-nose designed for quick-
draw use; adopted by many police departments.

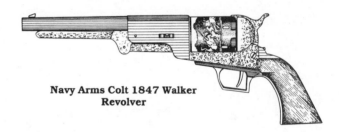

Navy Arms Colt 1847 Walker
Revolver

Navy Arms Colt 1847 Walker Revolver
Caliber: 44. Barrel: 9 inches. Rolled cylinder scene.
Blued and color casehardened finish. Brass square-
back trigger guard. Weight: 4½ pounds.
Standard Revolver. **$160**
Single Cased Set **240**

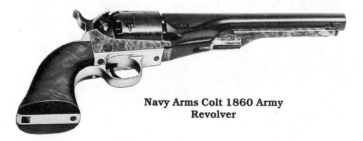

Navy Arms Colt 1860 Army
Revolver

Navy Arms Colt 1860 Army Revolver
Caliber: 44. Six-shot. Barrel: 8 inches, round. Overall
length: 13⅝ inches. Weight: 2 lbs. 9 oz. Brass trigger
guard. Steel back strap. Color casehardened loading le-

Navy Arms Colt 1860 Army Revolver (cont.)
ver and hammer. Rebated cylinder engraved with naval scene.

Standard Revolver........................... **$105**
Single Cased Set 175
Double Cased Set 290

Navy Arms LeMat Army Model Revolver **$375**
Caliber: 44. Nine-shot lightly engraved cylinder. 65-caliber single-shot lower barrel makes it a 10-shot double-barreled revolver. Barrel: 7⁵/₈ inches. Overall length: 14 inches. Weight: 3 lbs. 7 oz. Checkered pistol grip. Blued barrels. Color casehardened hammer, trigger. Fixed lanyard loop in butt plate. This is patterned after the 42-caliber double-barreled revolver designed by New Orleans doctor Jean Francois LeMat. Originally patented in 1856, it was popular with Confederate officers. (*See* photo, opposite.)

Navy Arms LeMat Cavalry Model Revolver ... **$375**
Same general specifications as Army Model, except for finger spur trigger guard and large swivel lanyard loop at butt plate. (*See* photo, opposite.)

Navy Arms LeMat Navy Model Revolver...... **$375**
Same general specifications as Army Model, except for rear sight. (*See* photo, opposite.)

Navy Arms Reb Model 1860
Revolver

Navy Arms Reb Model 1860 Revolver
Calibers: 36 and 44. Barrel: 7¹/₄ inches, round. Overall length: 13 inches. Brass frame, backstrap and trigger guard. Blued barrel. This is a replica of the Confederate Griswold & Gunnison Army revolver produced by Samuel Griswold from 1862 to 1864. Made by Navy Arms from 1958 to date.

Standard Revolver........................... **$ 75**
Single Cased Set 145
Double Cased Set 225

Navy Arms Remington Deluxe 1858
Revolver

Navy Arms Remington Deluxe 1858
Revolver **$190**
Caliber: 44. Barrel: 8 inches with progressive rifling. Overall length: 14¹/₄ inches. Weight: 2 lbs. 14 oz. Adjustable front sight. Steel construction finished in charcoal blue. Walnut stocks. Brass trigger guard.

Navy Arms Remington 1858
Stainless Steel Revolver

Navy Arms Remington 1858 Stainless Steel
Revolver **$170**
Same specifications as standard model, except made in all stainless steel.

Navy Arms Remington New Model Army Revolver
Calibers: 36 or 44. Barrel: 8 inches. Overall length: 13¹/₂ inches. Weight: 2 lbs. 9 oz. Blued finish. Nickel finish in 44 caliber.

Standard Revolver........................... **$105**
Single Cased Set 175
Double Cased Set 295

Navy Arms Remington Target
Model Revolver

Navy Arms Remington Target Model
Revolver **$120**
Caliber: 44 percussion. Based on the Army Model, this revolver has target sights.

Navy Arms Rogers & Spencer Navy
Revolver

Navy Arms Rogers & Spencer Navy Revolver . **$130**
Caliber: 44. Six-shot. Barrel: 7¹/₂ inches, octagonal. Overall length: 13³/₄ inches. Weight: 3 pounds. Hinged-type loading lever assembly. Two-piece walnut grips. Blued finish. Casehardened hammer and lever.

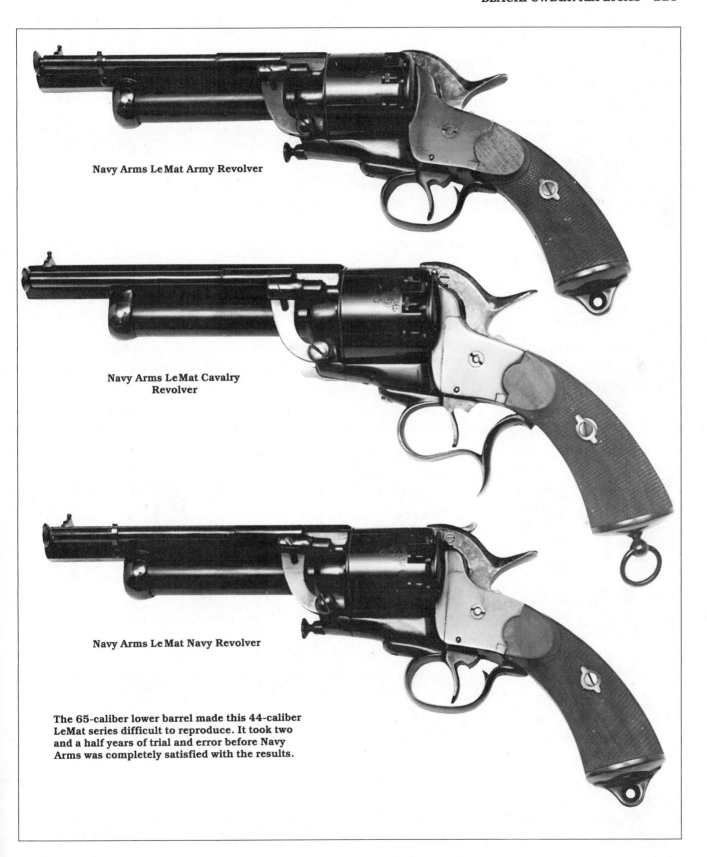

Navy Arms LeMat Army Revolver

Navy Arms LeMat Cavalry
Revolver

Navy Arms LeMat Navy Revolver

The 65-caliber lower barrel made this 44-caliber
LeMat series difficult to reproduce. It took two
and a half years of trial and error before Navy
Arms was completely satisfied with the results.

LONG ARMS

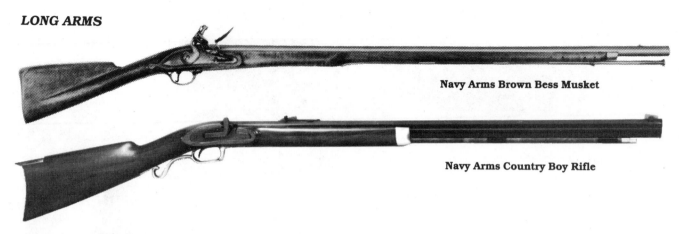

Navy Arms Brown Bess Musket

Navy Arms Country Boy Rifle

Navy Arms Brown Bess Musket **$280**
Caliber: 75. Flintlock. Barrel: 42 inches, brown, polished. Overall length: 59 inches. Weight: 9½ pounds. Brass furniture. Patterned after the American Revolutionary favorite, this replica Brown Bess bears the Colonial Williamsburg mark of authenticity.

Navy Arms Country Boy Rifle **$160**
Calibers: 32, 36, 45 or 50. Barrel: 26 inches. Weight: 5½ pounds. Hooked breech and fully adjustable hunting sights.

Navy Arms Buffalo Hunter

Navy Arms No. 2 Creedmoor Target Rifle

Navy Arms Buffalo Hunter **$200**
Caliber: 58 percussion. Barrel: 26 inches; precision-rifled of ordnance steel. Weight: 8 pounds. Color casehardened lock and hammer. Walnut-tone wood stock. Discontinued 1986.

Navy Arms Creedmoor No. 2 Target Rifle **$445**
Caliber: 45/70. Barrel: 30 inches, tapered. Overall length: 46 inches. Weight: 9 pounds. Color casehardened rolling block receiver. Checkered walnut stock and forend. Blued barrel. Hooded front sight and Creedmoor tang sight.

Navy Arms Enfield 1853 Rifle Musket

Navy Arms Enfield 1853 Rifle Musket **$340**
Caliber: 557. Barrel: 39 inches; cold-forged with 3-groove rifling; three-band. Overall length: 55 inches.

Weight: 9 pounds. Fixed front sight; graduated rear sight. Walnut stock with brass furniture. This was popular during the Civil War on both sides of the Mason/Dixon line because of its quality and accuracy.

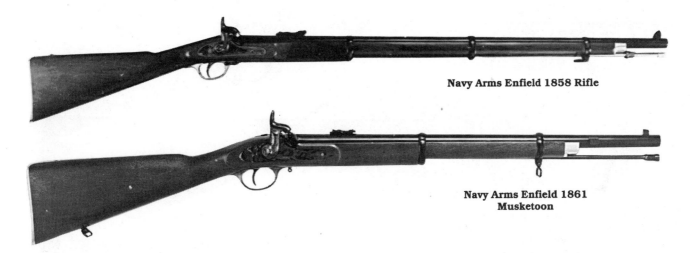

Navy Arms Enfield 1858 Rifle

Navy Arms Enfield 1861
Musketoon

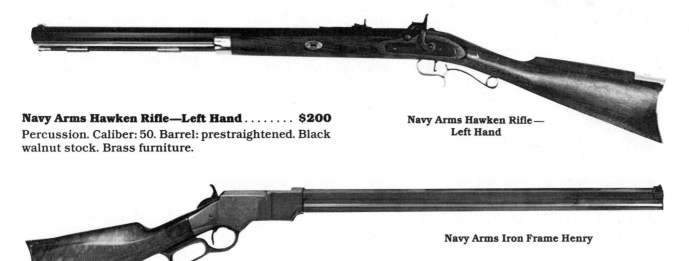

Navy Arms Hawken Rifle—
Left Hand

Navy Arms Iron Frame Henry

Navy Arms Enfield 1858 Rifle **$310**
Caliber: 557. Barrel: 33 inches, 5-grooved; progressive rifling. Overall length: 48¹/₂ inches. Weight 8 lbs. 8 oz. Fixed front sight; graduated rear sight. Walnut stock with brass furniture. Heavy constructed rifle adopted by the British Admiralty in the late 1850s.

Navy Arms Hawken Rifle—Left Hand **$200**
Percussion. Caliber: 50. Barrel: prestraightened. Black walnut stock. Brass furniture.

Navy Arms Henry Carbine
Reproduction of the arm used by the Kentucky Cavalry. Calibers: 44 rimfire or 44/40. Barrel: 23⁵/₈ inches; octagonal. Overall length: 39 inches. Weight: 8¹/₄ pounds. Brass frame. Blued barrel. Oil-stained American walnut stock. Limited deluxe edition of 50 has original styled engraving, silver-plated frame and deluxe American walnut stock.
Henry Carbine . . . . **$ 550**
Engraved Model **1375**

Navy Arms Enfield 1861 Musketoon **$235**
Caliber: 557. Barrel: 24 inches; 5-grooved, cold-forged. Overall length: 40¹/₄ inches. Weight: 7 lbs. 8 oz. Fixed front sight; graduated rear sight. Walnut stock with brass furniture. Front and rear sling loops. Limited collector's edition, individually serial numbered.

Navy Arms Henry, Iron Frame Model **$625**
Same general specifications as Henry Carbine, except with iron frame, barrel length of 24 inches, overall length of 43 inches, and weight of 9¹/₄ pounds.

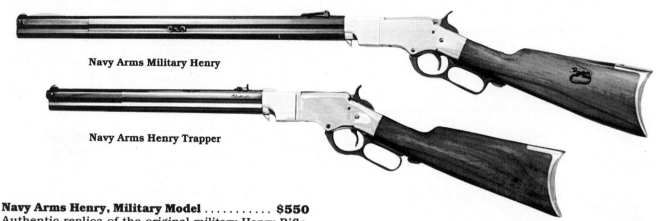

Navy Arms Military Henry

Navy Arms Henry Trapper

Navy Arms Henry, Military Model **$550**
Authentic replica of the original military Henry Rifle,
complete with bar swivels on the barrel and stock. Calibers: 44 rimfire or 44/40. Barrel: 24 inches, octagonal.
Overall length: 43 inches. Weight: 9¼ pounds. Brass
frame. Blued barrel.

Navy Arms Henry Trapper **$550**
Same general specifications as the Henry Carbine, except with shorter (16½ inches) barrel, overall length of
34½ inches and weight of 7¼ pounds.

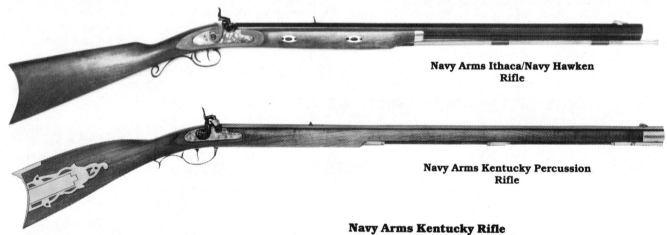

Navy Arms Ithaca/Navy Hawken
Rifle

Navy Arms Kentucky Percussion
Rifle

Navy Arms Kentucky Rifle
Calibers: 45 or 50. Barrel: 35 inches. Overall length: 51
inches. Weight: 6 lbs. 14 oz. Color casehardened lock.
Ornate brass patchbox, brass trigger guard and stock
fittings. Walnut stock.
Flintlock **$205**
Percussion **195**

Navy Arms Ithaca/Navy Hawken Rifle **$280**
Calibers: 50 or 54. Barrel: 31½ inches, octagonal.
Buckhorn-style rear sight; blade front sight. Color
casehardened percussion lock. Blued barrel and furniture, except nose cap and escutcheons. Walnut
stock.

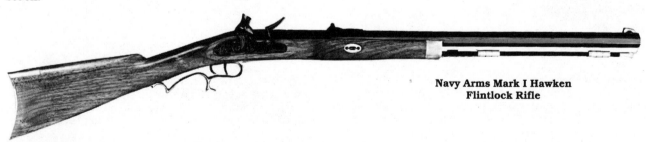

Navy Arms Mark I Hawken
Flintlock Rifle

Navy Arms Mark I Hawken Flintlock Rifle **$210**
Calibers: 50 or 54. Barrel: 32 inches, octagonal. Overall
length: 49 inches. Weight: about 9 pounds. Double-set

triggers. Fancy finger spur trigger guard. Hooked
breech. Hawken-style toe and butt plates. Engraved
blued lock. American walnut stock. Brass furniture.
Discontinued 1986.

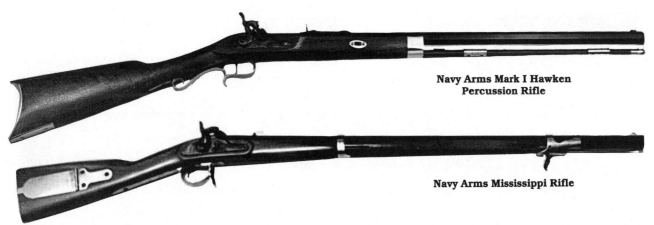

Navy Arms Mark I Hawken
Percussion Rifle

Navy Arms Mississippi Rifle

Navy Arms Mark I Hawken Percussion Rifle. . $200
Calibers: 50 or 54. Barrel: 26 inches; octagonal, precision rifled, "pre-straightened." Overall length: 43 inches. Weight: about 9 pounds. Fancy finger spur trigger guard. Blade front sight; rear sight with elevation leaf. American walnut stock. Discontinued 1986.

Navy Arms Mississippi Rifle Model 1841 . . . . $205
Caliber: 58 percussion. Barrel: 32½ inches. Overall length: 48½ inches. Weight: 9½ lbs. Walnut stock. Furnished in brass, including patch box for tools and spare parts. Patterned after the rifle used by the Mississippi Regiment at the Battle of Buena Vista (1847) during the Mexican War.

Navy Arms Morse Rifle

Navy Arms Morse Muzzleloading Rifle $125
Calibers: 45, 50 or 58. Barrel: 26 inches; "pre-straightened" precision-rifled ordnance steel. Overall length: 41½ inches. Brass action. Oil-finished American walnut stock.

Navy Arms Parker-Hale 451
Volunteer Rifle

Navy Arms Parker-Hale Model 1853 Three-Band Musket $370
Caliber: 577. Barrel: 39 inches. Overall length: 55 inches. Weight: 9 pounds. Adjustable globe front and ladder-type rear sights with interchangeable leaves. Hand-checkered walnut stock.

Navy Arms Parker-Hale Model 1858 Two-Band Musket $345
Caliber: 577. Barrel: 33 inches. Overall length: 48½ inches. Weight: 8½ pounds. Globe front and ladder-type adjustable rear sights with interchangeable leaves. Hand-checkered walnut stock.

Navy Arms Parker-Hale Model 1861 Musketoon $280
Caliber: 577. Barrel: 24 inches. Overall length: 40¼ inches. Weight: 7½ pounds. Adjustable globe front and ladder-type rear sights with interchangeable leaves. Hand-checkered walnut stock.

Navy Arms Parker-Hale 451 Volunteer Rifle . $450
Caliber: 451. Barrel is rifled by the cold-forged method, making one turn in 20 inches. Weight: 9½ pounds. Sights are adjustable: globe front and ladder-type rear with interchangeable leaves. Hand-checkered walnut stock.

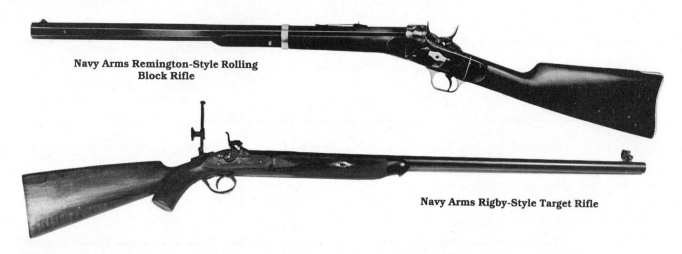

Navy Arms Remington-Style Rolling
Block Rifle

Navy Arms Rigby-Style Target Rifle

**Navy Arms Remington-Style Rolling Block
Rifle.** **$295**
Calibers: 45/70 and 50/70. Barrels: 18, 26 or 30 inches;
full octagonal or half-round. Open sights. Drilled and
tapped for Creedmoor sight.

Navy Arms Rigby-Style Target Rifle **$375**
Caliber: 451. Barrel: 32 inches. Adjustable target front
sight; adjustable vernier rear sight. Color casehardened breech plug, hammer lock plate and escutcheons.
Hand-checkered walnut stock.

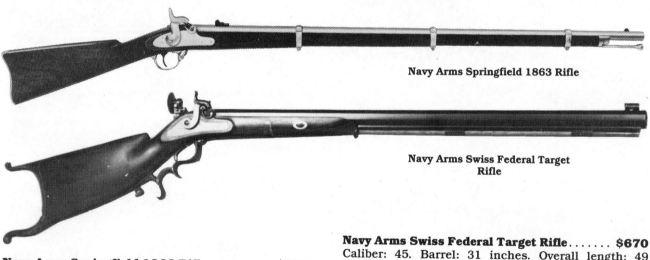

Navy Arms Springfield 1863 Rifle

Navy Arms Swiss Federal Target
Rifle

Navy Arms Springfield 1863 Rifle **$340**
Caliber: 58. Barrel: 40 inches; 3-band, precision-rifled.
Overall length: 56 inches. Weight: 9½ pounds. Walnut
stock with polished metal lock and stock fittings. With
bayonet and scabbard add $30.

Navy Arms Swiss Federal Target Rifle **$670**
Caliber: 45. Barrel: 31 inches. Overall length: 49
inches. Weight: 16¼ pounds. Adjustable rear peep
sight. Adjustable five-lever, double-set trigger system.
Walnut stock, color casehardened furniture. An exact
replica of the Swiss target rifles used in European com-
petitions during the 1880s.

Navy Arms Whitworth Military
Target Rifle

Navy Arms Whitworth Military Target Rifle . . **$450**
Caliber: 451. Barrel: 36 inches; hexagonal bore with a
pitch of 1 turn in 20 inches; cold-forged from ordnance

steel. Weight: 9½ pounds. Globe front sight; open military target rifle rear sight has interchangeable blades.
Walnut stock is hand-checkered.

Navy Arms Zouave Rifle

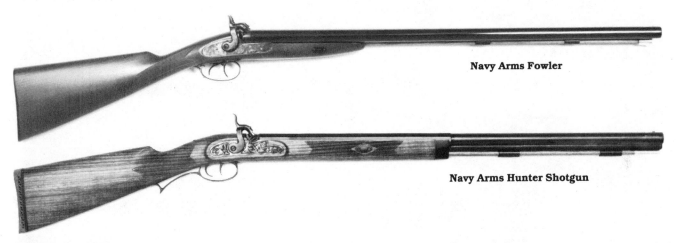

Navy Arms Fowler

Navy Arms Hunter Shotgun

Navy Arms Zouave Rifle. **$200**
Military-style percussion rifle. Caliber: 58. Barrel: 32$\frac{1}{2}$ inches. Overall length: 48$\frac{1}{2}$ inches. Color casehardened lock. Blued barrel. Brass fitting and patch box. Discontinued 1986.

Navy Arms Classic Side-by-Side Shotgun. . . . **$270**
Gauge: 10 or 12. Barrels: 28 inches. Weight: 7 lbs. 12 oz. Color casehardened lock, plates and hammers. All internal parts are steel. Hand-checkered walnut stock. Blued barrel.

Navy Arms Fowler **$185**
Gauge: 12. Barrels: 28 inches; blued, cylinder bore. Side-by-side. Overall length: 44$\frac{1}{2}$ inches. Weight: 7$\frac{1}{2}$ pounds. Bead front sight. Checkered stock, color casehardened engraved locks.

Navy Arms Hunter Shotgun. **$185**
Gauge: 20. Barrel: 28$\frac{1}{2}$ inches; round, chrome-lined. Bead front sight. Walnut stock with checkering at wrist and forend. Rubber butt pad. Engraved and color casehardened percussion lock. Double-set triggers.

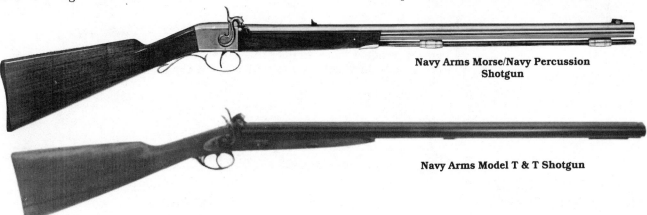

Navy Arms Morse/Navy Percussion
Shotgun

Navy Arms Model T & T Shotgun

Navy Arms Morse/Navy Single-Barrel Percussion Shotgun **$125**
Gauge: 12. Barrel: 26 inches. Overall length: 43 inches. Weight: 5 lbs. 12 oz. Brass receiver. Bead front sight. American walnut stock.

Navy Arms Model T & T Shotgun. **$250**
Percussion. Barrels: 28 inches. Turkey and Trap side-by-side is choked full/full. Color casehardened locks. Checkered, oil-finished walnut stock.

SHILOH SHARPS
Big Timber, Montana

Originally of Farmingdale, New York, Shiloh has undergone a metamorphosis in ownership as many other companies in the firearms industry. Known for a number of years for their "Sharps Old Reliable" metallic cartridge rifles, they are now owned by C. Sharps Arms Co., Inc.

Shiloh Sharps Model 1863 Sporting Rifle . . . $540
Caliber: 54. Barrel: 30 inches; tapered octagonal. Weight: 9 pounds. Schnabel-style forend. Blade front sight; sporting rear sight with elevation leaf; optional Tang sight. Adjustable double-set triggers, curved trigger plate.

Shiloh Sharps Model 1863
Sporting Rifle

Shiloh Sharps New Model 1863
Military Carbine

Shiloh Sharps New Model 1863
Military Rifle

Shiloh Sharps New Model 1863 Military Carbine. **$470**
Calibers: 45, 50 and 54 (standard). Barrel: 22 inches, round. Weight: 8 lbs. 12 oz. Blade front sight; Lawrence rear sight with elevation leaf. Military forend with barrel band. Military-style straight grip stock. Walnut finish.

Shiloh Sharps New Model 1863 Military Rifle. **$550**
Calibers: 45, 50 and 54 (standard). Barrel: 30 inches, round, with 3 barrel bands. Weight: 8 lbs. 12 oz. Blade front sight; Lawrence rear sight with elevation leaf. Straight-grip, military-style buttstock. Steel butt plate and patch box. Sling swivels.

Shiloh Sharps Model 1874
Business Rifle

Shiloh Sharps Model 1874 Business Rifle . . . $495
Calibers: 45-70, 45-90, 45-120, 50-70, 50-90, 50-140. Barrel: 28 inches; heavy, tapered round. Weight: 9 lbs.

8 oz. Schnabel-style forend. Adjustable double-set triggers. Blade front sight; sporting rear sight with elevation leaf. Straight-grip buttstock oil-finished in American walnut. Dark blued barrel.

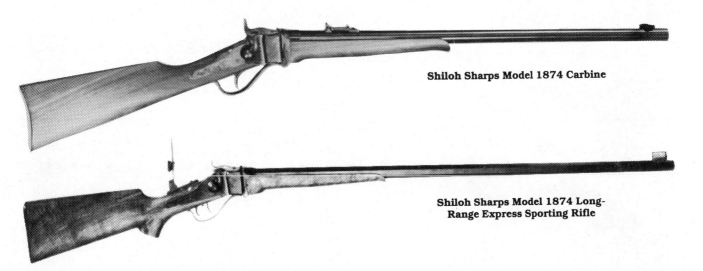

Shiloh Sharps Model 1874 Carbine

Shiloh Sharps Model 1874 Long-Range Express Sporting Rifle

Shiloh Sharps Model 1874 Carbine $510
Calibers: 45-70 and 45-90. Barrel: 24 inches, round. Weight: 8 lbs. 4 oz. Single trigger. Blade front sight; sporting rear sight. Straight-grip, oil-finished buttstock. Schnabel-style forend. Steel rifle butt plate. Dark blued barrel.

Shiloh Sharps Model 1874 Long-Range Express Sporting Rifle $635
Calibers: 45-70-$2^{1}/_{10}$", 45-90-$2^{4}/_{10}$", 45-100-$2^{6}/_{10}$", 45-110-$2^{7}/_{8}$", 45-120-$3^{1}/_{4}$", 50-110-$2^{1}/_{2}$", 50-140-$3^{1}/_{4}$". Barrel: 34 inches; medium-weight, tapered octagonal. Overall length: 51 inches. Weight: 10 lbs. 8 oz. Double-set triggers with adjustable set. Globe front sight; sporting Tang rear sight. Shotgun-style buttstock with pistol grip and cheek rest with accent line. Tapered forend with schnabel tip. Oil-finished American black walnut stock.

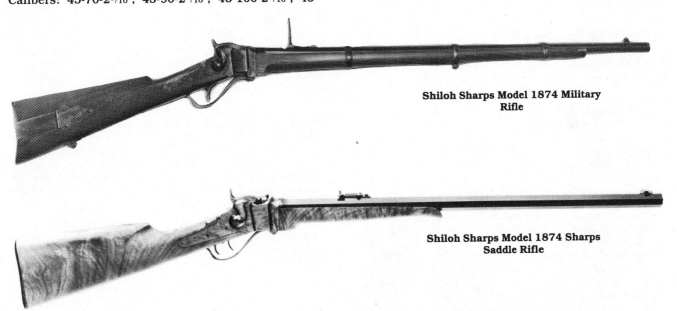

Shiloh Sharps Model 1874 Military Rifle

Shiloh Sharps Model 1874 Sharps Saddle Rifle

Shiloh Sharps Model 1874 Military Rifle $630
Calibers: 45-70 and 50-70. Barrel: 30 inches, round. Weight: 8 lbs. 2 oz. Blade front sight; Lawrence-style rear sight. Military-type forend with 3 barrel bands. Dark blued barrel. Oil-finished wood stock. Sling swivels.

Shiloh Sharps Model 1874 Sharps Saddle Rifle $590
Calibers: 40-50, 40-70 Sharps bottleneck, 45-70, 45-90. Barrel: 26 inches, tapered octagonal. Weight: 9 pounds. Double-set triggers. Blade front sight; sporting buckhorn rear sight. Straight-grip stock of select premium black walnut. Blued barrel.

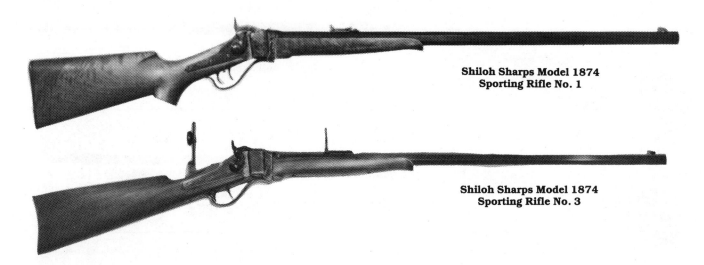

Shiloh Sharps Model 1874
Sporting Rifle No. 1

Shiloh Sharps Model 1874
Sporting Rifle No. 3

**Shiloh Sharps Model 1874 Sporting Rifle
No. 1** **$620**
Calibers: 45-70, 45-90, 45-120, 50-70, 50-90, 50-140.
Barrel: 28 or 30 inches, tapered octagonal. Weight: 9
lbs. 8 oz. Adjustable double-set triggers. Blade front
sight; sporting rear sight with elevation leaf. Sporting
schnabel-style forend. Pistol-grip shotgun-style buttstock of oil-finished American walnut. Blue-black barrel.

**Shiloh Sharps Model 1874 Sporting Rifle
No. 3** **$540**
Similar to the Sporting Rifle No. 1 in the same calibers.
Differences are: 30-inch barrel; weight of 9 lbs. 12 oz.;
straight-grip stock with rifle butt plate; sporting Tang
sight.

STOEGER INDUSTRIES
South Hackensack, New Jersey

Stoeger Industries began in 1918 as A. F. Stoeger,
Inc., of New York City. Established by Austrian-born
Alexander Stoeger, the firm distributed a wide variety
of sporting arms produced by both foreign and domes-
tic manufacturers. Stoeger for many years was the ex-
clusive import agent of Luger pistols into the U.S. and
Canada and, in fact, the company actually owned the
Luger name. Stoeger's offerings expanded to include
ammunition, accessories, gun parts and the famous
"Stoegerol," a multi-purpose solvent, cleaner and lu-
bricant. The company became the Stoeger Arms Corporation and it publicized its wares in the "Stoeger
Catalog," which first appeared in 1924. Through the
years the book evolved into the best-selling SHOOTER'S
BIBLE, containing the same successful ingredients that
has made "Stoeger" a household word among gun enthusiasts.

The company relocated several times and finally settled in northeastern New Jersey in 1962, after which
time its name eventually changed to the more encom-
passing Stoeger Industries. As "America's Great Gun
House," Stoeger was one of the first to distribute
blackpowder replica arms and did so until the late
1960s.

HANDGUNS

Stoeger Brown Bess Flintlock Pistol **$130**
Flintlock. Caliber: 65. Barrel: 9 inches, round. Overall
length: 15½ inches. Weight: 2 lbs. 15 oz. Polished steel
surfaces on side plates. Brass trigger guard, butt plate
and ramrod brackets. Walnut-finished mahogany
stock. Made during 1960s.

Stoeger Kentuckian Flintlock Pistol **$160**
Casehardened and engraved flintlock action. Caliber:
44. Barrel: 9½ inches, octagonal. Overall length: 15¼
inches. Weight: 40 ounces. Brass front sight; blued
steel rear sight. Single-piece select walnut stock. Solid
brass trigger guard and barrel cap; brass ramrod tip
and rimrod holders. Made during 1960s.

Stoeger Kentuckian Percussion Pistol **$160**
Same general specifications as the Kentuckian flintlock version, except has percussion lock. Made from
1966 to 1968.

**Stoeger Renegade Double Barrel Percussion
Pistol** **$140**
Casehardened frame with engraved side plates and
hammers. Calibers: 36 or 44. Barrel: 8¼ inches. Overall length: 13¼ inches. Weight: 31½ ounces. Double
triggers. Engraved brass trigger guard and butt cap.
Wooden ramrod with brass tip. Single-piece selected
walnut stock. Blued steel barrel. Made during 1960s.

LONG ARMS

Stoeger Buccaneer Gun **$200**
Model 4910. Flintlock. Caliber: 12 bore. Barrel: 51 inches, round. Weight: 9 lbs. 3 oz. Fixed front sight. Red-painted walnut stock. Assembled with antique locks of the Napoleonic Wars. Distributed by Stoeger from the mid-1900s to about 1968.

Stoeger Double Barrel Flintlock Shotgun **$360**
Model 5033. Double flintlocks. Gauge: 14. Barrels: 31 inches. Weight: 6 lbs. 14 oz. Front bead sight. Walnut stock and forend. Distributed by Stoeger from the mid-1900s to about 1968.

Stoeger Elephant Flintlock Gun **$200**
Model 6494. Flintlock. Gauge: 4. Barrel: 34 inches, round. Weight: 9 lbs. 14 oz. Distributed by Stoeger from the mid-1900s to about 1968.

Stoeger Flintlock Shotgun Model 4957B **$200**
Gauge: 14. Barrel: 33 inches, round. Weight: 6 pounds. Checkered walnut stock. Polished iron fittings. Distributed by Stoeger from the mid-1900s to about 1968.

Stoeger Flintlock Shotgun Model 6475W **$175**
Gauge: 14. Barrel: 36 inches, round. Weight: 7 lbs. 8 oz. Checkered walnut stock. Distributed by Stoeger from the mid-1900s to about 1968.

Stoeger Single Shot Flintlock Shotgun **$165**
Model 6475. Flintlock. Gauge: 14. Barrel: 36 inches, round. Weight: 8½ pounds. Front bead sight. Quality walnut stock. Distributed by Stoeger from the mid-1900s to about 1968.

STURM, RUGER & COMPANY, INC.
Southport, Connecticut

Sturm, Ruger entered into the firearms manufacturing industry shortly after World War II, and achieved remarkable success with its .22 rimfire autoloaders and single-action revolvers. With a track record of advanced design capabilities coupled with moderate pricing standards, it was no surprise that after a while they ventured into the blackpowder reproduction arena.

The Ruger Old Army Cap and Ball Revolver is an adaptation of the Ruger Black Hawk SA revolver, with the original design changed to percussion ignition and a loading lever added. It is probably the only modern-design percussion revolver in existence, and is considered to be far superior in both strength and design to any original-design replicas currently under manufacture.

Ruger Old Army Cap & Ball
Revolver

Ruger Old Army Cap and Ball Revolver **$145**
Percussion ignition. Caliber: 44 (.443-inch bore; .451-inch groove). Six-shot cylinder. Barrel: 7½ inches; six grooves; right twist, 1 in 16 inches. Weight: 46 ounces. Adjustable rear target sight; ramp front sight. Stainless steel nipples. American walnut grips. Finish: polished all over; blued and anodized.

Ruger Old Army Cap & Ball
Revolver— Stainless

**Ruger Old Army Cap and Ball Stainless
Revolver** **$210**
Same general specifications as blued model, except all metal is stainless steel.

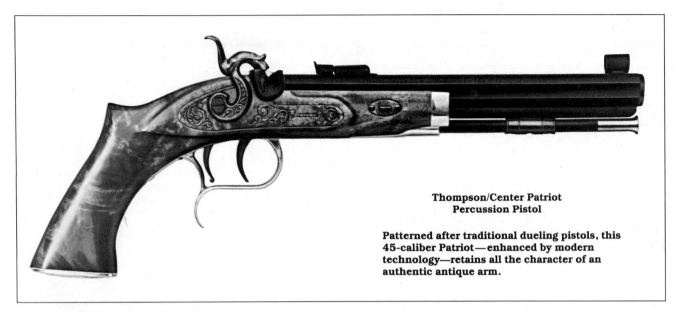

**Thompson/Center Patriot
Percussion Pistol**

Patterned after traditional dueling pistols, this 45-caliber Patriot—enhanced by modern technology—retains all the character of an authentic antique arm.

THOMPSON/CENTER ARMS
Rochester, New Hampshire

A division of the K. W. Thompson Tool Company, Inc., Thompson/Center Arms boasts its own modern investment casting foundry plus a complete gun-making facility. The firm is well-known for its "Contender" pistol, a long-range, high-power handgun that has been popular with hunters for about 20 years. The following listing shows the quality muzzleloaders they also produce.

Thompson/Center Patriot Pistol **$175**
Caliber: 45 percussion. Barrel: 9 inches; octagonal, $^{13}/_{16}$ inch across the flats. Weight: 36 ounces. Color casehardened lock with dolphin-shaped hammer. Hooked breech. Double-set triggers. Adjustable Patridge-type target rear sight. Engraved solid brass trim. Select American black walnut stock. Patterned after traditional dueling pistols. (*See* photo, above.)

LONG ARMS

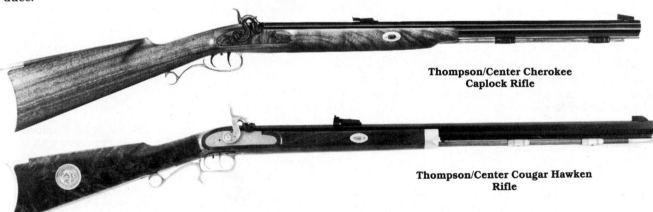

**Thompson/Center Cherokee
Caplock Rifle**

**Thompson/Center Cougar Hawken
Rifle**

Thompson/Center Cherokee Caplock Rifle . . . **$195**
Calibers: 32, 36 or 45 percussion. Barrel: 24 inches; octagonal, $^{13}/_{16}$ inch across the flats. Weight: about 6 pounds. Adjustable double-set triggers. Open hunting-style adjustable sights. Solid brass trim. Select American walnut stock with contoured cheekpiece on left-hand side. Patterned after an early New England hunting rifle.

Thompson/Center Cougar Hawken Rifle **$295**
Caplock percussion presentation grade. Caliber: 50. Barrel: 28 inches, octagonal. Pewter-like stainless steel furniture: hammer, lock, butt plate, double triggers, trigger guard, forend cap and thimbles. Stock of finest grade American black walnut has stainless steel medallion of cougar inletted on right side.

**Thompson/Center Hawken
Caplock Percussion Rifle**

**Thompson/Center Hawken Caplock Percussion
Rifle.** **$235**
Color casehardened percussion lock. Calibers: 45, 50
or 54. Barrel: 28 inches; octagonal, $^{15}/_{16}$ inch or 1 inch
(54 cal.) across the flats. Hooked breech. Adjustable
double-set triggers. Open hunting sights. Solid brass
trim. Stock of select American black walnut with left-
side cheekpiece. Patterned after the American rifles of
the early 1800s.

Thompson/Center Hawken Flintlock Rifle. **$245**
*Same general specifications as Hawken Percussion
model, except with flintlock ignition system in 50 caliber.*

**Thompson/Center Renegade
Caplock Percussion Rifle**

**Thompson/Center New Englander Percussion
Rifle.** **$150**
Caliber: 50 percussion. Barrel: 26 inches, round; rifled
one turn in 48 inches. Weight: 7 lbs. 15 oz. Adjustable
iron sights. Straight-grip stock of select American
black walnut. Blued barrel.

**Thompson/Center Renegade Caplock Percussion
Rifle.** **$195**
Caplock percussion rifle made of modern steel with in-
vestment cast parts. Calibers: 50 or 54. Barrel: 26
inches; octagonal, 1 inch across the flats; precision-rifled carbine-style. Weight: about 8 pounds. Hooked
breech system. Coil spring lock with engraved lock
plate and hammer. Double-set triggers. Adjustable Patridge-style hunting sights. Select American black walnut stock.

Thompson/Center Renegade Flintlock Rifle . . **$210**
*Same general specifications as Renegade Percussion
model, except with flintlock ignition system in 50 caliber.*

Thompson/Center Renegade Musket. **$195**
*Same general specifications as Renegade Caplock Per-
cussion Rifle, except available in 56 caliber with 26-
inch smoothbore musket barrel.*

**Thompson/Center Renegade Single Trigger
Hunter Rifle.** **$180**
*Same general specifications as Renegade Caplock Per-
cussion Rifle, except available in 50 caliber with single
trigger and shotgun-style trigger guard.*

**Thompson/Center Seneca
Percussion Rifle**

Thompson/Center Seneca Percussion Rifle. . . **$225**
Patterned after early New England hunting rifles, but
made with color casehardened lock. Calibers: 36 or 45
percussion. Octagonal barrel. Weight: about 6 pounds.
Hooked breech. Double-set triggers. Adjustable hunting sights. Solid brass trim. Select American walnut
stock.

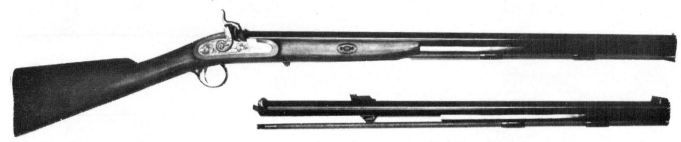

Thompson/Center New Englander
Shotgun

Thompson/Center New Englander Shotgun... **$150**
Gauge: 12 percussion. Barrel: 28 inches, round, with improved cylinder choke. Weight: 6 lbs. 8 oz. Hooked breech system. Color casehardened coil spring lock. Blued steel finish. Straight-grip stock of select American black walnut.

TRADITIONS INC.
Deep River, Connecticut

In addition to muzzleloading replicas, Traditions also offers pistol and rifle kits and blackpowder accessories.

Traditions' Trapper Pistol **$75**
Calibers: 36, 45 or 50. Barrel: 10 inches; octagonal, $7/8$ inch across the flats. Overall length: $14^3/4$ inches. Weight: $3^1/4$ lbs. Adjustable sear-engagement percussion lock with fly and bridle. Double-set triggers. Blade front sight; adjustable rear sight. Blued barrel. Select hardwood stock. Brass furniture, including finger spur trigger guard.

LONG ARMS

Traditions' Frontier Carbine
Calibers: 45 or 50. Flintlock or percussion. Barrel: octagonal, $15/16$ inch across the flats; rifled one turn in 66 inches. Overall length: 40 inches. Weight: 6 lbs. 7 oz. Double-set triggers. Hooked breech. Dovetailed blade front sight; Patridge-style open rear. Solid brass furniture. Blued steel. Select hardwood stock.
Flintlock **$140**
Percussion................................. **130**

Traditions' Frontier Rifle
Same general specifications as Frontier Carbine, except overall length is 44 inches and weight is 6 lbs. 14 oz.
Flintlock **$140**
Percussion................................. **130**

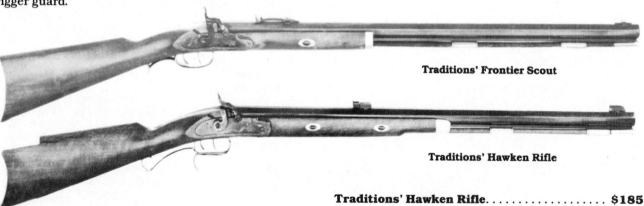

Traditions' Frontier Scout

Traditions' Hawken Rifle

Traditions' Frontier Scout
Same general specifications as the Frontier Rifle, except has shorter trigger pull and shortened stock; barrel is 26 inches long, overall length 40 inches, weight 5 lbs. 8 oz., fully adjustable rear sight.
Flintlock **$120**
Percussion................................. **110**

Traditions' Hawken Rifle................... **$185**
Calibers: 50, 54 or 58 percussion. Barrel: $32^1/4$ inches; octagonal, 1 inch across the flats, rifled 1 turn in 66 inches. Overall length: $49^1/2$ inches. Weight: 9 lbs. 2 oz. Hooked breech. Double-set triggers. Authentic Hawken-style trigger guard with finger spur. Dovetailed blade front sight; Patridge-style open rear. Solid brass furniture. Blued steel. Walnut stock with beavertail cheekpiece.

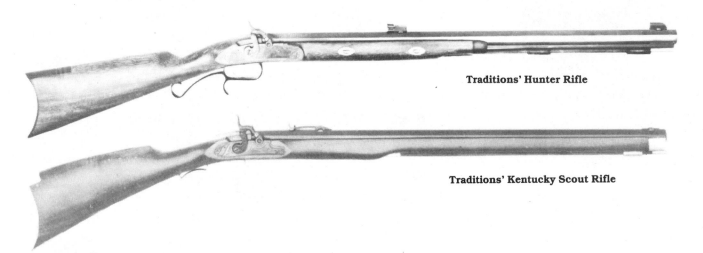

Traditions' Hunter Rifle

Traditions' Kentucky Scout Rifle

Traditions' Hunter Rifle **$185**
Calibers: 50 or 54. Percussion lock with adjustable
sear engagement. Barrel: 28 inches; octagonal, 1 inch
across the flats, rifled one turn in 66 inches. Overall
length: 44 inches. Weight: 8 lbs. 10 oz. Hooked breech.
Double-set triggers. Dovetailed blade front sight; Patridge-style open rear. Black-chromed brass with German silver wedge plates and stock ornaments. Walnut
stock with contoured beavertail cheekpiece.

Traditions' Kentucky Scout Rifle **$100**
Calibers: 45 or 50. Percussion lock with adjustable
sear engagement. Barrel: 26 inches; octagonal, $7/8$ inch
across the flats, rifled one turn in 66 inches. Overall
length: 40 inches. Weight: $5^1/2$ pounds. Double-set triggers. Blade front sight; adjustable rear sight. Sold
brass furniture. Blued steel. Select hardwood stock.

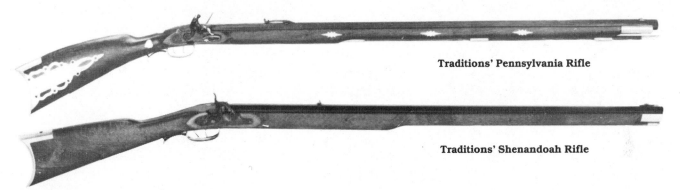

Traditions' Pennsylvania Rifle

Traditions' Shenandoah Rifle

Traditions' Pennsylvania Rifle
A handsomely reproduced rifle, approved for Revolu-
tionary War reenactment groups. Calibers: 45 or 50.
Flintlock or percussion. Barrel: $40^1/2$ inches; octago-
nal, $7/8$ inch across the flats, rifled one turn in 66
inches. Overall length: 57 inches. Weight: 9 lbs. 13 oz.
Double-set triggers. Blade front sight; adjustable rear.
Solid brass furniture, including patch box. Blued steel.
Select hardwood stock with beavertail-style cheek-
piece.
Flintlock **$215**
Percussion **208**

Traditions' Shenandoah Rifle
Reproduction of the 18th-century hunting rifle. Caliber: 50. Flintlock or percussion. Barrel: $33^1/2$ inches;
octagonal, $7/8$ inch across the flats, rifled one turn in 66

inches. Overall length: 48 inches. Weight: $7^1/4$ pounds.
Color casehardened lock with V-type mainspring. Dou-
ble-set triggers. Solid brass furniture. Blade front
sight; fixed rear. One-piece, select hardwood stock.
Flintlock **$145**
Percussion **138**

Traditions' Fowler Shotgun **$180**
American adaptation of the classic English fowler.
Gauge: 12. Barrel: 28 or 32 inches; octagonal tapered
to round. Overall length: $48^1/4$ inches. Weight: 5 lbs. 6
oz. V-type mainspring lock with color casehardened
lock plate. Brass bead front sight. German silver wedge
plate. Blued trigger guard, tang and buttplate. Fine-
grained walnut stock checkered at the wrist.

CHAPTER FIVE
OBSOLETE CARTRIDGES

Most antique cartridge collections probably evolved by the accumulation of odds and ends that accompanied collector firearms. For example, a collector purchases a Winchester Model 1886 Rifle chambered for .40-82 Winchester. Along with this rifle comes a partial box of original factory-loaded ammunition. Later the gun is sold or traded, but the cartridges remain. Another arm is purchased, say, a Remington Rolling Block Single Shot Rifle chambered for the Remington .44-100-500 cartridge. Again, a few cartridges are included in the deal. Eventually, after several purchases of this nature, the collector has what might be called a cartridge collection, which grew more or less by accident. The collection continues to expand in a generalized fashion, now more deliberately, but still without much purpose or reason; anything that seems collectible is thrown into the collection.

If enough interest exists, the collector will probably start specializing in one area of cartridge collecting; for example, by brand, country of origin, caliber, or perhaps in military ammunition. The study of only one small group of cartridges will reveal all kinds of information heretofore unknown to the collector. He will learn facts that will help him identify headstamps, case metals, bullet shapes and designs, just to name a few.

At this point, the cartridge collector will start looking for the best ways to catalog and store the collection, build up trading stock, maintain the collection, and similar details. He or she will also be looking for methods of evaluating the worth of the collections.

Not too many years ago, obsolete cartridges of all types could be found in attics, basements, at flea markets, gun shows, and other places...all for a relatively reasonable price. However, many of the early obsolete cartridges have risen in price to the point where many beginning collectors are eliminated at the outset. The investment required to purchase and maintain such a collection can be very discouraging to the would-be collector. Still, these rare specimens will be found from time to time, and rather than collect them, the finder may wish to sell them to an established cartridge collector.

The prices that follow are based on the average value of a single cartridge of original factory loaded ammunition in good, clean condition. Fired cases also have some collector value, which is usually considered to be about 20 percent of the value shown for the loaded case of the more common cartridges, and up to 80 percent of the value shown for the more rare cases. These prices are considered to be the replacement value of each round, and also what a collector might be willing to pay for the round. However, when selling large lots of ammo, or when selling to a dealer, the buyer will usually expect a discount of somewhere between 25 and 50 percent.

Full boxes of loaded factory ammunition usually command a premium, since full boxes (especially those that are sealed) are becoming more difficult to find, and also because the box itself often has collector value.

This cartridge section is grouped as follows:

CENTERFIRE RIFLE CARTRIDGES

.219 Winchester Zipper $1.25
Bullet Diameter: .224 inch
Bullet Weight: 56 grains
Muzzle Velocity: 3110 fps
Case Length: 1.94 inches
Neck Diameter: .252 inch
Shoulder Diameter: .364 inch
Base Diameter: .421 inch
Rim Diameter: .497 inch
Overall Length: 2.26 inches
Manufactured from 1936 to 1962.

.22 Savage High-Power $1.25
Bullet Diameter: .228 inch
Bullet Weight: 70 grains
Muzzle Velocity: 2800 fps
Case Length: 2.05 inches
Neck Diameter: .252 inch
Shoulder Diameter: .360 inch
Base Diameter: .416 inch
Rim Diameter: .500 inch
Overall Length: 2.51 inches
Made from 1912 to 1936. Reintroduced in recent years by Norma.

.22 Winchester Centerfire .... $.85
Bullet Diameter: .228 inch
Bullet Weight: 45 grains
Muzzle Velocity: about 1500 fps
Case Length: 1.39 inches
Neck Diameter: .241 inch
Shoulder Diameter: .278 inch
Base Diameter: .295 inch
Rim Diameter: .342inch
Overall Length: 1.61 inches
Manufactured from 1885 to 1936.

.22 Extra Long Maynard (.22-8 Model 1882)...........$1.60
Bullet Diameter: .228 inch
Bullet Weight: 45 grains
Muzzle Velocity: about 1100 fps
Case Length: 1.17 inches
Neck Diameter: .252 inch
Shoulder Diameter: Straight
Base Diameter: .252 inch
Rim Diameter: .310 inch
Overall Length: 1.41 inches
Made for the Model 1882 Maynard Rifle.

.22-8 Maynard (1873) $14.00
Same general specifications as .22 Extra Long Maynard, above, except has large Maynard rim, typical of the 1873 cartridges.

.22-15-60 Stevens $3.75
Bullet Diameter: .226 inch
Bullet Weight: 60 grains
Muzzle Velocity: about 1150 fps
Case Length: 2.01 inches
Neck Diameter: .243 inch
Shoulder Diameter: Straight
Base Diameter: .265 inch
Rim Diameter: .342 inch
Overall Length: 2.26 inches
Introduced in 1896.

.236 Navy $7.25
Bullet Diameter: .244 inch
Bullet Weight: 112 grains
Muzzle Velocity: 2560 fps
Case Length: 2.35 inches
Neck Diameter: .278 inch

.236 Navy (cont.)
Shoulder Diameter: .402 inch
Base Diameter: .445
Rim Diameter: .448 inch
Overall Length: 3.11 inches
Manufactured 1895 to 1935.

.25 Remington........$1.25
Bullet Diameter: .257 inch
Bullet Weight: 100 and 117 grains
Muzzle Velocity: 2330 and 2125 fps, respectively
Case Length: 2.04 inches
Neck Diameter: .280 inch
Shoulder Diameter: .355 inch
Base Diameter: .420 inch
Rim Diameter: .421 inch
Overall Length: 2.54 inches
Made from 1906 to about 1952.

.25-20 Single Shot $1.00
Bullet Diameter: .257 inch
Bullet Weight: 86 grains
Muzzle Velocity: 1410 fps
Case Length: 1.63 inches
Neck Diameter: .275 inch
Shoulder Diameter: .296 inch
Base Diameter: .315 inch
Rim Diameter: .378 inch
Overall Length: 1.9 inches
Manufactured from 1882 to 1936.

.25-21 Stevens $4.25
Bullet Diameter: .257 inch
Bullet Weight: 86 grains
Muzzle Velocity: 1470 fps
Case Length: 2.05 inches
Neck Diameter: .280 inch
Shoulder Diameter: Straight
Base Diameter: .300 inch
Rim Diameter: .376 inch
Overall Length: 2.30 inches
Introduced in 1897.

.25-25 Stevens $4.00
Bullet Diameter: .257 inch
Bullet Weight: 86 grains
Muzzle Velocity: 1500 fps
Case Length: 2.37 inches
Neck Diameter: .282 inch
Shoulder Diameter: Straight
Base Diameter: .323 inch
Rim Diameter: .376 inch
Overall Length: 2.63 inches
Introduced about 1895.

.28-30-120 Stevens $4.50
Bullet Diameter: .285 inch
Bullet Weight: 120 grains
Muzzle Velocity: 1500 fps
Case Length: 2.51 inches
Neck Diameter: .309 inch
Shoulder Diameter: Straight
Base Diameter: .357 inch
Rim Diameter: .412 inch
Overall Length: 2.82 inches
Manufactured from 1900 to 1918.

.32 Ballard Extra Long $1.50
Bullet Diameter: .317 inch
Bullet Weight: 115 grains
Muzzle Velocity: 1200 fps
Case Length: 1.24 inches
Neck Diameter: .318 inch
Shoulder Diameter: Straight
Base Diameter: .321 inch
Rim Diameter: .369 inch
Overall Length: 1.80 inches
Manufactured from 1879 to 1920.

.25-36 Marlin.........$2.50
Bullet Diameter: .257 inch
Bullet Weight: 117 grains
Muzzle Velocity: 1855 fps
Case Length: 2.12 inches
Neck Diameter: .281 inch
Shoulder Diameter: .358 inch
Base Diameter: .416 inch
Rim Diameter: .499 inch
Overall Length: 2.50 inches
Manufactured from 1895 to 1922.

.30 Newton $3.00
Bullet Diameter: .308 inch
Bullet Weight: 180 grains
Muzzle Velocity: 2860 fps
Case Length: 2.52 inches
Neck Diameter: .340 inch
Shoulder Diameter: .491 inch
Base Diameter: .523 inch
Rim Diameter: .525 inch
Overall Length: 3.35 inches
Manufactured from 1913 to 1938.

.32 Ideal $1.50
Bullet Diameter: .323 inch
Bullet Weight: 150 grains
Muzzle Velocity: 250 fps
Case Length: 1.77 inches
Neck Diameter: .344 inch
Shoulder Diameter: Straight
Base Diameter: .348 inch
Rim Diameter: .411 inches
Overall Length: 2.25 inches
Manufactured from 1903 to 1936.

.256 Newton $2.50
Bullet Diameter: .264 inch
Bullet Weight: 129 grains
Muzzle Velocity: 2760 fps
Case Length: 2.44 inches
Neck Diameter: .290 inch
Shoulder Diameter: .430 inch
Base Diameter: .469
Rim Diameter: .473 inch
Overall Length: 3.40 inches
Manufactured from 1913 to 1938.

.30-30 Wesson....... $29.00
Bullet Diameter: .308 inch
Bullet Weight: 165 grains
Muzzle Velocity: 1250 fps
Case Length: 1.66 inches
Neck Diameter: .329 inch
Shoulder Diameter: .330 inch
Base Diameter: .380 inch
Rim Diameter: .440 inch
Overall Length: 2.50 inches
Manufactured from 1881 to the early 1900s.

.32 Long Rifle $5.00
Bullet Diameter: .317 inch
Bullet Weight: 85 grains
Muzzle Velocity: 875 fps
Case Length: .82 inch
Neck Diameter: .318 inch
Shoulder Diameter: Straight
Base Diameter: .321 inch
Rim Diameter: .369 inch
Overall Length: 1.35 inches
Made from 1875 to about 1900.

.275 H&H Magnum.....$4.50
Bullet Diameter: .284 inch
Bullet Weight: 140 and 175 grains
Muzzle Velocity: 2660 fps
Case Length: 2.50 inches
Neck Diameter: .290 inch
Shoulder Diameter: .375 inch
Base Diameter: .513 inch
Rim Diameter: .532 inch
Overall Length: 3.30 inches
Manufactured from 1912 to 1939.

.30-40 Wesson....... $30.00
Bullet Diameter: .308 inch
Bullet Weight: 170 grains
Muzzle Velocity: 1700 fps
Case Length: 1.63 inch
Neck Diameter: .329 inch
Shoulder Diameter: .381 inch
Base Diameter: .377 inch
Rim Diameter: .436 inch
Overall Length: 2.39 inches
Manufactured from 1880 to the 1890s.

.32 Remington $1.00
Bullet Diameter: .320 inch
Bullet Weight: 170 grains
Muzzle Velocity: 2220 fps
Case Length: 2.04 inches
Neck Diameter: .344 inch
Shoulder Diameter: .396 inch
Base Diameter: .420 inch
Rim Diameter: .421 inch
Overall Length: 2.57 inches
Made from 1906 to the 1970s.

.32 Winchester Self-Loading . . . . **$.75**
Bullet Diameter: .320 inch
Bullet Weight: 165 grains
Muzzle Velocity: 1400 fps
Case Length: 1.28 inches
Neck Diameter: .343 inch
Shoulder Diameter: Straight
Base Diameter: .346 inch
Rim Diameter: .388 inch
Overall Length: 1.88 inches
Made from 1905 to the 1920s.

.32-30 Remington **$4.50**
Bullet Diameter: .312 inch
Bullet Weight: 125 grains
Muzzle Velocity: 1380 fps
Case Length: 1.64 inches
Neck Diameter: .332 inch
Shoulder Diameter: .357 inch
Base Diameter: .378 inch
Rim Diameter: .437 inch
Overall Length: 2.01 inches
Manufactured from 1884 to 1912.

.32-35 Stevens (Maynard) **$4.50**
Bullet Diameter: .312 inch
Bullet Weight: 165 grains
Muzzle Velocity: 1400 fps
Case Length: 1.88 inches
Neck Diameter: .339 inch
Shoulder Diameter: Straight
Base Diameter: .402 inch
Rim Diameter: .503 inch
Overall Length: 2.29 inches
Manufactured from 1885 to 1936.

.32-40 Bullard **$3.00**
Bullet Diameter: .315 inch
Bullet Weight: 150 grains
Muzzle Velocity: 1495 fps
Case Length: 1.85 inches

.32-40 Bullard (cont.)
Neck Diameter: .332 inch
Shoulder Diameter: .413 inch
Base Diameter: .453 inch
Rim Diameter: .510 inch
Overall Length: 2.26 inches
Manufactured from 1886 to 1900.

.32-40 Remington **$2.85**
Bullet Diameter: .309 inch
Bullet Weight: 150 grains
Muzzle Velocity: 1350 fps
Case Length: 2.13 inches
Neck Diameter: .330 inch
Shoulder Diameter: .358 inch
Base Diameter: .453 inch
Rim Diameter: .535 inch
Overall Length: 3.25 inches
Manufactured from 1870 to 1911.

.32-40 Winchester . . . . . . **$.75**
Bullet Diameter: .320 inch
Bullet Weight: 165 grains
Muzzle Velocity: 1440 fps
Case Length: 2.13 inches
Neck Diameter: .338 inch
Shoulder Diameter: Straight
Base Diameter: .424 inch
Rim Diameter: .506 inch
Overall Length: 2.59 inches
Manufactured from 1884 to date.

.33 Winchester **$2.00**
Bullet Diameter: .338 inch
Bullet Weight: 200 grains
Muzzle Velocity: 2200 fps
Case Length: 2.11 inches
Neck Diameter: .365 inch
Shoulder Diameter: .443 inch
Base Diameter: .508 inch
Rim Diameter: .610 inch
Overall Length: 2.80 inches
Manufactured from 1902 to 1940.

.35 Newton **$5.00**
Bullet Diameter: .358 inch
Bullet Weight: 250 grains
Muzzle Velocity: 2660 fps
Case Length: 2.52 inches
Neck Diameter: .383 inch
Shoulder Diameter: .498 inch
Base Diameter: .523 inch
Rim Diameter: .525 inch
Overall Length: 3.35 inches
Manufactured 1915 to 1936.

.35 Winchester **$3.25**
Bullet Diameter: .358 inch
Bullet Weight: 250 grains
Muzzle Velocity: 2200 fps
Case Length: 2.41 inches
Neck Diameter: .378 inch
Shoulder Diameter: .412 inch
Base Diameter: .457 inch
Rim Diameter: .539 inch
Overall Length: 3.16 inches
Manufactured 1903 to 1962.

.35 Winchester Self-Loading **$1.00**
Bullet Diameter: .351 inch
Bullet Weight: 180 grains
Muzzle Velocity: 1450 fps
Case Length: 1.14 inches
Neck Diameter: .374 inch
Shoulder Diameter: Straight
Base Diameter: .378 inch
Rim Diameter: .405 inch
Overall Length: 1.64 inches
Manufactured 1905 to 1922.

.35-30 Maynard Model 1865 . . . . **$30.00**
Same general specifications as Model 1873, except for rim size and ignition system.

.35-30 Maynard Model 1873 . . . . **$15.00**
Same general specifications as Model 1882, except for large 1873 rim.

.35-30 Maynard
Model 1882 . . . . $7.50
Bullet Diameter: .359 inch
Bullet Weight: 250 grains
Muzzle Velocity: 1280 fps
Case Length: 1.63 inches
Neck Diameter: .395 inch
Shoulder Diameter: Straight
Base Diameter: .400 inch
Rim Diameter: .494 inch
Overall Length: 2.03 inches
Made from 1882 to about 1900.

.38 Ballard, Extra
Long $2.00
Bullet Diameter: .375 inch
Bullet Weight: 146 grains
Muzzle Velocity: 1275 fps
Case Length: 1.63 inches
Neck Diameter: .378 inch
Shoulder Diameter: Straight
Base Diameter: .379 inch
Rim Diameter: .441 inch
Overall Length: 2.06 inches
Introduced in 1885.

.38-40 Remington-
Hepburn. $3.75
Bullet Diameter: .372 inch
Bullet Weight: 245 grains
Muzzle Velocity: 1200 fps
Case Length: 1.77 inches
Neck Diameter: .395 inch
Shoulder Diameter: Straight
Base Diameter: .454
Rim Diameter: .537 inch
Overall Length: 2.32 inches
Introduced in 1875.

.35-40 Maynard
Model 1873 . . . . $28.00
Bullet Diameter: .360 inch
Bullet Weight: 250 grains
Muzzle Velocity: 1200 fps
Case Length: 2.10 inches
Neck Diameter: .390 inch
Shoulder Diameter: Straight
Base Diameter: .403 inch
Rim Diameter: .764 inch
Overall Length: 2.57 inches
Manufactured from 1873 to
    1882.

.38 Long Centerfire $1.00
Bullet Diameter: .375 inch
Bullet Weight: 150 grains
Muzzle Velocity: 1050 fps
Case Length: 1.03 inches
Neck Diameter: .378 inch
Shoulder Diameter: Straight
Base Diameter: .379 inch
Rim Diameter: .441 inch
Overall Length: 1.45 inches
Manufactured from 1875 to
    1900.

.38-45 Bullard $6.00
Bullet Diameter: .373 inch
Bullet Weight: 190 grains
Muzzle Velocity: 1390 fps
Case Length: 1.80 inches
Neck Diameter: .397 inch
Shoulder Diameter: .448 inch
Base Diameter: .454 inch
Rim Diameter: .526 inch
Overall Length: 2.26 inches
Introduced in 1887.

.35-40 Maynard
Model 1882 . . . . $14.00
Bullet Diameter: .360 inch
Bullet Weight: 250 grains
Muzzle Velocity: 1350 fps
Case Length: 2.06 inches
Neck Diameter: .395 inch
Shoulder Diameter: Straight
Base Diameter: .400
Rim Diameter: .492 inch
Overall Length: 2.53 inches
Made from 1882 to about 1900.

.38-35 Stevens $5.00
Bullet Diameter: .375 inch
Bullet Weight: 215 grains
Muzzle Velocity: 1255 fps
Case Length: 1.62 inches
Neck Diameter: .402 inch
Shoulder Diameter: Straight
Base Diameter: .403 inch
Rim Diameter: .492 inch
Overall Length: 2.43 inches
Manufactured from 1875 to
    1890.

.38-45 Stevens $5.50
Bullet Diameter: .363 inch
Bullet Weight: 210 grains
Muzzle Velocity: 1420 fps
Case Length: 1.76 inches
Neck Diameter: .395 inch
Shoulder Diameter: Straight
Base Diameter: .455 inch
Rim Diameter: .522 inch
Overall Length: 2.24 inches
Manufactured from 1875 to the
    1880s.

.38-50 Ballard $6.00
Bullet Diameter: .376 inch
Bullet Weight: 255 grains
Muzzle Velocity: 1321 fps
Case Length: 2.0 inches
Neck Diameter: .395 inch
Shoulder Diameter: Straight
Base Diameter: .425 inch
Rim Diameter: .502 inch
Overall Length: 2.72 inches
Manufactured from 1876 to 1884.

.38-56 Winchester $3.00
Bullet Diameter: .376 inch
Bullet Weight: 255 grains
Muzzle Velocity: 1395 fps
Case Length: 2.10 inches
Neck Diameter: .403 inch
Shoulder Diameter: .447 inch
Base Diameter: .506 inch
Rim Diameter: .606 inch
Overall Length: 2.50 inches
Manufactured from 1887 to 1936.

.40-60 Maynard
Model 1882 . . . . $20.00
Bullet Diameter: .417 inch
Bullet Weight: 330 grains
Muzzle Velocity: 1370 fps
Case Length: 2.20 inches
Neck Diameter: .448 inch
Shoulder Diameter: Straight
Base Diameter: .454 inch
Rim Diameter: .533 inch
Overall Length: 2.75 inches
Introduced in 1882.

.38-50 Maynard
Model 1882 . . . . $13.00
Bullet Diameter: .375 inch
Bullet Weight: 255 grains
Muzzle Velocity: 1325 fps
Case Length: 1.97 inches
Neck Diameter: .415 inch
Shoulder Diameter: Straight
Base Diameter: .421 inch
Rim Diameter: .500 inch
Overall Length: 2.38 inches
Introduced in 1882.

.40-50 Sharps
(Necked) $6.25
Bullet Diameter: .403 inch
Bullet Weight: 265 grains
Muzzle Velocity: 1460 fps
Case Length: 1.72 inches
Neck Diameter: .424 inch
Shoulder Diameter: .489 inch
Base Diameter: .501 inch
Rim Diameter: .580 inch
Overall Length: 2.37 inches
Introduced in 1875.

.40-60 Winchester $4.00
Bullet Diameter: .404 inch
Bullet Weight: 210 grains
Muzzle Velocity: 1560 fps
Case Length: 1.87 inches
Neck Diameter: .425 inch
Shoulder Diameter: .445 inch
Base Diameter: .506 inch
Rim Diameter: .630 inch
Overall Length: 2.10 inches
Manufactured from 1876 to 1897.

.38-50 Remington-
Hepburn. $3.50
Bullet Diameter: .376 inch
Bullet Weight: 255 grains
Muzzle Velocity: 1320 fps
Case Length: 2.23 inches
Neck Diameter: .392 inch
Shoulder Diameter: Straight
Base Diameter: .454 inch
Rim Diameter: .535 inch
Overall Length: 3.07 inches
Introduced in 1883.

.40-50 Sharps
(Straight) $6.00
Bullet Diameter: .403 inch
Bullet Weight: 265 grains
Muzzle Velocity: 1410 fps
Case Length: 1.88 inches
Neck Diameter: .421 inch
Shoulder Diameter: Straight
Base Diameter: .454 inch
Rim Diameter: .554 inch
Overall Length: 2.63 inches
Introduced in 1880.

.40-65 Winchester $3.00
Bullet Diameter: .406 inch
Bullet Weight: 260 grains
Muzzle Velocity: 1420 fps
Case Length: 2.10 inches
Neck Diameter: .423 inch
Shoulder Diameter: Straight
Base Diameter: .504 inch
Rim Diameter: .604 inch
Overall Length: 2.48 inches
Manufactured from 1887 to 1935.

.40-70 Maynard...... $20.00
Bullet Diameter: .417 inch
Bullet Weight: 270 grains
Muzzle Velocity: 1645 fps
Case Length: 2.42 inches
Neck Diameter: .450 inch
Shoulder Diameter: Straight
Base Diameter: .451 inch
Rim Diameter: .535 inch
Overall Length: 2.88 inches
Manufactured from 1882 to 1900.

.40-70 Peabody "What Cheer" $30.00
Bullet Diameter: .408 inch
Bullet Weight: 380 grains
Muzzle Velocity: 1420 fps
Case Length: 1.76 inches
Neck Diameter: .428 inch
Shoulder Diameter: .551 inch
Base Diameter: .581 inch
Rim Diameter: .662 inch
Overall Length: 2.85 inches
Manufactured from 1878 to 1898.

.40-70 Remington......$5.00
Bullet Diameter: .405 inch
Bullet Weight: 330 grains
Muzzle Velocity: 1420 fps
Case Length: 2.25 inches
Neck Diameter: .434 inch
Shoulder Diameter: .500 inch
Base Diameter: .503 inch
Rim Diameter: .595 inch
Overall Length: 3.00 inches
Manufactured from 1880 to 1897.

.40-70 Sharps (Necked).............$7.00
Bullet Diameter: .403 inch
Bullet Weight: 330 grains
Muzzle Velocity: 1420 fps
Case Length: 2.25 inches
Neck Diameter: .426 inch
Shoulder Diameter: .500 inch
Base Diameter: .503 inch
Rim Diameter: .595 inch
Overall Length: 3.02 inches
Manufactured 1876 to 1900.

.40-70 Sharps (Straight).............$6.00
Bullet Diameter: .403 inch
Bullet Weight: 330 grains
Muzzle Velocity: 1260 fps
Case Length: 2.50 inches
Neck Diameter: .420 inch
Shoulder Diameter: Straight
Base Diameter: .453 inch
Rim Diameter: .533 inch
Overall Length: 3.18 inches
Manufactured 1880 to 1900.

.40-70 Winchester $5.00
Bullet Diameter: .405 inch
Bullet Weight: 330 grains
Muzzle Velocity: 1380 fps
Case Length: 2.40 inches
Neck Diameter: .430 inch
Shoulder Diameter: .496 inch
Base Diameter: .504 inch
Rim Diameter: .604 inch
Overall Length: 2.85 inches
Manufactured 1894 to 1906.

.40-72 Winchester $3.50
Bullet Diameter: .406 inch
Bullet Weight: 330 grains
Muzzle Velocity: 1400 fps
Case Length: 2.60 inches

.40-72 Winchester (cont.)
Neck Diameter: .431 inch
Shoulder Diameter: Straight
Base Diameter: .460 inch
Rim Diameter: .518 inch
Overall Length: 3.15 inches
Manufactured 1895 to 1936.

.40-75 Bullard.........$8.00
Bullet Diameter: .413 inch
Bullet Weight: 258 grains
Muzzle Velocity: 1500 fps
Case Length: 2.09 inches
Neck Diameter: .432 inch
Shoulder Diameter: Straight
Base Diameter: .505inch
Rim Diameter: .606 inch
Overall Length: 2.54 inches
Introduced in 1887.

.40-82 Winchester $3.50
Bullet Diameter: .406 inch
Bullet Weight: 260 grains
Muzzle Velocity: 1490 fps
Case Length: 2.40 inches
Neck Diameter: .428 inch
Shoulder Diameter: .448 inch
Base Diameter: .502 inch
Rim Diameter: .604 inch
Overall Length: 2.77 inches
Manufactured 1885 to 1935.

.40-85 Ballard.........$7.50
Bullet Diameter: .413 inch
Bullet Weight: 330 grains
Muzzle Velocity: 1400 fps
Case Length: 2.04 inches
Neck Diameter: .430 inch
Shoulder Diameter: .551 inch
Base Diameter: .569 inch
Rim Diameter: .622 inch
Overall Length: 2.55 inches
Manufactured 1878 to 1900.

.40-90 Ballard........$7.00
Bullet Diameter: .403 inch
Bullet Weight: 370 grains
Muzzle Velocity: 1425 fps
Case Length: 2.94 inches
Neck Diameter: .425 inch
Shoulder Diameter: Straight
Base Diameter: .477 inch
Rim Diameter: .545 inch
Overall Length: 3.81 inches
Introduced in 1878.

.40-90 Sharps (Necked)..............$8.00
Bullet Diameter: .403 inch
Bullet Weight: 370 grains
Muzzle Velocity: 1475 fps
Case Length: 2.63 inches
Neck Diameter: .435 inch
Shoulder Diameter: .500 inch
Base Diameter: .506 inch
Rim Diameter: .602 inch
Overall Length: 3.44 inches
Introduced in 1876.

.401 Winchester.......$1.50
Bullet Diameter: .406 inch
Bullet Weight: 200 grains
Muzzle Velocity: 2135 fps
Case Length: 1.50 inches
Neck Diameter: .428 inch
Shoulder Diameter: Straight
Base Diameter: .429 inch
Rim Diameter: .457 inch
Overall Length: 2.0 inches
Manufactured from 1910 to 1936.

.40-90 Bullard........$8.00
Bullet Diameter: .413 inch
Bullet Weight: 330 grains
Muzzle Velocity: 1440 fps
Case Length: 2.04 inches
Neck Diameter: .430 inch
Shoulder Diameter: .551 inch
Base Diameter: .569 inch
Rim Diameter: .622 inch
Overall Length: 2.55 inches
Manufactured from 1878 to 1900.

.40-90 Sharps (Straight)............ $14.00
Bullet Diameter: .403 inch
Bullet Weight: 370 grains
Muzzle Velocity: 1390 fps
Case Length: 3.25 inches
Neck Diameter: .425 inch
Shoulder Diameter: Straight
Base Diameter: .477 inch
Rim Diameter: .546 inch
Overall Length: 4.06 inches
Made from 1885 to the early 1900s.

.405 Winchester.......$2.50
Bullet Diameter: .412 inch
Bullet Weight: 300 grains
Muzzle Velocity: 2200 fps
Case Length: 2.58 inches
Neck Diameter: .436 inch
Shoulder Diameter: Straight
Base Diameter: .461 inch
Rim Diameter: .543 inch
Overall Length: 3.18 inches
Made from 1904 to about 1973.

.44 Ballard, Extra Long................ $11.00
Bullet Diameter: .428 inch
Bullet Weight: 265 grains
Muzzle Velocity: 1320 fps
Case Length: 1.58 inches
Neck Diameter: .442 inch
Shoulder Diameter: .463 inch
Base Diameter: .468 inch
Rim Diameter: .515 inch
Overall Length: 1.96 inches
Made from 1876 to the early 1900s.

.40-90 Peabody "What Cheer"........ $65.00
Bullet Diameter: .408 inch
Bullet Weight: 500 grains
Muzzle Velocity: 1250 fps
Case Length: 2.00 inches
Neck Diameter: .433 inch
Shoulder Diameter: .546 inch
Base Diameter: .596 inch
Rim Diameter: .659 inch
Overall Length: 3.37 inches
Made from 1877 to the early 1900s.

.40-110 Winchester Express............. $25.00
Bullet Diameter: .403 inch
Bullet Weight: 260 grains
Muzzle Velocity: 1600 fps
Case Length: 3.25 inches
Neck Diameter: .428 inch
Shoulder Diameter: .485 inch
Base Diameter: .543 inch
Rim Diameter: .651 inch
Overall Length: 3.63 inches
Made from 1886 to the early 1900s.

.44 Evans, Long...... $12.00
Bullet Diameter: .419 inch
Bullet Weight: 280 grains
Muzzle Velocity: 1200 fps
Case Length: 1.54 inches
Neck Diameter: .434 inch
Shoulder Diameter: Straight
Base Diameter: .449 inch
Rim Diameter: .509 inch
Overall Length: 2.0 inches
Made from 1877 to the early 1900s.

.44 Evans, Short $10.00
Bullet Diameter: .419 inch
Bullet Weight: 215 grains
Muzzle Velocity: 850 fps
Case Length: .99 inch
Neck Diameter: .439 inch
Shoulder Diameter: Straight
Base Diameter: .440 inch
Rim Diameter: .509 inch
Overall Length: 2.0 inches
Manufactured from 1875 to 1925.

.44 Henry $8.00
Bullet Diameter: .423 inch
Bullet Weight: 200 grains
Muzzle Velocity: 1150 fps
Case Length: .88 inch
Neck Diameter: .443 inch
Shoulder Diameter: Straight
Base Diameter: .445 inch
Rim Diameter: .523 inch
Overall Length: 1.36 inches
Manufactured from 1866 to 1900.

.44 Long, Centerfire .. $20.00
Bullet Diameter: .439 inch
Bullet Weight: 227 grains
Muzzle Velocity: —
Case Length: 1.09 inches
Neck Diameter: .440 inch
Shoulder Diameter: Straight
Base Diameter: .441 inch
Rim Diameter: .506 inch
Overall Length: 1.65 inches
Manufactured from 1875 to 1898.

.44 WCF $1.00
Bullet Diameter: .427 inch
Bullet Weight: 200 grains
Muzzle Velocity: 1150 fps
Case Length: 1.31 inches

.44 WCF (cont.)
Neck Diameter: .443 inch
Shoulder Diameter: Straight
Base Diameter: .471 inch
Rim Diameter: .525 inch
Overall Length: 1.55 inches
Manufactured from 1873 to date.

**.44 Wesson, Extra
Long $10.00**
Bullet Diameter: .440 inch
Bullet Weight: 250 grains
Muzzle Velocity: 1340 fps
Case Length: 1.63 inches
Neck Diameter: .441
Shoulder Diameter: Straight
Base Diameter: .441 inch
Rim Diameter: .510 inch
Overall Length: 2.19 inches
Manufactured from 1876 to 1897.

.44-40 Extra Long ... $35.00
Bullet Diameter: .428 inch
Bullet Weight: 250 grains
Muzzle Velocity: 1420 fps
Case Length: 1.575 inches
Neck Diameter: .442 inch
Shoulder Diameter: Straight
Base Diameter: .468 inch
Rim Diameter: .515 inch
Overall Length: 1.96 inches
Introduced in the late 1800s.

**.44-60 Peabody
Creedmoor........... $20.00**
Bullet Diameter: .447 inch
Bullet Weight: 395 grains
Muzzle Velocity: 1250 fps
Case Length: 1.89 inches
Neck Diameter: .464 inch
Shoulder Diameter: .502 inch
Base Diameter: .518 inch
Rim Diameter: .628 inch
Overall Length: 2.56 inches
Made from 1877 to the early 1900s.

**.44-60 Sharps
(Necked)............... $5.00**
Bullet Diameter: .447 inch
Bullet Weight: 395 grains
Muzzle Velocity: 1250 fps
Case Length: 1.88 inches
Neck Diameter: .464 inch
Shoulder Diameter: .502 inch
Base Diameter: .515 inch
Rim Diameter: .630 inch
Overall Length: 2.55 inches
Manufactured in the 1800s.

.44-60 Winchester $4.00
Bullet Diameter: .447 inch
Bullet Weight: 395 grains
Muzzle Velocity: 1250 fps
Case Length: 1.89 inches
Neck Diameter: .464 inch
Shoulder Diameter: .502 inch
Base Diameter: .518 inch
Rim Diameter: .628 inch
Overall Length: 2.56 inches
Introduced in 1874.

.44-70 Maynard...... $50.00
Bullet Diameter: .445 inch
Bullet Weight: 430 grains
Muzzle Velocity: 1300 fps
Case Length: 2.21 inches
Neck Diameter: .466 inch
Shoulder Diameter: Straight
Base Diameter: .499 inch
Rim Diameter: .601 inch
Overall Length: 2.87 inches
Introduced in 1882.

**.44-75 Ballard
Everlasting $4.00**
Bullet Diameter: .445 inch
Bullet Weight: 405 grains
Muzzle Velocity: 1250 fps
Case Length: 2.50 inches
Neck Diameter: .487 inch
Shoulder Diameter: Straight
Base Diameter: .497 inch
Rim Diameter: .603 inch
Overall Length: 3.0 inches
Introduced in 1876.

.44-77 Remington (or Sharps) $7.50
Bullet Diameter: .446 inch
Bullet Weight: 365 grains
Muzzle Velocity: 1460 fps
Case Length: 2.25 inches
Neck Diameter: .467 inch
Shoulder Diameter: .502 inch
Base Diameter: .516 inch
Rim Diameter: .625 inch
Overall Length: 3.05 inches
Introduced in 1875.

.44-85 Wesson $4.00
Bullet Diameter: .446 inch
Bullet Weight: 390 grains
Muzzle Velocity: 1450 fps
Case Length: 2.88 inches
Neck Diameter: —
Shoulder Diameter: Straight
Base Diameter: —
Rim Diameter: —
Overall Length: 3.31 inches
Introduced in 1881.

.44-90 Remington Special $23.00
Bullet Diameter: .442 inch
Bullet Weight: 550 grains
Muzzle Velocity: 1250 fps
Case Length: 2.44 inches
Neck Diameter: .466 inch
Shoulder Diameter: .504 inch
Base Diameter: .506 inch
Rim Diameter: .628 inch
Overall Length: 3.08 inches
Manufactured from 1873 to 1910.

.44-90 Remington (Straight)............ $20.00
Bullet Diameter: .442 inch
Bullet Weight: 520 grains
Muzzle Velocity: 1435 fps
Case Length: 2.60 inches
Neck Diameter: .465 inch
Shoulder Diameter: Straight
Base Diameter: .506 inch
Rim Diameter: .628 inch
Overall Length: 3.08 inches
Introduced in 1880.

.44-90 Sharps (Necked)............ $10.00
Bullet Diameter: .446 inch
Bullet Weight: 500 grains
Muzzle Velocity: 1270
Case Length: 2.63 inches
Neck Diameter: .468 inch
Shoulder Diameter: .504 inch
Base Diameter: .517 inch
Rim Diameter: .625 inch
Overall Length: 3.30 inches
Manufactured from 1873 to 1878.

.44-95 Peabody "What Cheer" $37.00
Bullet Diameter: .443 inch
Bullet Weight: 550 grains
Muzzle Velocity: 1310 fps
Case Length: 2.31 inches
Neck Diameter: .465 inch
Shoulder Diameter: .550 inch
Base Diameter: .580 inch
Rim Diameter: .670 inch
Overall Length: 3.32 inches
Introduced in 1875.

.44-100 Ballard...... $15.00
Bullet Diameter: .445 inch
Bullet Weight: 535 grains
Muzzle Velocity: 1400 fps
Case Length: 2.81 inches

.44-100 Ballard (cont.)
Neck Diameter: .485 inch
Shoulder Diameter: Straight
Base Diameter: .498 inch
Rim Diameter: .597 inch
Overall Length: 3.25 inches
Manufactured 1876 to 1880.

.44-100 Remington Creedmoor........... $12.00
Bullet Diameter: .442 inch
Bullet Weight: 550 grains
Muzzle Velocity: 1380 fps
Case Length: 2.60 inches
Neck Diameter: .465 inch
Shoulder Diameter: Straight
Base Diameter: .503 inch
Rim Diameter: .568 inch
Overall Length: 3.97 inches
Introduced in 1880.

.44-100 Wesson $5.00
Bullet Diameter: .445 inch
Bullet Weight: 550 grains
Muzzle Velocity: 1375 fps
Case Length: 3.38 inches
Neck Diameter: —
Shoulder Diameter: Straight
Base Diameter: —
Rim Diameter: —
Overall Length: 3.85 inches
Introduced in 1881.

.45-50 Peabody (Sporting) $20.00
Bullet Diameter: .454 inch
Bullet Weight: 290 grains
Muzzle Velocity: 1300 fps
Case Length: 1.54 inches
Neck Diameter: .478 inch
Shoulder Diameter: .508 inch
Base Diameter: .516 inch
Rim Diameter: .634 inch
Overall Length: 2.08 inches
Manufactured 1873 to 1897.

.45-60 Winchester $3.00
Bullet Diameter: .454 inch
Bullet Weight: 300 grains
Muzzle Velocity: 1315 fps
Case Length: 1.89 inches
Neck Diameter: .479 inch
Shoulder Diameter: Straight
Base Diameter: .508 inch
Rim Diameter: .629 inch
Overall Length: 2.15 inches
Manufactured 1879 to 1935.

.45-70 Van Choate ... $38.00
Bullet Diameter: .457 inch
Bullet Weight: 420 grains
Muzzle Velocity: 1250 fps
Case Length: 2.25 inches
Neck Diameter: .475 inch
Shoulder Diameter: Straight
Base Diameter: .50 inch
Rim Diameter: .60 inch
Overall Length: 2.91 inches
Manufactured 1872 to 1912.

.45-75 Sharps
(Straight)........... $14.00
Bullet Diameter: .457 inch
Bullet Weight: 400 grains
Muzzle Velocity: 1330 fps
Case Length: 2.10 inches
Neck Diameter: .453 inch
Shoulder Diameter: Straight
Base Diameter: .50 inch
Rim Diameter: .60 inch
Overall Length: 2.90 inches
Introduced in 1876.

.45-75 Winchester $3.00
Bullet Diameter: .454 inch
Bullet Weight: 350 grains
Muzzle Velocity: 1383 fps
Case Length: 1.86 inches

.45-75 Winchester (cont.)
Neck Diameter: .478 inch
Shoulder Diameter: .547 inch
Base Diameter: .559 inch
Rim Diameter: .616 inch
Overall Length: 2.25 inches
Manufactured from 1876 to 1935.

.45-82 Winchester $6.00
Bullet Diameter: .457 inch
Bullet Weight: 405 grains
Muzzle Velocity: 1468 fps
Case Length: 2.40 inches
Neck Diameter: .477 inch
Shoulder Diameter: Straight
Base Diameter: .501 inch
Rim Diameter: .597 inch
Overall Length: 2.88 inches
Introduced about 1886.

.45-85 Winchester $6.00
Bullet Diameter: .457 inch
Bullet Weight: 350 grains
Muzzle Velocity: 1510 fps
Case Length: 2.40 inches
Neck Diameter: .477 inch
Shoulder Diameter: Straight
Base Diameter: .501 inch
Rim Diameter: .597 inch
Overall Length: 2.88 inches
Introduced about 1886.

.45-90 Winchester $4.00
Bullet Diameter: .457 inch
Bullet Weight: 300 grains
Muzzle Velocity: 1554 fps
Case Length: 2.40 inches
Neck Diameter: .477 inch
Shoulder Diameter: Straight
Base Diameter: .501 inch
Rim Diameter: .597 inch
Overall Length: 2.88 inches
Introduced in 1886.

.45-100 Ballard...... $20.00
Bullet Diameter: .454 inch
Bullet Weight: 550 grains
Muzzle Velocity: 1370 fps
Case Length: 2.81 inches

.45-100 Ballard (cont.)
Neck Diameter: .487 inch
Shoulder Diameter: Straight
Base Diameter: .498 inch
Rim Diameter: .597 inch
Overall Length: 3.25 inches
Manufactured from 1878 to 1889.

.45-100 Remington .. $12.00
Bullet Diameter: .452 inch
Bullet Weight: 500 grains
Muzzle Velocity: —
Case Length: 2.63 inches
Neck Diameter: .490 inch
Shoulder Diameter: .550 inch
Base Diameter: .558 inch
Rim Diameter: .645 inch
Overall Length: 3.26 inches
Introduced in 1880.

.45-100 Sharps
(Straight)........... $24.00
Bullet Diameter: .453 inch
Bullet Weight: 550 grains
Muzzle Velocity: 1360 fps
Case Length: 2.40 inches
Neck Diameter: .472 inch
Shoulder Diameter: Straight
Base Diameter: .507 inch
Rim Diameter: .60 inch
Overall Length: 2.85 inches
Introduced in 1876.

.45-120 Sharps (3¹/₄″
Straight) $24.00
Bullet Diameter: .451 inch
Bullet Weight: 500 grains
Muzzle Velocity: 1520 fps
Case Length: 3.25 inches
Neck Diameter: .490 inch
Shoulder Diameter: Straight
Base Diameter: .506 inch
Rim Diameter: .597 inch
Overall Length: 4.16 inches
Manufactured from 1878 to 1881.

.45-125 Winchester . . $29.00
Bullet Diameter: .456 inch
Bullet Weight: 300 grains
Muzzle Velocity: 1690 fps
Case Length: 3.25 inches
Neck Diameter: .470 inch
Shoulder Diameter: .521 inch
Base Diameter: .533 inch
Rim Diameter: .601 inch
Overall Length: 3.63 inches
Introduced in 1886.

.50 U.S. Carbine $6.50
Bullet Diameter: .515 inch
Bullet Weight: 400 grains
Muzzle Velocity: 1200 fps
Case Length: —
Neck Diameter: —
Shoulder Diameter: —
Base Diameter: —
Rim Diameter: —
Overall Length: —
Introduced in 1870.

.50-50 Maynard. $8.00
Bullet Diameter: .513 inch
Bullet Weight: 350 grains
Muzzle Velocity: 1270 fps
Case Length: 1.37 inches
Neck Diameter: .535 inch
Shoulder Diameter: Straight
Base Diameter: .563 inch
Rim Diameter: .661 inch
Overall Length: 1.91 inches
Introduced in 1882.

.50-70 Musket (.50 Govt). $14.00
Bullet Diameter: .515 inch
Bullet Weight: 450 grains
Muzzle Velocity: 1260 fps
Case Length: 1.75 inches

.50-70 Musket (cont.)
Neck Diameter: .535 inch
Shoulder Diameter: Straight
Base Diameter: .565 inch
Rim Diameter: .660 inch
Overall Length: 2.25 inches
Manufactured from 1866 to 1873.

.50-90 Sharps $25.00
Bullet Diameter: .509 inch
Bullet Weight: 335 grains
Muzzle Velocity: 1475 fps
Case Length: 2.50 inches
Neck Diameter: .528 inch
Shoulder Diameter: Straight
Base Diameter: .565 inch
Rim Diameter: .663 inch
Overall Length: 3.20 inches
Introduced in 1875.

.50-95 Winchester $7.50
Bullet Diameter: .513 inch
Bullet Weight: 300 grains
Muzzle Velocity: 1557 fps
Case Length: 1.92 inches
Neck Diameter: .533 inch
Shoulder Diameter: .553 inch
Base Diameter: .562 inch
Rim Diameter: .627 inch
Overall Length: 2.26 inches
Introduced in 1879.

.50-100 Winchester $8.00
Bullet Diameter: .512 inch
Bullet Weight: 450 grains
Muzzle Velocity: 1475 fps
Case Length: 2.40 inches
Neck Diameter: .534 inch
Shoulder Diameter: Straight
Base Diameter: .551 inch
Rim Diameter: .607 inch
Overall Length: 2.75 inches
Manufactured 1899 to 1935.

.50-105 Winchester $9.00
Bullet Diameter: .512 inch
Bullet Weight: —
Muzzle Velocity: —
Case Length: 2.40 inches
Neck Diameter: .534 inch
Shoulder Diameter: Straight
Base Diameter: .551 inch
Rim Diameter: .607 inch
Overall Length: 2.75 inches
Manufactured 1899 to 1935.

.50-110 Winchester . . $10.00
Bullet Diameter: .512 inch
Bullet Weight: 300 grains
Muzzle Velocity: 1605 fps
Case Length: 2.40 inches
Neck Diameter: .534 inch
Shoulder Diameter: Straight
Base Diameter: .551 inch
Rim Diameter: .607 inch
Overall Length: 2.75 inches
Manufactured 1899 to 1935.

.50-115 Bullard $10.00
Bullet Diameter: .512 inch
Bullet Weight: 300 grains
Muzzle Velocity: 1539 fps
Case Length: 2.19 inches
Neck Diameter: .547 inch
Shoulder Diameter: .577 inch
Base Diameter: .585 inch
Rim Diameter: .619 inch
Overall Length: 2.56 inches
Introduced in 1886.

.50-140 Sharps. $50.00
Bullet Diameter: .509 inch
Bullet Weight: 473 grains
Muzzle Velocity: 1580 fps
Case Length: 3.25 inches
Neck Diameter: .528 inch
Shoulder Diameter: Straight
Base Diameter: .565 inch
Rim Diameter: .665 inch
Overall Length: 3.94 inches
Manufactured 1880 to 1884.

.50-140 Winchester
Express $125.00
Bullet Diameter: .512 inch
Bullet Weight: 473 grains
Muzzle Velocity: 1580 fps
Case Length: 3.25 inches
Neck Diameter: .528 inch
Shoulder Diameter: Straight
Base Diameter: .551 inch
Rim Diameter: .652 inch
Overall Length: 3.95 inches
Introduced in 1887.

.58 U.S. Musket
(Berdan)............ $27.00
Bullet Diameter: .589 inch
Bullet Weight: 530 grains
Muzzle Velocity: 1100 fps
Case Length: 1.65 inches
Neck Diameter: .625 inch
Shoulder Diameter: Straight
Base Diameter: .646 inch
Rim Diameter: .740 inch
Overall Length: 2.15 inches
Introduced in 1869.

.55-100 Maynard $12.00
Bullet Diameter: .551 inch
Bullet Weight: 530 grains
Muzzle Velocity: 1410 fps
Case Length: 1.94 inches
Neck Diameter: .582 inch
Shoulder Diameter: Straight
Base Diameter: .590 inch
Rim Diameter: .718 inch
Overall Length: 2.56 inches
Introduced in 1882.

.70-150
Winchester $150.00
Bullet Diameter: .705 inch
Bullet Weight: —
Muzzle Velocity: —
Case Length: 2.28 inches
Neck Diameter: .725 inch
Shoulder Diameter: .790 inch
Base Diameter: .805 inch
Rim Diameter: .870 inch
Overall Length: 2.63 inches
Introduced in 1888.

.58 Berdan Carbine .. $10.00
Bullet Diameter: .589 inch
Bullet Weight: 530 grains
Muzzle Velocity: 925 fps
Case Length: 1.59 inches
Neck Diameter: .625 inch
Shoulder Diameter: Straight
Base Diameter: .646 inch
Rim Diameter: .740 inch
Overall Length: 2.09 inches
Introduced in 1869.

THE DISCOVERY AND HISTORY OF GUNPOWDER

The origin of gunpowder, the only explosive known until the middle of the 19th century, is uncertain. There is a theory that it was known in China many centuries before its first appearance in Europe, and that knowledge of it gradually worked westward. Legend goes back to the time of Alexander the Great, who, it is asserted, refused to attack the Oxydracae, a race occupying the country between the Hyphasis and the Ganges, because they "lived under the protection of the gods and overthrew their enemies with thunder and lightning, which they shot forth from their walls."

Some authorities regard Greek Fire, rather extensively used in the defense of Constantinople in the seventh century, as a form of gunpowder, but it may have been merely an incendiary mixture, to which crude nitre was added to make it burn more fiercely. On the strength of passages in the works of Roger Bacon, an English monk who lived in the 13th century, he is spoken of as the inventor of gunpowder. In his late works, "Opus Tertium," "De Secretis," and "Opus Magnus," published about 1270, there is no doubt that he was acquainted with explosive mixtures of sulphur, charcoal, and nitre, the ingredients of gunpowder.

Berthold Schwartz, a monk of Freiburg, Germany, studied the writings of Bacon regarding explosives, and manufactured gunpowder while experimenting. He has commonly been credited as the inventor, and at any rate the honor is due to him for making known some properties of gunpowder. Its adoption in Central Europe quickly followed his announcement, which is supposed to have taken place about 1320. It is probable that gunpowder was well known in Spain and Greece many years prior to its being used in Central and Northern Europe.

The early uses of gunpowder, however, were confined to warfare, no use being made of it for sporting purposes for several hundred years. In the late 1300s, frequent references to gunpowder were made in literature, often in a way which makes it evident that the properties of gunpowder as a propellant were widely known.

MANUFACTURING GUNPOWDER

The manufacture of gunpowder was carried out originally by the very crude method of pounding the ingredients together by hand in mortars. But edge runners were introduced toward the end of the 16th century, which greatly facilitated the incorporating or milling process. During this century, the process of "corning" or "granulating" was introduced, whereby grains of standard size are assured.

In manufacturing gunpowder, care is required in the selection of material. The potassium nitrate, or nitre, should be chemically pure. The sulphur must contain no nonvolatile matter, and must be free from sulphuric acid. The quantity of the powder depends considerably on the quality of the charcoal, so that it is customary for powder mills to prepare their own.

The composition of gunpowder varies widely with the different grades manufactured. Coarse grains are used for blasting, and fine grains for gunpowder. The composition of French military powders remained the same from 1598 until the adoption of modern smokeless powders, which developed from Schoenbein's discovery of guncotton in 1846. From this, Vielle, a French chemist, invented smokeless powder in 1886, which possesses the ability to burn without creating much smoke.

Almost all sporting powder propellants today are smokeless powders. These can be divided into two classes, the dense powders and the bulk powders, both being used in rifle shooting and in shotguns. Although smokelessness characterizes these powders, it is their superior power that is of prime importance. While black gunpowder imparts to the projectile an initial velocity of 1,700 feet per second, initial velocities of over 3,000 foot seconds have been attained with smokeless powders.

Another division of smokeless powders into types is the nitroglycerin smokeless powders and the nitrocellulose. Both nitroglycerin and nitrocellulose powders consist of colloidal masses of gelatined nitrocellulose that have been pressed into ribbons, cords, tubes, or sheets, these being frequently cut into flakes when intended for use with small arms.

Nitroglycerin was discovered in 1846 by Sobrero, an Italian chemist, but nothing was done about it until Alfred Noble recognized its possibilities for blasting. Later, he found it was possible to mix and treat nitrocellulose dissolved in nitroglycerin, so that a hard colloid substance could be produced. This substance had all the properties that made it desirable as a rifle propellant. This led to the production in 1888 of ballistite, the first propellant of this class.

Today, nitroglycerin powders are manufactured for use in both shotguns and rifles. They usually are referred to as double-base powders, possessing the advantages of regular ballistics, and are less liable to produce back-flash than nitrocellulose powders. They keep extremely well.

OBSOLETE METRIC CARTRIDGES

5.6 X 33mm Rook $5.00
Bullet Diameter: .222 inch
Bullet Weight: 65 grains
Muzzle Velocity: 1500 fps
Case Length: 1.311 inches
Neck Diameter: .247 inch
Shoulder Diameter: .318 inch
Base Diameter: .325 inch
Rim Diameter: .326 inch
Overall Length: 1.62 inches
Manufactured from 1899 to
    1936.

5.6 X 33R Rook $5.25
Bullet Diameter: .222 inch
Bullet Weight: 65 grains
Muzzle Velocity: 1500 fps
Case Length: 1.311 inches
Neck Diameter: .247 inch
Shoulder Diameter: .318 inch
Base Diameter: .325 inch
Rim Diameter: .366 inch
Overall Length: 1.62 inches
Manufactured from 1898 to
    1934.

6.5 X 40R $2.75
Bullet Diameter: .248 inch
Bullet Weight: 100 grains
Muzzle Velocity: 1200 fps
Case Length: 1.58 inches
Neck Diameter: .290 inch
Shoulder Diameter: —
Base Diameter: .396 inch
Rim Diameter: .451 inch
Overall Length: 2.07 inches
Made from the late 1800s to
    1920.

6.5 X 53.5 Daudeteau . . $3.50
Bullet Diameter: .264 inch
Bullet Weight: 150 grains
Muzzle Velocity: 2400 fps
Case Length: 2.09 inches
Neck Diameter: .298 inch
Shoulder Diameter: .466 inch
Base Diameter: .490 inch
Rim Diameter: .524 inch
Overall Length: 3.02 inches
Made from 1895 to at least 1898.

6.5 X 48R Sauer $3.25
Bullet Diameter: .260 inch
Bullet Weight: 126 grains
Muzzle Velocity: 1150 fps
Case Length: 1.88 inches
Neck Diameter: .284 inch
Shoulder Diameter: Straight
Base Diameter: .433 inch
Rim Diameter: .495 inch
Overall Length: 2.43 inches
Introduced in the late 1880s.

6.5 X 58R Sauer $3.00
Bullet Diameter: .260 inch
Bullet Weight: 126 grains
Muzzle Velocity: 2000 fps
Case Length: 2.296 inches
Neck Diameter: .290 inch
Shoulder Diameter: Straight
Base Diameter: .433 inch
Rim Diameter: .532 inch
Overall Length: 3.07 inches
Manufactured 1900 to 1950.

**7.5 X 53.5 Schmidt-Rubin
Model 90 . . . . $16.00**
Bullet Diameter: .307 inch
Bullet Weight: 210 grains
Muzzle Velocity: 1980 fps
Case Length: 2.106 inches
Neck Diameter: .360 inch
Shoulder Diameter: —
Base Diameter: .486 inch
Rim Diameter: .489 inch
Overall Length: —
Introduced in the 1880s.

**8mm Bergmann No. 1
Automatic Pistol $4.00**
Bullet Diameter: .319 inch
Bullet Weight: —
Muzzle Velocity: —
Case Length: .905 inch
Neck Diameter: .342 inch
Shoulder Diameter: —
Base Diameter: .412 inch
Rim Diameter: —
Overall Length: —
Manufactured 1893 to 1898.

8 X 42R $4.50
Bullet Diameter: .318 inch
Bullet Weight: 157 grains
Muzzle Velocity: 1780 fps
Case Length: 1.65 inch
Neck Diameter: .347 inch
Shoulder Diameter: .423 inch
Base Diameter: .468 inch
Rim Diameter: .525 inch
Overall Length: 2.28 inches
Manufactured 1888 to 1940.

8 X 48R Sauer $5.00
Bullet Diameter: .316 inch
Bullet Weight: 196 grains
Muzzle Velocity: 1670 fps
Case Length: 1.88 inches
Neck Diameter: .344 inch
Shoulder Diameter: —
Base Diameter: .432 inch
Rim Diameter: .500 inch
Overall Length: 2.58 inches
Made from the late 1800s to the
    1960s.

8 X 51mm Mauser $3.00
Bullet Diameter: .316 inch
Bullet Weight: 154 grains
Muzzle Velocity: 2070 fps
Case Length: 1.98 inches
Neck Diameter: .344 inch
Shoulder Diameter: .436
Base Diameter: .467 inch
Rim Diameter: .467 inch
Overall Length: 2.67 inches
Introduced in 1888.

8 X 51R Mauser $7.00
Bullet Diameter: .316 inch
Bullet Weight: 196 grains
Muzzle Velocity: 2100 fps
Case Length: 1.98 inches
Neck Diameter: .344 inch
Shoulder Diameter: .436 inch
Base Diameter: .467 inch
Rim Diameter: .515 inch
Overall Length: 2.68 inches
Manufactured 1888 to 1960.

9 X 70R Mauser $4.00
Bullet Diameter: .357 inch
Bullet Weight: 217 grains
Muzzle Velocity: 2480 fps
Case Length: 2.76 inches
Neck Diameter: .385 inch
Shoulder Diameter: .418 inch
Base Diameter: .467 inch
Rim Diameter: .525 inch
Overall Length: 3.37 inches
Introduced in 1900.

**11 X 60R Japanese
Murata $16.00**
Bullet Diameter: .432 inch
Bullet Weight: —
Muzzle Velocity: —
Case Length: 2.36 inches
Neck Diameter: .465 inch
Shoulder Diameter: —
Base Diameter: .542 inch
Rim Diameter: .631 inch
Overall Length: —
Introduced in 1884.

11.15 X 58R Werndl ...$9.00

Bullet Diameter: .452 inch
Bullet Weight: 370 grains
Muzzle Velocity: 1440 fps
Case Length: 2.29 inches
Neck Diameter: .466 inch
Shoulder Diameter: —
Base Diameter: .545 inch
Rim Diameter: .617 inch
Overall Length: —
Introduced in 1877.

11.43 X 55R
Turkish $12.00

Bullet Diameter: .447 inch
Bullet Weight: 486 grains
Muzzle Velocity: 1260 fps
Case Length: 2.3 inches
Neck Diameter: .474 inch
Shoulder Diameter: —
Base Diameter: .582 inch
Rim Diameter: .644 inch
Overall Length: —
Introduced in 1874.

RIMFIRE
CARTRIDGES

.22 Extra Long........$1.25

Bullet Diameter: .223 inch
Bullet Weight: 40 grains
Muzzle Velocity: 1060 fps
Case Length: .750 inch
Neck Diameter: .225 inch
Shoulder Diameter: Straight
Base Diameter: .225 inch
Rim Diameter: .275 inch
Overall Length: 1.16 inches
Manufactured 1881 to 1935.

.22 Remington
Automatic .... $.50

Bullet Diameter: .223 inch
Bullet Weight: 45 grains
Muzzle Velocity: 950 fps
Case Length: .663 inch
Neck Diameter: .245 inch
Shoulder Diameter: Straight
Base Diameter: .245 inch
Rim Diameter: .290 inch
Overall Length: .920 inch
Manufactured from 1914 to 1946.

.22 Remington Special .. $.25

Bullet Diameter: .224 inch
Bullet Weight: 40 grains
Muzzle Velocity: 1440 fps
Case Length: .960 inch
Neck Diameter: .242 inch
Shoulder Diameter: Straight
Base Diameter: .243 inch
Rim Diameter: .295 inch
Overall Length: 1.17 inches
Manufactured from 1890 to date.

.22 Winchester
Automatic .... $.35

Bullet Diameter: .222 inch
Bullet Weight: 45 grains
Muzzle Velocity: 1055 fps
Case Length: .665 inch
Neck Diameter: .250 inch
Shoulder Diameter: Straight
Base Diameter: .250 inch
Rim Diameter: .310 inch
Overall Length: .915 inch
Manufactured from 1903 to date.

.22 Winchester Rimfire
(WRF) .... $.25

Bullet Diameter: .224 inch
Bullet Weight: 45 grains
Muzzle Velocity: 1400 fps
Case Length: .960 inch
Neck Diameter: .242 inch
Shoulder Diameter: Straight
Base Diameter: .243 inch
Rim Diameter: .295 inch
Overall Length: 1.17 inches
Manufactured from 1891 to date.

.25 Short............... $.50

Bullet Diameter: .246 inch
Bullet Weight: 43 grains
Muzzle Velocity: 750 fps
Case Length: .468 inch
Neck Diameter: .245 inch
Shoulder Diameter: Straight
Base Diameter: .245 inch
Rim Diameter: .290 inch
Overall Length: .780 inch
Manufactured 1860 to 1921.

.25 Stevens............$1.25

Bullet Diameter: .251 inch
Bullet Weight: 67 grains
Muzzle Velocity: 1200 fps
Case Length: 1.125 inches
Neck Diameter: .276 inch
Shoulder Diameter: Straight
Base Diameter: .276 inch
Rim Diameter: .333 inch
Overall Length: 1.395 inches
Manufactured 1895 to 1942.

.25 Stevens Short .... $.50

Bullet Diameter: .251 inch
Bullet Weight: 65 grains
Muzzle Velocity: 950 fps
Case Length: .599 inch
Neck Diameter: .275 inch
Shoulder Diameter: Straight
Base Diameter: .276 inch
Rim Diameter: .333 inch
Overall Length: .877 inch
Manufactured 1902 to 1942.

.30 Long $2.50
Bullet Diameter: .288 inch
Bullet Weight: 75 grains
Muzzle Velocity: 750 fps
Case Length: .613 inch
Neck Diameter: .288 inch
Shoulder Diameter: Straight
Base Diameter: .288 inch
Rim Diameter: .340 inch
Overall Length: 1.020 inches
Manufactured from 1873 to 1916.

.30 Long with Merwin Base $30.00

.30 Short..............$4.00
Bullet Diameter: .286 inch
Bullet Weight: 58 grains
Muzzle Velocity: 700 fps
Case Length: .515 inch
Neck Diameter: .292 inch
Shoulder Diameter: Straight
Base Diameter: .292 inch
Rim Diameter: .346 inch
Overall Length: .822 inch
Manufactured from 1862 to 1920.

.32 Extra Long........$7.50
Bullet Diameter: .316 inch
Bullet Weight: 90 grains
Muzzle Velocity: 1050 fps
Case Length: 1.12 inches
Neck Diameter: .317 inch
Shoulder Diameter: Straight
Base Diameter: .318 inch
Rim Diameter: .378 inch
Overall Length: 1.570 inches
Manufactured from 1875 to 1918.

.32 Extra Short $1.00
Bullet Diameter: .316 inch
Bullet Weight: 54 grains
Muzzle Velocity: 650 fps
Case Length: .398 inch
Neck Diameter: .318 inch
Shoulder Diameter: Straight
Base Diameter: .317 inch
Rim Diameter: .367 inch
Overall Length: .645 inch
Manufactured 1871 to 1920.

.32 Long $2.00
Bullet Diameter: .316 inch
Bullet Weight: 90 grains
Muzzle Velocity: 950 fps
Case Length: .791 inch
Neck Diameter: .318 inch
Shoulder Diameter: Straight
Base Diameter: .318 inch
Rim Diameter: .377 inch
Overall Length: 1.216 inches
Manufactured 1861 to 1975.

.32 Long Rifle $5.00
Bullet Diameter: .312 inch
Bullet Weight: 80 grains
Muzzle Velocity: 975 fps
Case Length: .937 inch
Neck Diameter: .318 inch
Shoulder Diameter: Straight
Base Diameter: .318 inch
Rim Diameter: .377 inch
Overall Length: 1.222 inches
Manufactured 1900 to 1924.

.32 Short..............$.50
Bullet Diameter: .316 inch
Bullet Weight: 58 grains
Muzzle Velocity: 700 fps
Case Length: .575 inch

.32 Short (cont.)
Neck Diameter: .318 inch
Shoulder Diameter: Straight
Base Diameter: .318 inch
Rim Diameter: .377 inch
Overall Length: .948 inch
Manufactured from 1861 to 1973.

.38 Extra Long........$5.25
Bullet Diameter: .375 inch
Bullet Weight: 150 grains
Muzzle Velocity: 1250 fps
Case Length: 1.480 inches
Neck Diameter: .378 inch
Shoulder Diameter: Straight
Base Diameter: .378 inch
Rim Diameter: .435 inch
Overall Length: 2.025 inches
Manufactured 1871 to 1917.

.38 Long $4.00
Bullet Diameter: .375 inch
Bullet Weight: 150 grains
Muzzle Velocity: 750 fps
Case Length: .873 inch
Neck Diameter: .376 inch
Shoulder Diameter: Straight
Base Diameter: .376 inch
Rim Diameter: .435 inch
Overall Length: 1.380 inches
Manufactured 1866 to 1932.

.38 Short..............$3.75
Bullet Diameter: .375 inch
Bullet Weight: 125 grains
Muzzle Velocity: 700 fps
Case Length: .768 inch
Neck Diameter: .376 inch
Shoulder Diameter: Straight
Base Diameter: .376 inch
Rim Diameter: .436 inch
Overall Length: 1.185 inches
Manufactured 1868 to 1941.

.41 Long $5.00
Bullet Diameter: .405 inch
Bullet Weight: 163 grains
Muzzle Velocity: 700 fps
Case Length: .635 inch
Neck Diameter: .407 inch
Shoulder Diameter: Straight
Base Diameter: .407 inch
Rim Diameter: .468 inch
Overall Length: .985 inch
Manufactured from 1873 to 1923.

.44 Extra Long....... $18.00
Bullet Diameter: .446 inch
Bullet Weight: 218 grains
Muzzle Velocity: 1250 fps
Case Length: 1.250 inches
Neck Diameter: .456 inch
Shoulder Diameter: Straight
Base Diameter: .457 inch
Rim Diameter: .524 inch
Overall Length: 1.843 inches
Manufactured from 1874 to 1888.

.44 Short.............$1.50
Bullet Diameter: .446 inch
Bullet Weight: 200 grains
Muzzle Velocity: 525 fps
Case Length: .688 inch
Neck Diameter: .445 inch
Shoulder Diameter: Straight
Base Diameter: .445 inch
Rim Diameter: .519 inch
Overall Length: 1.20 inches
Manufactured from 1865 to 1923.

.41 Short.............$3.00
Bullet Diameter: .405 inch
Bullet Weight: 130 grains
Muzzle Velocity: 425 fps
Case Length: .467 inch
Neck Diameter: .406 inch
Shoulder Diameter: Straight
Base Diameter: .406 inch
Rim Diameter: .468 inch
Overall Length: .913 inch
Manufactured from 1863 to 1942.

.44 Henry Flat $5.00
Bullet Diameter: .446 inch
Bullet Weight: 200 grains
Muzzle Velocity: 1125 fps
Case Length: .875 inch
Neck Diameter: .445 inch
Shoulder Diameter: Straight
Base Diameter: .446 inch
Rim Diameter: .519 inch
Overall Length: 1.345 inches
Manufactured from 1861 to 1934.

.50 Remington Navy .. $28.00
Bullet Diameter: .510 inch
Bullet Weight: 290 grains
Muzzle Velocity: 600 fps
Case Length: .860 inch
Neck Diameter: .535 inch
Shoulder Diameter: Straight
Base Diameter: .562 inch
Rim Diameter: .642 inch
Overall Length: 1.280 inches
Manufactured from 1865 to 1880.

.41 Swiss.............$3.75
Bullet Diameter: .418 inch
Bullet Weight: 310 grains
Muzzle Velocity: 1325 fps
Case Length: 1.52 inches
Neck Diameter: .445 inch
Shoulder Diameter: —
Base Diameter: .539 inch
Rim Diameter: .620 inch
Overall Length: 2.205 inches
Manufactured from 1869 to 1942.

.44 Long $6.00
Bullet Diameter: .451 inch
Bullet Weight: 220 grains
Muzzle Velocity: 825 fps
Case Length: 1.094 inches
Neck Diameter: .455 inch
Shoulder Diameter: Straight
Base Diameter: .458 inch
Rim Diameter: .525 inch
Overall Length: 1.842 inches
Manufactured from 1862 to 1923.

.56-46 Spencer $30.00
Bullet Diameter: .465 inch
Bullet Weight: 330 grains
Muzzle Velocity: 1200 fps
Case Length: 1.035 inches
Neck Diameter: .478 inch
Shoulder Diameter: .555 inch
Base Diameter: .558 inch
Rim Diameter: .641 inch
Overall Length: 1.595 inches
Manufactured from 1866 to 1869.

.56-50 Spencer $7.50
Bullet Diameter: .512 inch
Bullet Weight: 350 grains
Muzzle Velocity: 1250 fps
Case Length: 1.156 inches
Neck Diameter: .543 inch
Shoulder Diameter: Straight
Base Diameter: .556 inch
Rim Diameter: .639 inch
Overall Length: 1.632 inches
Manufactured from 1864 to 1920.

.56-52 Spencer $5.00
Bullet Diameter: .512 inch
Bullet Weight: 400 grains
Muzzle Velocity: 1200 fps
Case Length: 1.035 inches
Neck Diameter: .540 inch
Shoulder Diameter: Straight
Base Diameter: .559 inch
Rim Diameter: .639 inch
Overall Length: 1.50 inches
Manufactured from 1866 to 1920.

.56-56 ....$7.50
Bullet Diameter: .550 inch
Bullet Weight: 350 grains
Muzzle Velocity: 1200 fps
Case Length: .875 inch
Neck Diameter: .560 inch
Shoulder Diameter: Straight
Base Diameter: .560 inch
Rim Diameter: .645 inch
Overall Length: 1.545 inches
Manufactured from 1862 to 1920.

OBSOLETE SHOTSHELLS

"Shotshells" or simply "shells" as they are known in the U.S. are termed "cartridges" in England. They are made of paper or plastic tubes encased within a brass head, which is flanged so it can be grasped by the extractor. Inside is a base wad which, when the brass head is crimped, binds the tube, base wad and brass head together. This prevents the backwards escape of powder gas through the shell. Both the brass head and base wad are perforated with a hole that accepts the primer and allows it to ignite the powder inside the case.

The shotshell, once primed, receives a powder charge over which are pressed two or more wads at considerable pressure. Many manufacturers insert a cup and wad directly over the powder charge, which effectively prevents pattern-disrupting gas leakage into the shot column. A charge of shot is next placed over the wads and the unfilled end of the tube is crimped over the shot, making the shell ready for use.

Some earlier shotshells, often referred to as "punkin balls," were loaded with round balls for deer-sized game. The rifled slug did not come into use until later in the 20th century.

Loaded Paper Shotshell

Paper and Brass Cases
4 Gauge Paper Case $5.00
8 Gauge Paper Case 4.75
10 Gauge
  Paper Case 1.00
  Brass Case 5.00
12 Gauge
  Paper Case 1.00
  Brass Case 4.00
12 Gauge Black Powder
  Paper Case 3.00
14 Gauge Brass Case 14.00
16 Gauge
  Paper Case .... .75
  Brass Case 1.50
20 Gauge Paper Case ..... .75
24 Gauge Paper Case 5.00
28 Gauge
  Paper Case 1.00
  Brass Case 3.00
32 Gauge Paper Case 5.00
.410 Bore
  Paper Case .... .50
  Brass Case 2.00
9mm Rimfire Shotshells
  Paper.................1.00
  Brass.................1.00

Brass Shell

BIBLIOGRAPHY

BOOKS

Baer, Larry. **The Parker Gun.** North Hollywood: Beinfeld Publishing Inc., 1974, 1976.

Blackmore, Howard L. **British Military Firearms 1650–1850.** Arco Publishing Co., 1961.

Blair, Claude. **Pollard's History of Firearms.** New York: Macmillan Pub. Co., 1983.

Brown, M. L. **Firearms in Colonial America.** Washington D.C.: Smithsonian Institution Press, 1980.

Brownell, F. & Son. **Gunsmith Kinks.** Montezuma, Ill.: F. Brownell & Son., 1983.

Buchanan, Lamont. **A Pictorial History of the Confederacy.** New York: Crown Publishers, Inc., 1951.

Butler, David F. **The American Shotgun.** New York: The Winchester Press, 1973.

Byron, David. **Firearm Price Guide.** Crown-House of Collectibles, 1978–1980.

Chapel, Charles E. **The Gun Collector's Handbook of Values.** New York: Coward, McCann & Geoghegan, 1963 and other editions.

Cope, Kenneth L. **Stevens Pistols and Pocket Rifles.** Ottawa, Ontario: Museum Restoration Service, 1971.

Datig, Fred A. **Cartridges for Collectors, Vol I.** 1956.

—**Cartridges for Collectors, Vol. II.** 1958.

—**Cartridges for Collectors, Vol. III.** Alhambra, Ca.: Borden Publishing Co., 1967.

Edwards, William B. **Civil War Guns. (Illus.)** Harrisburg, Pa.: The Stackpole Co., 1962.

Flayderman, Norm. **Flayderman's Guide to Antique American Firearms, Third Edition.** Northfield, Ill.: DBI Books, Inc., 1983.

George, John Nigel. **English Pistols & Revolvers.** New York: Arco Publishing Co., 1962.

Gun Digest, 1953–1987 Editions. Northfield, Ill.: DBI Books, Inc.

Haven, Charles T., and Belden, Frank A. **A History of The Colt Revolver.** New York: Bonanza Books, 1940, 1978.

House of Collectibles. **The Official 1981 Price Guide to Antique & Modern Firearms.** Orlando, Fla.: House of Collectibles, 1981.

Hughes, James B. **Mexican Military Arms: The Cartridge Period, 1866–1967.** Houston: Deep River Armory, Inc., 1968.

Johnson, James R. **Kentucky Rifles & Pistols.** Golden Age Arms Co., 1976.

Keith, Elmer. **Six Guns.** New York: Bonanza Books, 1955, 1961.

Kentucky Rifles and Pistols, 1750–1850. Published by Golden Age Arms Co. and James R. Johnston for the Kentucky Rifle Association, 1976.

Konig, Klaus-Peter, and Hugo, Martin. **Waffen Sammeln: Die Wichtigsten Pistolen und Revolver seit 1850.** Stuttgart: Motorbuch Verlag Stuttgart, 1983.

Lindsay, Merrill. **The Kentucky Rifle.** New York: Arma Press for the York County, Pennsylvania Historical Society, 1972.

—**The Lure of Antique Arms.** New York: David McKay, Inc., 1976.

Lord, Francis A. **Civil War Collector's Encyclopedia. (Illus.)** Secaucus, N.J.: Castle Books, 1965.

—**Uniforms of the Civil War.** San Diego, Calif.: A. S. Barnes & Co., Inc., 1970.

Madis, George. **The Winchester Book.** Brownsboro, Tex.: George Madis, 1979.

Merino, Angel Hernandez. **El Tiro Con Armas de Avancarga Hoy.** Leon, Spain: Everest, S.A., 1983.

Maxwell, Samuel L., Sr. **Lever Action Magazine Rifles.** Dallas: Samuel L. Maxwell Sr., 1976.

Moore, Warren. **Weapons of the American Revolution. . . and Accoutrements.** New York: Funk & Wagnalls, 1967.

Neumann, George C. **The History of Weapons of the American Revolution.** New York: Harper & Row, 1967.

Nonte, George. **Black Powder Guide.** So. Hackensack, N.J.: Stoeger Publishing Co., 1976.

Peterson, Harold L. **A History of Firearms.** New York: Charles Scribner's Sons, 1961.

Pioneer Press. **Cartridge Broadsheets.**

Ramage, Kenneth. **Lyman Black Powder Handbook.** Middlefield, Conn.: Lyman Products Corp., 1981.

Reynolds, Major E. G. B. **The Lee-Enfield Rifle.** New York: Arco Pub. Co., 1962.

Rywell, Martin. **American Antique Pistols and Their Current Prices.** Union City, Tenn.: Pioneer Press, 1966. 17th Edition, 1974.

—**American Antique Rifles and Their Current Prices.** Union City, Tenn.: Pioneer Press, 1975.

—**Confederate Guns and Their Current Prices.**
Union City, Tenn.: Pioneer Press, 1974.

Schroeder, Joseph J., Jr. **Gun Collector's Digest.**
Northfield, Ill.: DBI Books, Inc., 1983.

—**Rare Selections From Old Gun Catalogs.**

Sellers, Frank M., and Smith, Samuel E. **American
Percussion Revolvers.** Ontario, Canada: Museum
Restoration Service, 1971.

—**Sharps Firearms.** Denver, Colo.: Sellers
Publications, 1982.

Serven, James E. **Colt Firearms From 1836.** Santa
Ana, Calif.: Foundation Press, 1974.

Sharpe, Philip B. **The Rifle in America.** New
York: William Morrow and Co., 1938.

Shooter's Bible, Volumes 75–80. So. Hackensack,
N.J.: Stoeger Pub. Co., 1984–1988.

Shumaker, P. L. **Colt's Variations of the Old Model
Pocket Pistol 1848–1872.** Borden Pub. Co./Fadco
Pub Co., 1966.

Smith, James A., and Swanson, Elmer. **The Antique
Pistol Book.** Speedwell Publishing Co., 1948.

Smith, W. H. B. **Small Arms of the World.** Harrisburg,
Pa.: Stackpole Pub., 1973.

Stelle & Harrison. **Gunsmith's Manual.** Reprint of
circa 1890 Gunsmith's Manual.

The Story of American Hunting and Firearms. New
York: Sunrise Books/E.P. Dutton & Company, Inc.,
1959, 1976.

Time-Life Editors. **The Gunfighters.** New
York: Time-Life Books, 1974.

Traister, John. **How To Buy and Sell Used Guns.**
South Hackensack, N.J.: Stoeger Publishing Co.,
1983.

U.S. Cartridge Co. **U.S. Cartridge Company's
Collection of Firearms.** Old Greenwich, Conn.: WE
Inc.

Virgines, George E. **Saga of the Colt Six-Shooter and
the Famous Men Who Used It.** Frederick Fell, Inc.,
1969.

West, Bill. **Remington Arms & History.** Whittier,
Calif.: Bill West, 1970.

—**Winchester Handbook Volume I.** Whittier,
Calif.: Bill West, 1966.

Wilson, R. L. **The Colt Heritage: The Official History
of Colt Firearms from 1836 to the Present.** New
York: Simon and Schuster, 1979.

ANTIQUE ARMS CATALOGS

**Colt's Revolving and Breechloading Firearms,
1896.** Hartford, Conn.: Colt's Patent Fire Arms
Mfg. Co.

Francis Bannerman Sons Catalogue, 1936. New
York: Francis Bannerman Sons, 1936.

Forehand Arms Company, 1896. Stoney Creek,
Ontario: Fortress Publications Inc.

**Forehand & Wadsworth Illustrated Catalogue of
Fire-Arms, 1880.** Stoney Creek, Ontario: Fortress
Publications Inc.

Fourteen Old Gun Catalogs. Chicago, Ill.: The Gun
Digest Association, Inc., 1962.

**Great Western Gun Works Illustrated Catalogue
No. 40, 1888-89.** J.H. Johnston. Northfield,
Ill.: Reprint by Gun Digest, 1966.

Hopkins and Allen Catalog

Ithaca Gun Catalog, 1915.

Iver Johnson Firearms, Catalog No. 19A. Iver
Johnson's Arms and Cycle Works.
Boston: McGrath-Sherrill Press.

Lefever Arms Co., 1889. Stoney Creek,
Ontario: Fortress Publications Inc.

Marlin Fire Arms Catalog, 1897. New Haven,
Conn.: Marlin Fire Arms Co., 1897.

Maynard Breech-Loading Firearms, 1880. Holyoke,
Mass.: Transcript Book and Job Printing House,
1880.

E. C. Meacham Arms Co., 1884. Reprint by Gun
Digest Co.

**Remingtons' Illustrated Catalog and Reduced Price
List, 1877.** Ilion, N.Y.: Citizen Steam Printing
Establishment, 1877.

Remington Catalogs of 1885, 1902, 1906.

L.C. Smith Breech-Loading Guns, 1889. Stoney
Creek, Ontario: Fortress Publications Inc.

Smith & Wesson Catalog, 1901. Springfield,
Mass.: Smith & Wesson, 1901.

**Winchester Repeating Arms Co. Catalogs of 1891,
1893, 1905.** New Haven, Conn.: Winchester
Repeating Arms Co.

INDEX

268 *ANTIQUE GUNS—THE COLLECTOR'S GUIDE*

R
Randall, Joseph C., Percussion Rifle, 117
Raphael Revolver, 88
Rappahannock Forge
Flintlock Musket, 154
Flintlock Pistol, 82
Reid, James, 40, 51
SA "Knuckle-Duster" Revolver, 51
Single Action Revolvers, 51
Remington Arms Co., 18, 51, 117, 163.
See also **Mexican Military Rifles** and
individual replica manufacturers
Handguns
Model 1861 Army Revolver, 51
Model 1861 Navy Revolver, 51
Model 1865 Navy Pistol, 51
Model 1867 Navy Breech-Loading, 82
Model 1867 Navy Single Shot, 51
Model 1871 Army Pistol, 83
Model 1875 SA Army Revolver, 52
Model 1890 SA Army Revolver, 52
Model 1891 Single Shot Target Pistol, 52
Army Revolver, 89
Navy Revolver, 89
Double Repeating Deringer, 52
Improved Navy Revolver, 52
Iroquois Revolver, 52
New Model No. 1 Revolver, 52
New Model No. 2 Revolver, 52
New Model No. 3 Revolver, 53
New Model No. 4 Revolver, 53
New Model Police Revolver, 53
New Pocket Revolver, 54
SA Belt Revolver, 54
Vest Pocket Pistols, 54
-Elliot Pepperbox Deringer, 54
-Elliot Single Shot Deringer, 54
-Elliot "Zig-Zag" Deringer, 55
-Rider DA Pocket Pistol, 55
-Rider New Model Magazine Pistol, 55
Rifles
No. 1 Military Rifle, 118
No. 1 Sporting, 117
No. 2 Sporting, 118
No. 3 (Hepburn) Sporting, 118
No. 3 (Hepburn) Creedmoor and
Schuetzen, 118
No. 3 (Hepburn) High Power, 118
No. 4 Single Shot, 119
Light Baby Carbine, 119
"Split Breech" Carbine, 119
Springfield Model, 119
U.S. Navy Carbine, 119
-Lee Bolt Action Sporting, 119, 137
Shotguns
Model 1874 Side-by-Side Breech-
Loading, 182
Model 1882 Double Barrel, 182
Model 1889 Double Barrel, 182
Model 1894 Double Barrel, 182
Model 1900 Double Barrel, 182
Single Barrel Breech-Loading, 181
Single Barrel Muzzle Loading, 181
**Remington, E. (Eliphalet), & Sons
Co.,** 51, 87, 117
Revolutionary War Flintlock Musket, 158
Rev-O-Noc, 172
Richards, Westley & Co. Ltd.
Side-by-Side Shotgun, 183
Single Barrel Shotgun, 183
Richardson Flintlock Pistol, 55
Richardson & Overman, 109, 161

Richmond
Confederate Carbine, 156
Confederate Navy Musketoon, 156
Confederate Pistol, 78
Confederate Rifled Musket, 156
Richter, Charles, 172
Rickard Arms Company, 172
Rider, Joseph, 55
Rifle Cartridges, Obsolete Centerfire, 241
Rifle Magazines, Successful, 137
Rigby, John, Dueling Pistols (Pair), 55
Rigdon & Ansley Confederate Revolver, 78
Rigdon, C. H., and Leech, Thomas,
Confederate Revolver, 78
Rimfire Cartridges, Obsolete, 255
Riverside Arms Co. Single Shot
Shotgun, 183
Robbins & Lawrence, 111, 121
Robertson Double Barrel Percussion
Shotgun, 183
Robinson Arms Mfg. Co. Robinson-Sharps
Confederate Carbine, 156
Rodman, Richard, 185
Rogers and Spencer, 50
Army Revolver, 89
Navy Revolver Replica, 222
Root, Elisha King, 29. *See also* **Colt
Handguns**
Royal Service, 172
Ruger. *See* **Sturm, Ruger & Co.**
Rummel, 172
Rupertus, Jacob
Double Barrel Derringer, 55
Eight-Shot Pepperbox, 55
SA Revolvers, 56
Singleshot Derringers, 56
Russian Military Model 1891 Mosin-
Nagant Bolt Action Rifles, 119

S
Saint Louis Arms Co., 174
**Savage (Arthur W.) Repeating Arms
Co.,** 89, 119, 125, 126
Handguns Navy Revolver, 89
Rifles
Model 1892 Repeating Military, 119
Model 1895 Carbine, 119
Model 1895 Repeating Military, 119
Model 1895 Sporting, 119
Model 1899 Repeating Mil. Carbine, 119
Model 1899 Repeating Mil., 119
Model 1899 Sporting, 120
Scheaner, William, American Kentucky
Flintlock Rifles, 154
Schneelock, Otto, Sporting Target
Rifle, 120
Schofield, Col. G.W., /S&W Revolvers, 63,
89
**Schneider (William S.) & Glassick
(Frederick G.)** Confederate Revolver, 78
Scott, W & C, and Son,, 185
Double Barrel Percussion Shotgun, 183
Segallas Flintlock Pocket Pistol, 56
Sears, Roebuck & Co., 167
Sharps, C., & Company, 56. *See also*
Sharps Rifle Co.
Handguns
Breech-Loading Single Shot Pistol, 56
Bryce Revolver, 56
Model 1 Four-Barrel Pepperbox, 57
Model 2 Four-Barrel Pepperbox, 57
Model 3 Four-Barrel Pepperbox, 57
Model 4 Four-Barrel Pepperbox, 57

Sharps, C., & Co. Handguns (cont.)
Percussion Revolver, 57
Pistol Rifle, 57
Sharps, C., Arms Co., Inc., 230
Sharps, Christian, 42, 56, 120
**Sharps (Christian) & Hankins
(William),** 56, 57, 120, 124
Model 1861 Navy Rifle, 124
Model 1862 Cavalry Carbine, 125
Pepperbox Pistols, 57
Sharps Rifle Company, 120
Model 1851 Boxlock Hunting, 121
Model 1851 "Original" Model Breech-
Loading Percussion, 121
Model 1852 Slanting Breech
Carbine, 121
Model 1855 Slanting Breech
Carbine, 121
Model 1859 Breech-Loading Percussion
Carbine, 121
Model 1859 Breech-Loading Percussion
Carbine, 121
Model 1859 BL Percussion Military, 121
Model 1859 Vertical Breech Percussion
Carbine, 121
Model 1863 BL Percussion Carbine, 121
Model 1863 BL Percussion Military, 121
Model 1867 BL Carbine, 121
Model 1868 BL Sporting, 121
Model 1869 BL Carbine, 121
Model 1869 BL Military, 121
Model 1870 BL Carbine, 122
Model 1870 BL Military, 122
Model 1873 Creedmoor, 122
Model 1874 Business, 122
Model 1874 Creedmoor Rifles, 122
Model 1874 Military, 122
Model 1875, 122
Model 1876 BL Sporting, 122
Model 1876 Long Range Rifles, 122
Model 1876 Mid-Range Rifles, 123
Model 1877 Rifle, 123
Model 1878 Business, 123
Model 1878 Hunter's, 123
Model 1878 Express, 123
Model 1878 Long Range, 123
Model 1878 Mid Range, 123
Model 1878 Military, 123
Model 1878 Officer's, 124
Model 1878 Short Range, 124
Model 1878 Sporting, 124
Breech-Loading Cartridge Carbine, 124
"Business", 122
Commercial Breech-Loading Mil., 124
Shattuck, C. S., Pocket Revolvers, 57
Sherrard (Joseph) & Taylor (Pleasant)
Confederate Revolver, 78
Shiloh Sharps Replicas
Model 1863 Sporting Rifle, 230
Model 1874 Business Rifle, 230
Model 1874 Carbine, 231
Model 1874 Long-Range Express
Sporting, 231
Model 1874 Military Rifle, 231
Model 1874 Sharps Saddle, 231
Model 1874 Sporting No. 1, 232
Model 1874 Sporting No. 3, 232
New Model 1863 Military Carbine, 230
New Model 1863 Military Rifle, 230
Shotshells, Obsolete, 258
Shue's Special, 172
Siber, Jean Frederick, 194
Sickels Arms Company, 174

FIREARMS THAT APPEAR ON THE COVER

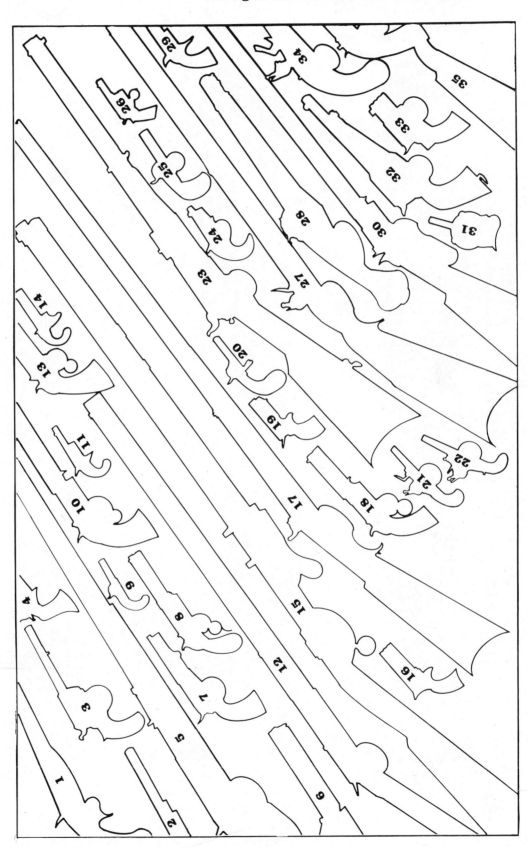

IDENTIFICATION OF FIREARMS THAT APPEAR ON THE COVER

1. Flobert 22 Caliber Target Pistol
2. Colt Texas Paterson Revolver
3. Colt Lightning Model Revolver
4. Colt Root Model Revolver
5. Winchester Model 1886 Lever Action Repeating Rifle
6. Collier Revolving Flintlock Pistol of 1820 (rare)
7. Manhattan Percussion Revolver
8. Smith & Wesson Experimental Small-Frame Magazine Pistol (rare)
9. Boxlock Percussion Muff-Gun with folding trigger
10. Large-frame Volcanic Magazine Pistol by New Haven Arms Company with custom ivory grips
11. Colt Third Model Thuer Deringer
12. Robinson First Model Repeating Magazine Rifle (rare)
13. Large-frame Volcanic Magazine Pistol by Volcanic Repeating Arms Company with fancy scroll engraving
14. First Model Deringer Pistol by National Arms Company
15. R. B. McDowell exact copy of the Walter Hunt Magazine Repeater. Only one is known to exist, in the Winchester Collection of the Buffalo Bill Historical Society in Cody, Wyoming.
16. Rupertus 1864 Patent 8-Barrel Pepperbox
17. Kentucky Rifle converted from flintlock to percussion
18. Small-frame Volcanic Magazine Pistol by New Haven Arms Company with fancy scroll engraving
19. Sharps Model 1 Four-shot Pepperbox
20. Double Barrel Percussion Muff-Gun with folding triggers
21. English all-metal flint box lock Vest Pocket Pistol with fancy engraving
22. English all-metal flint boxlock Vest Pocket Pistol with fancy engraving, marked "GALLAS, LONDON"
23. Colt Revolving Rifle of 1855
24. Williamson's Breech-Loading Deringer of 1866
25. Belgian-proofed (Liège) Boxlock Percussion Muff-Gun (maker unknown)
26. European-made Ring Trigger Rimfire Revolver (with Liège proof mark)
27. Kentucky Flintlock Rifle
28. Engraved, gold-plated Italian Wheel-Lock Pistol, marked "BORTOLO CHINELLI, GARDONE" (rare)
29. Five-shot Rimfire Pepperbox Revolver (patented in 1866) by Continental Arms Co. of Norwich, Conn.
30. Volcanic 41 Caliber Carbine made by New Haven Arms Company (rare)
31. Palm Pistol patented by Jacques Turbiaux, marked "THE PROTECTOR-MINN. FIRE ARMS CO." Often called the "Chicago Squeezer."
32. Remington Model 1875 Single Action Army Revolver with fancy engraving, pearl grips and gold and silver plating
33. The Reform Pistol, marked "Brevete/D.R.P./serial number/form of eagle." Shoots .25 ACP cartridges; four barrels elevate with each shot.
34. U.S. Model 1836 Johnson 54 Caliber Flintlock Pistol
35. Volcanic 41 Caliber Pistol Carbine manufactured by Volcanic Repeating Arms Company (rare)